To

Mercyhurst College Library

with compliments and best wishes

from

P. J. Lennox

May 28, 1927

THE GLORIES

OF

IRELAND

EDITED BY

JOSEPH DUNN, Ph.D.,

AND

P. J. LENNOX, Litt.D.,

PROFESSORS AT THE CATHOLIC UNIVERSITY OF AMERICA

PHOENIX, LIMITED
WASHINGTON, D. C.
1914

TO

THE IRISH RACE

IN

EVERY LAND

Ireland:

"All thy life has been a symbol; we can only read a part:
God will flood thee yet with sunshine for the woes that
drench thy heart."

JOHN BOYLE O'REILLY.

PREFACE

We had at first intended that this should be a book without a preface, and indeed it needs none, for it speaks in no uncertain tones for itself; but on reconsideration we decided that it would be more seemly to give a short explanation of our aim, our motives, and our methods.

As a result of innumerable inquiries which have come to us during our experience as educators, we have been forced to the conclusion that the performances of the Irish race in many fields of endeavor are entirely unknown to most people, and that even to the elect they are not nearly so well known as they deserve to be. Hence there came to us the thought of placing on record, in an accessible, comprehensive, and permanent form, an outline of the whole range of Irish achievement during the last two thousand years.

In undertaking this task we had a twofold motive. In the first place, we wished to give to people of Irish birth or descent substantial reason for that pride of race which we know is in them, by placing in their hands an authoritative and unassailable array of facts as telling as any nation in the world can show. Our second motive was that henceforward he who seeks to ignore or belittle the part taken by men and women of Irish birth or blood in promoting the spread of religion, civilization, education, culture, and freedom should sin, not in ignorance, but against the light, and that from a thousand quarters at once champions armed with the panoply of knowledge should be able to spring to his confutation.

To carry out in a satisfactory manner over a field so immense our lawfully ambitious aim was, as we realized at the outset, not possible to any two men who are primarily engaged, as we are, in other work of an exacting nature. Therefore, to render feasible the execution of our undertaking, we decided to invite the collaboration of many scholars and specialists, each of whom could, out of the fullness of information, speak with authority on some particular phase of the general subject. We are glad to say that the eminent writers to whom we addressed ourselves answered with promptitude and alacrity to our call, and have supplied us with such a body of material as to enable us to bring out a book that is absolutely unique.

From each contributor we asked nothing but a plain verifiable statement of facts, and that, we think, is exactly what they have given us, for, while we do not make ourselves personally responsible for everything set down in the following pages, we believe that what stands written therein bears every mark of careful research and of absolute reliability.

Although on many of our subjects little more remains to be said than what appears in the text, yet the treatment on the whole does not claim to be exhaustive, and therefore each writer has, at our request, appended to his contribution a short and carefully selected bibliography, so that those who are interested may have a guide for further reading. For our part, we consider these lists of works of reference to be a highly useful feature.

It is a glorious thing for us, who are proud, one of us of his Irish descent and the other of his Irish birth, to think that the sons and daughters of mother Erin have so conspicuously distinguished themselves in such varied spheres of activity in every age and in so many lands, and that we were privileged to make public the record of their achievements in a form never before attempted.

We have other works in contemplation, and some actually in preparation, which will go far to strengthen the claims put forward in this book. In the meantime, we trust that the reception accorded to it will be such as to encourage us to persevere in making still better known the Glories of Ireland.

JOSEPH DUNN

P. J. LENNOX

Catholic University of America,
  Washington, D. C.

November, 1914

CONTENTS

THE ROMANCE OF IRISH HISTORY

By Sir Roger Casement, C. M. G.

THE history of Ireland remains to be written, for the purpose of Irishmen remains yet to be achieved.

The struggle for national realization, begun so many centuries ago, is not ended; and if the long story offers a so frequent record of failure, it offers a continuous appeal to the highest motives and a constant exhibition of a most pathetic patriotism linked with the sternest courage.

Irish wars, throughout all time, have been only against one enemy, the invader, and, ending so often in material disaster, they have conferred always a moral gain. Their memory uplifts the Irish heart; for no nation, no people, can reproach Ireland with having wronged them.

When, at the dawn of the Christian era, we first hear of Ireland from external sources, we learn of it as an island harboring free men, whose indomitable love of freedom was hateful to the spirit of imperial exploitation.

Agricola's advice to the empire-builders of his day was that Rome should "war down and take possession of Ireland, so that freedom might be put out of sight."

It was to meet this challenge of despotism that the Scotic clans of Alba turned to their motherland for help, and the sea was "white with the hurrying oars" of the men of Erin speeding to the call of their Highland kinsmen, threatened with imperial servitude.

The first external record we possess thus makes it clear that when the early Irish went forth to carry war abroad, it was not to impose their yoke on other peoples, or to found an empire, but to battle against the Empire of the World in the threatened cause they held so dear at home.

In this early Roman reference to Ireland we get the keynote to all later Irish history—a warring down on the one hand, so that freedom might be put out of sight; an eternal resistance, on the other, so that it might be upheld.

It was this struggle that Ireland sought to maintain against every form of attack, down through Danish, Norman, Tudor,

Stuart, and Cromwellian assault, to the larger imperialism of the nineteenth century, when, as Thierry, the historian of the Norman Conquest, tells us, it still remained the one "lost cause" of history that refused to admit defeat. "This indomitable persistency, this faculty of preserving through centuries of misery the remembrance of lost liberty and of never despairing of a cause always defeated, always fatal to those who dared to defend it, is perhaps the strangest and noblest example ever given by any nation."

The resources Ireland opposed to her invaders have been unequal to the founding of a great state, but have preserved a great tradition. The weakness of Ireland lay in the absence of a central organization, a state machine that could mobilize the national resources to defend the national life. That life had to depend for its existence, under the stress of prolonged invasion, on the spontaneous patriotism and courage of individuals. At times one clan alone, or two clans, maintained the struggle. Arrayed against them were all the resources of a mighty realm—shipping, arms, munitions of war, gold, statecraft, a widespread and calculating diplomacy, the prestige of a great Sovereign and a famous Court—and the Irish clan and its chieftain, by the sheer courage of its members, by their bodily strength and hardihood and feats of daring, for years kept the issue in doubt.

When Hugh O'Neill, leagued with Red Hugh O'Donnell, challenged the might of Elizabeth, he had nothing to rely upon but the stout hearts and arms of the men of Tir-owen and Tir-Conail. Arms and armaments were far from Ulster. They could be procured only in Spain or elsewhere on the continent. English shipping held the sea; the English mint the coinage. The purse of England, compared to that of the Ulster princes, was inexhaustible. Yet for nine years the courage, the chivalry, the daring and skill of these northern clansmen, perhaps 20,000 men in all, held all the might of England at bay. Had the Spanish king at any time during the contest made good his promise to lend effective aid to the Irish princes, O'Neill would have driven Elizabeth from Ireland, and a sovereign State would today be the guardian of the freedom of the western seas for Europe and the world. It took "the best army in Europe" and a vast treasure, as Sir John Davies asserted, to conquer two Ulster clans three hundred years ago. The naked valor of the Irishman excelled the armed might of Tudor England; and the struggle that gave the empire of the seas to Britain was won not in the essay of battle, but in the assay of the mint.

It is this aspect of the Irish fight for freedom that dignifies an otherwise lost cause. Ever defeated, yet undefeated, a long-remembering race believes that these native qualities must in the end prevail. The battle has been from the first one of manhood against might. The State Papers, the official record of English rule in Ireland, leave us rarely in doubt. We read in that record that, where the appeal was to the strength or courage of the opposing men, the Irish had nothing to fear from English arms.

Thus the Earl of Essex, in a despatch to Elizabeth, explained the failure of his great expedition in 1599 against O'Neill and O'Donnell. "These rebels . . . have (though I do unwillingly confess it) better bodies and perfecter use of their arms than those men whom your Majesty sends over." The flight of the Earls in 1607 left Ireland leaderless, with nothing but the bodies and hearts of the people to depend on. In 1613 we read, in the same records, a candid admission that, although the clan system had been destroyed and the great chiefs expropriated, converted, or driven to flight, the people still trusted to their own stout arms and fearless hearts:

"The next rebellion, whenever it shall happen, doth threaten more danger to the State than any heretofore, when the cities and walled towns were always faithful; (1) because they have the same bodies they ever had and therein they had and have advantage of us; (2) from infancy they have been and are exercised in the use of arms; (3) the realm by reason of the long peace was never so full of youths; (4) that they are better soldiers than heretofore their continental employment in wars abroad assures us, and they do conceive that their men are better than ours."

And when that "next rebellion" came, the great uprising of the outraged race in 1641, what do we find? Back from the continent sails the nephew of the great O'Neill, who had left Ireland a little boy in the flight of the Earls, and the dispossessed clansmen, robbed of all but their strength of body and heart, gathered to the summons of Owen Roe.

Again it was the same issue: the courage and hardihood of the Irishman to set against the superior arms, equipment, and wealth of a united Britain. Irish valor won the battle; a great state organization won the campaign. England and Scotland combined to lay low a resurgent Ireland; and again the victory was not to the brave and skilled, but to the longer purse and the implacable mind. Perhaps the most vivid testimony to these innate qualities of the Irishman is to be found in a typically Irish challenge issued in the course of this ten years' war from 1641 to 1651. The document has a lasting interest, for it displays not only the "better body" of the Irishman, but something of his better heart and chivalry of soul.

One Parsons, an English settler in Ireland, had written to a friend to say, among other things, that the head of a colonel of an Irish regiment then in the field against the English would not be allowed to stick long on its shoulders. The letter was intercepted by the very regiment itself, and a captain in it, Felim O'Molloy, wrote back to Parsons:

"I will doe this, if you please. I will pick out 60 men and fight against 100 of your choise men, if you do but pitch your campe one mile out of your towne, and then, if you have the victory, you may threaten my colonel; otherwise do not reckon your chickens before they be hatched."

It was this same spirit of daring, this innate belief in his own manhood, that for three hundred years made every Irishman the custodian of his country's honor.

An Irish state had not been born; that battle had still to be fought; but the romantic effort to achieve it reveals ever an unstained record of personal courage. Freedom has not come to Ireland; it has been "warred down and kept out of sight"; but it has been kept in the Irish heart, from Brian Boru to Robert Emmet, by a long tale of blood shed always in the same cause. Freedom is kept alive in man's blood only by the shedding of that blood. It was this they were seeking, those splendid "scorners of death", the lads and young men of

Mayo, who awaited with a fearless joy the advance of the English army fresh from the defeat of Humbert in 1798. Then, if ever, Irishmen might have run from a victorious and pitiless enemy, who having captured the French general and murdered, in cold blood, the hundreds of Killala peasants who were with his colors, were now come to Killala itself to wreak vengeance on the last stronghold of Irish rebellion.

The ill-led and half-armed peasants, the last Irishmen in Ireland to stand in open, pitched fight for their country's freedom, went to meet the army of General Lake, as the Protestant bishop who saw them says, "running upon death with as little appearance of reflection or concern as if they were hastening to a show."

The influences that begot this reverence for freedom lie in the island itself no less than in the remote ancestry of the people. Whoever looks upon Ireland cannot conceive it as the parent of any but freemen. Climate and soil here unite to tell man that brotherhood, and not domination, constitutes the only nobility for those who call this fair shore their motherland. The Irish struggle for liberty owes as much, perhaps, to the continuing influence of the same lakes and rivers and the same mountains as to the survival of any political fragments of the past. Irish history is inseparably the history of the land, rather than of a race; and in this it offers us a spectacle of a continuing national unity that long-continuing disaster has not been able wholly to efface or wholly to disrupt.

To discover the Europe that existed before Rome we must turn to the East, Greece, and to the West, Ireland.

Ireland alone among western lands preserves the recorded tradition, the native history, the continuity of mind, and, until yesterday, of speech and song, that connect the half of Europe with its ancestral past. For early Europe was very largely Celtic Europe, and nowhere can we trace the continuous influence of Celtic culture and idealism, coming down to us from a remote past, save in Ireland only.

To understand the intellect of pre-Roman Gaul, of Spain, of Portugal, and largely of Germany, and even of Italy, we must go to Ireland. Whoever visits Spain or Portugal, to investigate the past of those countries, will find that the record stops where Rome began. Take England in further illustration. The first record the inhabitants of England have of the past of their island comes from Roman invasion. They know of Boadicea, of Cassivelaunus, the earliest figures in their history, from what a foreign destroyer tells them in an alien tongue.

All the early life of Celtiberians and Lusitanians has passed away from the record of human endeavor, save only where we find it recorded by the Italian invaders in their own speech, and in such terms as imperial exploitation ever prescribes for its own advancement and the belittlement of those it assails. Ireland alone among all western nations knows her own past, from the very dawn of history and before the romance of Romulus began, down to the present day, in the tongue of her own island people and in the light of her own native mind. Early Irish history is not the record of the clan-strivings of a petty and remote population, far from the centre of civilization. It is the authentic story of all western civilization before the warm solvent of Mediterranean blood and iron melted and moulded it into another and rigid shape.

The Irishman called O'Neill, O'Brien, O'Donnell, steps out of a past well-nigh co-eval with the heroisms and tragedies that uplifted Greece and laid Troy in ashes, and swept the Mediterranean with an Odyssey of romance that still gives its name to each chief island, cape, and promontory of the mother sea of Europe. Ireland, too, steps out of a story just as old. Well nigh every hill or mountain, every lake or river, bears the name today it bore a thousand, two thousand, years ago, and one recording some dramatic human or semi-divine event.

The songs of the Munster and Connacht poets of the eighteenth and nineteenth centuries gave to every cottage in the land the ownership as well as the tale of an heroic ancestry. They linked the Ireland of yesterday with the Ireland of Finn and Oscar, of Diarmid and Grainne, of Deirdre and the Sons of Usnech, of Cuchulainn the Hound of Ulster. A people bred on such soul-stirring tales as these, linked by a language "the most expressive of any spoken on earth" in thought and verse and song with the very dawn of their history, wherein there moved, as familiar figures, men with the attributes of gods—great in battle. grand in danger, strong in loving, vehement in death—such a people could never be vulgar, could never be mean, but must repeat, in their own time and in their own manhood, actions and efforts thus ascribed as a vital part of their very origin. Hence the inspiration that gave the name of Fenian, in the late nineteenth century, to a band of men who sought to achieve by arms the freedom of Ireland. The law of the Fenian of the days of Marcus Aurelius was the law of the Fenian in the reign of Victoria—to give all —mind, body, and strength of purpose—to the defense of his country, "to speak truth and harbor no greed in his heart."

Some there are who may deny to Finn and his Fenians of the second and third centuries corporeal existence; yet nothing is surer than that Ireland claims these ancestral embodiments of an heroic tradition by a far surer title of native record than gives to the Germans Arminius, to the Gauls, Ariovistus, to the British, Caractacus. This conception of a national life, one with the land itself, was very clear to the ancient Irish, just as it has been and is the foundation of all later national effort.

"If ever the idea of nationality becomes the subject of a thorough and honest study, it will be seen that among all the peoples of antiquity, not excluding the Hellenes and the Hebrews, the Irish held the clearest and most conscious and constant grasp of that idea; and that their political divisions, instead of disproving the existence of the idea, in their case intensely strengthen the proof of its existence and emphasize its power.

In the same way the remarkable absence of insular exclusiveness, notwithstanding their geographical position, serves to bring their sense of nationality into higher relief.

Though pride of race is evident in the dominant Gaelic stock, their national sentiment centres not in the race, but altogether in the country, which is constantly personified and made the object of a sort of cult.

It is worth noting that just as the Brehon Laws are the laws of Ireland without distinction of province or district; as the language of Irish literature is the language of Ireland without distinction of dialects; as the Dindshenchus contains the topographical legends of all parts of Ireland, and the Festilogies commemorate the saints of all Ireland; so the

Irish chronicles from first to last are histories of the Irish nation. The true view of the Book of Invasions is that it is the epic of Irish Nationality." (Professor Eoin MacNeill, in a letter to Mrs. A. S. Green, January, 1914.)

The "Book of Invasions", which Professor MacNeill here speaks of, was compiled a thousand years ago. To write the history of later Ireland is merely to prolong the "Book of Invasions", and thus bring the epic of Irish resistance down to our own day. All Irish valor and chivalry, whether of soul or of body, have been directed for a thousand years to this same end. It was for this that Sarsfield died at Landen no less than Brian at Clontarf. The monarch of Ireland at the head of a great Irish army driving back the leagued invaders from the shores of Dublin Bay in 1014, and the exiled leader in 1693, heading the charge that routed King William's cause in the Netherlands, fell on one and the same battlefield. They fought against the invader of Ireland.

We are proudly told that the sun never sets on the British Empire. Wherever an Irishman has fought in the name of Ireland it has not been to acquire fortune, land, or fame, but to give all, even life itself, not to found an empire, but to strike a blow for an ancient land and assert the cause of a swordless people. Wherever Irishmen have gone, in exile or in fight, they have carried this image of Ireland with them. The cause of Ireland has found a hundred fields of foreign fame, where the dying Irishman might murmur with Sarsfield, "Would that this blood were shed for Ireland", and history records the sacrifice as made in no other cause.

Ireland, too, owns an empire on which the sun never sets.

REFERENCES:

Sigerson: Bards of the Gael and Gall; O'Callaghan: History of the Irish Brigades; Mitchel: Life of Hugh O'Neill; Green: The Making of Ireland and its Undoing, Irish Nationality, The Old Irish World; Taylor: Life of Owen Roe O'Neill; Todhunter: Life of Patrick Sarsfield; Hyde: Love Songs of Connacht, Religious Songs of Connacht; O'Grady: Bog of Stars, Flight of the Eagle; Ferguson: Hibernian Nights' Entertainment; Mitchel: History of Ireland, in continuation of MacGeoghegan's History.

THE ISLAND OF SAINTS AND SCHOLARS

By Canon D'Alton, M. R. I. A., LL.D.

UNLIKE the natives of Britain and Scotland, the Irish in pre-Christian times were not brought into contact with Roman institutions or Roman culture. In consequence they created and developed a civilization of their own that was in some respects without equal. They were far advanced in the knowledge of metal-work and shipbuilding; they engaged in commerce; they loved music and had an acquaintance with letters; and when disputes arose among them, these were settled in duly constituted courts of justice, presided over by a trained lawyer, called a brehon, instead of being settled by the stern arbitrament of force. Druidism was their pagan creed. They believed in the immortality and in the transmigration of souls; they worshipped the sun and moon, and they venerated mountains, rivers, and wells; and it would be difficult to find any ministers of religion who were held in greater awe than the Druids.

Commerce and war brought the Irish into contact with Britain and the continent, and thus was Christianity gradually introduced into the island. Though its progress at first was not rapid, there were, by 431, several Christian churches in existence, and in that year Palladius, a Briton and a bishop, was sent by Pope Celestine to the Irish who already believed in Christ. Discouraged and a failure, Palladius returned to Britain after a brief stay on his mission, and then, in 432, the same Pope sent St. Patrick, who became the Apostle of Ireland.

Because of the great work he did, St. Patrick is one of the prominent figures of history; and yet, to such an extent has the dust of time settled down on his life and acts that the place and year of his birth, the schools in which he was educated, and the year of his death, are all matters of dispute. There is, however, no good reason to depart from the traditional account, which is, that the Apostle was born at Dumbarton in Scotland, in the year 372; that in 388 he was captured by the Irish king Niall, who had gone on a plundering raid into Scotland; that he was brought to Ireland and sold as a slave, and that as such he served a pagan chief named Milcho who lived in what is now the county of Antrim; that from Antrim he escaped and went back to his own country; that he had many visions urging him to return to Ireland and preach the Gospel there; that, believing these were from God, he went to France, and there was educated and ordained priest, and later consecrated bishop; and then, accompanied by several ecclesiastics, he was sent to Ireland.

From Wicklow, where he landed, he proceeded north and endeavored, but in vain, to convert his old pagan master Milcho; thence he proceeded south by Downpatrick and Dundalk to Slane in Meath, where, in sight of Tara, the high-king's seat, he lighted the paschal fire. At Tara he confounded the Druids in argument, baptized the high-king and the chief poet; and then, turning north and west, he crossed the Shannon into Connacht, where he spent seven years. From Connacht he passed into Donegal, and thence through Tyrone and Antrim, after which he entered Munster, and remained there seven years. Finally, he returned to Armagh, which he made his episcopal see, and died at Saul, near Downpatrick, in 493.

St. Patrick wrote two short works, both of which have survived, his *Confession* and his *Epistle to Coroticus*. In neither are there any graces of style, and the Latin is certainly not that of Cicero or Livy. But in the *Confession* the character of the author himself is completely revealed—his piety, his zeal, his self-sacrifice, his courage in face of every danger and every trial. Not less remarkable was the skill with which he handled men and used pagan institutions for the purposes of Christianity; and equally so was the success with which his bloodless apostolate was crowned.

One great difficulty which St. Patrick had was to provide the people with a native ministry. At first he selected the chief men—princes, brehons, bards—and these, with little training and little education, he ordained. Thus, slenderly equipped with knowledge, the priest, with his ritual, missal, and a catechism, and the bishop, with his crozier and bell, went forth to do battle for the Lord. This condition of things was soon ended. In 450 a college was founded at Armagh, which in a short time grew to be a famous school, and attracted students from afar. Other schools were founded in the fifth century, at Noendrum, Louth, and Kildare. In the sixth century arose the famous monastic schools of Clonfert, Clonard, Clonmacnois, Arran, and Bangor; while the seventh century saw the rise of Glendalough and Lismore.

St. Patrick was educated in Gaul, at the monasteries of Marmoutier and Lerins; and, perhaps as a result, the monastic character of the early Irish church was one of its outstanding features; moreover it was to the prevalence of the monastic spirit, the desire for solitude and meditation, that so many of the great monastic establishments owed their existence. Fleeing from society and its attractions, and wishing only for solitude and austerity, some holy man sought out a lonely retreat, and there lived a life of mortification and prayer. Others came to share his poverty and vigils; a grant of land was then obtained from the ruling chief, the holy man became abbot and his followers his monks; and a religious community was formed destined soon to acquire fame. It was thus that St. Finnian established Clonard on the banks of the Boyne, and St. Kieran, Clonmacnois by the waters of the Shannon; and thus did St. Enda make the wind-swept Isles of Arran the home and the resting place of so many saints. Before the close of the sixth century, 3,000 monks followed the rule of St. Comgall at Bangor; and in the seventh century, St. Carthage made Lismore famous and St. Kevin attracted pious men from afar to his lonely retreat in the picturesque valley of Glendalough.

And there were holy women as well as holy men in Ireland. St. Brigid was held in such honor that she is often called the Mary of the Gael. Even in St. Patrick's day, she had founded a convent at Kildare, beside which was a monastery of which St. Conleth was superior; and she founded many other convents in addition to that at Kildare. Her example was followed by St. Ita, St. Fanchea, and many others; and if at the close of the sixth century there were few districts which had not monasteries and monks, there were few also which had not convents and nuns.

Nor was this all. Fired with missionary zeal, many men left

Ireland to plant the faith in distant lands. Thus did St. Columcille settle in Iona, whence he converted the Picts. Under his successors, St. Aidan and his friends went south to Lindisfarne to convert Northumbria in England; and the ninth abbot of Iona was the saintly Adamnan, whose biography of St. Columcille has been declared by competent authority to be the best of its kind of which the whole Middle Ages can boast. Nor must it be forgotten that the monasteries of Luxeuil and Bobbio owed their origin to St. Columbanus; that St. Gall gave his name to a town and canton in Switzerland; that St. Fridolin labored on the Rhine and St. Fursey on the Marne; and that St. Cathaldus was Bishop of Tarentum, and is still venerated as the patron of that Italian see.

And if we would know what was the character of the schools in which these men were trained, we have only to remember that Colgu, who had been educated at Clonmacnois, was the master of Alcuin; that Dicuil the Geographer came from the same school; that Cummian, Abbot and Bishop of Clonfert, combated the errors about the paschal computation with an extent of learning and a wealth of knowledge amazing in a monk of the seventh century; and that at the close of the eighth century two Irishmen went to the court of Charlemagne and were described by a monk of St. Gall as "men incomparably skilled in human learning". The once pagan Ireland had by that time become a citadel of Christianity, and was rightfully called the School of the West, the Island of Saints and Scholars.

With this state of progress and prosperity the Danes played sad havoc. Animated with the fiercest pagan fanaticism, they turned with fury against Christianity, and especially against monks and religious foundations. Armagh, Clonmacnois, Bangor, Kildare, and many other great monastic establishments thus fell before their fury. Ignorance, neglect of religion, and corruption of manners followed, and from the eighth to the twelfth century there was a noted falling off in the number of Irish scholars. At home indeed were Cormac and Maelmurra, O'Hartigan and O'Flynn, and abroad was John Scotus Erigena, whose learning was so great that it excited astonishment even at Rome. The love of learning and zeal for religion lived on through this long period of accumulated disasters. After the triumph of Brian Boru at Clontarf, there was a distinct revival of piety and learning; and, when a century of turmoil followed Brian's fall and religion again suffered, nothing was wanted to bring the people back to a sense of their duty but the energy and reforming zeal of St. Malachy.

Gerald Barry, the notorious Anglo-Norman, who visited Ireland towards the close of the twelfth century, has been convicted out of his own mouth when he states that Ireland was a barbarous nation when his people came there. He forgot that a people who could illuminate the Book of Kells and build Cormac's Chapel could not be called savages, nor could a church be lost to a sense of decency and dignity that numbered among its children such a man as St. Laurence O'Toole. Abuses there were, it is true, consequent on long continued war, though these abuses were increased rather than lessened by the coming of the Anglo-Normans, and to such an extent that for more than two centuries there is not a single great name among Irish scholars except Duns Scotus.

The fame of Duns Scotus was European, and the Subtle Doctor, as he was called, became the great glory of the Franciscan, as his rival St. Thomas was the great glory of the Dominican, order. But he left no successor, and from his death, at the opening of the fourteenth century, till the seventeenth century the number of Irish scholars or recognized Irish saints was small. Yet, in the midst of disorders within, and despite oppression from without, at no time did the love of learning disappear in Ireland; nor was there ever in the Irish church either heresy or schism.

The attempted reformation by Henry VIII and his daughter Elizabeth produced martyrs like O'Hurley and O'Hely; and there were many more martyrs in the time of the Stuarts, and especially under the short but sanguinary rule of Cromwell.

Those were the days of the penal laws, when they who clung to the old religion suffered much. But nothing could shake their faith; neither the proclamations of Elizabeth and James, the massacres of Cromwell, nor the ferocious proscriptions of the eighteenth century. The priest said Mass, though his crime was punishable by death, and the people heard Mass, though theirs also was a criminal offence; and the school-master, driven from the school, taught under a sheltering hedge. The clerical student, denied education at home, crossed the sea, to be educated at Louvain or Salamanca or Seville, and then, perhaps loaded with academic honors, he returned home to face poverty and persecution and even death. The Catholic masses, socially ostracised, degraded, and impoverished, shut out from every avenue to ambition or enterprise, deprived of every civil right, knowing nothing of law except when it oppressed them and nothing of government except when it struck them down, yet clung to the religion in which they were born. And when, in the latter half of the eighteenth century, the tide turned and the first dawn of toleration appeared on the horizon, it was found that the vast majority of the people were unchanged, and that, after two centuries of the most relentless persecution since the days of Diocletian, Ireland was, in faith and practice, a strongly Catholic nation still.

On a soil constantly wet with the blood and tears of its chil-dren, it would be vain to expect that scholarship could flourish. And yet the period had its distinguished Irish scholars both at home and abroad. At Louvain, in the sixteenth century, were Lombard and Creagh, who both became Archbishops of Armagh, and O'Hurley who became Archbishop of Cashel. An even greater scholar than these was Luke Wadding, the eminent Franciscan who founded the convent of St. Isidore at Rome. At Louvain was John Colgan, a Franciscan like Wadd-ing, a man who did much for Irish ecclesiastical history. And at home in Ireland, as parish priest of Tybrid in Tipperary, was the celebrated Dr. Geoffrey Keating the historian, once a student at Salamanca. John Lynch, the renowned opponent of Gerald Barry the Welshman, was Archdeacon of Tuam. And in the ruined Franciscan monastery of Donegal, the Four Masters, aided and encouraged by the Friars, labored long and patiently, and finally completed the work which we all know as the *Annals of the Four Masters*. This work, originally written in Irish, remained in manuscript in Louvain till the middle of the nineteenth century, when it was edited and translated into English by John O'Donovan, one of Ireland's greatest Irish scholars, with an ability and completeness quite worthy of the original.

On the Anglo-Irish side there were also some great names, and especially in the domain of history, notably Stanyhurst and Hammer, Moryson and Campion and Davies, and, above all, Ussher and Ware. James Ware died in 1666, and though a Protestant and an official of the Protestant government, and living in Ireland in an intolerant age and in an atmosphere charged with religious rancor, he was, to his credit be it said, to a large extent free from bigotry. He dealt with history and antiquities, and wrote in no party spirit, wishing only to be fair and impartial, and to set out the truth as he found it. James Ussher, Archbishop of Armagh, was a much abler man and a much greater scholar than Ware. His capacity for research, his profound scholarship, the variety and extent of his learning raised him far above his co-religionists, and he has been rightly called the Great Luminary of the Irish Protestant church. It is regrettable that his fine intellect was darkened by bigotry and intolerance.

Far different was the character of another Protestant bishop, the great Berkeley, of Cloyne, a patriot, a philosopher, and a scholar, who afterwards left money and books for a scholarship, which is still in existence, at the then infant Yale College in New England. He lived in the first half of the eighteenth century, when the whole machinery of government was ruthlessly used to crush the Catholics. But Berkeley had little sympathy with the penal laws; he had words of kindness for the Catholics, and undoubtedly wished them well. Nor must Swift be forgotten, for though he took little pride in being an Irishman, he hated and despised those who oppressed Ireland, and is rightly regarded as one of the greatest of her sons.

The short period during which Grattan's parliament existed was one of great prosperity. It was then that Maynooth College was established for the education of the Irish priesthood. But Catholics, though free to set up schools, were still shut out from the honors and emoluments of Trinity College, the one university at that time in Ireland. Still, Charles O'Connor, MacGeoghegan, and O'Flaherty were great Catholic scholars in the latter part of the eighteenth century.

In the following century, while Protestant ascendancy was still maintained, the Catholics had greater scope. Away back in the days of Queen Elizabeth, Campion found Latin widely spoken among the peasantry, and Father Mooney met country lads familiar with Virgil and Homer. In 1670, Petty had a similar story to tell, in spite of all the savageries of Cromwell and the ruin which necessarily followed. And in the eighteenth century the schoolmaster, though a price was set on his head, was still active. With an inherited love of learning, the Irish in the nineteenth century would have made rapid progress had they been rich. But their impoverishment by the penal laws made it impossible for them to set up an effective system of primary education, and until the national school system came into existence in 1831, they had to rely on the hedge-schools. Secondary education fared better, for the bishops, relying with confidence on the generosity of their flocks, were soon able to establish diocesan colleges. And in higher education, equally determined efforts were made by the establishment of the Catholic University under Cardinal Newman. But in this field of intellectual effort, in spite of the energy and zeal of the bishops, in spite of the great generosity of the people, so many of whom were poor, and in spite of the fame of Newman, it is failure rather than success which the historian has to record.

Nor has the love of the Irish for religion, any more than their love of learning, been lessened or enfeebled by time. The mountain side as the place for Mass in the penal days gradually gave way to the rude stone church without steeple or bell; and when steeple and bell ceased to be proscribed, and the people were left free to erect suitable houses of sacrifice and prayer, the fine churches of the nineteenth century began gradually to appear. The unfettered exercise of freedom of religious worship, the untiring efforts of a zealous clergy and episcopate, the unstinted support of a people, who out of their poverty grudged nothing to God or to God's house, formed an irresistible combination, and all over the country beautiful churches are now to be found.

In every diocese in Ireland, with scarcely an exception, there is now a stately cathedral to perpetuate the renown of the patron saint of that diocese, and even parish churches have been built not unworthy to be the churches of an ancient see. At Armagh, a cathedral has been built which does honor to Irish architecture, and worthily commemorates the life and labors of St. Patrick, the founder of the primatial see; at Thurles, a cathedral stands, the chief church of the southern province, statelier far than any which ever stood on the Rock of Cashel; at Tuam, a noble building, associated with the memory of John MacHale, the Lion of the Fold of Judah, perpetuates the name of St. Jarlath; at Queenstown, the traveller, going to America or returning from it to the old land, has his attention attracted to the splendid cathedral pile sacred to St. Colman, the patron saint of the diocese of Cloyne; and if we would see how splendid even a parish church may be, let us visit the beautiful church in Drogheda, dedicated to the memory of Oliver Plunkett.

Nor are these things the only evidence we have that zeal for religion among the Irish has survived centuries of persecution. Columbanus and Columcille have still their successors, eager and ready as they were to bring the blessings of the Gospel to distant lands. In recent years an Irish-born Archbishop of Sydney has been succeeded by an Irish-born Archbishop; an Irishman rules the metropolitan see of Adelaide; and an Irish-born Archbishop of Melbourne has as his coadjutor a former president of the College of Maynooth. In South Africa, the work of preaching and teaching and ruling the church is largely the work of Irish-born men. In the great Republic of the West the three cardinal-archbishops at the head of the Catholic Church have the distinctively Irish names of Gibbons and Farley and O'Connell; and in every diocese throughout the United States the proportion of priests of Irish birth or descent is large.

Nor must the poorer Irish be forgotten. How much does the Catholic Church, both in Ireland and in America, owe to the generosity of Irish-American laborers and servant girls! Out of their scanty and hard-earned pay they have contributed much not only towards the building of the plain wooden church in the rural parishes, but also of the stately cathedrals of American cities. And many a church in old Ireland owes its completion and its adornment to the dollars given by the poor but generous Irish exiles.

And if the zeal of the Irish for religion has thus survived to the twentieth century, so also in an equally remarkable degree has their zeal for learning. We have evidence of this in the numerous primary schools in every parish, filled with eager pupils and presided over by hard working teachers; in the colleges where the sciences and the classics are studied with the same energy as in the ancient monastic schools; and in Maynooth College, which is the foremost ecclesiastical college in the world. And if there are now new universities, the National and the Queen's, sturdy and vigorous in their youth, this does not imply that Trinity College suffers from the decreptitude of age. For among those whom she sent forth in recent times are Dowden and Mahaffy and Lecky, to name but three, and these would do credit to any university in Europe.

It would be difficult to find in any age of Irish history a greater pulpit orator than the famous Dominican, Father Tom Burke, or a more delightful essayist than Father Joseph Farrell; and who has depicted Irish clerical life more faithfully than the late Canon Sheehan, whose fame as a novelist has crossed continents and oceans? O'Connell was a great orator as well as a great political leader, and Dr. Doyle and Archbishop John MacHale were scholars as well as statesmen and bishops. We have thus an unbroken chain of great names, a series of Irishmen whom the succeeding ages have brought forth to enlighten and instruct lesser men; and Ireland, in the twentieth century, is not less attached to religion and learning than she was when Clonmacnois flourished and the saintly Carthage ruled at Lismore.

REFERENCES :

Joyce: Social History of Ancient Ireland (Dublin, 1903); Lanigan: Ecclesiastical History of Ireland (Dublin, 1822); Healy: Ireland's Ancient Schools and Scholars (Dublin, 1896), Life and Writings of St. Patrick (Dublin, 1905); Bury: St. Patrick and his Place in History (London, 1905); Ussher's Works (Dublin, 1847); Reeves: Adamnan's Life of St. Columba (Dublin, 1851); Worsae: The Danes in Ireland (London, 1852); Moran: Essays on the Early Irish Church

(Dublin, 1864) ; Stokes: Ireland and the Anglo-Norman Church (London, 1897) ; Mant: History of the Church of Ireland (London, 1841) ; Bagwell: Ireland under the Tudors (London, 1885-90) ; Moran: Persecutions under the Puritans (Callan, 1903) ; Murphy: Our Martyrs (Dublin, 1896) ; Meehan: Franciscan Monasteries of the Seventeenth Century (Dublin, 1870) ; Lecky: History of Ireland in the Eighteenth Century (London, 1902) ; O'Connell's Correspondence (London, 1888) ; Wyse: History of the Catholic Association (London, 1829) ; Doyle: Letters on the State of Ireland (Dublin, 1826) ; O'Rorke: Irish Famine (Dublin, 1902) ; Gavan Duffy: Young Ireland (London, 1880) ; Plunkett: Ireland in the New Century (London, 1904) ; O'Riordan: Catholicity and Progress in Ireland (London, 1905) ; MacCaffery: History of the Church in the Nineteenth Century (Dublin, 1909) ; Healy: Centenary History of Maynooth College (Dublin, 1905) ; D'Alton: History of Ireland (London, 1910).

IRISH MONKS IN EUROPE

By Rev. Columba Edmonds, O. S. B.

ST. PATRICK'S work in Ireland was chiefly concerned with preaching the faith and establishing monasteries which served as centres of education. The great success that attended these efforts earned for Ireland the double title of Island of Saints and a Second Thebaid.

The monastic institutions organized by St. Patrick were characterized from their commencement by an apostolic zeal that knew no bounds. Sufficient scope was not to be found at home, so it was impatient to diffuse itself abroad.

SCOTLAND: Hence in the year 563 St. Columcille, a Donegal native of royal descent, accompanied by twelve companions, crossed the sea in currachs of wickerwork and hides, and sought to land in Caledonia. They reached the desolate Isle of Iona on the day preceding Whitsunday.

Many years before, colonies of Irishmen had settled along the western parts of the present Scotland. The settlement north of the Clyde received the name of the Kingdom of Dalriada. These Dalriadan Irish were Christian at least in name, but their neighbors in the Pictish Highlands were still pagans. Columcille's apostolate was to be among both these peoples. Adamnan says that Columcille came to Caledonia "for the love of Christ's name", and well did his after-life prove the truth of this statement. He had attained his forty-fourth year when King Conall, his kinsman, bestowed Iona upon him and his brethren. The island, situated between the Dalriadans and the Picts of the Highlands, was conveniently placed for missionary work. A numerous community recruited from Ireland, with Columcille as its Abbot, soon caused Iona to become a flourishing centre from which men could go forth to preach Christianity. Monasteries and hermitages rapidly sprang up in the adjacent islands and on the mainland. These, together with the Columban foundations in Ireland, formed one great religious federation, in which the Celtic apostles of the northern races were formed under the influence of the holy founder.

St. Columcille recognized the need of securing permanence for his work by obtaining the conversion of the Pictish rulers, and thus he did not hesitate to approach King Brude in his castle on the banks of the River Ness. St. Comgall and St. Canice were Columcille's companions on his journey through the great glen, now famous for the Caledonian Canal. The royal convert Brude was baptized, and by degrees the people followed the example set them. Opposition, however, was keen and aggressive, and it came from the official representatives of Pictish paganism—the Druids.

Success, too, attended Columcille's ministrations among the Dalriadans, and on the death of their king, Aidan Gabhran, who succeeded to the throne, sought regal consecration from the hands of Columcille. In 597 the saint died, but not before he had won a whole kingdom to Christ and covered the land with churches and monasteries. Today his name is held in honor not by Irishmen alone, but by the Catholics and non-Catholics of the land of his adoption.

There are other saints who either labored in person with Columcille or perpetuated the work he accomplished in Caledonia; and their names add to the glory of Ireland, their birthland. Thus St. Moluag (592) converted the people of Lismore, and afterwards died at Rosemarkie; St. Drostan, St. Columcille's friend and disciple, established the faith in Aberdeenshire and became abbot of Deer; St. Kieran (548) evangelized Kintyre; St. Mun (635) labored in Argyleshire; St. Buite (521) did the same in Pictland; St. Maelrubha (722) preached in Ross-shire; St. Modan and St. Machar benefited the dwellers on the western and eastern coasts respectively; and St. Fergus in the eighth century became apostle of Forfar, Buchan, and Caithness.

DISTANT ISLANDS: But Irish monks were mariners as well as apostles. Their hide-covered currachs were often launched in the hope of discovering solitudes in the ocean. Adamnan records that Baitan set out with others in search of a desert in the sea. St. Cormac sought a similar retreat and arrived at the Orkneys. St. Molaise's holy isle guards Lamlash Bay, off Arran. The island retreats of the Bass, Inchkeith, May, and Inchcolm, in the Firth of Forth, are associated with the Irish saints Baldred, Adamnan, Adrian, and Colum-cille. St. Maccaldus, a native of Down, became bishop of the Isle of Man.

Remarkable, too, is the fact that Irish monks sailed by way of the Faroe Islands to distant Iceland. These sailor-clerics, who settled on the southeast of the island, were spoken of by later Norwegians as "papar." After their departure—they were probably driven away by Norwegian pagans—these Ice-landic apostles "left behind them Irish books, bells, and croziers, wherefrom one could understand they were Irish-men."

But St. Brendan, the voyager, is the most wonderful of the mariner monks of Ireland. He accomplished apostolic work in both Wales and Scotland, but his seafaring instincts urged him to make missionary voyages to regions hitherto unknown. Some writers, not without reason, have actually maintained that he and his followers traveled as far as the American shore. Be this as it may, the tradition of the discoveries of this Irish monk kept in mind the possibly existing western land, and issued at last in the discovery of the great continent of America by Columbus.

NORTHUMBRIA: Turn now to Northumbria. Adamnan writes that St. Columcille's name was honored not only in Gaul, Spain, and Italy, but in Rome itself. England, however, owes to it a special veneration, because of the widespread apostolic work accomplished within her borders by Colum-cille's Irish disciples. The facts are as follows: Northumbrian Christianity was well-nigh exterminated through the victory of Penda the pagan over Edwin the Christian, A. D. 633. St. Paulinus, its local Roman apostle, was driven permanently from his newly founded churches. Meanwhile Oswald and his brother Edwith sought refuge among the Irish monks of Iona, and received baptism at their hands. Edwith died and Oswald became heir to the throne. A battle was fought. The day before he met the pagan army, between the Tyne and the Solway, Oswald beheld St. Columcille in vision saying to him: "Be strong and of good faith; I will be with thee." The result of this vision of the abbot of Iona was that a consider-able part of England received the true faith. Oswald was victorious; he united the kingdoms of Deira and Bernicia, and became overlord of practically all England, with the exception of Kent. There was evangelization to be done, and St. Oswald turned to Iona. In response to his appeal, the Irish bishop, St. Aidan, was sent with several companions. They were established on the island of Lindisfarne, in sight of the royal residence at Bamborough. These monks labored in union with, and even seemed to exceed in zeal, the Roman missionaries in the south under St. Augustine. However great the enthusiasm they had displayed for conversions in Iona, they displayed still greater on the desolate isle of Lindisfarne. In the first instance St. Aidan and his monks evangelized Northumbria. Want of facility in preaching in the Anglo-Saxon tongue was at first an obstacle, but it was speedily overcome, for king Oswald himself, who knew both Gaelic and English, came forward and acted as interpreter.

When St. Aidan died in 651, Iona sent St. Finan, another Irish bishop, to succeed him. Finan spread the faith beyond the borders of Northumbria and succeeded so well that he himself baptized Penda, king of the Mid-Angles, and Sigebert, king of the East Saxons. Diuma and Cellach, Irish monks, assisted by three Anglo-Saxon disciples of St. Aidan, consolidated the mission to the Mercians.

ANGLIA: While Christianity was thus being restored in Northumbria, other Irish apostles were teaching it in East Anglia. St. Fursey, accompanied by his brother St. Foillan and St. Ultan and the priests Gobham and Dicuil, landed in England in 633, and began to labor in the eastern portions of Anglia. In his monastery at Burghcastle, in Suffolk, the convert king Sigebert made his monastic profession, and in the same house many heavenly visions were vouchsafed to its founder.

The South Saxons had in Dicuil an apostle who founded the monastery of Bosham in Sussex, whence originated the episcopal see of Chichester. Another Irish monk named Maeldubh settled among the West Saxons and became the founder of Malmesbury Abbey and the instructor of the well-known St. Aldhelm.

Thus did Irish monks contribute to the conversion of Great

Britain and its many distant islands. They built up the faith by their holy lives, their preaching, and their enthusiasm, and wisely provided for its perpetuation by educating a native clergy and by the founding of monastic institutions.

They were not yet satisfied, so they turned towards other lands to bring to other peoples the glad tidings of salvation.

GAUL: In 590 St. Columbanus, a monk of Bangor in Ireland, accompanied by twelve brethren, arrived in France, having passed through Britain. After the example of St. Columcille in Caledonia, they traveled to the court of Gontram, king of Burgundy, in order to secure his help and protection. During the course of the journey they preached to the people, and all were impressed with their modesty, patience, and devotion. At that epoch Gaul was sadly in need of such missionaries, for, owing partly to the invasion of barbarians and partly to remissness on the part of the clergy, vice and impiety everywhere prevailed. Columbanus, because of his zeal, sanctity, and learning, was well fitted for the task that lay before him. One of his early works in Burgundy was the founding of the monastery of Luxeuil, which became the parent of many other monasteries founded either by himself or by his disciples. Many holy men came from Ireland to join the community, and so numerous did the monks of Luxeuil become that separate choirs were formed to keep up perpetual praise— the "laus perennis". But Columbanus did not remain at Luxeuil. In his strict uncompromising preaching he spared not even kings, and he preferred to leave his flourishing monastery rather than pass over in silence the vices of the Merovingians. He escaped from the malice of Brunehaut, and, being banished from Burgundy, made his way to Neustria, and thence to Metz. Full of zeal, he resolved to preach the faith to the pagans along the Rhine, and with this purpose set out with a few of his followers. They proceeded as far as the Lake of Zurich, and finally established themselves at Bregentz, on the Lake of Constance.

By this time his disciple St. Gall had learned the Alemannian dialect, which enabled him to push forward the work of evangelization. But Columbanus felt that he was called to labor in other lands while vigor remained to him, so, bidding his favorite follower farewell, he crossed the Alps and arrived at Milan in northern Italy. King Agilulph and his queen, Theodelinda, gave the Irish abbot a reverent and kind welcome. His zeal was still unspent, and he worked much for the conversion of the Lombard Arians. Here he founded, between Milan and Genoa, the monastery of Bobbio, which as a centre of knowledge and piety was long the light of northern Italy. In this monastery he died in the year 615, but not before the arrival of messengers from King Clothaire, inviting him to return to Luxeuil, as his enemies were now no more. But he could not go; all he asked was protection for his dear monks at Luxeuil.

It has been said most truly that Ireland never sent a greater son to do God's work in foreign lands than Columbanus. The fruit of his labors remained; and for centuries after his death his influence was widely felt throughout Europe, especially in France and Italy. His zeal for the interests of God was unbounded, and this was the secret of his immense power. Some of his writings have come down to us, and comprise his Rule for Monks, his Penitential, sixteen short sermons, six letters, and several poems, all in Latin. His letters are of much value as evidence of Ireland's ancient belief in papal supremacy.

SWITZERLAND: Gall, Columbanus's disciple, remained in Switzerland. In a fertile valley, lying between two rivers and surrounded by hills, he laid the beginnings of the great abbey which afterwards bore his name and became one of the most famous monasteries in Christendom. St. Gall spent thirty years of his life in Helvetia, occupying himself in teaching, preaching, and prayer. He succeeded where others had failed, and that which was denied to Columbanus was reserved for Gall, his disciple, and the latter is entitled the Apostle of Alemannia.

Other districts had their Irish missionaries and apostles. Not far from St. Gall, at Seckingen, near Basle, St. Fridolin was a pioneer in the work of evangelization.

Towards the close of the seventh century St. Kilian, an Irishman, with his companions, Totnan and Colman, arrived in Franconia. He was martyred in Würtzburg, where he is honored as patron and apostle.

Sigisbert, another Irish follower of St. Columbanus, spread the faith among the half-pagan people of eastern Helvetia, and founded the monastery of Dissentis in Rhaetia.

St. Ursanne, a little town on the boundaries of Switzerland, took its origin from another disciple of St. Columbanus.

OTHER APOSTLES AND FOUNDERS: Desire for solitary life drew St. Fiacre to a hermitage near Meaux, where he transformed wooded glades into gardens to provide vegetables for poor people. This charity has earned for Fiacre the title of patron saint of gardeners.

St. Fursey, the illustrious apostle of East Anglia, crossed over to France, where he travelled and preached continuously. He built a monastery at Lagny-sur-Marne, and was about to return to East Anglia when he died at Mézerolles, near Doullens. St. Gobham followed his master's example, and like him evangelized and founded monasteries. St. Etto (Zé) acted in like manner. St. Foillan and St. Ultan, brothers of St. Fursey, became apostles in southern Brabant.

The monastery of Honau, on an island near Strasburg, and that of Altomünster, in Bavaria, owe their foundation to the Irish monks Tuban and Alto, respectively.

Not far from Luxeuil was the Abbey of Lure, another great Irish foundation, due to Deicolus (Desle, Dichuill), a brother of St. Gall and a disciple of St. Columbanus. So important was this house considered in later times that its abbot was numbered among the princes of the Holy Roman Empire.

Rouen, in Normandy, felt the influence of the Irish monks through the instrumentality of St. Ouen; and the monasteries of Jouarre, Rebais, Jumièges, Leuconaus, and St. Vandrille were due at least indirectly to Columbanus or his disciples.

Turning to Belgium, it is recorded that St. Romold preached the faith in Mechlin, and St. Livinus in Ghent. Both came from Ireland.

St. Virgilius, a voluntary exile from Erin, "for the love of Christ", established his monastery at Salzburg, in Austria. He became bishop there, and died in 781.

Moreover, the Celtic Rule of Columbanus was carried into Picardy by St. Valery, St. Omer, St. Bertin, St. Mummolin, and St. Valdelenus; but the Irish Caidoc and Fricor had already preceded them, their work resulting in the foundation of the Abbey of St. Riquier.

ITALY: Something yet remains to be said of the monks of Ireland in Italy. Anterior to St. Columbanus's migration, his fellow countryman, St. Frigidian (or Fridian), had taken up his abode in Italy at Monte Pisana, not far from the city of Lucca, where he became famed for sanctity and wisdom. On the death of the bishop of Lucca, Frigidian was compelled to occupy the vacant see. St. Gregory the Great wrote of him that "he was a man of rare virtue". His teachings and holy life not only influenced the lives of his own flock, but brought to the faith many heretics and pagans. In Lucca this Celtic apostle is still honored under the name of St. Frediano.

St. Pellegrinus is another Irish saint who sought solitude at Garfanana in the Apennines; and Cathaldus, a Waterford saint, in 680, became Bishop of Taranto, which he governed for many years with zeal and great wisdom. His co-worker was Donatus, his brother, who founded the church at Lecce in the Kingdom of Naples.

Of the two learned Irishmen, Clemens and Albinus, who resided in France in the eighth century, Albinus was sent into Italy, where at Pavia he was placed at the head of the school attached to St. Augustine's monastery. Dungal, his compatriot, was a famous teacher in the same city. Lothair thus ordained concerning him: "We desire that at Pavia, and under the superintendence of Dungal, all students should assemble from Milan, Brescia, Lodi, Bergamo, Novara, Vercelli, Tortona, Acqui, Genoa, Asti, Como."

It was this same Dungal who presented the Bangor psalter to Bobbio; therefore it may be reasonably conjectured that he came from the very monastery that produced Columbanus, Gall, and Comgall.

Fiesole, in Tuscany, venerates two Irish eighth-century saints, Donatus and Andrew. The former was educated at Iniscaltra, and Andrew was his friend and disciple. After visiting Rome, they lingered at Fiesole. Donatus was received with great honor by clergy and people and was requested to fill their vacant bishopric. With much hesitation he took upon himself the burden, which he bore for many years. His biographer says of him that "he was liberal in almsgiving, sedulous in watching, devout in prayer, excellent in doctrine, ready in speech, holy in life." Andrew, who was his deacon, founded the church and monastery of St. Martin in Mensola, and is known in Fiesole as St. Andrew of Ireland, or St. Andrew the Scot, that is, the Irishman.

HOSPITALIA: Thus Irish monks were to be found in France, Belgium, Switzerland, Germany, and Italy, and even in Bulgaria. So numerous were they and so frequent their travels through the different countries of Europe that hospices were founded to befriend them. These institutions were known as "Hospitalia Scottorum ("Hospices for the Irish"), and their benefactors were not only pious laymen but the highest ecclesiastical authorities. Sometimes the hospices were diverted to purposes other than those originally intended, and then Church Councils would intervene in favor of the lawful inheritors. Thus in 845 we read that the Council of Meaux ordered the hospices in France to be restored to the dispossessed Irishmen. In the twelfth century Ireland still continued to send forth a constant succession of monk-pilgrims, renowned for faith, austerity, and piety.

RATISBON: Special monasteries were erected to be peopled by the Irish. The most renowned of these dates from 1067, when Marianus Scotus ("Marianus the Irishman"), with his companions, John and Candidus, left his native land and arrived in Bavaria. These holy men were welcomed at Ratisbon by the Bishop Otto; and on the advice of Murcherat, an Irish recluse, took up their residence near St. Peter's church at the outskirts of the city. Novices flocked from Ireland to join them and a monastery was erected to receive the community. In a short time this had to be replaced by a still larger one, which was known to future ages as the Abbey of St. James's of the Scots (that is, Irish) at Ratisbon. How prolific was this parent foundation is evidenced from its many offshoots, the only surviving monasteries on the continent for many centuries intended for Irish brethren. These, besides St. James's at Erfurt and St. Peter's at Ratisbon, comprised St. James's at Würtzburg, St. Giles's at Nuremberg, St. Mary's at Vienna, St. James's at Constance, St. Nicholas's at Memmingen, Holy Cross at Eichstatt, a Priory at Kelheim and another at Oels in Silesia, all of which were founded during the twelfth or thirteenth century, and formed a Benedictine congregation approved of by Pope Innocent III., and presided over by the Abbot of Ratisbon. These Irish houses, with their long lines of Celtic abbots, in the days of their prosperity did much work that was excellent and civilizing, and rightly deserve a remembrance in the achievements of Ireland's ancient missionaries.

Ratisbon and its dependent abbeys, as is set forth in the papal briefs of 1248, possessed priories in Ireland, and, from these, novices were usually obtained.

But evil days came for the Congregation of St. James, and now it is extinct. The subjugation of Ireland to England, says Wattenbach, contributed no doubt to the rapid decline of the Scotic (that is, Irish) monasteries. For from Ireland they had up till then been continually receiving fresh supplies of strength. In this their fatherland the root of their vitality was to be found. Loss of independence involved loss of enterprise.

SCHOLARSHIP AND INFLUENCE: Irish monks were not only apostles of souls, but also masters of intellectual life. Thus in the seventh century the Celtic monastery of Luxeuil became the most celebrated school in Christendom. Monks from other houses and sons of the nobility crowded to it. The latter were clearly not intended for the cloister, but destined for callings in the world.

There were outstanding men among these missionaries from Ireland. St. Virgilius of Salzburg in the eighth century taught the sphericity of the earth and the existence of the Antipodes. It was this same teaching that Copernicus and later astronomers formulated into the system now in vogue.

St. Columcille himself was a composer of Latin hymns and a penman of no mean order, as the Book of Kells, if written by him, sufficiently proves. In all the monasteries which he founded, provision was made for the pursuit of sacred learning and the multiplication of books by transcription. The students of his schools were taught classics, mechanical arts, law, history, and physics. They improved the methods of husbandry and gardening; supplied the people, whom they helped to civilize, with implements of labor; and taught them the use of the forge, an accomplishment belonging to almost every Irish monk.

The writings of Adamnan, who spent most of his life outside his native land, show that he was familiar with the best Latin authors, and had a knowledge of Greek as well. His "Vita S. Columbae" ("Life of St. Columcille") has made his name immortal as a Latin writer. His book "De Locis Sanctis" ("On the Holy Places") contains information he received from the pilgrim bishop Arculfus, who had been driven by a tempest to take refuge with the monks of Iona. On account of the importance of the writings of Adamnan and because of his influence in secular and ecclesiastical affairs of importance, few will question his right to a distinguished place among the saintly scholars of the West.

Irish monks, abroad as well as at home, were pre-eminently students and exponents of Holy Scripture. Sedulius wrote a commentary on the Epistles of St. Paul; John Scotus Erigena composed a work, "De Praedestinatione" ("Concerning Predestination"); Dungal was not only an astronomer, but also an excellent theologian, as is clear from his defence of Catholic teaching on the invocation of saints and the veneration of their relics. His knowledge of Sacred Scripture and of the Fathers is exceedingly remarkable.

St. Columbanus, besides other works, is said to have composed an exposition of the Psalms, which is mentioned in the catalogue of St. Gall's library, but which cannot now be identified with certainty. The writings of this abbot are said to have brought about a more frequent use of confession both in the world and in monasteries; and his legislation regarding the Blessed Sacrament fostered eucharistic devotion.

Marianus Scotus is the author of a commentary on the Psalms, so precious that rarely was it allowed to pass beyond the walls of the monastic library. His commentary on St. Paul's Epistles is regarded as his most famous production. Herein he shows acquaintance with Saints Jerome, Augustine, Gregory, and Leo, with Cassiodorus, Origen, Alcuin, Cassian, and Peter the Deacon. He completed the work on the 17th

May, 1079, and ends the volume by asking the reader to pray
for the salvation of his soul.

TRANSCRIPTION: In all the monasteries a vast number
of scribes were continually employed in multiplying copies of
the Sacred Scriptures. These masterpieces of calligraphy,
written by Irish hands, have been scattered throughout the
libraries of Europe, and many fragments remain to the present
day. The beauty of these manuscripts is praised by all, and
the names of the best transcribers often find mention in monastic annals. The work was irksome, but it was looked upon as a
privilege and meritorious.

It remains to speak of that glorious monument of the Irish
monks, the abbey of St. Gall, in Switzerland. It was here
that Celtic influence was most felt and endured the longest.
Within its walls for centuries the sacred sciences were taught
and classic authors studied. Many of its monks excelled as
musicians and poets, while others were noted for their skill
in calligraphy and the fine arts. The library was only in its
infancy in the eighth century, but gradually it grew, and eventually became one of the largest and richest in the world. The
brethren were in correspondence with all the learned houses
of France and Italy, and there was constant mutual inter-
change of books, sacred and scientific, between them.

They manufactured their own parchment from the hides of
the wild beasts that roamed in the forests around them, and
bound their books in boards of wood clamped with iron or
ivory.

Such was the monastery of St. Gall, which owes its incep-
tion to the journey through Europe of the great Columbanus
and his monk-companions—men whose lives, according to
Bede, procured for the religious habit great veneration, so that
wherever they appeared they were received with joy, as God's
own servants. "And what will be the reward," asks the
biographer of Marianus Scotus, "of these pilgrim-monks who
left the sweet soil of their native land, its mountains and
hills, its valleys and its groves, its rivers and pure fountains,
and went like the children of Abraham without hesitation into
the land which God had pointed out to them?" He answers
thus: "They will dwell in the house of the Lord with the

ɪnd archangels of God forever; they will behold the
gods in Sion, to whom be honor and glory for ever and

REFERENCES:

Lanigan: Ecclesiastical History of Ireland (Dublin, 1829);
Montalembert: Monks of the West (Edinburgh, 1861); Moran:
Irish Saints in Great Britain (Dublin, 1903); Dalgairns: Apostles
of Europe (London, 1876); Healy: Ireland's Ancient Schools and
Scholars (Dublin, 1890); Barrett: A Calendar of Scottish Saints
(Fort Augustus, 1904); Stokes: Six Months in the Apennines (London, 1892), Three Months in the Forests of France (London, 1895);
Fowler: Vita S. Columbæ (Oxford, 1894); Wattenbach: Articles in
Ulster Journal of Archæology, vol. 7 (Belfast, 1859); Gougaud: Les
Chrétientés celtiques (Paris, 1911); Hogan: Articles in Irish Ecclesiastical Record, 1894, 1895; Drane: Christian Schools and Scholars (London, 1881).

THE IRISH AND THE SEA

By William H. Babcock, LL.B.

THE beginning of Irish navigation, like the beginning of everything else, is hidden in the mist of antiquity. Vessels of some kind obviously must have borne the successive waves of immigrants or invaders to the island. Naturally they would remain in use afterwards for trade, travel, exploration, and war. Irish ships may have been among those of the Breton fleet that Cæsar dispersed at Vannes after an obstinate struggle. Two or three centuries later we find Niall of the Nine Hostages making nautical descents on the neighboring shores, especially Britain: and there is every probability that ships of the island conveyed some at least of the "Scots" (Irish) whom Gildas in the sixth century describes as joining the Picts in furiously storming the Roman wall.

The equally adventurous but more pacific work of exploration went on also, if we may judge by that extraordinary series of Irish sea-sagas, the *Imrama,* comprising the Voyages of Bran, Maelduin, the Hui Corra, and St. Brendan—the last-mentioned deservedly the most famous. These vary in their literary merits and in the merits of their several parts, for they have been successively rewritten at different periods, receiving always something of the color, belief, and adornment which belonged to the writer's time; but under all may be dimly traced, as in a palimpsest, the remote pagan original. At their best they embody a lofty and touching poetry very subtle and significant, as when we read of Bran's summoning by a visitant of supernatural beauty to the isles of undying delight, where a thousand years are but as a day; his return with a companion who had been overcome by longing for Ireland and home; the man's falling to ashes at the first touch of the native soil, as though he had been long dead; and the flight of Bran and his crew from the real living world to the islands of the blessed. At least equally fine and stirring is St. Brendan's interview with the exiled spirit of Heaven, whose "sin was but little", so that he and his fellows were given only the pleasing penance of singing delightfully, in the guise of beautiful birds, the praises of

showed them mercy and grace, amid the charms
paradise. "Then all the birds sang evensong, so
an heavenly noise to hear."

very surprising that St. Brendan's legend, with such
qualities in prose and verse, made itself at home in many
lands and languages, and became for centuries a widespread
popular favorite and matter of general belief, also influencing
the most permanent literature of a high contemplative cast,
which we might suppose to be out of touch with it altogether.
Certain of its more unusual incidents are found even in Arab
writings of romance founded on fact, as in Edrisi's narrative
of the Magrurin explorers of Lisbon and the adventures of
Sinbad related in the Arabian Nights; but perhaps here we
have a case of reciprocal borrowing such as may well occur
when ships' companies of different nations meet.

The most conspicuous, insistent, and repeated feature of
all these *Imrama* is a belief in Atlantic islands fair enough
or wonderful enough to tempt the shore dwellers of Ireland far away and hold them spell-bound for years. It is
easy to ascribe these pictures to sunset on the ocean, or the
wonders of mirage; but all the time, within long sailing distance, there actually were islands of delightful climate and
exceeding beauty. These had been occasionally reached from
the Mediterranean ever since early Carthaginian times, as
classical authors seem to tell us; why not also from Ireland,
perhaps not quite so distant? It is undoubted that the
Canary Islands were never really altogether forgotten, and the
same is probably true of the Madeiras and all three groups of
Azores, though the knowledge that lingered in Ireland was a
distorted glimmering tradition of old voyages, occasionally
inciting to new ventures in the same field.

Some have supposed, though without sufficient evidence, that
Saint Brendan even made his way to America, and parts of that
shore line in several different latitudes have been selected as
the scene of the exploit. His first entry into serious geography
is in the fine maps of Dulcert, 1339, and the Pizigani, 1367,
both of which plainly label Madeira, Porto Santo, and Las
Desertas—"The Fortunate Islands of St. Brandan." That
there may be no possibility of misunderstanding, the Pizigani

brothers present a full-length portrait of the holy navigator himself bending over these islands with hands of benediction. The inscription, though not the picture, was common, thus applied, on the maps of the next century or two, and no other interpretation of his voyage found any place until a later time.

Of course the fourteenth century was a long way from the sixth, when the voyage was supposed to have been made, and we cannot take so late a verdict as convincing proof of any fact. But it at least exhibits the current interpretation of the written narrative among geographers and mariners, the people best able to judge; and here the interval was much less. The story itself seems to corroborate them in a general way, if read naturally. One would say that it tells of a voyage to the Canaries, of which one is unmistakably "the island under Mount Atlas", and that this was undertaken by way of the Azores and Madeira, with inevitable experience of great beauty in some islands and volcanic terrors in others. Madeira may well have been pitched upon by the interpreters as the suitable scene of a particularly long tarrying by the way. Of course magic filled out all gaps of real knowledge, and wonders grew with each new rewriting.

Whatever Brendan did, there is no doubt that Irish mariner-monks, incited by the great awakening which followed St. Patrick's mission, covered many seas in their frail vessels during the next three or four centuries. They set up a flourishing religious establishment in Orkney, made stepping stones of the intervening islands, and reached Iceland some time in the eighth century, if not earlier. The Norsemen, following in their tracks as always, found them there, and the earliest Icelandic writings record their departure, leaving behind them books, bells, and other souvenirs on an islet off shore which still bears their name.

Did they keep before the Norsemen to America too? At least the Norsemen thought so. For centuries the name Great Ireland or Whitemen's Land was accepted in Norse geography as meaning a region far west of Ireland, a parallel to Great Sweden (Russia), which lay far east of Sweden. The saga of Thorfinn Karlsefni, first to attempt colonizing America, makes it plain that his followers believed Great Ireland to be somewhere in that region, and it is explicitly located near Wineland by the twelfth century Landnamabok. Also there were specific tales afloat of a distinguished Icelander lost at sea, who was afterward found in a western region by an Irish vessel long driven before the storm. The version most relied on came through one Rafn, who had dwelt in Limerick; also through Thorfinn, earl of the Orkneys.

Brazil, the old Irish *Breasail,* was another name for land west of Ireland—where there is none short of America—on very many medieval maps, of which perhaps a dozen are older than the year 1400, the earliest yet found being that of Dalorto, 1325. Usually it appears as a nearly circular disc of land opposite Munster, at first altogether too near the Irish coast, as indeed the perfectly well-known Corvo was drawn much too near the coast of Spain, or as even in the sixteenth century, when Newfoundland had been repeatedly visited, that island was shifted by divers mapmakers eastward towards Ireland, almost to the conventional station of Brazil. Also, not long afterwards, the maps of Nicolay and Zaltieri adopted the reverse treatment of transferring Brazil to Newfoundland waters, as if recognizing past error and restoring its proper place.

The name Brazil appears not to have been adopted by the Norsemen, but there is one fifteenth century map, perhaps of 1480, preserved in Milan, which shows this large disc-form "Brazil" just below Greenland ("Illa Verde"), in such relation that the mapmaker really must have known of Labrador under the former name and believed that it could be readily reached from that Norse colony.

It seems altogether likely that "Brazil" was applied to the entire outjutting region of America surrounding the Gulf of St. Lawrence—that part of this continent which is by far the nearest Ireland. Besides the facts above stated, certain coincidences of real geography and of these old maps favor that belief, and they are quite unlikely to have been guessed or invented. Thus certain maps, beginning with 1375, while keeping the circular external outline of Ireland, reduce the land area to a mere ring, enclosing an expanse of water dotted with islands; and certain other maps show it still nearly circular externally, and solid, but divided into two parts by a curved channel nearly from north to south. The former exposition is possible enough to one more concerned with the nearly enclosed Gulf of St. Lawrence and its islands than with its two comparatively narrow outlets; the second was afterward repeated approximately by Gastoldi's map illustrating Ramusio when he was somehow moved to minimize the width of the Gulf, though well remembering the straits of Belle Isle and Cabot. There are some other coincidences, but it is unnecessary to dwell on them. Land west of Ireland must be either pure fancy or the very region in question, and it is hardly believable that fancy could guess so accurately as to two different interpretations of real though unusual geography and give them right latitude, with such an old Irish name (Brazil) as might naturally have been conferred in the early voyaging times. That an extensive region, chiefly mainland, should be represented as an island is no objection, as anyone will see by examining the maps which break up everything north of South America in the years next following the achievements of Columbus and Cabot. There was a natural tendency to expect nothing but islands short of Asia.

It seems likely, therefore, that America was actually reached by the Irish even before the Norsemen and certainly long before all other Europeans.

REFERENCES :

Babcock: Early Norse Visits to North America, Smithsonian Publication 2138 (1913) ; Baring-Gould: Curious Myths of the Middle Ages; Beauvois: The Discovery of the New World by the Irish; Cantwell: Pre-Columbian Discoveries of America; Daly: The Legend of St. Brandan, Celtic Review, vol. I, A Sequel to the Voyage of St. Brandan, Celtic Review, Jan. 13, 1909; Hardiman: The History of Galway; Hull: Irish Episodes of Icelandic History; Joyce: The Voyage of Maelduin; Nutt: The Voyage of Bran; Stokes: The Voyage of Maelduin (*Revue Celtique*, vol. 9), Voyage of Snedgus (*Revue Celtique*, vol. 9), Voyage of the Hui Corra (*Revue Celtique*, vol. 14) ; Moran: Brendaniana.

IRISH LOVE OF LEARNING

By Rev. P. S. Dinneen, M. A., R. U. I.

"THE distinguishing property of man," says Cicero, "is to search for and follow after truth. Therefore, when disengaged from our necessary cares and concerns, we desire to see, to hear, and to learn, and we esteem knowledge of things obscure or wonderful as indispensable to our happiness." (*De Officiis* I., 4).

I claim for the Irish race that throughout their history they have cut down their bodily necessities to the quick, in order to devote time and energy to the pursuit of knowledge; that they have engaged in intellectual pursuits, not infrequently of a high order, on a low basis of material comfort; that they have persevered in the quest of learning under unparalleled hardships and difficulties, even in the dark night of "a nation's eclipse", when a school was an unlawful assembly and school-teaching a crime. I claim, moreover, that, when circumstances were favorable, no people have shown a more adventurous spirit or a more chivalrous devotion in the advancement and spread of learning.

Love of learning implies more than a natural aptitude for acquiring information. It connotes a zest for knowledge that is recondite and attainable only at the expense of ease, of leisure, of the comforts and luxuries of life, and a zeal for the cultivation of the mental faculties. It is of the soul and not of the body; it refines, elevates, adorns. It is allied to sensibility, to keenness of vision, to the close observation of mental phenomena. Its possessor becomes a citizen of the known world. His mind broadens; he compares, contrasts, conciliates; he brings together the new and the old, the near and the distant, the permanent and the transitory, and weaves from them all the web of systematized human thought.

I am not here concerned with the extent of Ireland's contribution to the sum of human learning, nor with the career of her greatest scholars; I am merely describing the love of learning which is characteristic of the race, and which it seems best to present in a brief study of distinct types drawn from various periods of Irish history.

In the pre-Christian period the Druid was the chief representative of the learning of the race. He was the adviser of kings and princes, and the instructor of their children. His knowledge was of the recondite order and beyond the reach of ordinary persons. The esteem in which he was held by all classes of the people proves their love for the learning for which he stood.

Patrick came: and with him came a wider horizon of learning and greater facilities for the acquisition and diffusion of knowledge. Monastic schools sprang up in all directions—at Clonard, Armagh, Clonmacnois, Bangor, Lismore, Kildare, Innisfallen. These schools were celebrated throughout Europe in the earlier middle ages, and from the fifth to the ninth century Ireland led the nations of Europe in learning and deserved the title of the "Island of Saints and Scholars." Our type is the student in one of these monastic schools. He goes out from his parents and settles down to study in the environs of the monastery. He is not rich; he resides in a hut; his time is divided between study, prayer, and manual labor. He becomes a monk, only to increase in devotion to learning and to accentuate his privations. He copies and illuminates manuscripts. He memorizes the Psalms. He glosses the Vulgate Scriptures with vernacular notes. He receives ordination, and, realizing that there are benighted countries ten times as large as his native land beyond the seas, and, burning with zeal for the spread of the Gospel and the advancement of learning, sails for Britain, or passes into Gaul, or reaches the slopes of the Apennines, or the outskirts of the Black Forest. The rest of his life is devoted to the foundation of monasteries to which schools are attached, to the building of churches, and to the diffusion around him of every known branch of knowledge. He may have taken books from Ireland over seas, and, of these, relics are now to be found among the treasures of the ancient libraries of Europe. Columcille, Columbanus, Adamnan, Gall, Virgilius occur to the mind in dwelling on this type.

The hereditary *seanchaidhe,* who treasured up the traditional lore of the clan and its chief, was held in high honor and enjoyed extraordinary privileges. He held a freehold. He was high in the graces of the chief, and officiated at his inauguration.

An important type is the Irish ecclesiastical student abroad in the penal days. School teaching, unless at the sacrifice of Faith, was a crime in Ireland, and the training required for the priesthood had to be obtained on the continent. The Irish out of their poverty established colleges in Rome (1628), Salamanca (1593), Seville (1612), Alcala (1590), Lisbon (1593), Louvain (1624), Antwerp (1629), Douai (1577), Lille (1610), Bordeaux (1603), Toulouse (1659), Paris (1605), and elsewhere. As late as 1795 these colleges contained 478 students, and some of them are still in existence. The young student in going abroad risked everything. He often returned watched by spies, with his life in danger. Yet the supply never failed; the colleges flourished; and those who returned diffused around them not only learning but the urbanity and refinement which were a striking fruit and mark of their studies abroad.

Another type is the Irish scribe. In the days of Ireland's fame and prosperity and of the flood-tide of her native language, he was a skilled craftsman, and the extant specimens of his work are unsurpassed of their kind. But I prefer to look at him at a later period, when he became our sole substitute for the printer and when his diligence preserved for us all that remains of a fading literature. He was miserably poor. He toiled through the day at the spade or the plough, or guided the shuttle through the loom. At night, by the flare of the turf-fire or the fitful light of a splinter of bogwood, he made his copy of poem or tract or tale, which but for him would have perished. The copies are often ill-spelt and ill-written, but with all their faults they are as noble a monument to national love of learning as any nation can boast of.

In our gallery of types we must not forget the character whom English writers contemptuously called the "hedge-schoolmaster." The hedge-school in its most elemental state was an open-air daily assemblage of youths in pursuit of knowledge. Inasmuch as the law had refused learning a fitting temple in which to abide and be honored, she was led by her votaries into the open, and there, beside the fragrant hedge, if you will, with the green sward for benches, and the canopy of heaven for dome, she was honored in Ireland, even as she had been honored ages before in Greece, in Palestine, and by our primordial Celtic ancestors themselves. The hedge-schoolmaster conducted the rites, and the air resounded with the sonorous hexameters of Virgil and the musical odes of Horace.

In the Irish-speaking portions of the country the hedge-schoolmaster was often also a poet who wrote mellifluous songs in Irish, which were sung throughout the entire district. and sometimes earned him enduring fame. Eoghan Ruadh O'Sullivan and Andrew MacGrath, called *An Mangaire Sugach* or "the Jolly Pedlar," are well-known instances of this type.

The poor scholar is another type that under varying forms and under various circumstances has ever trod the stage of Irish history. From an ancient Irish manuscript (See O'Curry, *Manners and Customs,* II, 79, 80) we learn that Adamnan, the biographer of St. Columcille, and some other youths studied at Clonard and were supported by the neighborhood. The poor scholar more than any other type embodies the love of learning of the Irish race. In the schools which preceded the National, he appeared in a most interesting stage of development. He came from a distance, attracted by the reputation of a good teacher and the regularity of a well-conducted school. He came, avowedly poor. His only claim on the generosity of his teacher and of the public was a marked aptitude for learning and an ardent desire for study and cultivation of mind. He did not look for luxuries. He was satisfied, if his bodily wants were reasonably supplied, even with the inconveniences of frequent change of abode. A welcome was extended to him on all sides. His hosts and patrons honored his thirst for knowledge and tenacity of purpose. He was expected to help the students in the house where he found entertainment, and it may not have been unpleasing to him on occasion to display his talents before his host. When school was over, it was not unusual to find him surrounded by a group of school-companions, each pressing his claim to entertain him for the night.

Despite the hospitality of his patrons, the poor scholar often felt the bitterness of his dependent state, but he bore it with equanimity, his hand ever eagerly stretched out for the prize of learning. What did learning bring him? Why was he so eager to bear for its sake

> "all the thousand aches
> That patient merit of the unworthy takes"?

Sometimes he became a priest; sometimes his life was purposeless and void. But he was ever urged onward by the fascination of learning and of the cultivation of the nobler part of his nature.

As might have been expected, the Irish who have emigrated to the American and Australian continents have given touching proof of their devotion to the cause of learning. I have space only for a few pathetic examples.

An Irish workman in the United States, seeing my name in connection with an Irish Dictionary, wrote to me a few years ago to ask how he might procure one, as, he said, an Italian in the works had asked him the meaning of *Erin go bragh,* and he felt ashamed to be unable to explain it.

A man who, at the age of three, had emigrated from Clare in the famine time, wrote to me recently from Australia in the Irish language and character.

An old man named John O'Regan of New Zealand, who had been twelve years in exile in the United States and forty-eight on the Australian continent, with failing eyesight, in a letter that took him from January to June of the year 1906 to write, endeavored to set down scraps of Irish lore which he had carried with him from the old country and which had clung to his memory to the last.

"In my digging life in the quarries," he says, "books were not a part of our swag (prayerbook excepted). In 1871, when I had a long seat of work before me, I sent for McCurtin's Dictionary to Melbourne. It is old and wanting in the introductory part, but for all was splendid and I loved it as my life." (See *Gaelic Journal,* Dec., 1906.)

REFERENCES:

Joyce: A Social History of Ancient Ireland (2 vols., 2d ed., Dublin, 1913); Healy: Ireland's Ancient Schools and Scholars (Dublin,

1890), Maynooth College Centenary History (Dublin, 1895);
O'Curry: Manners and Customs of the Ancient Irish, (3 vols., Dublin and London, 1873), Manuscript Materials of Irish History, reissue (Dublin, 1873); Carleton: Traits and Stories of the Irish
Peasantry, especially vol. 3, The Poor Scholar; Montalembert: The
Monks of the West, authorized translation, (7 vols., London, 1861);
Meyer: Learning in Ireland in the Fifth Century (Dublin, 1913);
Dinneen: Poems of Eoghan Ruadh O'Sullivan, Introduction (Dublin, 1902), The Maigue Poets, Introduction (Dublin, 1906); Boyle:
The Irish College in Paris 1578-1901, with a brief sketch of the
other Irish Colleges in France (Dublin, 1901); Irish Ecclesiastical
Record, new series, vol. VIII, 307, 465; 3rd series, vol. VII, 350,
437, 641.

IRISH MEN OF SCIENCE

By Sir Bertram C. A. Windle, Sc.D., M.D.,
President, University College, Cork.

WE may divide our survey of the debt owed to Ireland by science into three periods: the earliest, the intermediate, and the latest.

In the earliest period the names which come before us are chiefly those of compilers such as Augustin, a monk and an Irishman who wrote at Carthage, in Africa, in the seventh century, a Latin treatise on *The Wonderful Things of the Sacred Scripture,* still extant, in which, in connection with Joshua's miracle, a very full account of the astronomical knowledge of the period, Ptolemaic, but in many ways remarkably accurate, is given. There are, however, three distinguished names. Virgil the Geometer, *i. e.,* Fergil (O'Farrell), was Abbot of Aghaboe, went to the continent in 741, and was afterwards Bishop of Salzburg. He died in 785. He is remembered by his controversies with St. Boniface, one of which is concerned with the question of the Antipodes. Virgil is supposed to have been the first to teach that the earth is spherical. So celebrated was he that it has been thought that a part of the favor in which the author of the *Aeneid* was held by medieval churchmen was due to a confusion between his name and that of the geometer, sometimes spoken of as St. Virgil.

Dicuil, also an Irish monk, was the author of a remarkable work on geography, *De Mensura Provinciarum Orbis Terrae,* which was written in 825, and contains interesting references to Iceland and especially to the navigable canal which once connected the Nile with the Red Sea. He wrote between 814 and 816 a work on astronomy which has never been published. It is probable, but not certain, that he belonged to Clonmacnois.

Dungal, like the two others named above, was an astronomer. He probably belonged to Bangor, and left his native land early in the ninth century. In 811 he wrote a remarkable work, *Dungali Reclusi Epistola de duplici solis eclipsi anno 810 ad Carolum Magnum.* This letter, which is still extant, was written at the request of Charlemagne, who considered its

author to be the most learned astronomer in existence and
most likely to clear up the problem submitted to him.

Before passing to the next period, a word should be said as
to the medieval physicians, often if not usually belonging to
families of medical men, such as the Leahys and O'Hickeys,
and attached hereditarily to the greater clans. These men
were chiefly compilers, but such works of theirs as we have
throw light upon the state of medical knowledge in their day.
Thus there is extant a treatise on *Materia Medica* (1459),
written by Cormac MacDuinntsleibhe (Dunleavy), hereditary
physician to the clan of O'Donnell in Ulster. A more interesting work is the *Cursus Medicus,* consisting of six books on
Physiology, three on Pathology, and four on Semeiotica,
written in the reign of Charles I. of England by Nial O'Glacan,
born in Donegal, and at one time physician to the king of
France.

O'Glacan's name introduces us to the middle period, if
indeed it does not belong there. *Inter arma silent leges,* and
it may be added, scientific work. The troublous state of Ireland
for many long years fully explains the absence of men of
science in any abundance until the end of the eighteenth century. Still there are three names which can never be forgotten,
belonging to the period in question. Sir Hans Sloane was
born at Killileagh, in Ulster, in 1660. He studied medicine
abroad, went to London where he settled, and was made a
Fellow of the Royal Society. He published a work on the
West Indies, but his claim to undying memory is the fact that
it was the bequest of his most valuable and extensive collections to the nation which was the beginning and foundation of
the British Museum, perhaps the most celebrated institution
of its kind in the world. Sloane's collection, it should be added,
contained an immense number of valuable books and manuscripts, as well as of objects more usually associated with the
idea of a museum. He died in 1753.

The Hon. Robert Boyle was born at Lismore, in the county
Waterford, in 1627, being the fourteenth child of the first
Earl of Cork. On his tombstone he is described as "The
Father of Chemistry and the Uncle of the Earl of Cork", and,
indeed, in his *Skyptical Chimist* (1661), he assailed, and for

the time overthrew, the idea of the alchemists that there was a *materia prima,* asserting as he did that theory of chemical "elements" which held good until the discoveries in connection with radium led to a modification in chemical teaching. This may be said of Boyle, that his writings profoundly modified scientific opinion, and his name will always stand in the forefront amongst those of chemists. He made important improvements in the air-pump, was one of the earliest Fellows of the Royal Society, and founded the "Boyle Lectures." He died in 1691.

Sir Thomas Molyneux was born in Dublin, in 1661, of a family which had settled in Ireland about 1560-70. He practised as a physician in his native city, was the first person to describe the Irish Elk and to demonstrate the fact that the Giant's Causeway was a natural and not, as had been previously supposed, an artificial production. He was the author of many other scientific observations. He died in 1733.

We may now turn to more recent times, and it will be convenient to divide our subjects according to the branch of science in which they were distinguished, and to commence with

MATHEMATICIANS,

of whom Ireland may boast of a most distinguished galaxy.

Sir William Rowan Hamilton (b. in Dublin 1805, d. 1865), belonged to a family, long settled in Ireland, but of Scottish extraction. He was a most precocious child. He read Hebrew at the age of seven, and at twelve, had studied Latin, Greek, and four leading continental languages, as well as Persian, Syriac, Arabic, Sanscrit, and other tongues. In 1819 he wrote a letter to the Persian ambassador in that magnate's own language. After these linguistic contests, he early turned to mathematics, in which he was apparently self-taught; yet, in his seventeenth year he discovered an error in Laplace's *Mécanique Céleste.* He entered Trinity College where he won all kinds of distinctions, being famous not merely as a mathematician, but as a poet, a scholar, and a metaphysician. He was appointed Professor of Astronomy and Astronomer Royal whilst still an undergraduate. He predicted "conical refraction," afterwards experimentally proved by another Irishman, Humphrey Lloyd. He twice received the Gold Medal of the Royal Society: (i) for optical discoveries; (ii) for his theory of a general method of dynamics, which resolves an extremely abstruse problem relative to a system of bodies in motion. He was the discoverer of a new calculus, that of Quaternions, which attracted the attention of Professor Tait of Edinburgh, and was by him made comprehensible to lesser mathematicians. It is far too abstruse for description here.

Sir George Gabriel Stokes (born in Sligo 1819, d. 1903) was, if not the greatest mathematician, at least among the greatest, of the last hundred years. He was educated in Cambridge, where he spent the rest of his life, being appointed Lucasian Professor of Mathematics in 1849, and celebrating the jubilee of that appointment in 1899. He was member of parliament for his University, and for a time occupied the presidential chair of the Royal Society. He devoted himself, *inter alia,* to optical work, and is perhaps best known by those researches which deal with the undulatory theory of light. It was on this subject that he delivered the Burnett lectures in Aberdeen (1883-1885).

James McCullagh, the son of a poor farmer, was born in Tyrone in 1809, d. 1847. His early death, due to his own hand in a fit of insanity, cut short his work, but enough remains to permit him to rank amongst the great mathematicians of all time, his most important work being his memoir on surfaces of the second order.

Humphrey Lloyd (b. in Dublin 1800, d. 1881), F. R. S. His father was Provost of Trinity College, Dublin, a position subsequently occupied also by the son. Lloyd's work was chiefly concerned with optics and magnetism, and it was in connection with the former that he carried out what was probably the most important single piece of work of his life, namely, the experimental proof of the phenomenon of conical refraction which had been predicted by Sir William Hamilton. He was responsible for the erection of the Magnetic Observatory in Dublin, and the instruments used in it were constructed under his observation and sometimes from his designs or modifications. He was also a meteorologist of distinction.

George Salmon (b. in Dublin 1819, d. 1904), like the last mentioned subject, was, at the time of his death, Provost of Trinity College, Dublin. Besides theological writings, he contributed much to mathematical science, especially in the directions of conic sections, analytic geometry, higher plane curves, and the geometry of three dimensions. He was a Fellow of the Royal Society, and received the Copley and Royal medals, as well as distinctions from many universities and learned societies.

John Casey (b. Kilkenny 1820, d. 1891), F. R. S., was educated at a National School and became a teacher in one in later years. Entirely self-taught as a mathematician, he raised himself from the humble position which he occupied to be a university professor (in the Catholic University of Ireland, and afterwards in the Royal University), and earned the highest reputation as one of the greatest authorities on plane geometry. He was a correspondent of eminent mathematicians all over the world.

Henry Hennessey (b. in Cork 1826, d. 1901), F. R. S., was also a professor in the Catholic University of Ireland and afterwards in the Royal College of Science in Dublin. He was a writer on mathematics, terrestrial physics, and climatology.

Benjamin Williamson (b. in Cork 1827), F. R. S., is a Senior Fellow of Trinity College, Dublin, and a distinguished writer on mathematical subjects, especially on the differential, integral, and infinitesimal calculuses.

Sir Joseph Larmor (b. in Antrim 1857), F. R. S., was educated at Queen's College, Belfast, and in Cambridge, in which last place he has spent his life as a professor. He now represents the University in parliament and is secretary to the Royal Society. He is well-known for his writings on the ether and on other physical as well as mathematical subjects.

ASTRONOMERS.

William Parsons, Earl of Rosse (b. in York 1800, d. 1867), F. R. S., was a very distinguished astronomer who experimented in fluid lenses and made great improvements in casting specula for reflecting telescopes. From 1842-45 he was engaged upon the construction, in his park at Parsonstown, of his great reflecting telescope 58 feet long. This instrument, which cost £30,000, long remained the largest in the world. He was president of the Royal Society from 1848 to 1854.

Sir Howard Grubb (b. 1844), F. R. S., is known all over the world for his telescopes and for the remarkable advances which he has made in the construction of lenses for instruments of the largest size.

Sir Robert Ball (b. in Dublin 1840, d. 1913), F. R. S. Originally Lord Rosse's astronomer at Parsonstown, he migrated as professor to Trinity College, Dublin, and subsequently became Lowndean Professor of Astronomy at Cambridge. He was a great authority on the mathematical theory of screws, and his popular works on astronomy have made him known to a far wider circle of readers than those who can grapple with his purely scientific treatises.

William Edward Wilson (b. Co. Westmeath 1851, d. 1908), F. R. S. A man of independent means, he erected, with the help of his father, an astronomical observatory at his residence. In this well-equipped building he made many photographic researches, especially into the nature of nebulae. He also devoted himself to solar physics, and wrote some remarkable papers on the sudden appearance in 1902 of the star Nova Persei. He was the first to call attention to the probability that radium plays a part in the maintenance of solar heat. In fact, the science of radio-activity was engaging his keenest interest at the time of his early death.

A. A. Rambaut (b. Waterford 1859), F. R. S., formerly Astronomer Royal for Ireland and now Radcliffe Observer at Oxford, is one of the leading astronomers of the day.

PHYSICISTS.

Lord Kelvin, better known as Sir William Thompson (b. Belfast 1824, d. 1907), F. R. S. Amongst the greatest physicists who have ever lived, his name comes second only to that of Newton. He was educated at Cambridge, became professor of natural philosophy in Glasgow University in 1846, and celebrated the jubilee of his appointment in 1896. To the public his greatest achievement was the electric cabling of the Atlantic Ocean, for which he was knighted in 1866. His electrometers and electric meters, his sounding apparatus, and his mariners' compass are all well-known and highly valued instruments. To his scientific fellows, however, his greatest achievements were in the field of pure science, especially in connection with his thermodynamic researches, including the doctrine of the dissipation or degradation of energy. To this brief statement may be added mention of his work in connection with hydrodynamics and his magnetic and electric discoveries. His papers in connection with wave and vortex movements are also most remarkable. He was awarded the Royal and Copley medals and was an original member of the Order of Merit. He received distinctions from many universities and learned societies.

George Francis Fitzgerald (b. Dublin 1851, d. 1901), F. R. S., was fellow and professor of natural philosophy in Trinity College, Dublin, where he was educated. He was the first person to call the attention of the world to the importance of Hertz's experiment. Perhaps his most important work, interrupted by his labors in connection with education and terminated by his early death, was that in connection with the nature of the ether.

George Johnston Stoney (b. King's Co. 1826, d. 1911), F. R. S., after being astronomer at Parsonstown and professor of natural philosophy at Galway, became secretary to the Queen's University and occupied that position until the dissolution of the university in 1882. He wrote many papers on geometrical optics and on molecular physics, but his great claim to remembrance is that he first suggested, "on the basis of Faraday's law of Electrolysis, that an absolute unit of quantity of electricity exists in that amount of it which attends each chemical bond or valency and gave the name, now generally adopted, of electron to this small quantity." He proposed the electronic theory of the origin of the complex ether vibrations which proceed from a molecule emitting light.

John Tyndall (b. Leighlin Bridge, Co. Carlow, 1820, d. 1893), F. R. S., professor at the Royal Institution and a fellow-worker in many ways with Huxley, especially on the subject of glaciers. He wrote also on heat as a mode of motion and was the author of many scientific papers, but will, perhaps, be best remembered as the author of a Presidential Address to the British Association in Belfast (1874), which was the high-water mark of the mid-Victorian materialism at its most triumphant moment.

CHEMISTS.

Richard Kirwan (b. Galway 1733, d. 1812), F. R. S. A man of independent means, he devoted himself to the study of chemistry and mineralogy and was awarded the Copley medal of the Royal Society. He published works on mineralogy and on the analysis of mineral waters, and was the first in Ireland to publish analyses of soils for agricultural purposes, a research which laid the foundation of scientific agriculture in Great Britain and Ireland.

Maxwell Simpson (b. Armagh 1815, d. 1902), F. R. S., held the chair of chemistry in Queen's College, Cork, for twenty years and published a number of papers in connection with his subject and especially with the behavior of cyanides, with the study of which compounds his name is most associated.

Cornelius O'Sullivan (b. Brandon, 1841, d. 1897), F. R. S., was for many years chemist to the great firm of Bass & Co., brewers at Burton-on-Trent, and in that capacity became one of the leading exponents of the chemistry of fermentation in the world.

James Emerson Reynolds (b. Dublin 1844), F. R. S., professor of chemistry, Trinity College, Dublin, for many years, discovered the primary thiocarbamide and a number of other chemical substances, including a new class of colloids and several groups of organic and other compounds of the element silicon.

Among others only the names of the following can be mentioned:—

Sir Robert Kane (b. Dublin 1809, d. 1890), professor of chemistry in Dublin and founder and first director of the Museum of Industry, now the National Museum. He was president of Queen's College, Cork, as was William K. Sullivan (b. Cork 1822, d. 1890), formerly professor of chemistry in the Catholic University. Sir William O'Shaughnessy Brooke, F. R. S. (b. Limerick 1809, d. 1889), professor of chemistry and assay master in Calcutta, is better known as the introducer of the telegraphic system into India and its first superintendent.

BIOLOGISTS.

William Henry Harvey (b. Limerick 1814, d. 1866), F. R. S., was a botanist of very great distinction. During a lengthy residence in South Africa, he made a careful study of the flora of the Cape of Good Hope and published *The Genera of South African Plants*. After this he was made keeper of the Herbarium, Trinity College, Dublin, but, obtaining leave of absence, travelled in North and South America, exploring the coast from Halifax to the Keys of Florida, in order to collect materials for his great work, *Nereis Boreali-Americana*, published by the Smithsonian Institution. Subsequently he visited Ceylon, Australia, Tasmania, New Zealand, and the Friendly and Fiji Islands, collecting algae. The results were published in his *Phycologia Australis*. At the time of his death he was engaged on his *Flora Capensis*, and was generally considered the first authority on algae in the world.

William Archer (b. Co. Down 1827, d. 1897), F. R. S., devoted his life to the microscopic examination of freshwater organisms, especially desmids and diatoms. He attained a very prominent place in this branch of work among men of science. Perhaps his most remarkable discovery was that of Chlamydomyxa labyrinthuloides (in 1868), "one of the most remarkable and enigmatical of all known microscopic organisms."

George James Allman (b. Cork 1812, d. 1898), F. R. S., professor of botany in Trinity College, Dublin, and afterwards Regius Professor of natural history in the University of Edinburgh, published many papers on botanical and zoological subjects, but his great work was that on the gymnoblastic Hydrozoa, "without doubt the most important systematic work dealing with the group of Coelenterata that has ever been produced."

Amongst eminent living members of the class under consideration may be mentioned Alexander Macalister (b. Dublin 1844), F. R. S., professor of anatomy, first in Dublin and now in Cambridge, an eminent morphologist and anthropologist, and Henry Horatio Dixon (b. Dublin), F. R. S., professor of botany in Trinity College, an authority on vegetable physiology, especially problems dealing with the sap.

GEOLOGISTS.

Samuel Haughton (b. Carlow 1821, d. 1897), F. R. S., after earning a considerable reputation as a mathematician and a geologist, and taking Anglican orders, determined to study medicine and entered the school of that subject in Trinity College. After graduating he became the reformer, it might even be said the re-founder, of that school. He devoted ten years to the study of the mechanical principles of muscular action, and published his *Animal Mechanism,* probably his greatest work. He will long be remembered as the introducer of the "long drop" as a method of capital execution. He might have been placed in several of the categories which have been dealt with, but that of geologist has been selected, since in the later part of his most versatile career he was professor of geology in Trinity College, Dublin.

Valentine Ball (b. Dublin 1843, d. 1894), F. R. S., a brother of Sir Robert, joined the Geological Survey of India, and in that capacity became an authority not only on geology but also on ornithology and anthropology. His best known work is *Jungle-Life in India.* In later life he was director of the National Museum, Dublin.

MEDICAL SCIENCE.

Very brief note can be taken of the many shining lights in Irish medical science. Robert James Graves (1796-1853), F. R. S., after whom is named "Graves's Disease", was one of the greatest of clinical physicians. His *System of Clinical Medicine* was a standard work and was extolled by Trousseau, the greatest physician that France has ever had, in the highest terms of appreciation.

William Stokes (1804-1878), Regius Professor of Medicine in Trinity College, and the author of a *Theory and Practice of Medicine,* known all over the civilized world, was equally celebrated.

To these must be added Sir Dominic Corrigan (1802-1880), the first Catholic to occupy the position of President of the College of Physicians in Dublin, an authority on heart disease, and the first adequate describer of aortic patency, a form of ailment long called "Corrigan's Disease". "Colles's Fracture" is a familiar term in the mouths of surgeons. It derives its name from Abraham Colles (1773-1843), the first surgeon in the world to tie the innominate artery, as "Butcher's Saw", a well-known implement, does from another eminent surgeon, Richard Butcher, Regius Professor in Trinity College in the seventies of the last century.

Sir Rupert Boyce (1863-1911), F. R. S., though born in London, had an Irish father and mother. Entering the medical profession, he was assistant professor of pathology at University College, London, and subsequently professor of pathology in University College, Liverpool, which he was largely instrumental in turning into the University of Liverpool. He was foremost in launching and directing the Liverpool School of Tropical Medicine, which has had such widespread results all over the world in elucidating the problems and checking the ravages of the diseases peculiar to hot countries. It was for his services in this direction that he was knighted in 1906.

Sir Richard Quain (b. Mallow 1816, d. 1898), F. R. S., spent most of his life in London, where he was for years the most prominent physician. He wrote on many subjects, but the *Dictionary of Medicine,* which he edited and which bears his name, has made itself and its editor known all over the world.

Sir Almroth Wright (b. 1861), F. R. S., is the greatest living authority on the important subject of vaccino-therapy, which, indeed, may be said to owe its origin to his researches, as do the methods for measuring the protective substances in the human blood. He was the discoverer of the anti-typhoid injection which has done so much to stay the ravages of that disease.

ENGINEERING.

Bindon Blood Stoney (1828-1909), F. R. S., made his reputation first as an astronomer by discovering the spiral character of the great nebula in Andromeda. Turning to engineering, he was responsible for the construction of many important works, especially in connection with the port of Dublin. He was brother of G. J. Stoney.

Sir Charles Parsons (b. 1854), F. R. S., fourth son of the third Earl of Rosse, is the engineer who developed the steam turbine system and made it suitable for the generation of electricity, and for the propulsion of war and mercantile vessels. If he has revolutionized traffic on the water, so on the land has John Boyd Dunlop (still living), who discovered the pneumatic tire with such wide-spread results for motor-cars, bicycles, and such means of locomotion.

MISCELLANEOUS.

Admiral Sir Leopold McClintock (b. Dundalk 1819, d. 1907), F. R. S., was one of the great Arctic explorers, having spent eleven navigable seasons and six winters in those regions. He was the chief leader and organizer of the Franklin searches. From the scientific point of view he made a valuable collection of miocene fossils from Greenland, and enabled Haughton to prepare the geological map and memoir of the Parry Archipelago.

John Ball (b. Dublin 1818, d. 1889), F. R. S., educated at Oscott, passed the examination for a high degree at Cambridge, but, being a Catholic, was excluded from the degree itself and any other honors which a Protestant might have attained to. He travelled widely and published many works on the natural history of Europe and South America from Panama to Tierra del Fuego. He was the first to suggest the utilization of the electric telegraph for meteorological purposes connected with storm warnings.

Space ought to be found for a cursory mention of that strange person, Dionysius Lardner (1793-1859), who by his *Lardner's Cyclopaedia* in 132 vols., his *Cabinet Library,* and his *Museum of Science and Art,* did much to popularize science in an unscientific day.

REFERENCES :

The principal sources of information are the National Dictionary of Biography; the Obituary Notices of the Royal Society (passages in inverted commas are from these) ; "Who's Who" (for living persons) ; Healy: Ireland's Ancient Schools and Scholars; Hyde: Literary History of Ireland; Joyce: Social History of Ancient Ireland; Moore: Medicine in the British Isles.

LAW IN IRELAND

By Laurence Ginnell, B. L., M. P.

A DISTINCTION. Ireland having been a self-ruled country for a stretch of some two thousand years, then violently brought under subjection to foreign rule, regaining legislative independence for a brief period toward the close of the
eighteenth century, then by violence and corruption deprived
of that independence and again brought under the same foreign
rule, to which it is still subject, the expression "Law in Ireland" comprises the native and the foreign, the laws devised
by the Irish Nation for its own governance and the laws imposed upon it from without: two sets, codes, or systems proper
to two entirely distinct social structures having no relation
and but little resemblance to each other. Whatever may be
thought of either as law, the former is Irish in every sense,
and vastly the more interesting historically, archæologically,
philologically, and in many other ways; the latter being English law in Ireland, and not truly Irish in any sense.

ORIGIN AND CHARACTER OF IRISH LAW. *Sean-
chus agus Féineachus na hEireann* = *Hiberniae Antiquitates et
Sanctiones Legales* = The Ancient Laws and Decisions of the
Féini, of Ireland. *Sen* or *sean* (pronounced shan) = "old,"
differs from most Gaelic adjectives in preceding the noun it
qualifies. It also tends to coalesce and become a prefix.
Seanchus (shanech-us) = "ancient law." *Féineachus* (fainech-
us) = the law of the *Féini,* who were the Milesian farmers,
free members of the clans, the most important class in the ancient Irish community. Their laws were composed in their contemporary language, the *Bearla Féini,* a distinct form of
Gaelic. Several nations of the Aryan race are known to have
cast into metre or rhythmical prose their laws and such other
knowledge as they desired to communicate, preserve, and trans-
mit, before writing came into use. The Irish went further and,
for greater facility in committing to memory and retaining
there, put their laws into a kind of rhymed verse, of which they
may have been the inventors. By this device, aided by the isolated geographical position of Ireland, the sanctity of age, and

the apprehension that any change of word or phrase might change the law itself, these archaic laws, when subsequently committed to writing, were largely preserved from the progressive changes to which all spoken languages are subject, with the result that we have today, embedded in the Gaelic text and commentaries of the *Senchus Mór,* the *Book of Aicill,* and other law works, available in English translations made under a Royal Commission appointed by Government in 1852, and published, at intervals extending over forty years, in six volumes of "Ancient Laws and Institutions of Ireland," a mass of archaic words, phrases, law, literature, and information on the habits and manners of the people, not equalled in antiquity, quantity, or authenticity in any other Celtic source. In English they are commonly called Brehon Laws, from the genitive case singular of *Brethem* = "judge", genitive *Brethemain* (pronounced brehun), as Erin is an oblique case of Eire, and as Latin words are sometimes adopted in the genitive in modern languages which themselves have no case distinctions. It is not to be inferred from this name that the laws are judge-made. They are rather case law, in parts possibly enacted by some of the various assemblies at which the laws were promulgated or rehearsed, but for the most part simple declarations of law originating in custom and moral justice, and records of judgments based upon "the precedents and commentaries", in the sort of cases common to agricultural communities of the time, many of the provisions being as inapplicable to modern life as modern laws would be to ancient life. A reader is impressed by the extraordinary number and variety of cases with their still more numerous details and circumstances accumulated in the course of long ages, the manner in which the laws are inextricably interwoven with the interlocking clan system, and the absence of scientific arrangement or guiding principle except those of moral justice, clemency, and the good of the community. This defect in arrangement is natural in writings intended, as these were, for the use of judges and professors, experts in the subjects with which they deal, but makes the task of presenting a concise statement of them difficult and uncertain.

SOCIETY LAW. The law and the social system were inseparable parts of a complicated whole, mutually cause and consequence of each other. *Tuath, clann, cinel, cine,* and *fine* (pronounced thooah, clong, kinnel, kineh, and fin-yeh) were terms used to denote a tribe or set of relatives, in reality or by adoption, claiming descent from a common ancestor, forming a community occupying and owning a given territory. *Tuath* in course of time came to be applied indifferently to the people and to their territory. *Fine,* sometimes designating a whole tribe, more frequently meant a part of it, occupying a distinct portion of the territory, a potential microcosm or nucleus of a clan, having limited autonomy in the conduct of its own immediate affairs. The constitution of this organism, whether as contemplated by the law or in the less perfect actual practice, is alike elusive, and underwent changes. For the purpose of illustration, the *fine* may be said to consist, theoretically, of the "seventeen men" frequently mentioned throughout the laws, namely, the *flaithfine* = chief of the *fine;* the *geilfine* = his four fullgrown sons or other nearest male relatives; the *deirbhfine, tarfine,* and *innfine,* each consisting of four heads of families in wider concentric circles of kinship, say first, second, and third cousins of the *flaithfine.* The *fine* was liable, in measure determined by those circles, for contracts, fines, and damages incurred by any of its members so far as his own property was insufficient, and was in the same degree entitled to share advantages of a like kind accruing. Intermarriage within this *fine* was prohibited. The modern term "sept" is applied sometimes to this group and sometimes to a wider group united under a *flaith* (flah) = "chief", elected by the *flaithfines* and provided, for his public services, with free land proportionate to the area of the district and the number of clansmen in it. *Clann* might mean the whole Irish nation, or an intermediate homogeneous group of *fines* having for wider purposes a *flaith* or *ri-tuatha* = king of one *tuath,* elected by the *flaiths* and *flaithfines,* subject to elaborate qualifications as to person, character, and training, which limited their choice, and provided with a larger portion of free land. This was the lowest chief to whom the title *ri, righ* (both pr. ree) = *rex.* or "king", was applied. A group of these kinglets connected by blood or territory or policy, and their *flaiths*, elected, from a still narrower circle of specially trained men within their own rank, the *ri-mor-tuatha* = king of the territory so composed, to whose office a still larger area of free land was attached. In turn, kings of this class, with their respective sub-kings and *flaiths*, elected from among the *riogh-dhamhna* (ree-uch-dhowna) = *materia principum* or "king-timber", a royal *fine* specially educated and trained, a *ri-cuighidh* (ree coo-ee-hee) supreme over five *ri-mor-tuathas* = roughly, a fourth of Ireland. These, with their respective principal supporters, elected the *ard-ri* = "supreme king", of Ireland, who for ages held his court and national assemblies at Tara and enjoyed the kingdom of Meath for his mensal land. Usually the election was not direct to the king-ship, but to the position of *tanaiste* = " second" (in authority), heir-apparent to the kingship. This was also the rule in the learned professions and "noble" arts, which were similarly endowed wth free land. The most competent among those specially trained, whether son or outsider, should succeed to the position and land. All such land was legally indivisible and inalienable and descended in its entirety to the successor, who might, or might not, be a relative of the occupant. The beneficiaries were, however, free to retain any land that belonged to them as private individuals.

Membership of the clan was an essential qualification for every position; but occasionally two clans amalgamated, or a small *fine*, or desirable individual, was co-opted into the clan— in other words, naturalized. The rules of kinship determined *eineachlann* (ain-yach-long) = "honor value", the assessed value of status, with its correlative rights, obligations, and lia-bilities in connection with all matters civil and criminal; largely supplied the place of contract; endowed members of the clan with birthrights; and bound them into a compact social, politi-cal, and mutual insurance copartnership, self-controlled and self-reliant. *Eineachlann* rested on the two-fold basis of kin-ship and property, expanding as a clansman by acquisition of property and effluxion of time progressed upward from one grade to another; diminishing if he sank; vanishing if for crime he was expelled from the clan.

FOSTERAGE. To our minds, one of the most curious customs prevalent among the ancient Irish was that of *iarrad,* called also *altar* = "fosterage"—curious in itself and in the fact that in all the abundance of law and literature relating to it no logically valid reason is given why wealthy parents normally put out their children, from one year old to fifteen in the case of a daughter and to seventeen in the case of a son, to be reared in another family, while perhaps receiving and rearing children of other parents sent to them. As modern life does not comprise either the custom or a reason for it, we may assume that fosterage was a consequence of the clan system, and that its practice strengthened the ties of kinship and sympathy. This conjecture is corroborated by the numerous instances in history and in story of fosterage affection proving, when tested, stronger than the natural affection of relatives by birth. What is more, long after the dissolution of the clans, fosterage has continued stealthily in certain districts in which the old race of chiefs and clansmen contrived to cling together to the old sod; and the affection generated by it has been demonstrated, down to the middle of the nineteenth century. The present writer has heard it spoken of lovingly, in half-Irish, by simple old people, whom to question would be cruel and irreverent.

LAND LAW. The entire territory was originally, and always continued to be, the absolute property of the entire clan. Not even the private residence of a clansman, with its *maighin digona* = little lawn or precinct of sanctuary, within which himself and his family and property were inviolable, could be sold to an outsider. Private ownership, though rather favored in the administration of the law, was prevented from becoming general by the fundamental ownership of the clan and the birthright of every free-born clansman to a sufficiency of the land of his native territory for his subsistence. The land officially held as described was not, until the population became numerous, a serious encroachment upon this right. What remained outside this and the residential patches of private land was classified as cultivable and uncultivable. The former was the common property of the clansmen, but was held and used in severalty for the time being, subject to *gabhail-cine* (gowal-kinneh) = clan-resumption and redistribution by authority of an assembly of the clan or *fine* at intervals of from one to three years, according to local customs and circumstances, for the purpose of satisfying the rights of young clansmen and dealing with any land left derelict by death or forfeiture, compensation being paid for any unexhausted improvements. The clansmen, being owners in this limited sense, and the only owners, had no rent to pay. They paid tribute for public purposes, such as the making of roads, to the *flaith* as a public officer, as they were bound to render, or had the privilege of rendering—according to how they regarded it—military service when required, not to the *flaith* as a feudal lord, which he was not, but to the clan, of which the *flaith* was head and representative.

The uncultivable, unreclaimed forest, mountain, and bog-land was common property in the wider sense that there was no several appropriation of it even temporarily by individuals. It was used promiscuously by the clansmen for grazing stock, procuring fuel, pursuing game, or any other advantage yielded by it in its natural state.

Kings and *flaiths* were great stock-owners, and were allowed to let for short terms portions of their official lands. What they more usually let to clansmen was cattle to graze either on private land or on a specified part of the official land, not measured, but calculated according to the number of beasts it was able to support. A *flaith* whose stock for letting ran short hired some from a king and sublet them to his own people. A *féine, aithech,* or *ceile* (kailyeh), as a farmer was generally called, might hire stock in one of two distinct ways: saer = "free", which was regulated by the law, left his status unimpaired, could not be terminated arbitrarily or unjustly, under which he paid one-third of the value of the stock yearly for seven years, at the end of which time what remained of the stock became his property, and in any dispute relating to which he was competent to sue or defend even though the *flaith* gave evidence; or *daer* = "bond", which was matter of bargain and not of law, was subject to onerous conditions and contingencies, including maintenance of kings, *flaiths,* or brehons, with their retinues, on visitations, of disbanded soldiers, etc., under which the stock always remained the property of the *flaith,* regarding which the *ceile* could not give evidence against that of the *flaith,* which degraded the *ceile* and his *fine* and impaired their status; a bargain therefore which could not be entered into without the sanction of the *fine.* This prohibition was rendered operative by the legal provision that in case of default the *flaith* could not recover from the *fine* unless their consent had been obtained. The letting of stock, especially of *daer*-stock, increased the *flaith's* power as a lender over borrowers, subject, however, to the check that his rank and *eineachlann* depended on the number of independent clansmen in his district.

Though workers in precious metals, as their ornaments show, the ancient Irish did not coin or use money. Sales were by barter. All payments, tribute, rent, fulfilment of contract, fine, damages, wages, or however else arising, were made in kind—horses, cows, store cattle, sheep, pigs, corn, meal, malt, bacon, salt beef, geese, butter, honey, wool, flax, yarn, cloth, dye-plants, leather, manufactured articles of use or ornament, gold, and silver—whatever one party could spare and the other find a use for.

Tributes and rent, being alike paid in kind and to the same person, were easily confused. This tempted the *flaith,* as the system relaxed, to extend his official power in the direction of ownership; but never to the extent of enabling him to evict a clansman. For a crime a clansman might be expelled from clan and territory; but, apart from crime, the idea of eviction from one's homestead was inconceivable. Not even when a *daer-ceile,* or "unfree peasant", failed to make the stipulated payments could the *flaith* do more than sue as for any other debt; and, if successful, he was bound, in seizing, to leave the family food-material and implements necessary for living and recovering.

LAW OF DISTRAINING. *Athgabail* (ăh-gowil) = "distress", was the universal legal mode of obtaining anything due, or justice or redress in any matter, whether civil or criminal, contract or tort. Every command or prohibition of the law, if not obeyed, was enforced by *athgabail.* The brehons reduced all liabilities of whatsoever origin to material value to be re-

covered by this means. Hence its great importance, the vast
amount of space devoted to it in the laws, and the fact that
the law of distress deals incidentally with every other branch
of law and reveals best the customs, habits, and character of
the people. A claimant in a civil case might either summon his
debtor before a brehon, get a judgment, and seize the amount
adjudged, or, by distraining first at his own risk, force the
defendant either to pay or stop the seizure by submitting the
matter in dispute to trial before a brehon, whom he then could
choose. There was no officer corresponding to a sheriff to
distrain and realize the amount adjudged; the person entitled
had to do it himself, accompanied by a law-agent and wit-
nesses, after, in "distress with time", elaborate notices at
intervals of time sufficient to allow the defendant to consider
his position and find means of satisfying the claim if he could.
In a proper case his hands were strengthened by very explicit
provisions of the law. "If a man who is sued evades justice,
knowing the debt to be due of him, double the debt is payable
by him." In urgent cases "immediate distress" was allowed.
In either case the property seized—usually cattle—was not
taken to the plaintiff's home, but put into a pound, and by
similar easy stages became his property to the amount of the
debt. The costs were paid out of what remained, and any ultimate remainder was returned. On a *fuidir* (foodyir) = serf
or other unfree person resident in the territory incurring liability to a clansman, the latter might proceed against the *flaith*
on whose land the defendant lived, or might seize immediately
any property the defendant owned, and if he owned none,
might seize him and make him work off the debt in slavery.

Seizure of property of a person of higher rank than the
plaintiff had to be preceded by *troscead* (truscah) = fasting
upon him. This consisted in waiting at the door of the defendant's residence without food until the debt was paid or a
pledge given. The laws contained no process more strongly
enforced than this. A defendant who allowed a plaintiff properly fasting to die of hunger was held by law and by public
opinion guilty of murder, and completely lost his *eineachlann*.
Both text and commentary declare that whoever refuses to
cede a just demand when fasted upon shall pay double that

amount. If the faster, having accepted a pledge, did not in due course receive satisfaction of his claim, he forthwith distrained, taking and keeping double the amount of the debt. The law did not allow those whom it at first respected to trifle with justice.

Troscead is believed to have been of druidical origin, and it retained throughout, even in Christian times, a sort of supernatural significance. Whoever disregarded it became an outcast and incurred risks and dangers too grave to be lightly faced. Besides being a legal process, it was resorted to as a species of elaborate prayer, or curse,—a kind of magic for achieving some difficult purpose. This mysterious character enhanced its value in a legal system deficient in executive power.

NON-CITIZENS. From what precedes it will be understood that there were in ancient Ireland from prehistoric times people not comprised in the clan organization, and therefore not enjoying its rights and advantages or entitled to any of its land, some of whom were otherwise free within certain areas, while some were serfs and some slaves. Those outsiders are conjectured to have originated in the earlier colonists subdued by the Milesians and reduced to an inferior condition. But the distinction did not wholly follow racial lines. Persons of pre-Milesian race are known to have risen to eminence, while Milesians are known to have sunk, from crime or other causes, to the lowest rank of the unfree. Here and there a *daer-tuath* = "bond community", of an earlier race held together down to the Middle Ages in districts in which conquest had left them and to which they were restricted. Beyond that restriction, exclusion from the clan and its power, some peculiarities of dialect, dress, and manners, and a tradition of inferiority such as still exists in certain parishes, they were not molested, provided they paid tribute, which may have been heavy.

There were also *bothachs* = cottiers, and *sen-cleithes* = old adherents of a *flaith,* accustomed to serve him and obtain benefits from him. If they had resided in the territory for three generations, and been industrious, thrifty, and orderly, on a few of them joining their property together to the number of one hundred head of cattle, they could emancipate themselves by appointing a *flaithfine* and getting admitted to the clan. Till this was done, they could neither sue nor defend nor inherit, and the *flaith* was answerable for their conduct.

There being no prisons or convict settlements, any person of whatever race convicted of grave crime, or of cowardice on the field of battle, and unable to pay the fines imposed, captives taken in foreign wars, fugitives from other clans, and tramps, fell into the lowest ranks of the *fuidre* = "serfs." It was as a captive that Saint Patrick was brought in his youth to Ireland. The law allowed, rather than entitled, a *flaith* to keep unfree people for servile occupations and the performance of unskilled labor for the public benefit. In reality they worked for his personal profit, oftentimes at the expense of the clan. They lived on his land, and he was responsible for their conduct. By analogy, the distinctions *saer* and *daer* were recognized among them, according to origin, character, and means. Where these elements continued to be favorable for three generations, progress upward was made; and ultimately a number of them could club together, appoint a *flaithfine,* and apply to be admitted to the clan.

A *mog* was a slave in the strict sense, usually purchased as such from abroad, and legally and socially lower than the lowest *fuidir.* Giraldus Cambrensis, writing towards the close of the twelfth century, tells us that English parents then frequently sold their surplus children and other persons to the Irish as slaves. The Church repeatedly intervened for the release of captives and mitigation of their condition. The whole institution of slavery was strongly condemned as unChristian by the Synod held in Armagh in 1171.

CRIMINAL LAW. Though there are numerous laws relating to crime, to be found chiefly in the *Book of Aicill,* criminal law in the sense of a code of punishment there was none. The law took cognizance of crime and wrong of every description against person, character, and property; and its function was to prevent and restrict crime, and when committed to determine, according to the facts of the case and the respective ranks of the parties, the value of the compensation or reparation that should be made. It treated crime as a mode of

incurring liability; entitled the sufferer, or, if he was murdered, his *fine,* to bring the matter before a brehon, who, on
hearing the case, made the complicated calculations and ad-
justments rendered necessary by the facts proved and by the
grades to which the respective parties belonged, arrived at and
gave judgment for the amount of the compensation, armed
with which judgment, the plaintiff could immediately distrain
for that amount the property of the criminal, and, in his default, that of his *fine.* The *fine* could escape part of its liability by arresting and giving up the convict, or by expelling him
and giving substantial security against his future misdeeds.

From the number of elements that entered into the calcula-
tion of a fine, it necessarily resulted that like fines by no
means followed like crimes. Fines, like all other payments,
were adjudged and paid in kind, being, in some cases of the
destruction of property, generic—a quantity of that kind of
property. Large fines were usually adjudged to be paid in
three species, one-third in each, the plaintiff taking care to
inform correctly the brehon of the kinds of property the defendant possessed, because he could seize only that named, and
if the defendant did not possess it, the judgment was "a blind
nut." Crime against the State or community, such as wilful
disturbance of an assembly, was punished severely. These
were the only cases to which the law attached a sentence of
death or other corporal punishment. For nothing whatsoever
between parties did the law recognize any duty of revenge,
retaliation, or the infliction of personal punishment, but only
the payment of compensation. Personal punishment was regarded as the commission of a second crime on account of a
first. There was no duty to do this; but the right to do it
was tacitly recognized if a criminal resisted or evaded payment
of an adjudged compensation. Criminal were distinguished
from civil cases only by the moral element, the sufferer's right
in all cases to choose a brehon, the loss of *eineachlann,* partial
or whole according to the magnitude of the crime, the elements
used in calculating the amount of fine, and the technical terms
employed. *Dire* (djeereh) was a general name for a fine, and
there were specific names for classes of fines. *Eric* = reparation, redemption, was the fine for killing a human being, the

amount being affected by the distinction between murder and manslaughter and by other circumstances; but in no case was a violent death, however innocent, allowed to pass without reparation being made. A fine was awarded out of the property of the convict or of his *fine* to the *fine* of the person slain, in the proportions in which they were entitled to inherit his property, that being also according to their degrees of kinship and the degrees in which they were really sufferers. This gāve every clan and every clansman, in addition to their moral interest, a direct monetary interest in the prevention and suppression of crime. Hence the whole public feeling of the country was entirely in support of the law, the honor and interest of community and individual being involved in its maintenance. The injured person or *fine*, if unable to recover the fine, might, in capital cases, seize and enslave, or even kill, the convict. Probably restrained by the fact that, there being no officers of criminal law, they had to inflict punishment themselves, they sometimes imprisoned a convict in a small island, or sent him adrift on the sea in a *currach* or boat of hide. Law supported by public opinion, powerful because so inspired, powerful because unanimous, was difficult to evade or resist. It so strongly armed an injured person, and so utterly paralyzed a criminal, that escape from justice was hardly possible. The only way in which it was possible was by flight, leaving all one's property behind, and sinking into slavery in a strange place; and this in effect was a severe punishment rather than an escape.

FOREIGN LAW. The Danes and other Norsemen were the buccaneers of northwestern Europe from the eighth to the eleventh century. They conquered and settled permanently in Neustria, from them called Normandy, and conquered and ruled for a considerable time England and part of Scotland and the Isles. In Ireland they were little more than marauders, having permanent colonies only round the coast; always subject, nominally at least, to the *ard-ri* or to the local chief; paying him tribute when he was strong, raiding his territory when he was weak, and fomenting recurrent disorder highly prejudicial to law, religion, and civilization. They never made any pretence of extending their laws to Ireland, and their attempt to conquer the country was finally frustrated at Clontarf in 1014.

The Anglo-Norman invaders also seized the seaports. The earlier of them who went inland partially adopted in the second generation the Gaelic language, laws, and customs; as many non-Celtic Lowlanders of Scotland about the same period adopted the Gaelic language, laws, and customs of the Highlanders. Hence they did not make much impression on the Gaelic system, beyond the disintegrating effect of their imperfect adoption of it.

Into the eastern parts of Ireland, however, a fresh stream of English adventurers continued to flow, as aggressive and covetous as their means and prudence permitted; calling so much of the country as they were able to wrench from the Irish "the English Pale", which fluctuated in extent with their fortunes; and, when compelled to pay tribute to Irish chiefs, calling it "black rent", to indicate how they regarded it. Their greatest difficulty was to counteract the tendency of the earlier colonists to become Hibernicized—a most unwilling tribute to the superiority of the Irish race. They, and still more those in England who supported them, knew nothing of the Irish language, laws, and institutions but that they should all be impartially hated, uprooted, and supplanted by English people and everything English as soon as means enabled this to be done. This was the amiable purpose of the pompously-named "Statute of Kilkenny", passed by about a score of these colonists in 1367. Presuming to speak in the name of Ireland, the statute prohibited the English colonists from becoming Irish in the numerous ways they were accustomed to do, and excluded all Irish priests from preferment in the Church, partly because their superior virtue would by contrast amount to a censure. The purpose was not completely successful even within the Pale. Outside that precinct, the mass of the Irish were wholly unconscious of the existence of the "Statute of Kilkenny." But expressing, as the statute did correctly, the views of fresh adventurers, it became, in arrogance and in the pretension to speak for the whole of Ireland, a model for their future legislation and policy.

Under King Henry VI. of England, Richard, Duke of York, being Lord Deputy, the Parliament of the Pale, assembled in Dublin, repudiated the authority of the English Parliament in Ireland, established a mint, and assumed an attitude of almost complete independence. On the other hand, in 1494, under Henry VII., the Parliament of the Pale, assembled at Drogheda, passed Poyning's Act, extending all English laws to Ireland and subjecting all laws passed in Ireland to revision by the English Council. This, extended to the whole of Ireland as English power extended, remained in force until 1782. Henry VIII. was the first English sovereign to take practical measures for the pacific and diplomatic conquest of the whole of Ireland and the substitution of English for Irish institutions and methods. His daughter, Queen Elizabeth, continued and completed the conquest; but it was by drenching the country in blood, by more than decimating the Irish people, and by reducing the remnant to something like the condition of the ancient *fuidre*. Her policy prepared the ground for her successor, James I., to exterminate the Irish from large tracts, in which he planted Englishmen and Scotchmen, and to extend all English laws to Ireland and abolish all other laws. James's English attorney-general in Ireland, Sir John Davies, in his work, *A Discoverie of the True Causes, etc.*, says:

"For there is no nation of people under the sunne that doth love equall and indifferent [= impartial] justice better than the Irish; or will rest better satisfied with the execution thereof, although it bee against themselves; so as they may have the protection and benefit of the law, when uppon just cause they do desire it."

The ancient Irish loved their laws and took pride in obeying and enforcing them. The different attitude of the modern Irish towards foreign laws and administration is amply explained by the morally indefensible character of those laws and that administration, to be read in English statutes and ordinances and in the history of English rule in Ireland—a subject too vast and harrowing, and in every sense foreign to what has gone before, to be entered upon here. Though the Parliament of 1782-1800 was little more than a Pale Parliament, in which the mass of the Irish people had no representation whatever, one of its Acts, to its credit be it said, was an attempt to mitigate the Penal Laws and emancipate the oppressed Gaelic and Catholic population of Ireland. With the partial exception of that brief interval, law in Ireland has, during the last 360 years, meant English laws specially enacted for the destruction of any Irish trade or industry that entered into competition with a corresponding English trade or industry. In later times those crude barbarities have been gradually superseded by the more defensible laws now in force in Ireland, all of which can be studied in statutes passed by the Parliament, since the Union with Scotland, called British.

REFERENCES:

Pending the desirable work of a more competent Brehon Law Commission and translators, the subject must be studied in the six volumes of *Ancient Laws of Ireland*, produced by the first Commission, from 1865 to 1901, ignoring the long introductions and many of the notes. Whitley Stokes: Criticism of Atkinson's Glossary (London, 1903); R. Dareste: Etudes d'histoire de droit (Paris, 1889); d'Arbois de Jubainville and Paul Collinet: Etudes sur le droit celtique, 2 vols. (Paris, 1895); Joyce: Social History of Ancient Ireland, 2 vols. (London, 1913); Laurence Ginnell: The Brehon Laws (London, 1894).

IRISH MUSIC

By W. H. Grattan Flood, Mus. D., M. R. I. A., K. S. G.

PERHAPS nothing so strikingly brings home the association of Ireland with music as the fact that the harp is
emblazoned on the national arms. Ireland, "the mother of
sweet singers", as Pope writes; Ireland, "where", according to
St. Columcille, "the clerics sing like the birds"; Ireland can
proudly point to a musical history of over 2,000 years. The
Milesians, the De Dananns, and other pre-Christian colonists
were musical. Hecataeus (B. C. 540-475) describes the Celts
of Ireland as singing songs to the harp in praise of Apollo,
and Aethicus of Istria, a Christian philosopher of the early
fourth century, describes the culture of the Irish. Certain it
is that, even before the coming of St. Patrick, the Irish were
a highly cultured nation, and the national Apostle utilized
music and song in his work of conversion. In the early Lives
of the Irish Saints musical references abound, and the Irish
school of music attracted foreign scholars from the sixth to
the ninth century.

Hymnologists are familiar with the hymns written by early
Irish saints and laics, e. g., St. Sechnall, St. Columcille, St.
Molaise, St. Cuchuimne, St. Columbanus, St. Ultan, St. Colman, St. Cummain, St. Aengus, Dungal, Sedulius, Moengal,
and others. Who has not heard of the great music school of
San Gallen, founded by St. Gall, "the wonder and delight of Europe," whither flocked German students? One
of the Irish monks, Tuathal (Tutilo), composed numerous
sacred pieces, including the famous farced Kyrie, "Fons boni-
tatis", included in the Vatican edition of the *Kyriale* (1906).
Not alone did Irish monks propagate sacred and secular music
throughout France, Italy, Switzerland, Austria, Germany, and
the far North, but they made their influence felt in Lindisfarne, Malmesbury, Glastonbury, and other cities in England,
as also in Scotland. St. Aldhelm, one of the pupils of St.
Maeldubh, tells us that at the close of the seventh century,
"Ireland, synonymous with learning, literally blazed like the
stars of the firmament with the glory of her scholars."

During the ninth century we meet with twelve different forms of instruments in use by the Irish, namely:—the *Cruit* and *Clairseach* (small and large harp); *Timpan* (*Rotta* or bowed *cruit*); *Buinne* (oboe or bassoon); *Bennbuabhal* and *Corn* (horn); *Cuisleanna* and *Piob* (bagpipes); *Feadan* (flute or fife); *Guthbuinne* (bass horn); *Stoc* and *Sturgan* (trumpet); *Pipai* (single and double pipes); *Craoibh cuil* and *Crann cuil* (cymbalum); *Cnamha* (castanet); and *Fidil* (fiddle). The so-called "Brian Boru's Harp" really dates from the thirteenth century, and is now in Trinity College, Dublin, but there are numerous sculptured harps of the ninth and tenth centuries on the crosses at Graig, Ullard, Clonmacnois, Durrow, and Monasterboice.

Donnchadh, an Irish bishop of the ninth century, who died as abbot of St. Remigius, wrote a commentary on Martianus Capella, a well-known musical text book. Towering above all his fellows, John Scotus Erigena, in 867, wrote a tract *De Divisione Naturae,* in which he expounds *organum* or discant, nearly a hundred years before the appearance of the *Scholia Enchiriadis* and the *Musica Enchiriadis.* He also wrote a commentary on Martianus Capella, now in a Paris MS. of the ninth century.

The eulogy of Giraldus Cambrensis, or Gerald Barry, who came to Ireland in 1183, on Irish harpers and minstrels is too well known to be repeated, but Brompton and John of Salisbury are equally enthusiastic. Ground bass, or pedal point, and singing in parts, as well as bands of harpers and pipers, were in vogue in Ireland before the coming of the English. Dante, quoted by Galilei, testifies to the fact that Italy received the harp from Ireland; and, it may be added, the Irish harp suggested the pianoforte. In the Anglo-Norman ballad, "The Entrenchment of New Ross"—in 1265—allusion is made to pipes and flutes, and carols and dancing. Another poem, dating from about 1320, refers to Irish dances in a flattering manner.

John Garland (1190-1264) wrote a treatise on *Organum,* and outlined a scheme of dividing the interval, which developed into ornamentation, passing notes, and grace notes. The Dublin *Troper* of the thirteenth century has a number of farced Kyries and Glorias, also a collection of Sequences. A Dublin

Processionale of the fourteenth century contains the most elaborate form of the *Officium Sepulchri,* with musical notation on a four-line stave—the foundation of the Miracle Play of the Resurrection. Another Dublin *Troper* dates from 1360 and was used in St. Patrick's Cathedral. It contains the hymn, "Angelus ad Virginem", alluded to by Chaucer. The Christ Church Psaltery, about 1370, has musical notation and is exquisitely illuminated. Lionel Power, an Anglo-Irishman, wrote the first English treatise on music in 1395. Exactly a century later, in 1495, a music school was founded in Christ Church Cathedral, Dublin.

The Irish Annals of the thirteenth to the fifteenth century have numerous references to distinguished harpers and singers, and there are still sung many beautiful airs of this period, including "The Coulin" and "Eibhlin a ruin." John Lawless was a famous Irish organ-builder of the second half of the fifteenth century, and his successor, James Dempsey, built many fine organs between the years 1530 and 1565.

Notwithstanding the many penal enactments against Irish minstrels, all the great Anglo-Irish nobles of the Pale retained an Irish harper and piper in their service. Under date of 1480, we find Chief Justice Bermingham having an Irish harper to teach his family, as also "to harp and to dance." A century later "Blind Cruise, the harper"—Richard Cruise—composed a lamentation song on the fall of the Baron of Slane, the air of which is still popular. It is to the credit of the Irishman, William Bathe (who subsequently became a Jesuit), that he wrote the first printed English treatise on music, published in 1584—thus ante-dating by thirteen years Morley's work. Bathe wrote a second musical treatise in 1587, and he was the first to call measures by the name of bars. He also formulated methods of transposition and sight reading that may still be studied with profit.

Thomas Campion, the poet and composer, was born in Dublin in 1567, but spent nearly all his life in England. Other Irish composers, to mention only the most distinguished, were William Costello (madrigalist), Richard Gillic, Edward Shergold, and Walter Kennedy. Strange as it may seem, Queen Elizabeth retained in her service an Irish harper, Cormac Mac-

Dermot, from 1591 to 1603, and on the death of the queen he was given an annual pension of £46 10s. 10d.—nearly £500 a year of our present money.

Shakespeare refers to eleven Irish tunes, of which the famous "Callino Casturame" (*Cailin og a stuir me*) is still fresh. Irish dances were extremely popular at the English court from 1600 to 1603 and were introduced into the Masks. Shakespeare's "intrinsic friend," John Dowland of Dublin, was one of the greatest lutenists in Europe from 1590 to 1626. In the dedication of a song "to my loving countryman, Mr. John Foster the Younger, merchant of Dublin in Ireland," Dowland sufficiently indicates his nationality, and his compositions betray all the charm and grace of Irish melody. It is of interest to add that the earliest printed "Irish Dance" is in *Parthenia Inviolata,* of which work, published in 1613-4, there is only one copy known—now in the New York Public Library. From 1600-1602, Charles O'Reilly was harpist to the court of Denmark at 200 thalers a year. His successor was Donal *Dubh* ("the black") O'Cahill (1602-1610), who followed Anne of Denmark to the English court. Walter Quin of Dublin was music master to King James's eldest son, Prince Henry, from 1608 to 1611. Other noted harpers of the first half of the seventeenth century are: Rory *dall* ("the blind") O'Cahan; Nicholas *dall* Pierce; Tadhg MacRory; John, Rory, and Henry Scott; Owen MacKeenan; Owen MacDermot; Tadhg O'Coffey; and Father Robert Nugent, S. J. Darby Scott was harper to the Danish Court from 1621 till his death, at Copenhagen, on December 19, 1634. Pierce Ferriter, a "gentleman harper", was executed at Killarney in 1652. Myles O'Reilly and the two Connellans were famous harpers between the years 1660-1680. Evelyn, the English diarist, in 1668, praises the excellent performance on the harp of Sir Edward Sutton, who, in the following year, was granted by King Charles II. the lands of Confey, Co. Kildare. Two beautiful harps of this period are still preserved—the Fitzgerald Harp and the Fogarty Harp.

There are many exquisite airs of the seventeenth century, some of which have been incorporated in Moore's *Irish Melodies.* The titles of several airs of this epoch are of historical interest, *e. g.,* "Sarsfield's Lament," "Lament for Owen Roe O'Neill," "MacAlistrum's March," "Ned of the Hill," "The Breach of Aughrim," "Limerick's Lamentation," "Lilliburlero," "Ballinamona," "The Boyne Water," and "The Wild Geese." Irish tunes abound in the various editions of Playford's *Country Dances* from 1651 to 1720.

Turlogh O'Carolan (1670-1738), who has been styled "the last of the Irish bards", wrote and composed innumerable songs, also Planxties, Plearacas, and Lamentations. It is here merely necessary to note that twenty-six of O'Carolan's airs are included in Moore's *Irish Melodies,* although his claim to them has only recently been proved by the present writer. Goldsmith's eulogy of O'Carolan is well known.

The Jacobite period from 1710 to 1750 considerably influenced Irish minstrelsy, and some of the most delightful airs were adapted to Jacobite lyrics. "Seaghan buidhe," "An Sean duine," "Lament for Kilcash," "Ormonde's Lament," "Morin ni Chullenain," "All the Way to Galway" (the air of "Yankee Doodle"), "Caitlin ni Houlihan," "Balance a straw" ("The Wearing of the Green"), "St. Patrick's Day," "Plancam Peirbhig," are amongst the tunes in vogue at this period.

As early as 1685 the Hibernian Catch Club was established and still flourishes. Cecilian celebrations were held from 1727 to 1732, and a Dublin Academy of Music was founded in 1728. The Charitable and Musical Society (founded in 1723) built the Fishamble Street Music Hall in 1741, and assisted at the first performance of *The Messiah,* conducted by Handel himself, on 13th April, 1742. Kitty Clive, Peg Woffington, and Daniel Sullivan were noted Irish singers of this epoch, while John Clegg, Dr. Murphy, and Burke Thumoth were famous instrumentalists. In 1741 Richard Pockrich invented the Musical Glasses, for which Gluck wrote some pieces: it was afterwards improved by Benjamin Franklin. On the continent, Henry Madden was music director of the Chapel Royal at Versailles in 1744 (in succession to Campra), and was also canon of St. Quentin.

In 1764 the Earl of Mornington, Mus. D., was appointed first professor of music in Dublin University. A few years later Charles Clagget invented the valve-horn. Michael Kelly

of Dublin was specially selected by Mozart to create the parts
of Basilio and Don Curzio at the first performance of the opera
of *Figaro,* on May 1st, 1786. Kane O'Hara, Samuel Lee,
Owenson, Neale, Baron Dillon, Dr. Doyle, T. A. Geary,
Mahon, and the Earl of Westmeath were distinguished musicians—while the fame of Carter, Mountain, Moorehead, and
Dr. Cogan was not confined to Ireland.

Among native minstrels, Jerome Duigenan, Dominic Mon-
gan, Denis Hempson, Charles Byrne, James Duncan, Arthur
Victory, and Arthur O'Neill were celebrated as harpers. The
Belfast meeting of 1792 revived the vogue of the national
instrument. Nor was the bagpipe neglected. Even in America,
in 1778, Lord Rawdon had a band of pipers, with Barney
Thomson as Pipe Major. At home, Sterling, Jackson, Mac-
Donnell, Moorehead, Kennedy, and Macklin sustained the
reputation of this ancient instrument.

Ere the close of the eighteenth century John Field of Dublin was a distinguished pianist. He subsequently (1814) invented the nocturne, developed by Chopin. Sir John Stevenson (the arranger of the *Irish Melodies*), Tom Cooke, William
Southwell (inventor of the damper action for pianofortes),
Henry Mountain, Andrew Ashe (flautist), Barton, Rooke,
and Bunting were world-famed.

Among the Irish musicians of the last century the following
names are typical: Thomas Moore, J. A. Wade, Balfe (*Bohemian Girl*), Wallace (*Maritana*), Osborne, Sir Frederick
Ouseley, Scotson Clarke, Howard Glover, Horncastle, J. W.
Glover, Sir Robert Stewart, Augusta Holmes, R. M. Levey,
Joseph Robinson, Forde, Lover, Kearns, Allen, Barker, Tor-
rance, Molloy, Guernsey, Gilmore, Thunder, Harvey, Good-
man, Sir Arthur Sullivan (*Pinafore, Mikado*), Miss Davis,
Halliday (inventor of the Kent bugle), Latham, Duggan, Gas-
kin, Lacy, Pontet (Piccolomini), Hudson, Pigot, Horan,
Marks, and W. C. Levey. Famous vocalists like Catherine
Hayes, Mrs. Scott Fennell, Signor Foli (Foley), Barton Mc-
Guckin, Denis O'Sullivan, and William Ludwig deserve in-
clusion.

In our own day, it is only necessary to mention composers
like Sir Charles Villiers Stanford, Dr. C. Woods, Victor Her-

bert, Mrs. Needham, Dr. Sinclair, Norman O'Neill, and Arthur
O'Leary; singers like Egan, Burke, Plunket Greene, John Mac-
Cormack, P. O'Shea, Charles Manners, and Joseph O'Mara;
violinists like Maud McCarthy, Emily Keady, Arthur Darley,
and Patrick Delaney; organists like Dr. Charles Marchant,
Brendan Rogers, Dr. Jozé, and Professor Buck; writers like
Mrs. Curwen, Dr. Annie Patterson, Mrs. Milligan Fox, Professor Mahaffy, A. P. Graves, Dr. Collison, and G. B. Shaw;
and conductors like Hamilton Harty and James Glover.

REFERENCES:

Walker: Irish Bards (1786); O'Curry: Lectures (1870); Hardiman:
Irish Mistrelsy (2 vols., 1834); The Complete Petrie Collection
(3 vols., 1902-1904); Grattan Flood: History of Irish Music (3rd ed.,
1913), Story of the Harp (1906), Story of the Bagpipe (1911);
Mrs. Milligan Fox: Annals of the Irish Harpers (1911); Mason:
Song Lore of Ireland (1910); Armstrong: Musical Instruments
(2 vols., 1904-1908); O'Neill: Irish Folk Music (1911), Irish Minstrels and Musicians (1913).

IRISH METAL WORK

By Diarmid Goffey.

FROM the earliest times in the history of western Europe
Ireland has been renowned for her work in metal. The
first metal used was copper, and copper weapons are found in
Ireland dating from 2,000 B. C., or even earlier, the beautiful
designs of which show that the early inhabitants of the country were skilled workers in metal. Fields of copper exist all
along the southern seaboard of Ireland. Numbers of flat
copper celts, or axes, have been found modelled on the still
earlier stone implements. By degrees the influence of the
early stone axe disappears and axes of a true metal type are
developed. Primitive copper knives and awls are also abundant. The fineness of the early Irish copper work is seen at its
best in the numerous copper halberd blades found in Ireland.
These blades, varying from nine to sixteen inches in length,
were fastened at right angles by rivets into wooden shafts.
The blades show a slight sickle-like curve and are of the highest workmanship. Halberds somewhat similar in type have
been found in Spain, North Germany, and Scandinavia.

Between the years 2000 and 1800 B. C. the primitive metalworkers discovered that bronze, a mixture of tin and copper,
was a more suitable metal than pure copper for the manufacture of weapons; and the first period of the bronze age may be
dated from 1800 to 1500 B. C. The bronze celts at first differed little from those made of copper, but gradually the type
developed from the plain wedge-shaped celt to the beautiful
socketed celt, which appears on the scene in the last, or fifth,
division of the bronze age (900-350 B. C.). It was during
the age of bronze that spears came into general use, as did
the sword and rapier. The early spear-heads were simply
knife-shaped bronze weapons riveted to the ends of shafts,
but by degrees the graceful socketed spear-heads of the late
bronze age were developed.

Stone moulds for casting the early forms of weapons have
been found, but, as the art of metalworking became perfected,
the use of sand moulds was discovered, with the result that

there are no extant examples of moulds for casting the more developed forms of weapons. The bronze weapons—celts, swords, and spear-heads—are often highly decorated. In these decorations can be traced the connection between the early Irish civilization and that of the eastern Mediterranean. The bronze age civilization in Europe spread westward from the eastern Mediterranean either by the southern route of Italy, Spain, France, and thence to Ireland, or, as seems more probable, up the river Danube, then down the Elbe, and so to Scandinavia, whence traders by the north of Scotland introduced the motives and patterns of the Aegean into Ireland. Whichever way the eastern civilization penetrated into Ireland, it left England practically untouched in her primitive barbarity.

Of gold work, for which Ireland is especially famous, the principal feature in the bronze age was the lunula, a crescent-shaped flat gold ornament generally decorated at the ends of the crescent. These lunulae are found in profusion all over Ireland. A few have been found in Cornwall and Brittany, and a few in Scotland and Denmark. One has been found in Luxemburg and one in Hanover.

Gold collars are numerous in Ireland and also date from the bronze age. The earliest form of collar is the "torc" of twisted gold. Another type, later in date than the torc, is the gold ring-shaped collar. Two splendid examples of this latter type were found at Clonmacnois, the decoration of which, in *La Tène,* or trumpet, pattern, shows the connection between the Irish and continental designs.

A find of prehistoric gold ornaments in county Clare should be mentioned. An immense number was there discovered in 1854 hidden together in a cist, the value of the whole being estimated at over £3,000.

After the bronze age comes the iron age. The introduction of iron wrought a great change in metalworking, but, as iron is a metal very subject to oxidization, comparatively few early iron remains are found. There are some swords of an early pattern in the National Museum at Dublin.

It has been shown that the pre-Christian metalwork of Ireand is well worthy of attention, but it is to the early Christian metalworkers that Ireland owes her pre-eminent fame in this field. In early Christian Ireland metalworking was brought to a pitch rarely equalled and never excelled. The remains found, such as the Tara Brooch, the Cross of Cong, and the Ardagh Chalice, are among the most beautiful metalwork in the world. The wonderful interlaced patterns, which are typically Celtic, bewildering in their intricacy, and fascinating in the freedom and boldness of their execution, lend themselves readily to metal work.

The connecting link between the metalwork of the late pagan period and that of early Christian times is chiefly exemplified by the penannular brooches, of which great numbers have been found in Ireland. Examples of this characteristically Celtic ornament may be seen in all Celtic countries.

In its earliest form this brooch is simply a ring, with a gap in it, to which a pin is loosely attached by a smaller ring. Gradually the open ends of the ring, which need some enlargement in order to prevent the pin slipping off, became larger and ornamented. In time these became regular trumpet-shaped ends, generally ornamented with characteristic "trumpet" patterns. The next stage was to close the gap, leaving a ring with a crescent-shaped disc at one side. Space does not permit of the description of the numerous brooches found. It will be sufficient to describe the Tara Brooch, which is the crowning glory not only of the Irish but of any metal-worker's art.

The Tara Brooch, whose only connection with Tara is its name, was found near Drogheda; it is about seven inches in diameter and the pin about fifteen inches long. It is made of bronze covered with the most elaborate interlaced ornament in gold. The fineness of the interlaced work may be compared with, and is quite equal to, that of the best illuminated manuscripts; the freedom of its execution is amazing. Besides panels of ribbon ornament, which include spirals, plaited work, human heads, and animal forms, the front of the brooch is decorated with enamel and settings of amber and colored glass. The back of the brooch is, as is often the case in Irish work, decorated in a bolder manner than the front, and the "trumpet" pattern is there very marked. The head of the pin is also elaborately decorated. The minute and intricate style of the work is strikingly shown by the fact that, even after prolonged study, some patterns escaped notice and have only lately been discovered. Further, each of the gold lines is made of tiny gold balls, so small as only to be seen by means of a magnifying glass.

With the introduction of Christianity, the attention of artificers was turned to the manufacture of church vessels and shrines. Of these perhaps the most beautiful are the Ardagh Chalice, the Cross of Cong, and the Shrine of St. Patrick's Bell, though great numbers of other sacred ornaments, such as the Shrine of St. Lactan's Arm and the numerous bell shrines, are also fine examples of the work of an unsurpassed school of metalworkers.

The date of the Tara Brooch is not easy to determine, but it may probably be placed in the eighth century of our era. The Ardagh Chalice belongs probably to about the same date. It was found in a rath at Ardagh, county Limerick, in 1868. It measures 7 inches in height and 9½ in diameter. Around the cup is a band of fine filigree interlaced ornament in the form of panels divided by half beads of enamel. Below this are the names of the twelve Apostles in faint Celtic lettering. The two handles are beautifully decorated with panels of interwoven ornament, and on the sides are two circular discs divided into ornamented panels. The under side of the foot of the Chalice is also very beautifully decorated.

The shrines of the bells of the Irish saints are interesting examples of Irish metal work. As is fitting, the finest of these is the Shrine of St. Patrick's Bell. This was made by order of King Domnall O'Lachlainn between the years 1091 and 1105 to contain St. Patrick's bell, a square iron bell made of two plates of sheet iron riveted together. The shrine is made of bronze plates, to which gold filigree work and stones are riveted. The top of the shrine, curved to receive the handle of the bell, is of silver elaborately decorated. The back is overlaid with a plate of silver cut in cruciform pattern. Around the margin of the back is engraved the following inscription in Irish: "A prayer for Domnall Ua Lachlainn, by whom this bell [shrine] was made, and for Domnall, successor of Patrick, by whom it was made, and for Cathalan Ua Maelchallann, the keeper of the bell, and for Cudulig Ua Inmainen with his sons, who fashioned it." The whole is executed in a very fine manner and is the most beautiful object of its kind in existence. Another beautiful shrine, known as the Cross of Cong, made to enshrine a piece of the true cross presented by the pope in 1123, was made for King Turlogh O'Conor at about that date. It is 2 feet 6 inches high and 1 foot 6¾ inches wide. It is made of oak cased with copper and enriched with ornaments of gilded bronze. The ornamentation is of the typical Irish type, as on the Ardagh Chalice and the Shrine of St. Patrick's Bell. A quartz crystal set in the centre of the front of the cross probably held the relic.

It is clear from the succession of beautiful work executed from the eighth to the twelfth century, that there must have existed in Ireland during that period a school of workers in metal such as has seldom been equalled by any individual worker or guild before or since, and never excelled. The examples described are only the more famous of the remains of early Irish Christian art in metal, but they are surrounded by numerous examples of pins, brooches, and shrines, each worthy to rank with the finest productions of the metalworker. The Shrine of St. Moedoc (date uncertain) ought perhaps to be mentioned. On it are found several figures, including three nuns, men with books, sceptres, and swords, and a lifelike figure of a harper.

Besides articles of ornament, articles of use, such as bits for horses and household utensils, have been found, which show that the Irish smiths were as well able to produce articles for every-day use as the artificers were to create works of art in metal.

With the landing of the English in 1169 the arts and sciences in Ireland declined. Indeed, from that time on and for long afterwards, almost the only metalworkers needed were makers of arms and weapons of offense and defense.

REFERENCES:

British Museum, Bronze Age Guide; Coffey: Bronze Age in Ireland; Allen: Celtic Art; Abercrombie: Bronze Age Pottery; Wilde: Catalogue of the Royal Irish Academy's Collection; Allen: Christian Symbolism; Stokes: Christian Art in Ireland; Petrie: Ecclesiastical Architecture in Ireland; Coffey: Guide to the Celtic Antiquities of the Christian Period perserved in the National Museum, Dublin; Kane: Industrial Resources of Ireland; O'Curry: Manners and Customs of the Ancient Irish; Coffey: New Grange and other incised Tumuli in Ireland; Dechelette: Manuel d'Archéologie pré-historique; Ridgeway: Origin of Currency and Weight Standards.

IRISH MANUSCRIPTS

By Louis Ely O'Carroll, B. A., B. L.

IN the dark ages of Europe, whilst new civilizations were in the making and all was unrest, art and religion, like the lamp of the sanctuary, burned brightly and steadily in Ireland, and their rays penetrated the outer gloom. Scattered through the libraries of Europe are the priceless manuscripts limned by Irish scribes. The earliest missionaries to the continent, disciples of St. Columbanus and St. Gall, doubtless brought with them into exile beautiful books which they or their brothers of the parent monastery had wrought in a labor of love; or mayhap many a monk crossed the seas bearing the treasured volumes into hiding from the spoiling hands of the Dane. Yet, fortunately, in the island home where their beauty was born the most superb volumes still remain.

From almost prehistoric times the Irish were skilled artificers in gold and bronze, and, at the advent of Christianity, had already evolved and perfected that unique system of geometrical ornament which is known as Celtic design. The original and essential features of this system consisted in the use of spirals and interlacing strapwork, but later on this type was developed by transforming the geometrical fret into a scheme of imaginary or nondescript animals, portions of which, such as the tails and ears, were prolonged and woven in exquisite fancy through the border. The artistic features of Celtic book decoration consist chiefly of initial letters of this nature embellished with color. Amongst the ancient Irish there was a keen knowledge of color and an exceptional appreciation of color values. Thus it was that in the early centuries of Christian Ireland the learned monks, transcribing the Gospels and longing to make the book beautiful, were able to bring to their task an artistic skill which was hereditary and almost instinctive. The colors which they used were mostly derived from mineral substances and the black was carbon, made, it is conjectured, from charred fish-bones; but with them was combined some gummy material which made them cling softly to the vellum and has held for us their lustre for more than a thousand years. It is noteworthy that neither gold nor silver was used for book decoration, and this would appear to be a deliberate avoidance of the glitter and glare which distinguish eastern art.

The Book of Durrow (in the Library of Trinity College, Dublin) is the oldest specimen of Celtic illumination and, if not the work of St. Columcille, is certainly of as early a date. Each of the Gospels opens with a beautiful initial succeeded by letters of gradually diminishing size, and there are full page decorations embodying such subjects as the symbols of the Evangelists. The colors are rich and vivid and all the designs are of the purest and most Celtic character.

The Gospels of MacRegol (now in the Bodleian Library, Oxford) is the work of an Abbot of Birr who died A. D. 820. It is a volume of unusually large size, copiously ornamented with masterly designs and containing illuminated portraits of Saints Mark, Luke, and John. The first part of the book with the portrait of St. Matthew is missing.

The Book of Kells (in the Library of T. C. D.) is the all-surpassing masterpiece of Celtic illuminative art and is acknowledged to be the most beautiful book in the world. This copy of the four Gospels was long deemed to have been made by the saintly hands of Columcille, though it probably belongs to the eighth century. Into its pages are woven such a wealth of ornament, such an ecstasy of art, and such a miracle of design that the book is today not only one of Ireland's greatest glories but one of the world's wonders. After twelve centuries the ink is as black and lustrous and the colors are as fresh and soft as though but the work of yesterday. The whole range of colors is there—green, blue, crimson, scarlet, yellow, purple, violet—and the same color is at times varied in tone and depth and shade, thereby achieving a more exquisite combination and effect. In addition to the numerous decorative pages and marvellous initials, there are portraits of the Evangelists and full-page miniatures of the Temptation of Christ, His Seizure by the Jews, and the Madonna and Child surrounded by Angels with censers. Exceptionally beautiful are these angels and other angelic figures throughout the book, their wings shining with glowing colors amid woven patterns of graceful design. The portraits and miniatures and the numerous faces centred in initial letters are not to be adjudged by the standard of anatomical drawing and delineation of the human figure, but rather by their effect as part of a scheme of ornamentation; for the Celtic illuminator was imaginative rather than realistic, and aimed altogether at achieving beauty by means of color and design. The Book of Kells is the Mecca of the illuminative artist, but it is the despair of the copyist. The patience and skill of the olden scribe have baffled the imitator; for, on an examination with a magnifying glass, it has been found that, in a space of a quarter of an inch, there are no fewer than a hundred and fifty-eight interlacements of a ribbon pattern of white lines edged by black ones on a black ground. Surely this is the manuscript which was shown to Giraldus Cambrensis towards the close of the twelfth century and of whose illuminations he speaks with glowing enthusiasm; "they were," he says, "supposed to have been produced by the direction of an angel at the prayer of St. Brigid."

The Gospels of MacDurnan (now in the Archbishop's Library at Lambeth) is a small and beautiful volume which was executed by an abbot of Armagh who died in the year 891. A full-page picture of the Evangelist precedes each Gospel, and a composite border frames each miniature in a bewildering pattern of intertwining strapwork and wonderful designs of imaginary beasts. Ornamental capitals and rich borders give a special beauty to the initial pages of the Gospels.

The Book of Armagh (in the Library of T. C. D.) was carefully guarded and specially venerated through the ages in the erroneous belief that it was in part the handiwork of St. Patrick. It was written about the year 800, and would appear to have been copied from documents actually written by the patron saint of Ireland. The book is exceptionally interesting by reason of the fact that it contains St. Patrick's Confession, that beautiful story of how he found his mission, how the captive grew to love his captors, and how, after his escape, he came back to them bearing the lamp of Holy Faith. Although the ornamentation of the manuscript is infrequent, there are occasional beautiful examples which compare in richness with those in the Book of Kells.

The Liber Hymnorum (in the Franciscan Monastery, Dublin) contains a number of hymns associated with the names of Irish saints. The ornamentation consists of colored initials, designed with a striking use of fanciful animal figures interlaced and twined with delightful freedom around the main structural body.

The *Garland of Howth* and the *Stowe Missal* (both in Trinity College Library) belong to the eighth century and are beautiful examples of early illuminative art. The former, which is very incomplete, has only two ornamental pages left, each containing figure-representations inserted in the decorative work.

The *Gospels of St. Chad* (in the Cathedral Library at Lichfield) and the *Gospels of Lindisfarne,* which are "the glory of the British Museum", form striking examples of the influence of Celtic art. St. Chad was educated in Ireland in the school of St. Finian, where he acquired his training in book decoration. The Gospels of Lindisfarne were produced by the monks of Iona, where St. Columcille founded his great school of religion, art, and learning. This latter manuscript is second only to the Book of Kells in its glory of illuminative design, and, from its distinctive scheme of colors, the tones of which are light and bright and gay, it forms a contrast to the quieter shades and the solemn dignity of the more famous volume.

The Book of the Dun Cow, The Book of Leinster, and the other great manuscripts of the eleventh, twelfth, and thirteenth centuries are interesting as literature rather than as art, for they tell the history of ancient Erin and have garnered her olden legends and romantic tales. It is only the Gospels and other manuscripts of religious subjects that are illuminated. In the apparel of the ancient Irish, the number of colors marked the social rank: the king might wear seven colors, poets and learned men six; five colors were permitted in the clothes of chieftains, and thus grading down to the servant, who might wear but one. All this the scribe knew well. We can picture the humble servant of God, clad in a coarse robe of a single color, deep in his chosen labor of recording the life and teachings of his Master, and striving to endow this record with the glory of the seven colors which were rightly due to a King alone. As we gaze on his work today its beauty is instinct with life, and the patient love that gave it birth seems to cling to it still. The white magic of the artist's holy hands has bridged the span of a thousand years.

REFERENCES:

O'Curry: Lectures on the Manuscript Materials of Ancient Irish History (Dublin, 1861); Bruun: An Enquiry into the Art of the Illuminated Manuscripts of the Middle Ages, Part I, Celtic Illuminated Manuscripts (Edinburgh, 1897); Robinson: Celtic Illuminative Art in the Gospels of Durrow, Lindisfarne, and Kells (Dublin, 1908); Westwood: The Book of Kells, a lecture given in Oxford, November, 1886 (Dublin, 1887); Gougaud: Répertoire des fac-similés des manuscripts irlandais (Paris, 1913).

THE RUINS OF IRELAND

By Francis Joseph Bigger, M. R. I. A.

THE ruins of Ireland are her proudest monuments. They stand as a lasting revelation to all mankind—a distinct and definite proclamation that the Irish people, century after century, were able to raise and adorn some of the finest buildings in stone that western civilization has seen or known. It is recognized the world over that Irish art has a beauty and distinction all its own, in its own Irish setting unrivalled, throned in its own land, in its own natural surroundings. The shrines and gospels, the reliquaries and missals, the crosses and bells that are still existent, many in Ireland, others in every country in the world, attest beyond any dispute that Irish art-workers held a preëminent place in the early middle ages, and that works of Irish art are still treasured as unique in their day and time. No country has been plundered and desolated as Ireland has been. Dane, Norman, English—each in turn swept across the fair face of Ireland, carrying destruction in their train, yet withal Ireland has her art treasures and her ruins that bear favorable comparison with those of other civilizations.

In Dublin and in many private Irish collections can be found hand-written books of parchment, illuminated with glowing colors that time has scarce affected or the years caused to fade. On one page alone of the Book of Kells, ornament and writing can be seen penned and painted in lines too numerous even to count. They are there by the thousand; a magnifying glass is required to reveal even a fragment of them. Ireland produced these in endless number—every great library or collection in Europe possesses one or more examples.

As with books, so with reliquaries, crosses, and bells. When the Island of Saints and Scholars could produce books, it could make shrines and everything necessary to stimulate and hand down the piety and the patient skill of a people steeped in art-craft and religious feeling. What they could do on parchment—like the Books of Kells and Durrow—what they could produce in bronze and precious metals—like the Cross of Cong, the Shrine of Saint Patrick's Bell, the Tara Brooch, and the Chalice of Ardagh—not to write of the numberless bronze and gold articles of an age centuries long preceding their production—they could certainly vie with in stone.

Of this earlier work a word must go down. In Ireland still at the present day, after all the years of plunder she has undergone, more ancient gold art-treasures remain than in any other country, museum, or collection, most of them pre-Christian, and what the other countries do possess are largely Irish or of Celtic origin. We must have this borne into the minds of every one of Irish birth or origin, that this great treasure was battered into shape by Irish hands on Irish anvils, designed in Irish studios, ornamented with Irish skill for Irish use.

With such workmen, having such instincts and training, what of the housing and surroundings to contain them and give them a fit and suitable setting? The earliest stone structures in Ireland still remaining are the great stone cashels or circular walls enclosing large spaces—walls of great thickness, unmortared, in which there are vast quantities of masonry. Around their summits a chariot might be driven, inside their spaces horse races might be run. As a few examples, there are Staigue, in Kerry; Dun Angus, in Aran, off Galway; Aileach, above the walls of Derry. Of the earliest churches, cyclopean in construction and primitive in character, built of stone, with thick sloping walls from foundation to ridge, Gallerus still remains, and the Skelligs, those wondrous sea-girt rocks, preserve both church and cell almost perfect. There are many other examples, some of a later date, such as Temple Cronan and Maghera and Banagher in Derry, St. Finan's oratory in county Cork, St. Fechin's at Fore, and St. Molaise's at Devenish.

From the seventh, eighth, and ninth centuries, there are innumerable examples of oratories, some with stone roofs, others with roofs not so permanent, but all having the common features of an altar window facing the east, through which the sun fell at the beginning of the day to tell the early missioner that his hour of devotion had arrived, and a west door, through which the rays of the declining sun fell across the altar steps, speaking of a day that was closing. A south window was added close to the east end, and it, too, was a sun-dial; it told the hour of angelus, the mid-day, when the bell was rung and a calm reverence fell on all within its hearing. Such churches can still be seen at Aran and Inismurray, on the islands of Lough Derg, Lough Ri, and in many other places.

A few years later these oratories were too small for the growing faith, and larger churches were built, some using the older structure as chancels. Where the west door was built a circular arch was made and the new and old united. This can well be seen at Inis-na-ghoill in Lough Corrib, on the Aran Islands off Galway, at Glendalough, at Inis-cleraun in Lough Ri, at Clonmacnois, at Iniscaltra, and on many another island and promontory of the south and west.

During this time, and after, we find the most elaborate carvings on door and arch and window, equal in skill to what is found in book or metal work.

It must have been at this time that the Galls, or strangers, first invaded Ireland, bearing havoc in their train, for then it was that the *cloicteach,* or Round Towers, were built. It is now admitted by all Irish authorities of any repute, and that beyond dispute, that the Round Towers, the glory of Ireland, were built by Irish people as Christian monuments from which the bells might be rung, and as places of strength for the preservation of the valued articles used in Christian worship; here they might be safely stored. They were also used for the preservation of life in case of sudden attack and onslaught by unexpected enemies. All the towers are on ecclesiastical sites, many are incorporated in church buildings, such as those of Glendalough in Wicklow and Clonmacnois on the Shannon. The records of the construction of some of them in the tenth and eleventh centuries are still extant, and this is conclusive. There are today about seventy Round Towers in Ireland, and many have been destroyed.

The pillar towers of Ireland, how wondrously they stand
By the lakes and rushing rivers through the valleys of our land;
In mystic file, through the isle, they lift their heads sublime,
These gray old pillar temples—these conquerors of time.

Here was placed the holy chalice that held the sacred wine,
And the gold cross from the altar, and the relics from the shrine,
And the mitre shining brighter with its diamonds than the east,
And the crozier of the pontiff, and the vestments of the priest.

D. F. MacCarthy.

This was the time when the High Crosses of Ireland were carved and set up. They vie with the Round Towers in interest and in the display of skill. What the towers have in perfection, masonry and construction, the crosses have in artistic carving and symbolic design. No two crosses are alike; they are as varied as the clouds in an Irish sky or the pebbles on the beach or the flowers in a garden. They were carved in reverence by those who knew and esteemed their art, and lavished all their skill and knowledge on what they most valued and treasured. They were not set up as grave-marks merely—theirs was a higher and loftier mission. They were raised in places where some great event or period was to be commemorated—they were erected where some early disciple of the Cross could stand beside one of them and from any panel could tell the foundation of the Faith, for there in stone was story after story, from the Old Testament and the New, that gave him his text, and so, as at the Cross of the Scriptures at Clonmacnois, a missioner could preach on every recurring holy day from Christmas to Christmas, with ever his text in stone before him. Many a broken and mutilated cross has been set up in Ireland in recent years, proving that the heart of the Gael, no matter how rent and broken, is still inclined to bind up the broken wounds of her past glories.

With the religious orders there came to Ireland a widespread desire to add something to the older sanctuaries of the Gael, to widen their borders and strengthen their cords, and so the abbeys were founded. Here and there we find them still— by winding rivers, on rich meadows, in glens and glades, by the sea margin, or on the slopes of the rugged mountain. Their crumbling walls and broken windows can still be traced, their towers are still to be seen over tree tops and in the centre of many a slumbering town. By the shores of Donegal Bay the old Franciscan house, where the Four Masters compiled what is perhaps the most remarkable record possessed by any nation, is still clothed in ivy. At Kilconnell, in Galway, their old place is almost as they left it, but roofless, with the tears of the friars upon the altar steps. Clare Galway has a tower worth travelling half a continent to see. By the Boniet River, at Drumahaire, on the banks of Lough Gill, are the mason marks of the cloister builders, and the figure of St. Francis talking to the birds is still there. The abbey is roofless and empty, and so the birds of the air are his constant companions.

Space forbids, or endless abbeys might be described. The Black Abbey at Kilkenny, with its long row of Butler effigies, or the Cathedral of Saint Canice, still perfect, with its soaring round tower beside it, or the mystical seven light window of the Franciscan friary by the Nore, with the old mill-weirs running free to this day. How long could we ponder by the east window of Kilcooley, with tracery like a spider's web, and listen to the mystical bells, or gaze at the beautiful oriel at Feenagh, or stand at Jerpoint, with its spacious cloisters and stone-groined choir, with Saint Christopher in Irish marble beside us.

Cashel, one of the wonders of the world, grows up suddenly into sight on a high rock rising from level land crowned with buildings. A great abbey dominates; beside it clings that carved gem of a stone-roofed church, Cormac's Chapel. Round Tower and Cross are there, and many a sculptured tomb.

Not far from Cashel is the Abbey of Holy Cross, with its lovely mitred windows, shadowed in the river passing at its feet. The circular pillars and arches of Boyle Abbey are splendidly proportioned, whilst the cloisters of Sligo display in their long, shadowy recesses and ornamented pillars great dignity and beauty. The windows and monuments of Ennis Friary, founded by the O'Briens, are of unusual interest, the carving of figure-subjects being equal to the best of their age.

We have Thomastown and Callan, Dunbrody and Tintern, all having an individual charm and interest that not only dim the eye and make the blood course freely in every one of Irish stock when he looks upon what is and thinks of what was, but even in the coldest light give food for thought to every one desirous of knowing something of the growth and civilization of a great people.

Of the many castles and stout Irish strongholds it is hard to write in such a short paper as this. Those on the Boyne, such as Trim, for strong building and extent, excel in many ways. Carlingford, Carrickfergus, and Dunluce have by their size and picturesque situations ever appealed to visitors. They are each built on rocks jutting into the sea, Dunluce on a great perpendicular height, the Atlantic dashing below. Dunamace, near Maryborough, in the O'More country, appears like Cashel, but is entirely military. The famed walled cities of Kells, in Kilkenny, and Fore, in Westmeath, are remarkable. Each has an abbey, many towers, gates, and stout bastions. The great keeps of the midland lords, the towers of Granuaile on the west coast, and the traders' towers on the east coast, especially those of Down, afford ample material for a study of the early colonizing efforts of different invaders, as well as providing incidents of heroism and romance. These square battlemented towers can be seen here and there in every district.

Every portion of Ireland has its ruins. Earthworks, stone forts, prehistoric monuments, circular stone huts, early churches, abbeys, crosses, round towers, castles of every size and shape are to be found in every county, some one in every parish, all over Ireland. It is almost invidious to name any in particular where the number is so great.

REFERENCES:

Proceedings of Royal Irish Academy (Dublin); Proceedings of Society of Antiquaries (Dublin); Ulster Journal of Archæology, Old Series and New Series, edited by F. J. Bigger, Belfast; Wakeman: Handbook of Irish Antiquities (Dublin, 1891); Stokes: Early Christian Art in Ireland (Dublin, 1887); Petrie: Round Towers and Ancient Architecture of Ireland (Dublin, 1845).

MODERN IRISH ART

By D. J. O'Donoghue,
Librarian, University College, Dublin.

IT would be difficult to dispute, in view of her innumerable
and excellent artists, that there has always been in modern
times an art consciousness in Ireland, but it is impossible to
assert that there has been any artistic unity in her people. She
has produced no school, but merely a great number of brilliant
painters, sculptors, and engravers, chiefly for export. With
all our acknowledged artistic capacity, we have not, except in
one notable instance, produced a cumulative art effect. The
history of Irish art is almost uniformly a depressing narrative.
During a comparatively brief period in the eighteenth century—significantly enough, it was while the country enjoyed a
short spell of national life—there was something like a national
patronage of the artist, and the result is visible in the noble
public buildings and beautiful houses of the Irish capital, with
their universally admired mantelpieces, doors, ceilings, fan-
lights, ironwork, and carvings. In short, while Ireland had
even a partly unfettered control of her own concerns, the arts
were generously encouraged by her government and by the
wealthy individual. When other European capitals were mere
congeries of rookeries, Dublin, the centre of Irish political
life, possessed splendid streets, grandly planned. But there
was little solidarity among the artistic fraternity. Various
associations of artists were formed, which held together fairly
well until the flight of the resident town gentry after the
Union, and many admirable artists were trained in the schools
of the Royal Dublin Society, but, since the opening of the
nineteenth century, there has been almost no visible art effort
in Dublin. True, there have been many fine artists, who have
made a struggle to fix themselves in Dublin, but, as with the
Royal Hibernian Academy, of which the best of them were
members, the struggle has been a painful agony. Usually the
artist migrated to London to join the large group of Irishmen
working there; a few others went to America and obtained
an honored place in her art annals. Those who went to

England secured in many cases the highest rewards of the profession. Several, like Barry, Hone, Barrett, and Cotes, were founders or early members of the Royal Academy; one, Sir Martin Shee, became its President. Nevertheless, many distinguished artists remained in Dublin, where the arts of portrait-painting and engraving were carried to a high pitch of excellence.

This record must necessarily be of a chronological character, and can only take note of those whose works have actual value and interest, historical or other. Edward Luttrell (1650-1710) did some excellent work in crayon or pastel, while Garrett Murphy (fl. 1650-1716), Stephen Slaughter (d. 1765), Francis Bindon (d. 1765), and James Latham (1696-1747), have each left us notable portraits of the great Irish personages of their day. To fellow countrymen in London, Charles Jervas (1675?-1739), Thomas Hickey (d. 1816?), and Francis Cotes, R. A. (1725-1770), we owe presentments of other famous people. George Barrett, R. A. (1728-1784), one of the greatest landscapists of his time; Nathaniel Hone, R. A. (1718-1784), an eccentric but gifted painter, with an individuality displayed in all his portraits; James Barry, R. A. (1741-1806), still more eccentric, with grand conceptions imperfectly carried out in his great historical and allegorical pictures:—these, with Henry Tresham, R. A. (1749?1814), and Matthew Peters, R. A. (1742-1814), historical painters of considerable merit, upheld the Irish claim to a high place in English eighteenth century art. A little later, miniaturists such as Horace Hone, A. R. A. (1756-1825), George Chinnery (1774-1852), and Adam Buck (1759-1844), also worked with remarkable success in London. Among resident Irish artists, the highest praise can be given to the miniature painters, John Comerford (1770?1832) and Charles Robertson (1760-1821), and to the portrait-painters, Robert Hunter (fl. 1750-1803) and (especially) Hugh Douglas Hamilton (1739-1808), of whose work Ireland possesses many distinguished examples. Some day Hamilton's pictures will appeal to a far wider public than his countrymen can provide. One must omit the names of many clever Irish artists like the Wests, Francis and Robert, who were the most successful teachers of perhaps any time in Ireland, and come at once to that branch of art in which Ireland stands second to none—mezzotint-engraving.

One of the earliest engravers in this style was Edward Luttrell, already named as a painter, but it was John Brooks (fl. 1730-1756) who is justly considered the real founder of that remarkable group of Irish engravers whose work may be more correctly described as belonging to a school than any other of the period. For many years in Dublin, and afterwards in London, a succession of first-rate artists of Irish birth produced work which remains and always must remain one of the glories of Ireland. Limits of space allow only the bare mention of the names of James McArdell (1728?-1765), Charles Spooner (d. 1767), Thomas Beard (fl. 1728), Thomas Frye (1710-1762), Edward Fisher (1722-1785?), Michael Ford (d. 1765), John Dixon (1740?-1811), Richard Purcell (fl. 1746-1766), Richard Houston (1721?-1775), John Murphy (1748?-1820), Thomas Burke (1749-1815), Charles Exshaw (fl. 1747-1771), and Luke Sullivan (1705-1771)—artists of whom any country might be proud, and whose works have in most cases outlasted the remembrance of the persons whose likenesses they sought to reproduce. Separate monographs might be justifiably written on most of the gifted artists here enumerated, and one can only regret not being able in short space to compare and estimate their various qualities. Thomas Chambers, A. R. A. (1724?-1784), William Nelson Gardiner (1766-1814), James Egan (1799-1842), and William Humphreys (1794-1865) are other Irish engravers who cannot be overlooked in a survey of the art of the late eighteenth and early nineteenth centuries.

Contemporaneously with the remarkable development of the art of engraving arose a group of Irish architects. Rather earlier in point of time was Sir Edward Lovat Pearce (d. 1733), who was one of the chief architects of the Irish Parliament House, and Thomas Burgh (d. 1730), to whom we owe the Library of Trinity College, Dublin; but Thomas Cooley (1740-1784), designer of the handsome Royal Exchange of that city; Richard Castle (d. 1751), a foreigner who settled in Ireland and built a number of beautiful Irish residences; Francis Johnston (1761-1829), an excellent architect whose chief claim to remembrance, however, is as founder of the Royal Hibernian Academy; and, above all, James Gandon (1743-1823), whose superb Custom House, Four Courts, and part of the Irish Parliament House will perpetuate his name in Dublin while that city lasts—each helped to make the capital, even in its decay, one of the most interesting in Europe. Nor should we forget Thomas Ivory (d. 1786), whose Foundling Hospital is another of Dublin's many graceful edifices; nor Sir Richard Morrison (1767-1849) and his son William (1794-1838), much of whose work remains to testify to their skill and ingenuity.

Ecclesiastical architecture in Ireland is indebted to Patrick Byrne (fl. 1840), James J. McCarthy (d. 1882), J. B. Keane (d. 1859), and James Murray (1831-1863), for many well designed churches and chapels throughout Ireland; but the great names in modern Irish architecture are those of Benjamin Woodward (1815-1861), whose premature death was a serious loss to Irish art; Sir Thomas Deane (1792-1871); and his son, Sir Thomas Newenham Deane (1828-1899). The elder Deane was, with Woodward, the architect of the Oxford Museum and of the splendid Engineering Hall of Trinity College, Dublin, buildings which have elicited enthusiastic praise from John Ruskin and other eminent critics. Deserving of respectful mention, too, to come down to our own days, are Sir Thomas Drew (1838-1910) and William H. Lynn, who is still living.

In sculpture, again, Ireland has done memorable work. In the eighteenth century she gave us admirable craftsmen like Edward Smyth (1749-1812), John Hickey (1756-1795), and Christopher Hewitson (fl. 1772-1794), whose dignified monument of Bishop Baldwin is one of the most distinguished pieces of sculpture in Trinity College, Dublin. But it was not till the appearance of a later group of sculptors, including John Hogan (1800-1858), John Edward Carew (1785-1868), John Henry Foley, R. A. (1818-1874), and Patrick Mac-Dowell, R. A. (1799-1870), that Irish sculpture obtained more than local renown. Fortunately, most of the best work of Hogan and Foley remains in Ireland; that of Carew and MacDowell is chiefly to be found in the Houses of Parliament and other institutions in London. The incomparable "Goldsmith," "Burke," "Grattan," and other statues by Foley, together with an almost complete collection of casts of his other works, are in his native country. Hogan is represented in Dublin by his "Thomas Davis" and his "Dead Christ," to name but two of his principal works. The names at least of James Heffernan (1785-1847), of John Edward Jones (1806-1872), of Terence Farrell (1798-1876), of Samuel F. Lynn (1834-1876), and perhaps of Christopher Moore (1790-1863), an excellent sculptor of busts, may be set down here. Sir Thomas Farrell (1827-1900) and the living sculptors, John Hughes, Oliver Sheppard, and Albert Bruce Joy, are responsible for some of the more admirable of the public monuments of Dublin. It is much to be deplored that of the work of one of the greatest of Dublin-born artists, Augustus Saint Gaudens, we have only one example—the statue of Parnell. Ireland may surely claim him as one of her most gifted sons. And perhaps a word might be said in this place of some of the other Irishmen who made their home in America: of Hoban the architect who designed the White House at Washington, modelling it after Leinster House in Dublin; of painters like Charles Ingham, W. G. Wall, William Magrath, the Morans, James Hamilton, and Thomas Hovenden; and of sculptors like John Donoghue, John Flanagan, Andrew O'Connor, John F. Kelly, Jerome Connor, John J. Boyle, and Martin Milmore. But they belong rather to the history of American art than to that of Ireland.

Before leaving the subject of Irish sculpture, the work of the medallists, an allied branch of the art in which Irishmen did much valued work, should not be overlooked. The medals of William Mossop (1751-1805), of his son, William Stephen Mossop (1788-1827), and of John Woodhouse (1835-1892), to mention only three of its chief representatives in Ireland, are greatly prized by collectors.

Most modern Irish art of high importance has been largely produced out of Ireland, which has been perforce abandoned by those artists who have learned how little encouragement is to be met with at home. One can blame neither the artist nor the Irish public for this unfortunate result; there is sufficient reason in the political and economic condition of Ireland since the Union to explain the fact. But for this cause men like Daniel Maclise, R. A. (1806-1870), William Mulready, R. A. (1786-1863), Francis Danby, A. R. A. (1793-1861), and Alfred Elmore, R. A. (1815-1881), might have endeavored to emulate the spirit of James O'Connor (1792-1841), the landscapist, Richard Rothwell (1800-1868), a charming subject painter, and Sir Frederic W. Burton (1816-1900), one of the most distinguished artists of his time, who at least spent some of their active working career in their native land. The same words apply to artists who succeeded in other branches of the profession, men like John Doyle (1797-1868), a caricaturist with all the power, without the coarseness, of his predecessors; his son, Richard Doyle (1824-1883), a refined and delicate artist; John Leech (1817-1864), the humorist, a member of an Irish Catholic family; Paul Gray (1842-1866), who died before his powers had fully matured; and Matthew James Lawless (1837-1864), who also died too early. William Collins, R. A. (1788-1847) and Clarkson Stanfield, R. A. (1793-1867), both eminent representatives of English art, though of Irish extraction, more properly belong to England than to Ireland.

Not discouraged by the melancholy history of many gifted Irish artists, Ireland still produces men who are not unworthy of association with the best who have gone before. Our most recent losses have been heavy—notably those of Walter F. Osborne (1859-1903) and Patrick Vincent Duffy (1832-1909), but we still have artists of genius in the persons of Nathaniel Hone, a direct descendant of his famous namesake; John Butler Yeats; John Lavery, A. R. A.; and William Orpen, A. R. A. Many other names might be given, but already this attempt at a survey suffers by its enumeration of artists, who, however, could hardly be neglected in such a record.

Crowded as the list may be, it is a careful selection, and it demonstrates that, notwithstanding all the disadvantages under which Ireland suffers, the country has an almost unlimited capacity for fine achievement, and that, with prosperity and contentment, she may be expected to rival the most illustrious of art centres. It is only within living memory that any attempt has been made to direct the known artistic skill of the Irish people to industrial effort. But the remarkable success achieved in the modern designs for Irish lace in the English art competitions is an instance of what might be done generally in the applied arts. Though they are in their infancy, the new carpet and stained glass industries in Ireland also hold out considerable hope for the future. But one can only barely indicate what has been and might be done in the furtherance of Irish art. If we only had under one roof a judiciously made collection of all the best work done by Irish artists of all styles and periods, it would more eloquently justify our claim than endless columns of praise.

REFERENCES :

Anthony Pasquin [John Williams]: History of Professors of Painting in Ireland (1795); T. J. Mulvany: Life of James Gandon; John O'Keeffe: Reminiscences, vol. I; Taft: American Sculpture; W. G. Strickland: Dictionary of Irish Artists (2 vols., 1913).

IRELAND AT PLAY

By Thomas E. Healy,
Editor of "Sport," Dublin.

ON the face of the earth there is no nation in which the love of clean and wholesome sport is more strongly developed than in the Irish. Against us it cannot be urged that we take our pleasures sadly. We enter into them with entire self-abandon, whole-hearted enthusiasm, and genuine exuberance of spirit. There is nothing counterfeit about the Irishman in his play. His one keen desire is to win, be the contest what it may; and towards the achievement of that end he will strain nerve and muscle even to the point of utter exhaustion. And how the onlookers applaud at the spectacle of a desperately contested race, whether between horses, men, motorcars, bicycles, or boats, or of a match between football, hurling, or cricket teams! It matters not which horse, man, car, cycle, boat, or team is successful: the sport is the thing that counts; the strenuousness of the contest is what stimulates and evokes the rapturous applause. At such a moment it is good to be alive. Scenes similar to those hinted at may be witnessed on any sports-field or racetrack in our dear little Emerald Isle almost any day of the year. All is good fellowship; all is in the cause of sport.

No one can question that in some departments of horse-racing Ireland is today supreme. The Irish devotion to the horse is of no recent growth. Everybody knows how, in the dim and distant days when King Conor macNessa ruled at Emain, the war-steeds of the Ultonians neighed loudly in their stalls on the first dramatic appearance of Cuchulainn of Muirthemne at the northern court. Cuchulainn's own two steeds, Liath Macha, "the Roan of Macha", and Dub Sainglenn, "Black Sanglan", are celebrated in story and song:

> Never hoofs like them shall ring,
> Rapid as the winds of spring.

To read of the performances of Cuchulainn and his warhorses and his charioteer and friend, Laeg macRiangabra, at

the famous battle of Rosnaree, and again at the last fight between the Red Branch Knights and the forces of Queen Medb
of Connacht, does truly, in the words used by Sir Philip Sidney
in another connection, stir the heart like the sound of a
trumpet.

As time went on, the Irish war-horse became more and more
famous, and always carried his rider in gallant style. Stout
was the steed that, bestridden by Godfrey O'Donnell at the
battle of Credan-Kille, withstood the shock of Lord Maurice
Fitzgerald's desperate onslaught, and by his steadiness enabled
the Tyrconnell chieftain to strike senseless and unhorse his
fierce Norman foe. More celebrated still was the high-spirited
animal which Art MacMurrogh rode in 1399 to his ineffectual
parley with King Richard the Second's representative, the
Earl of Gloucester. The French chronicler who was a witness
of that historic scene tells us that a horse more exquisitely
beautiful, more marvellously fleet, he had never seen. "In
coming down," he says, "it galloped so hard that, in my opinion, I never saw hare, deer, sheep, or any other animal, I
declare to you for a certainty, run with such speed as it did."
Edmund Spenser, the poet of *The Faerie Queene,* writing in
1596, bears this striking testimony to the Irish horse-soldier
and inferentially to the Irish horse: "I have hearde some
greate warriours say, that, in all the services which they had
seene abroad in forrayne countreys, they never sawe a more
comely horseman than the Irish man, nor that cometh on more
bravely in his charge." The feats performed at the Battle of
the Boyne, in 1690, by the Irish horse-soldiers under Hamilton
and Berwick were really wonderful, and well-nigh turned disaster into victory on that memorable day which decided the
fate of nations as well as of dynasties. And surely those were
fleet and stout-hearted steeds that, on August 12, 1690, carried Sarsfield and his chosen five hundred on their dare-devil
midnight ride from the Keeper Hills to Ballyneety, where in
the dim morning twilight they captured and destroyed William
of Orange's wonderful siege-train, and thereby heartened the
defenders of beleaguered Limerick.

Writing in 1809, Lawrence, in his *History and Delineation
of the Horse,* said: "From Ireland alone we import [into

England] many saddle horses, as many perhaps as 1,500 in a year; upwards in some years. The Irish are the highest and steadiest leapers in the world. Ireland has bred some good racers, and the generality of Irish horses are, it appears, warmer tempered than our own; and, to use the expression, sharper and more frigate-built."

It is not to be wondered at therefore if in such a country there developed an ardent love of the noble sport of horse-racing. The Curragh of Kildare, the long-standing head-quarters of the Irish Turf Club, was celebrated far back in the eighteenth century as the venue of some great equine contests; and to this day, with its five important fixtures every year, it still holds pride of place. There are numerous other race-courses all over the country, from Punchestown, Leopardstown, Phoenix Park, and Baldoyle in the east to Galway in the west, and from The Maze in the north to rebel Cork in the south. Horse-racing has not inappropriately been termed the national pastime of Ireland. The number of people now giving their attention to it has called for a notable increase in the number of race-meetings, and stake-money is being put up on a more generous scale than at any previous time in the history of the sport. For example, the Irish Derby, run at the Curragh, was in 1914 worth £2,500; and there are besides several stakes of £1,500 and £1,000. The result of this forward policy is that increasing numbers come to our race-meetings and that the turf has never been more popular than it is today. Men and women of wealth and position find in the national pastime a pleasant method of employing their leisure, and in expending their surplus wealth in its pursuit and in the raising of horses of the highest class they realize that they confer a real benefit on the country.

It is, of course, now universally known that Ireland has an international reputation as a country eminently fitted for horse-breeding. If proof were needed, it would be found in the extensive purchases effected by English, French, Italian, German, Russian, and American buyers at the great Dublin Horse Show held in August every year. Horses bought in Ireland have seldom failed to realize their promise. The English classic races and many of the principal handicaps on the flat

have been often won by Irish-bred horses, such as Galtee
More, Ard Patrick, Orby, Kilwarlin, Barcaldine, Umpire,
Master Kildare, Kilsallaghan, Bendigo, Philomel, The Re-
jected, Comedy, Winkfield's Pride, Bellevin, Royal Flush,
Victor Wild, Bachelor's Button, Irish Ivy, and Hackler's
Pride. If only a few of the star performers are here set
down, it is not from lack of means to continue, but merely
from a desire to avoid the compilation of a mere string of
names. In France, too, the Irish racer has made his mark.
It is, however, in the four-and-a-half miles' Liverpool Grand
National Steeplechase, the greatest cross-country race in the
world, the supreme test of the leaper, galloper, and stayer,
that Irish-bred horses have made perhaps the most wonderful
record. The list of winners of that great event demonstrates
in an unmistakable manner that we are second to none in the
art of breeding steeplechase horses. Among many other noted
Irish-bred winners of this race there stand boldly forth the
names of The Lamb, Empress, Woodbrook, Frigate, Come
Away, Cloister, Wild Man from Borneo, and Manifesto. In
fact, it is the exception when another than an Irish-bred horse
annexes the blue riband of steeplechasing.

Closely allied to horse-racing is fox-hunting, and fox-
hunting, as well as the hunting of the stag and of the hare, has
flourished exceedingly in Ireland for a long time past. A
great deal of needed employment is one of the results. Dogs
are specially bred and trained for each of these branches of
sport. Irish foxhounds, staghounds, harriers, and beagles have
a high reputation. More native to the soil, and so interwoven
with the history of the country that it is often used as one of
its symbols, is the Irish wolfhound. This is probably the
animal to which Aurelius Symmachus, a Roman consul in
Britain, referred when, writing to his brother in Ireland in
A. D. 391, he acknowledged the receipt of seven Irish hounds.
The wolfhound played a sinister part in the Irish history of the
eighteenth century, for, as Davis says in his poem, "The
Penal Days":

> Their dogs were taught alike to run
> Upon the scent of wolf and friar.

The Irish wolfhound is now very scarce, and a genuine specimen is a valued and highly coveted possession. The greyhound, too, figures prominently in present-day sport, and in many parts of the country are held coursing meetings, which frequently result in several spirited contests. A famous Irish greyhound was Lord Lurgan's black and white dog, Master McGrath. Master McGrath achieved the rare distinction of winning the Waterloo Cup three times, in 1868, 1869, and 1871. When it is remembered that the Waterloo Cup is to coursing what the Liverpool Grand National is to steeplechasing, or the Epsom Derby to flat racing, the merit of this triple performance will at once be apparent.

Compared with the sports in which horse and hound participate, all other outdoor pastimes in Ireland take rather a minor place. Still, the Irishman's love of sport is diversified. Few there are who have not many inclinations, and as a nation our taste in sport is catholic. We take part in nearly every pastime; in many we excel. The prize ring has fallen from its high estate, nor is it the intention here to try to cast any glamour over it. The subject is introduced, in a passing way, for the sole purpose of showing that, in what at least used to be the manly art of self-defense, Ireland in days gone by as well as at the present time has more than held her own. The most conspicuous of the representatives of her race in this department are perhaps Heenan, Ryan, Sullivan, Corbett, Maher, McAuliffe, McFarland, and McGoorty. There is one other prize-fighter, Dan Donnelly by name, who became a sort of national hero, of whom all Irishmen of his day were not a little proud, because he laid the English champion low, and whose performance, now haloed by the antiquity of more than a hundred years, we may with equanimity, as without offense, contemplate, with perhaps a sigh for the good old times. The famous encounter between Donnell yand Cooper took place on the Curragh, and after eleven rounds of scientific boxing Donnelly knocked his opponent over the ropes and won the world's championship for the Emerald Isle. The spot where the battle came off has ever since been known as Donnelly's Hollow, and a neat monument there erected commemorates the Dublin man's pluck and skill. A ballad recounting the incidents of the fight and, as ballads go, not badly composed, had a wonderful vogue, and was sung at fair and market and other meeting place within the memory of men who are not now more than middle-aged.

A search in other domains of sport will be by no means barren of results. Take running, for instance. Who has not heard of the wondrous little Thomas Conneff from the short-grass county of Kildare? Who does not know of his brilliant performances on the track? We in Ireland, who had seen him defeat Carter, the great Canadian, over the four-mile course at Ballsbridge one summer's eve now nearly twenty golden years ago, knew his worth before he crossed the broad Atlantic to show to thousands of admiring spectators in America that Ireland was the breeder of fleet-footed sons, who lacked neither the courage, nor the thews and sinews, nor the staying power, to carry them at high speed over any distance of ground. May the earth lie light on Conneff, for in a small body he had a great heart! Then there was the mighty runner, James J. Daly, a true hero from Galway, the idol of the crowd in his native land as well as in the United States. Daly was the champion long distance cross-country runner of his day at home, and he showed before various nationalities in the Greater Ireland beyond the seas that he could successfully compete with the best from all countries.

In high jumping, Patrick Davin, P. Leahy, and Peter O'Connor were for long in the foremost rank; Daniel Ahearne was famous for his hop-step-and-jump performance; Maurice Davin, Matthew McGrath, and Patrick Ryan have, each in his own day, thrown the 16-pound hammer to record distance; in shot-putting there are Sheridan, Horgan, John Flanagan, and others bearing true Irish names, who are right in front; and before their time we had a redoubted champion in W. J. M. Barry. All previous performances in the shot-putting line have, however, been recently eclipsed by Patrick J. McDonald, of the Irish-American Club, who at Celtic Park, Long Island, on May 30, 1914, made a new world's record by putting the 18-pound shot 46 feet 2¾ inches. The climax of achievement was reached when T. F. Kiely won the all-round championship of the world at New York. The distinguished part taken by

Irishmen or sons of Irishmen in all departments of the Olympic games is so recent and so well known as to call for no comment. Ireland is far indeed from being degenerate in her athletes.

In international strife with England, Scotland, Wales, and France at Rugby football, Ireland has likewise won her spurs. She has never been beaten by the representatives of Gaul; and though for long enough she had invariably to succumb in competition with the other three countries, such is not the case nowadays, nor has it been for many years past. The Irish team has ever to be reckoned with. In Association football, too, Ireland is coming into her own. This branch of the game has developed enormously within a comparatively few seasons. The people flock in their thousands to witness matches for the principal league contests or cup ties. But the greatest crowds of all go to see Gaelic football, the national game; and to hurling, also distinctively Irish, they foregather in serried masses. Since the Gaelic Athletic Association was founded both football and hurling have prospered exceedingly. They are essentially popular forms of sport, and the muscular manhood of city and country finds in them a natural outlet for their characteristic Celtic vigor. The Gaelic Association has fostered and developed these sports, and has organized them on so sound a basis that interest in them is not confined to any particular district but spreads throughout the length and breadth of Ireland.

When the America Cup was to be challenged for, into the breach stepped the Earl of Dunraven and flung his gage to the holders of the trophy. This distinguished Irish nobleman furnished a contender in his Valkyrie II. in the fall of 1893, and his patriotic spirit in doing so stirred the sport-loving Irish nation to the greatest enthusiasm. His lordship was not successful, but he was not disheartened. He tried again with Valkyrie III., but again he was only second best, for, though his yacht sailed to victory in home waters, she proved unequal to the task of lifting the cup. No Englishman was prepared to tempt fortune, but not so that sterling Irishman, Sir Thomas Lipton, who, win or lose, would not have it laid to the charge of Ireland that an attempt should not be made. His Shamrock, Shamrock II., and Shamrock III.—surely a deep sense of patriotism prompted nomenclature such as that—each in succession went down to defeat; but Sir Thomas has not done yet. Like King Bruce, he is going to try again, and Shamrock IV. is to do battle with the best that America can range against her. All honor to Lord Dunraven and to Sir Thomas Lipton for their persistent efforts to engage in generous rivalry with the yachtsmen across the sea.

Lawn-tennis, cricket, and golf we play, and play well; to rowing many of us are enthusiastically devoted; and at handball our young men—and some not so young—are signally expert. The champion handball player has always been of Irish blood. Baseball we invented—and called it rounders. It is significant that the great American ball game is still played according to a code which is scarcely modified from that which may be seen in force any summer day on an Irish school field or village green. Perhaps something of hereditary instinct is to be traced in the fact that many of the best exponents of American baseball are the bearers of fine old Irish names.

This brief and cursory review of Ireland at Play must now conclude. It is scarcely more than a glossary, and not a complete one at that. It may, however, serve to show that Ireland's record in sport, like her record in so many other things set forth in this book, is great and glorious enough to warrant the insertion of this short chapter among those which tell of old achievements and feats of high emprize.

REFERENCES:

Racing—Irish Racing Calendar: 1790-1914, 124 vols. (Dublin, Brindley and Son); The Racing Calendar: 1774-1914 (London, Weatherby and Sons). Breeding—The General Stud Book: 1908-1913, 22 vols. (London, Weatherby and Sons). Racing and Breeding Generally—Cox: Notes on the History of the Irish Horse (Dublin, 1897). Boxing and Athletics—Files of *Sport* and *Freeman's Journal*.

THE FIGHTING RACE

By Joseph I. C. Clarke,
President, American Irish Historical Society.

I.—The Fighting Race at Home.

"War was the ruling passion of this people," says Mac-Geoghegan, meaning the Milesians who were the latest of the peoples that overran ancient Ireland up to the coming of Christ. How many races had preceded them remains an enigma of history not profitable to examine here, but whoever they were, or in what succession they arrived, they must, like all migrating people, have been prepared to establish themselves at the point of the spear and the edge of the sword. Two races certainly were mingled in the ancient Irish, the fair or auburn haired with blue eyes, and the dark haired with eyes of gray or brown. The Milesians appear to have reached Ireland through Spain. They came swiftly to power, more than a thousand years before our Lord, and divided the country into four provinces or kingdoms, with an *ard-ri,* or high-king, ruling all in a loose way as to service, taxes, and allegiance. The economic life was almost entirely pastoral. Riches were counted in herds of cattle. "Robustness of frame, vehemence of passion, elevated imagination," Dr. Leland says, signalized this people. Robust, they became athletic and vigorous and excelled in the use of deadly weapons; passionate, they easily went from litigation to blows; imaginative, they leaned toward poetry and song and were strong for whatever religion they practised. The latter was a polytheism brought close to the people through the Druids. Some stone weapons were doubtless still used; they had also brazen or bronze swords, and spears, axes, and maces of various alloys of copper and tin. Socially they remained tribal. Heads of tribes were petty kings, each with his stronghold of a primitive character, each with his tribal warriors, bards, harpers, and druids, and the whole male population more or less ready to take part in war.

The great heroes whose names have come down to us, such

as Finn, son of Cumhal, and Cuchulainn, were reared in a school of arms. Bravery was the sign of true manhood. A law of chivalry moderated the excess of combat. A trained militia, the Fianna, gave character to an era; the Knights of the Red Branch were the distinguishing order of chevaliers. The songs of the bards were songs of battle; the great Irish epic of antiquity was the *Táin Bó Cúalnge,* or Cooley Cattle-raid, and it is full of combats and feats of strength and prowess. High character meant high pride, always ready to give account of itself and strike for its ideals: "Irritable and bold", as one historian has it. They were jealous and quick to anger, but light-hearted laughter came easily to the lips of the ancient Irish. They worked cheerfully, prayed fervently to their gods, loved their women and children devotedly, clung passionately to their clan, and fought at the call with alacrity.

Nothing, it will be seen, could be further from the minds of such a people than submission to what they deemed injustice. The habit of a proud freedom was ingrained. Their little island of 32,000 square miles in the Atlantic Ocean, the outpost of Europe, lay isolated save for occasional forays to and from the coasts of Scotland and England. The Roman invasions of western Europe never reached it. England the Romans overran, but never Scotland or Ireland. Self-contained, Ireland developed a civilization peculiarly its own, the product of an intense, imaginative, fighting race. War was not constant among them by any means, and occupied only small portions of the island at a time, but, since the bards' best work was war songs and war histories, with much braggadocio doubtless intermixed, a different impression might prevail. Half of their kings may have been killed in broil or battle, and yet great wars were few. It is undoubted that Scotic, that is, Irish, invasion and immigration peopled the western shores of Scotland and gave a name to the country. In the first centuries of the Christian era they were the men who with the Picts fought the Romans at the wall of Severus. The Britons, it will be remembered, enervated by Roman dominance, had failed to defend their "border" when Rome first withdrew her legions.

At this time, too, began the first appearance of Ireland as a power on the sea. In the fourth century the high-king, Niall of the Hostages, commanding a large fleet of war galleys, invaded Scotland, ravaged the English coasts, and conquered Armorica (Brittany), penetrating as far as the banks of the Loire, where, according to the legend, he was slain by an arrow shot by one of his own men. One of the captives he brought from abroad on one of his early expeditions was a youth named Patrick, afterwards to be the Apostle of Ireland. Niall's nephew, Dathi, also ard-ri, was a great sea king. He invaded England, crossed to Gaul, and marched as far as the Alps, where he was killed by lightning. He was the last pagan king of Ireland. In perhaps a score of years after the death of Dathi, all Ireland had been converted to Christianity, and its old religion of a thousand years buried so deep that scholars find the greatest difficulty in recovering anything about it. This conservative, obstinate, jealous people overturned its pagan altars in a night, and, ever since, has never put into anything else the devotion, soul and body, of its sacrifices for religion. Christianity profoundly modified Irish life, softened manners, and stimulated learning. Not that the fighting propensities were obliterated. There were indeed many long and peaceful reigns, but the historians record neat little wars, seductive forays and "hostings", to use the new-old word, to the heart's content. The Irish character remained fixed in its essentials, but, under the influence of religious enthusiasm, Ireland progressed and prospered in the arts of peace. It would undoubtedly have shared the full progress of western Europe from this time on, but for its insularity. Hitherto its protection, it was now to be its downfall. A hostile power was growing of which it knew nothing.

The Norsemen—the hardy vikings of Norway, Sweden, and Denmark—had become a nation of pirates. Undaunted fighters and able mariners, they built their shapely long ships and galleys of the northern pine and oak, and swept hardily down on the coasts of England, Ireland, France, Spain, and Italy, and the lands of the Levant, surprising, massacring, plundering. In France (Normandy), in England, and lastly in Ireland they planted colonies. Their greatest success was in England, which

they conquered, Canute becoming king. Their greatest battles
and final defeat were in Ireland. From the end of the eighth
century to the beginning of the eleventh the four shores of
Erin were attacked in turn, and sometimes all together, by
successive fleets of the Norsemen. The waters that had been
Ireland's protection now became the high roads of the invaders. By the river Shannon they pushed their conquests
into the heart of the country. Dublin Bay, Waterford Harbor, Belfast Lough, and the Cove of Cork offered shelter to
their vessels. They established themselves in Dublin and
raided the country around. Churches and monasteries were
sacked and burned. To the end these Norsemen were robbers rather than settlers. To these onslaughts by the myriad
wasps of the northern seas, again and again renewed, the
Irish responded manfully. In 812 they drove off the invaders
with great slaughter, only to find fresh hordes descending a
year or two later. In the tenth century, Turgesius, the Danish
leader, called himself monarch of Ireland, but he was driven
out by the Irish king, Malachi. The great effort which really
broke the Danish power forever in Ireland was at the battle of Clontarf, on Dublin Bay, Good Friday, 1014, when King
Brian Boru, at the head of 30,000 men, utterly defeated the
Danes of Dublin and the Danes of oversea. Fragments of
the Northmen remained all over Ireland, but henceforth they
gradually merged with the Irish people, adding a notable element to itis blood. One of the most grievous chapters of
Irish history, the period of Norse invasion, literally shines
with Irish valor and tenacity, undimmed through six fighting generations. As Plowden says:

"Ireland stands conspicuous among the nations of the uni-
verse, a solitary instance in which neither the destructive hand
of time, nor the devastating arm of oppression, nor the widest
variety of changes in the political system of government
could alter or subdue, much less wholly extinguish, the national genius, spirit, and character of its inhabitants." This
is true not only of the Danish wars which ended nine hundred
years ago, but of many a dreadful century since and to this
very day.

Now followed a troubled period, Ireland weakened by loss

of blood and treasure, its government failing of authority through the defects of its virtues. It was inevitable, sooner or later, that England, as it became consolidated after its conquest by William the Norman, should turn greedy eyes on the fair land across the Irish sea. It was in 1169 that "Strongbow"—Richard, earl of Pembroke—came from England at the invitation of a discontented Irish chieftain and began the conquest of Ireland. Three years later came Henry II. with more troops and a Papal bull. After a campaign in Leinster, he set himself up as overlord of Ireland, and then returned to London. It was the beginning only. An English Lord Deputy ruled the "Pale", or portion of Ireland that England held more or less securely, and from that vantage ground made spasmodic war upon the rest of Ireland, and was forever warred on, in large attacks and small, by Irish chieftains.

The Irish were the fighting race now if ever. Without hope of outside assistance, facing a foe ever reinforced from a stronger, richer, more fully organized country, nothing but their stubborn character and their fighting genius kept them in the field. And century out and century in, they stayed, holding back the foreign foe four hundred years. It is worthy of note that it was the Norman English, racial cousins, as it were, of the Norsemen, who first wrought at the English conquest of Ireland. When some of these were seated in Irish places of pride, when a Butler was made Earl of Ormond and a Fitzgerald, Earl of Kildare, it was soon seen that they were merging rapidly in the Irish mass, becoming, as it was said, "more Irish than the Irish themselves." Many were the individual heroic efforts to strike down the English power. Here and there small Irish chiefs accepted the English rule, offsetting the Norman Irish families who at times were "loyal" and at times "rebel." The state of war became continuous and internecine, but three-fourths of Ireland remained unconquered. The idea of a united Ireland against England had, however, been lost except in a few exalted and a few desperate breasts. A gleam of hope came in 1316, when, two years after the great defeat of England by the Scotch under Robert the Bruce at Bannockburn, Edward, the victor-king's brother, came at the invitation of the northern Irish to Ireland with 6,000 Scots, landing near Carrick-fergus. He was proclaimed king of Ireland by the Irish who joined him. Battle after battle was won by the allies. Edward was a brilliant soldier, lacking, however, the prudence of his great brother, Robert. The story of his two years of fighting, ravaging, and slaying, is hard at this distance to reconcile with intelligible strategy. In the end, in 1318, the gallant Scot fell in battle near Dundalk, losing at the same time two-thirds of his army. For two years Scot and Irish had fought victoriously side by side. That is the fact of moment that comes out of this dark period.

The following century, like that which had gone before, was full of fighting. In 1399, on Richard II.'s second visit to Ireland, he met fierce opposition from the Irish septs. MacMorrough, fighting, harassing the king's army from the shelter of the Wicklow woods, fairly drove the king to Dublin. The sanguinary "Wars of the Roses"—that thirty years' struggle for the crown of England between the royal houses of York and Lancaster, 1455 to 1485—gave Ireland a long opportunity, which, however, she was too weak to turn to advantage; but fighting between Irish and English went on just the same, now in one province, now in another.

In the reign of Henry VIII. a revolt against England started within the Pale itself, when Lord Thomas Fitzgerald, known as Silken Thomas, went before the Council in Dublin and publicly renounced his allegiance. He took the field—a brave, striking figure—in protest against the king's bad faith in dealing with his father, the Earl of Kildare. At one time it looked as if the rebellion (it was the first real Irish rebellion) would prosper. Lord Thomas made combinations with Irish chieftains in the north and west, and was victor in several engagements. He finally surrendered with assurances of pardon, but, as in many similar cases, was treacherously sent a prisoner to London, where he was executed.

Queen Mary's reign was one of comparative quiet in Ireland. Her policy towards the Catholics was held to be of good augury for Ireland. The English garrison was reduced with impunity to 500 foot and a few horse; but another and darker day came with Elizabeth. Her coming to the throne, to-

(9)

gether with her fanatic devotion to the Reformation and an equal hatred of the old religion and all who clung to it, ushered in for Ireland two and a half centuries of almost unbroken misfortune. You cannot make people over. Some may take their opinions with their interest; others prefer to die rather than surrender theirs, and glory in the sacrifice. The proclamations of Elizabeth had no persuasion in them for the Irish. Her proscriptions were only another English sword at Ireland's throat. The disdain of the Irish maddened her. During her long reign one campaign after another was launched against them. Always fresh soldier hordes came pouring in under able commanders and marched forth from the Pale, generally to return shattered and worn down by constant harrying, sometimes utterly defeated with great slaughter. So of Henry Sidney's campaign, and so of the ill-fated Essex. Ulster, the stronghold of the O'Neills and the O'Donnells, remained unconquered down to the last years of Elizabeth's reign, although most of the greater battles were fought there. In Hugh O'Neill, Earl of Tyrone, and "Red" Hugh O'Donnell, prince of Tyrconnell, Ireland had two really great soldiers on her side. The bravery, generalship, prudence, and strategy of O'Neill were worthy of all praise, and Red Hugh fell little short of his great compatriot. In battle after battle for twenty years they defeated the English with slaughter. Ireland, if more and more devastated by campaigns and forays, became the grave of tens of thousands of English soldiers and scores of high reputations. Writing from Cork, the Earl of Essex, after a disastrous march through Leinster and Munster, says:

"I am confined in Cork . . . . but still I have been unsuccessful; my undertakings have been attended with misfortune . . . . The Irish are stronger and handle their arms with more skill than our people; they differ from us also in point of discipline. They likewise avoid pitched battles where order must be observed, and prefer skirmishes and petty warfare . . . . and are obstinately opposed to the English government."

They did not like attacking or defending fortified places, he also believed. It was only his experience. The campaigns of

Shane O'Neill, a bold but ill-balanced warrior, were full of
such attacks, but one potent cause for Irish reluctance to make
sieges a strong point of their strategy was that the strongest
fortresses were on the sea. An inexhaustible, powerful enemy
who held the sea was not in the end to be denied on sea or
land, but the Irish in stubborn despair or supreme indifference
to fate fought on. Religious rancor was added to racial hate.
Most of the English settlers, or "garrison," as they came to
be called, had become Protestants at the royal order. Ruin
perched upon Ireland's hills and made a wilderness of her fertile valleys. The Irish chieftains with their faithful followers moved from place to place in woods and hollows of the
hills. English colonists were settled on confiscated lands,
and were harried by those who had been driven from their
homes. It was war among graves. At last O'Neill made
composition with the government when all was lost in the
field, but the passionate Irish resolve never to submit still
stalked like a ghost, as if it could not perish.

When Elizabeth died it was thought that better things were
coming to Ireland with James I., the son of Mary, Queen of
Scots. Nothing of the kind. That curiously minded creature
at once made an ingenuous proclamation:

"Whereas his Majesty was informed that his subjects of
Ireland had been deceived by *a false report that his Majesty
was disposed to allow them liberty of conscience* and the free
choice of religion, now, etc." Fresh "transplanting" of English and Scotch settlers on the lands of the Irish was the gist
of his answer to the "false reports." So again the war of surprise, ambush, raid, and foray went on in a hundred places at
once, but the result was that the English power was even more
firmly seated than before.

In the time of Charles I. there were terrible slaughters
both of Protestants and Catholics. Patriotism and loyalty as
moving causes had disappeared, but religion fiercely took their
place. With Cromwell, the religious persecution took on an
apocalyptic note of massacre, but the Irish were still showing
that they were there with arms in their hands. The names of
Owen Roe O'Neill and his splendid victory, in 1646, at Ben-
burb over the English and Scotch, where he slew more than

3,000 men, and of another Hugh O'Neill, who made such a brilliant defense at Clonmel against Cromwell, shine brightly out of the darkness. But Ireland, parcelled out among the victors, was always the weaker after every campaign. Waves of war swept over her. She became mixed up in the rivalries of the English royal families, religion playing the most important part in the differences. It had armed Henry and Elizabeth, James and Charles against her. It gave edge to Cromwell's sword, and it led her into a great effort on behalf of James II. When William of Orange crossed the Boyne, all that followed for a century was symbolized. Athlone, Aughrim, Limerick, all places of great and fierce contests, were decided against her. French support of a kind had James, but not enough. Bravery and enthusiasm may win battles, but they do not carry through great campaigns. Once again God marched with the heaviest, best-fed, best-armed battalions. The great Tyrone dying in exile at Rome, Red Hugh O'Donnell perishing in Spain in the early days of the seventeenth century, were to prefigure the fighting and dying of half a million Irish warriors on continental soil for a hundred years after the fall of Limerick as the seventeenth century neared its close.

During that period the scattered bands of the Rapparees, half patriots, half robbers, hiding in mountain fastnesses, dispersing, reassembling, descending on the English estates for rapine or the killing of "objectionables," represented the only armed resistance of the Irish. It was generally futile although picturesque.

After the close of the Revolutionary War in America, Ireland received a new stimulation. The success of the patriots of the Irish parliament under Grattan, backed as they were by 100,000 volunteers and 130 pieces of cannon, in freeing Irish industry and commerce from their trammels, evoked the utmost malignity in England. Ireland almost at once sprang to prosperity, but it was destined to be short lived. A great conspiracy, which did not at first show above the surface, was set on foot to destroy the Irish parliament. This is not the place to follow the sinister machinations of the English, save to note that they forced both the Presbyterians and the Catholics of the north into preparations for revolt. The Society of United Irishmen was formed, and drew many of the brightest and most cultivated men in Ireland into its councils. It numbered over 70,000 adherents in Ulster alone. The government was alarmed, and began a systematic persecution of the peasantry all over Ireland. English regiments were put at "free quarters," that is, they forced themselves under order into the houses and cabins of the people with demands for bed and board. The hapless people were driven to fury. Brutal murders and barbarous tortures of men and women by the soldiers, savage revenges by the peasantry, and every form of violent crime all at once prevailed in the lately peaceful valleys. Prosecutions of United Irishmen and executions were many. It was all done deliberately to provoke revolt. In 1798 the revolt came. In the greater part of Ulster and Munster the uprising failed, but a great insurrection of the peasantry of Wexford shocked the country. Poorly armed, utterly undisciplined, without munitions of war, but 40,000 strong, they literally flung themselves pike in hand on the English regiments, sweeping everything before them for a time. Father John Murphy, a priest and patriot, was one of their leaders, but Beauchamp Bagenal Harvey was soon their commander-in-chief. At one time the "rebels" dominated the entire county save for a fort in the harbor and a small town or two, but it was natural that the commissariat should soon be in difficulties and their ammunition give out. The British general, Lake, with an army of 20,000 men and a moving column of 13,000, attacked the rebels on Vinegar Hill, and although the fight was heroic and bloody while it lasted, it was soon over and the British army was victorious. The rest was retreat, dispersal, and widespread cruelties and burnings and a long succession of murders. The "Boys of Wexford" under great difficulties had given a great account of themselves. Dark as was that page of history, it has been a glowing lamp to Irish disaffection ever since. It is the soul of the effort that counts, and the disasters do not discredit '98 in Irish eyes.

Voltaire, in his *Century of Louis XIV.*, made his reflection on the Irish soldier out of his limited knowledge of the Williamite war in Ireland. He says, "The Irish, whom we have seen such good soldiers in France and Spain, have always fought poorly at home"! They had not fought poorly at home. It took four hundred years of English effort to complete, merely on its face, the conquest of Ireland, and all of that long sweep of the sword of Time was a time of battle. The Irish were fought with every appliance of war, backed by the riches of a prospering, strongly organized country, and impelled persistently by the greed of land and love of mastery; but there was not a mountain pass in Ireland, not a square mile of plain, not a river-ford, scarce a hill that had not been piled high with English dead in that four hundred years at the hands of the Irish wielders of sword and spear and pike.

The Irish had not made their environment or their natures, and no power on earth could change them. Over greater England had swept the Romans, the Jutes, the Saxons, the Angles, the Norsemen, and the Normans. All found lodgment and all went to the making of England. Well, one might say, it had been for Ireland if she had developed that assimilating power which made her successive conquerors in process of time the feeders of her greatness, but the Irish would not and could not. Instead, they developed the pride of race that no momentary defeat could down. They became inured to battle and dreamt of battle when the peace of an hour was given them. When the four kings of Ireland were feasted in Dublin by King Richard II. of England, an English chronicler remarked, "Never were men of ruder manners"; but neither the silken array and golden glitter of Richard's peripatetic court nor the brave display of his thousand knights and thirty thousand archers filled them with longing for the one or fear of the other. They went back to their Irish hills and plains and fastnesses as obstinately Irish as ever.

They fought well at home, if unfortunately, the wonder being that they continued to fight. The heavens and the earth seemed combined against them.

II.—THE FIGHTING RACE ABROAD.

We next see Irish soldiers fighting abroad. The blood they had shed so freely for the Stuarts at the Boyne, at Athlone, at Aughrim, at Limerick was in vain. The king of France, if he sent armies to Ireland, demanded Irish troops in return. The transports that brought the French regiments over in May, 1690, took back over five thousand officers and men from Ireland, who formed the first Irish Brigade in the service of France. This, remember, was before the battle of the Boyne. The men were formed on their arrival in France into three regiments, those of Mountcashel, O'Brien, and Dillon, named after their commanders, and were sent to Savoy. The French aid to James in Ireland helped best in giving confidence to the raw Irish levies, but it was more than offset by the German troops brought over by William. The weakness, indecision, or worse, of James before Derry, his chicken-hearted failure to overwhelm Schomberg when he lay at his mercy before the arrival of William, ruined his chances. Remember that the Irish army, if defeated at the Boyne, was not broken, and was strong enough, when pursued by William, to repulse him with 500 killed and 1,000 wounded and to compel him to raise the siege of Limerick. The dash and skill of Patrick Sarsfield, Earl of Lucan, backed by Irish desperation, won the day. The French troops sailed home after William's retreat. In the next year's campaign occurred the crowning disasters of the war, but in any other country or with any other people than the English the terms of capitulation at Limerick, which were formulated by Ginkel and showed a soldier's respect for a brave and still powerful foe, would have ushered in an era of peace.

The Irish soldiers' distrust of the conquerors was shown in the fact that, since the stipulations allowed the free departure of the garrison with honors of war, 19,059 officers and men took service with France, and sailed in October, 1691, on the French fleet, which by the irony of fate had arrived in the Shannon too late, on the very day after the signing of the treaty of Limerick. Never in the whole course of the history of nations has more hideous treachery been shown than in the immediate breaking of that treaty; and dearly has England paid for it ever since, although, for the hundred years that followed, Ireland sank to the very depths under the penal laws, with her trade ruined, her lands stolen, her religion persecuted, and all education and enlightenment forbidden by abominable, drastic laws.

If, as has been computed, 450,000 Irish fought and died in the service of France between 1690 and 1745, a further 30,000 are to be added down to 1792. A French writer estimates the whole Irish contingent at 750,000, but, for a roster of seekers of glory from an impoverished people, the more reasonable half-million should surely suffice.

Long would be the story to follow the fighting fortunes of the Irish Brigades. Officered by Irish gentlemen and drilled to perfection, they soon came to hold in the French service the esteem that later was given to Irish regiments in the service of England. King Louis welcomed them heartily and paid them a higher wage than his native soldiers. No duty was too arduous or too dangerous for the Irish Brigades. Seldom were they left to rust in idleness. Europe was a caldron of wars of high ambitions.

The Irish regiments fought through the war in Flanders. At Landen, July 29, 1693, the French under the duke of Luxembourg defeated the English under William III. with a slaughter of 10,473 men, losing 8,000 men themselves. In the retreat, Ginkel, William's general in the Irish campaign, was almost drowned in the river Greete. The Irish Royal Regiment of Footguards, that of Dorrington, was the first corps to break through the English intrenchments, its gallant leader, Colonel Barrett, falling as he headed the charge. Here also was stricken Lieutenant-Colonel Nugent of Sheldon's Irish Regiment. Here also fell—saddest loss of all—Patrick Sarsfield, Earl of Lucan, brave, resourceful, a true unfaltering soldier and lover of his country. The legend of his life blood flowing before his eyes and his utterance, "Would it had been shed for Ireland", may and should be true, although he lived three days after the battle. Would, indeed, it had been shed for Ireland—after such a day!

It was in 1703 that the celebrated defence of Cremona lifted Irish renown to great heights throughout Europe. There were but 600 Irish troopers all told in that long day's work, and from the break of day till nightfall they held at bay Prince Eugene's army of 10,000 men. The two battalions of Bourke and

Dillon were surprised at early morn to learn that the Austrians
—and there were Irish officers among them—were in the town.
Major O'Mahony and his men ran from their beds to the
gates, and neither the foes without nor the foes within could
make them budge. Terribly they suffered under concentrated
attacks, but a withering fire from the Irish met every assault.
It was nightfall before relief came, and then the sons of Ireland who had held Cremona for the French were acclaimed
by all, but of their 600 they had lost nearly 350. Small wonder that the honor list that day was long. In Bourke's bat-
talion the specially distinguished were Captains Wauchop,
Plunkett, Donnellan, MacAuliffe, Carrin, Power, Nugent, and
Ivers; in Dillon's, Major O'Mahony, Captains Dillon, Lynch,
MacDonough, and Magee, and Lieutenants Dillon and Gib-
bon, John Bourke and Thomas Dillon. Major O'Mahony
was sent to Paris to carry the news of the victory to the king,
who presented him with a purse of 1,000 louis d'or, a pension of 1,000 livres, and the brevet of colonel.

So the history proceeds, the Irish regiments lost in the
array of the French forces, but showing here and there a
glint of charging bayonets, captured trenches, and gushes of
Irish blood. In 1703 the brigade regiments fought in Italy
and Germany under the Duc de Vendome. We hear of the
regiments of Berwick, Bourke, Dillon, Galmoy, and Fitzgerald
vigorously engaged. In Germany the story is of Sheldon's
Horse and two battalions of the regiments of Dorrington and
Clare. At the first battle of Blenheim, September 20, 1703,
the regiment of Clare lost one of its colors, rallied, charged
with the bayonet and recovered it, taking two colors from the
enemy. This was a French victory. Not so the great battle
of Blenheim, August, 1704, when Marlborough and Prince
Eugene severely defeated the French and Bavarians. Three
Irish battalions shared in the disaster. In 1705 at Cassano
in Italy an Irish regiment, finding itself badly galled by artillery fire from the opposite bank of the Adda, declared they
could stand it no longer, and thereupon jumped in, swam the
river, and captured the battery. In 1705 Colonel O'Mahony
of Cremona fame distinguished himself in Spain. In the
next year at the battle of Ramillies, in which Marlborough

with the Dutch defeated the French under Villeroi, Lord Clare's regiment captured the colors of the English Churchill regiment and of the Scottish regiment in the Dutch service. In the same year and the next, the Irish Brigade fought many battles in Spain. One cannot pursue the details of the engagements. Regiments ever decimated were ever recruited by the "Wild Geese" from Ireland—the adventurous Catholic youth of the country who sought congenial outlet for their love of adventure and glory. Many Irish also joined the French army after deserting from the English forces in Flanders.

It was, however, at Fontenoy, May 11, 1745, that the Irish Brigade rendered their most signal service to France. The English under the Duke of Cumberland, son of George II., with 55,000 men including a large German and Dutch auxiliary, met the French under Marshal Saxe, and in the presence of the French king Louis XV., near Tournai in Belgium. Saxe had 40,000 men in action and 24,000 around Tournai, which town was the objective of the English advance. Among the troops on the field were the six Irish regiments of Clare, Dillon, Bulkeley, Roth, Berwick, and Lally, all under Charles O'Brien, Viscount Clare, afterwards Marshal Thomond of France. After fierce cannonading on both sides and a check to the allies on their right and left, a great column of English veterans advanced on the French centre, breaking through with sheer force. They had thus reached high ground when some cannonading halted them. It was at this moment of gravest peril to the French that the Irish regiments with unshotted guns charged headlong up the slope on their ancient enemies, crying, "Remember Limerick and British Faith!" The great English column, already roughly handled by the cannon, broke and fled in wild disorder before that irresistible onslaught, and France had won a priceless victory, but the six Irish regiments lost one-third of their gallant men by a single volley as they followed their steel into the English lines.

When Charles Edward, the Stuart Pretender, landed in Scotland in 1745, he was followed by a small French force, including 500 Irishmen from the Brigade. Colonel John

O'Sullivan was much relied on by the prince in his extraordinary campaign. Sir Thomas Sheridan also distinguished himself. There were 475 Irish at the battle of Culloden, that foredoomed defeat of the Stuart cause, and two days later a score of Irish officers were among those who surrendered at Inverness.

In Spain at the beginning of the 18th century there were hundreds of Irish officers in the military service, and eight Irish regiments. Among the officers were thirteen Kellys, thirteen Burkes, and four Sheas. It seemed that Ireland had soldiers for the world. Don Patricio, Don Miguel, Don Carlos, Don Tadeo took the place of Patrick, Michael, Charles, and Thadeus. O'Hart gives a list of sixty descendants of the "Wild Geese" in places of honor in Spain. General Prim was a descendant of the Princes of Inisnage in Kilkenny. An O'Donnell was Duke of Tetuan and field marshal of Spain. Ambrose O'Higgins, born in county Meath, Ireland, was the foremost Spanish soldier in Chile and Peru; Admiral Patricio Lynch was one of its most distinguished sailors; and James McKenna its greatest military engineer. The son of O'Higgins was foremost among those who fought for Chilean independence and gained it, and one of his ablest lieutenants was Colonel Charles Patrick O'Madden of Maryland.

In Austria the Irish soldiers were particularly welcome. They count forty-one field-marshals, major-generals, generals of cavalry, and masters of ordnance of Irish birth in the Austrian service. O'Callaghan relates that on March 17, 1766, His Excellency Count Mahony (son of the O'Mahony of Cremona), ambassador from Spain to the court of Vienna, gave a grand entertainment in honor of St. Patrick, to which he invited all persons of condition who were of Irish descent. Among many others, there were present Count Lacy, President of the Council at War, the generals O'Donnell, McGuire, O'Kelly, Browne, Plunkett, and MacElligot, four chiefs of the Grand Cross, two governors, several knights military, six staff officers, and four privy councillors, with the principal officers of State. All wore Patrick's crosses in honor of the Irish nation, as did the whole court that day. Emperor Francis I. said: "The more Irish officers in the Austrian service the better; bravery will not be wanting; our troops will always be well disciplined." The Austrian O'Reillys and Taaffes were famous. It was the dragoon regiment of Count O'Reilly that by a splendid charge saved the remnant of the Austrian army at Austerlitz.

In the American war of the Revolution, General Charles Geoghegan of the Irish Brigade made the campaigns of Rochambeau and Lafayette. He received the order of the Cincinnati from Washington and was ever proud of it. Lieutenant General O'Moran also served in America. He was afterwards executed in the French Revolution, for the "Brigade" remained royalist to the end. General Arthur Dillon, who served in the Brigade, was also guillotined in 1794, crying, *"Vive le roi!"* At the foot of the scaffold a woman, probably Mme. Hébert, also condemned, stood beside him. The executioner told her to mount the steps. "Oh, Monsieur Dillon," she said, "pray go first." "Anything to oblige a lady," he answered gaily, and so faced his God.

Lord Macaulay, commenting upon these things and deploring the policies that brought them about, says with great significance:

"There were Irish Catholics of great ability, but they were to be found everywhere except in Ireland—at Versailles, at St. Ildefonso, in the armies of Frederic, in the armies of Maria Theresa. One exile (Lord Clare) became a marshal of France, another (General Wall) became Prime Minister of Spain .... Scattered all over Europe were to be found brave Irish generals, dexterous Irish diplomatists, Irish counts, Irish barons, Irish knights of St. Louis and St. Leopold, of the White Eagle, and of the Golden Fleece, who if they remained in the house of bondage, could not have been ensigns of marching regiments or freemen of petty corporations."

The old Irish brigades ended with the French monarchy. Battalions of the regiments of Dillon and Walsh were with the French fleet in the West Indies at Grenada and St. Eustache, also at Savannah, and under Rochambeau at Yorktown, but, except as to the officers, the surviving regiments of Berwick, Dillon, and Walsh were largely French. With the better times under Grattan's Parliament in Ireland, the soldier emigration to France had all but ceased. The Irish Volunteers of 1782 numbered 100,000 men, of whom an appreciable proportion were Catholics. Many Irish went into the English army and navy, but there was another stream of fighting emigrants, that which flocked to the standard of revolt against England in America, of which much was to be heard thereafter.

In the American colonies before the Revolution there were thousands of descendants of the Catholic Irish who had settled in Maryland and Pennsylvania during the seventeenth century, as well as hardy Irish Presbyterians from Ulster, who came in great multitudes during the first half of the eighteenth century. They had suffered persecution in Ireland for conscience sake from their fellow-Protestants. In Maine, New Hampshire, Massachusetts, Pennsylvania, and the Carolinas they constituted entire communities. The emigration of the Catholic or purely Celtic Irish to America in the seventeenth and eighteenth centuries was often compulsory. At any rate, after the middle of the eighteenth century it was large and became continuous—a true drift. Catholics and Presbyterians alike brought hostility to the English government with them, and their voices fed the storm of discontent. The Irish schoolmasters, of whom there were hundreds, were especially efficient in this. They came in every ship to the colonies. They had no love for England, for they had experienced in Ireland the tyranny of English law, and they would be more than human if they did not imbue the minds of the American children under their care with their own hatred of oppression and wrong and English domination. The log schoolhouse of the Irish teacher became the nursery of revolution. They were a very important factor, therefore, in the making of the Revolution, and many of them took an active part as soldiers in the field.

The Irish, both Catholics and Protestants, poured into the patriot ranks once the standard of revolt was raised in 1775. The Pennsylvania line, which General Lee called "the line of Ireland," was almost entirely Irish, and the rosters of several of the Maryland and Virginia regiments contain a remarkably large proportion of Irish names, in some cases running as high as 60 per cent. It is computed that the Irish furnished not less than a third of the whole American forces. A common cause blotted out all old religious prejudices between Irishmen in the American service. It was John Sullivan, of New Hampshire, son of a Limerick schoolmaster, who began the revolt by seizing the fort of William and Mary and its storehouses filled with that powder which charged the guns at Bunker Hill in the following year. It was Captain Jeremiah O'Brien, with his brothers, who made the first sea attack on the British off Machias, Maine, in May, 1775, an engagement which Fenimore Cooper calls "the Lexington of the Seas." There were fifteen Celtic Irish names among the Minute Men at the Battle of Lexington. Colonel Barrett, who commanded at Concord, was Irish. There were 258 Celtic Irish names on the rosters of the American forces at the battle of Bunker Hill. John Sullivan had been made a major-general, thereafter to be a notable figure in the war at Princeton, Trenton, Newport, and in his Indian campaign. The Connecticut line was thick with Irish names. Around Washington himself was a circle of brilliant Irishmen: Adjutant-General Edward Hand leading his rifles, Stephen Moylan his dragoons, General Henry Knox and Colonel Proctor at the head of his artillery, John Dunlop his body-guard, Andrew Lewis his brigadier-general, Ephraim Blaine his quartermaster, all of Irish birth or ancestry. Commodore John Barry, born in Wexford in 1739 and bred to the sea, was a ship captain in his early twenties, trading from Philadelphia. When the Continental Congress met, he at once volunteered, and was given command of the *Lexington,* the first American ship to capture a British war vessel. Later, after gallant fighting on sea and land, he was given command of the U. S. frigate *Alliance,* in which he crossed the Atlantic to France, and fought and captured in a rattling battle two British warships, the *Atlanta* and the *Trepasay.* He was the Father of the American navy, holding captain's certificate No. 1, signed by Washington himself—the highest rank then issued.

General Richard Montgomery, the brave and able soldier who fell at Quebec as he charged the heights, was an Irishman. General George Clinton, son of an Irishman, was a brigadier-general, governor of New York and twice Vice-President of the United States. Fifty-seven officers of New York regiments in the Revolution were Irish, and a large number of the officers in the Southern regiments of the line, as well as of the militia, were native Irish or of Irish descent. The rosters of the enlisted Irishmen of the New York regiments run into the thousands. Hundreds of Irish soldiers suffered in the prison ships of New York, the horrors of which served so conspicuously to stimulate American determination to carry the war to the only rightful conclusion. Washington always recognized America's debt to the Irish. "St. Patrick" he made the watchword in the patriot lines the night before the English evacuated Boston forever on the memorable 17th of March, 1776. After the war he was made, with his own consent, an honorary member of the Friendly Sons of St. Patrick. Major-General Richard Butler and his four brothers, all officers, and Brigadier-Generals John Armstrong, William Irvine, William Thompson, James Smith, and Griffith Rutherford all fought with distinction. All of these officers were Irish-born. It was in truth an Irish war, so far as Irish sentiment and whole-hearted service could make it. The record of Irish soldiers' names alone would fill volumes.

The thirst of the Irish race for the glory of war is shown in the large enlistments in the last quarter of the eighteenth century, and since, in the English army and navy. Grattan, in pleading for Ireland, claimed that a large percentage of the British forces were Irish. Wolfe Tone avers that there were 210 Irishmen out of 220 in the crew of a British frigate that overhauled his ship on its way to America. Bonaparte had in his armies an Irish Legion that did good service in Holland, Spain, Portugal, and Germany. Marshal Clarke, Duke of Feltre, French Minister of War in 1809, was Irish. Up and down the Spanish Peninsula, Irish blood was shed in abundance in the armies of Wellington. Never was more brilliant fighting done than that which stands to Irish credit from the lines of Torres Vedras to Badajos and Toulouse. Of the Waterloo campaign volumes have been written in praise of Irish valor. As Maxwell says in his *Tales of Waterloo*:—
"The victors of Marengo and Austerlitz reeled before the

charge of the Connaught Rangers." Wellington himself was Irish, as in the later wars of England Lord Gough, Lord Wolseley, Lord Roberts, Lord Kitchener, and General French came from Ireland. The Irish soldiers in the English service by a pitiful irony of fate helped materially to fasten the chains of English domination on the peoples of India in a long series of wars.

In America, the War of 1812 once more gave opportunity to the Fighting Race. The commanding figure of the war, which opened so inauspiciously for the United States, was General Andrew Jackson, the hero of the battle of New Orleans, and afterwards twice elected President of the United States. "Old Hickory", as he came to be lovingly called, was proud of his Irish father, and sympathized with the national longings of the Irish people. He was a splendid soldier, and his defeat of the English general, Pakenham, on January 8, 1815, which meant the control of the mouths of the Mississippi, as well as safeguarding the city of New Orleans, reflected the highest credit on his skill and unflagging energy. The English had superior numbers, between 8,000 and 9,000 men, against a scant 6,000 under Jackson, and their force was made up of veterans of the European wars. In command of the left of his line Jackson placed the gallant general William Carroll, born in Philadelphia, but of Irish blood, who was afterwards twice governor of Tennessee. The British general made the mistake of despising the soldier value of his enemy, yet before evening of that day he saw his artillery silenced and his lines broken, as he died of a wound on the field. The battle was actually fought after the signing of the treaty of peace at Ghent; it annihilated British pretensions in this part of the world, anyway.

After Commodore Perry, the victor in the battle of Lake Erie, and himself the son of an Irish mother, the northern naval glory of the War of 1812 falls to Lieutenant Thomas MacDonough, of Irish descent, whose victory on Lake Champlain over the British squadron was almost as important as Perry's. Admiral Charles L. Stewart ("Old Ironsides"), who commanded the frigate *Constitution* when she captured the *Cyane* and the *Levant,* fighting them by moonlight, was a great and renowned figure. His parents came from Ireland, and Charles Stewart Parnell's mother was the great sea-fighter's daughter. Lieutenant Stephen Cassin commanded the *Ticonderoga* and fought her well. Captain Johnston Blakely, who was born in Ireland, captured in the *Wasp* of 18 guns the much larger British *Reindeer* of 20 guns and 175 men in a splendid fight, and later sank the *Avon,* an 18-gun brig. After capturing a great prize, which he sent to Savannah, he sailed for the Spanish main and was never heard of more. Captain Boyle, in the privateer *Comet* of Baltimore, fought the *Hibernia,* of 18 guns, and later in the *Chasseur,* known as the phantom ship, so fast she sailed, took eighty prizes on the high seas. General A. E. Maccomb, who commanded victoriously at Plattsburg, was of Irish descent, and Colonel Robert Carr, who distinguished himself in the same campaign, was born in Ireland. Major George Croghan of Kentucky, the hero of Fort Stephenson, was the son of an Irish father who had been a soldier in the Revolution. Colonel Hugh Brady, of the 22nd Infantry, commanded at Niagara. He remained in the army and fought in Mexico. William McRee, of Irish descent, was General Browne's chief engineer in laying out the military works of the American army at Niagara.

Let it not be forgotten that in this memorable company brave Mrs. Doyle has a place. Her husband, Patrick Doyle, an Irish artilleryman, had been taken prisoner by the British in the affair at Queenston and had been refused a parole. Accordingly, when the guns were trained on the English lines before Fort Niagara, Mary, emulating the example of her countrywoman, "Molly" Pitcher, at Monmouth, determined to take her husband's place, and, regardless of flying British balls, tended a blacksmith's bellows all day, providing red-hot shot for the American gun battery, and sending a prayer with every shot into the British lines.

After the Queenston affair, it is well to note, the English doctrine of perpetual allegiance was abated. Twenty-three Irish-born men were among the captives of the English in that engagement. They were manacled to be sent to Ireland to be tried for treason, not as enemies taken in the field. Winfield Scott, then lieutenant-colonel, was also a prisoner with them.

He protested loudly against this infamous course. Upon his release he laid aside twenty-three British prisoners to be treated like the Irishmen, eye for eye and tooth for tooth. As a result, the Irish prisoners were exchanged.

Colonel John Allen, who fell at the head of the First Regiment of Kentucky Riflemen at the battle of the river Raisin on January 21, 1813, was one of the Irish Allens of Kentucky. His father and mother were natives of Ireland.

The Mexican War (1846-48) again showed Irish valor at the front. It was not a great war, though brilliantly fought and rich in territorial accessions. The campaigning comprised the work of two main expeditions and a subsidiary movement in California. One column, under General Zachary Taylor, penetrated northern Mexico and fought the battles of Matamoras, Palo Alto, and Resaca de la Palma, in May, 1846, with a force of 2,200 men; forced the evacuation of Monterey in September, his army swelled to 5,000; and defeated Santa Anna at Buena Vista in February, 1847. General Winfield Scott, with a naval expediton, attacked Vera Cruz from the sea in March, 1847, and took up the march, 13,000 strong, to Mexico City, fighting the battles of Cerro Gordo, Contreras, Churubusco, Molino del Rey, and Chapultepec, and entered Mexico City on September 14. General James Shields, born in Tyrone, Ireland, in 1810, was in command with his brigade under Scott. A brilliant soldier, he was severely wounded at Cerro Gordo and again at Chapultepec. He served as United States Senator after the war and again took the field in the Civil War, his forces defeating Stonewall Jackson at the first battle of Winchester in 1862. The glamour of chivalry lights the name of Phil Kearney. Here was a born soldier. He was a volunteer with the French in Algiers in 1839-40. He also commanded under Scott with brilliant bravery, and was brevetted major on the field for "gallant and meritorious conduct" at the battles of Contreras and Churubusco. In the French war with Austria in 1859-60, Kearney fought with the French, distinguishing himself at the decisive and bloody battle of Solferino. In the Civil War he was brigadier-general of New Jersey troops in 1861 and major-general in 1862, taking distinguished part in the battles of the Peninsula and second Bull Run, and was killed while reconnoitring at Chantilly. General Stephen W. Kearney, with the Army of the West, by dint of long marches, secured California among the fruits of the war. General Bennet Riley, born in Maryland of Irish ancestry, commanded a brigade at Contreras, making a wonderful charge, and also fought brilliantly at Cerro Gordo and Churubusco, and was brevetted brigadier-general. He attained the army rank in 1858. Major-General William O. Butler, under Zachary Taylor, was one of the heroes of Monterey. Born in Kentucky, son of Percival Butler of Kilkenny, who was one of the famous five Butler brothers of the Revolutionary War whom Washington once toasted as "The Butlers and their five sons," General Butler succeeded General Scott in command of the entire American army in Mexico in February, 1848. Another of clear Irish descent who fought under Zachary Taylor was Major-General George Croghan, whose father, born in Sligo, Ireland, had fought in the Revolution. He himself took part, as we have seen, in the War of 1812, and now was at the front before Monterey. Once, when a Tennessee regiment wavered under a hot converging fire, Croghan rushed to the front and, taking off his hat, shouted, "Men of Tennessee, your fathers conquered with Jackson at New Orleans. Come, follow me!" and they followed in a successful assault. Major-General Robert Paterson, who was born at Strabane, Ireland, and was the son of a '98 man, saw service in 1812, and became major-general of militia in Pennsylvania, whence he went to the Mexican War. He also lived to serve in the War of the States.

Among Irish-named officers mentioned honorably in official despatches are Major Edward H. Fitzgerald, Major Patrick J. O'Brien; Captain Casey, chosen to lead the first storming party at Chapultepec; Captains Hogan, Byrne, Kane, McElvin, McGill, Burke, Barny, O'Sullivan, McCarthy, McGarry, and McKeon. Captain Mayne Reid, the novelist, a native of Ireland, was in the storming of Chapultepec. Theodore O'Hara, the poet, served with the Kentucky troops and was brevetted major for gallantry at Contreras and Churubusco, while on the staff of General Franklin Pierce (afterwards President of the United States). O'Hara's magnificent poem, "The Bivouac of the Dead," has made his name immortal. It was written on the occasion of the interment at Frankfort, Ky., of the Kentucky dead of the Mexican War, where

> "Glory guards with solemn round
> The bivouac of the dead."

Irwin C. McDowell, who was brevetted captain at Buena Vista, commanded a corps in the Civil War. George A. McCall, brevetted lieutenant-colonel at Palo Alto, was a major-general in the Civil War. Francis T. Bryan was a hero of Buena Vista. Lieutenant-Colonel Thomas P. Moore and Captain James Hogan both won fame in the 3rd Dragoons. Lieutenant Thomas Claiborn of the Mounted Rifles became a colonel in the Confederate Army. Lieutenant-Colonel J. W. Geary fought brilliantly and was to be heard from later with renown.

Colonel John F. Reynolds of the 3rd Artillery lived to be major-general in the Civil War, and to fall gloriously at Gettysburg. Nor must we forget Major Folliot Lally's bravery at Cerro Gordo; Second Lieutenant Thomas W. Sweeny, a brigadier-general of the Civil War and the planner of the Fenian invasion of Canada in 1866; Lieutenant Henry B. Kelly of the 2nd Infantry, afterwards a Confederate colonel; Captain Martin Burke of the 1st Artillery, killed at Churubusco; nor Lieutenant William F. Barry of the 2nd Artillery, a brigadier-general in the Civil War. There were scores of other Irish named officers. In the whole American force of 30,000 engaged, the Irish born and Irish descended troops of all arms were numbered by thousands.

It was, however, in the Civil War that the flood of Irish valor and loyalty to the American Republic was at its height. The 2,800,000 enlistments on the Northern side stood probably for 1,800,000 individual soldiers serving during the four years of the war. Not less than 40 per cent. of these were Irish born or of Irish descent. Of the 337,800 men furnished by the State of New York, 51,206 were natives of Ireland out of the total of 134,178 foreign born, or 38 per cent. of the latter, while not less than 80,000 of Irish descent figured among the

203,600 native born soldiers. Of the 2,261 engagements in the war, few there were that saw no Irishmen in arms, and certainly, in every one of the 519 engagements that made Virginia a great graveyard, the Irish figured largely. Of the 1,000,516 mustered out in 1865, not less than 150,000 were natives of Ireland, while those of Irish descent numbered hundreds of thousands. They fought well everywhere, and it would require volumes to give the names and deeds of those who distinguished themselves more than their fellows.

One name, however, shines with a great blaze above them all, the name of Philip H. Sheridan, one of the three supreme soldiers of the Union, Ulysses S. Grant and William Tecumseh Sherman being the others. Had Ireland furnished only Sheridan to the Union cause, her service would be beyond reward. He was born in Albany, N. Y., in March, 1831, the year after his parents, John and Mary Sheridan, arrived there from the Co. Cavan, in Ireland. The family moved to Somerset, Perry Co., Ohio, the following year. There Philip began village life. How he gained the beginning of an education; worked in a grocery store; became a bookkeeper; longed for a West Point nomination and got it; how he worked through the Academy in 1853; served as lieutenant on the frontier, in Texas, California, and Oregon, until the outbreak of the Civil War, when he was promoted captain and ordered east, can be quickly told. His history until the fall of the Confederacy would need many long chapters. His military genius included all the requirements of a great captain, and his opportunties of exhibiting all his qualities in action came in rapid succession. In every service from quartermaster to army commander his talents shone. His tremendous vigor, incredible mental alertness, and genius for detail, added to his skill and outreach, continually set him forward. He stood 5 feet 5 inches high, but somehow looked taller, owing to his erect, splendid bearing. There was something in the full chest, the thick muscular neck, the heavy head, the dark blazing eyes, and the quick bodily movements that arrested attention. His name has come down to this generation mainly as a great cavalry leader, but he was a natural commander of all arms, a great tactician, a born strategist. His campaign of the Shenandoah Valley was a whirlwind of success. His great battles around Richmond were wonderful. General Grant's opinion of Sheridan, given thirteen years after the war, sums up the man. It is here quoted from J. R. Young's book, *Around the World with General Grant*. It runs, in part, as follows:

"As a soldier, as a commander of troops, as a man capable of doing all that is possible with any number of men, there is no man living greater than Sheridan. He belongs to the very first rank of soldiers, not only of our country but of the world. I rank Sheridan with Napoleon and Frederick and the great commanders in history. No man ever had such a faculty of finding things out as Sheridan, of knowing all about the enemy. He was always the best informed of his command as to the enemy. Then he had that magnetic quality of swaying men, which I wish I had, a rare quality in a general. I don't think anyone can give Sheridan too high praise."

Praise from U. S. Grant is praise indeed. A peculiar feature of the Civil War was the growth of the generals: Grant, Sherman, Sheridan, Thomas, Meade, all conspicuously experienced it. With Sheridan, however, one point is notable, namely, that he triumphed in every branch in each successive extension of the field of his duties, and he went from captain to major-general in three years of the regular army. His care for his men was constant. His troops were always the best fed, best clothed, best rested in the armies on either side, but on no troops was there more constant call for endeavor, and they were never found to fail him. In action he is described as severe, peremptory, dominating, but his determinations were mighty things, not to be interfered with. He wanted things done and done at once. His men of all grades soon conceded that he knew best what to do, and set about doing it accordingly. Out of action he was joyous of spirit, but, in fight or out of it, his alertness and his lightning-like decisions marked him apart from every other commander. His career in the Tennessee campaign was meteoric. Of his score and more of great conflicts, the most picturesque was his wonderful battle at Cedar Creek, to fight which he rode at breakneck speed "from Winchester twenty miles away" through the dust and debris of a broken army to the extreme front, rallying the scattered regiments and turning a defeat into a crushing victory, which recovered all that had been lost, taking 25 cannon and 1,200 prisoners, and driving for miles the lately victorious enemy under Early. Captain P. J. O'Keefe was one of the two who made the ride beside him. The battles of Waynesboro, Five Forks, and Sailor's Creek showed the same brilliant generalship on the part of Sheridan. His hold on the affection of the army and the admiration of the people continued to the day of his death, August 5, 1888, when he held the headship of the United States army as general in succession to the great Sherman.

General Sheridan, towards the end of the war, had a soldier's difference with Major-General George G. Meade, commander of the Army of the Potomac, but that did not blind "Little Phil" to the real merit of the victor in the tremendous three days' battle of Gettysburg, handling an army new to his hand against Robert E. Lee. The Meade family is of Irish descent. George Meade, the grandfather, came from Dublin and was a patriot in the American Revolutionary War. General Meade commanded a division at Antietam and a corps at Fredericksburg, and held command of the Army of the Potomac to the end of the war. He was a fine soldier and gentleman. Of quiet manners at most times, he was most irascible in the hour of battle, but his temper did not becloud his judgment. General James Shields and General Irwin McDowell, both fine Irish soldiers, have already been mentioned.

It would be hard to compass in a brief article even the names of the general officers of Irish blood in the Civil War. General John Logan, who fought with the western armies, is worthy of high and honorable mention, as is General Thomas Francis Meagher, a patriot in Ireland, a prisoner in Australia, a soldier of dash in the Civil War. Meagher's Irish Brigade left a record of valor unsurpassed: their charge at Fredericksburg up Marye's Heights alone should give them full meed of fame. General Michael Corcoran, a native of Ireland, commanded the wholly Irish 69th Regiment when it departed for the war in 1861, and after his exchange from a Confederate prison raised and organized the Corcoran Legion. Major-General McDowell McCook commanded brilliantly in the western campaigns. Who has not heard of the Fighting McCooks?—a family of splendid men and hardy warriors. Brigadier-General Thomas C. Devin was a superb cavalry commander, who led the first division of Sheridan's Shenandoah army through all its great operations. General James Mulligan of Illinois was of the true fighting breed. Colonel Timothy O'Meara led his superb Irish Legion from Illinois up Missionary Ridge. Brigadier-General C. C. Sullivan of western army fame was one of the five generals, headed by Rosecrans, who recommended Phil Sheridan for promotion to brigadier-general after the battle of Booneville as "worth his weight in gold." General Brannan was a gallant division commander in the Middle Tennessee campaign. Colonel William P. Carlin made a name at Stone River. General James T. Boyle, of the Army of the Ohio under Buell, was the brave man whose promotion to division commander left a vacancy for "Little Phil", that was to be an immediate stepping stone to higher opportunity. Brigadier-General McMillan, who commanded the second brigade at Cedar Creek; Colonel Thomas W. Cahill, 9th Connecticut; Lieutenant-Colonel Alfred Neafie of the 156th New York; Captain Charles McCarthy of the 175th New York; Lieutenant-Colonel Alex. J. Kenny of the 8th Indiana; Lieutenant Terrence Reilly of the Horse Artillery, all won distinction in the Shenandoah Valley. Such splendid fighters as General James R. O'Beirne, Colonel Guiney, Colonel Cavanagh, Colonel John P. Byron, Colonel Patrick Gleason, General Denis F. Burke, wrote their names red over a score of battle fields, but one cannot hope to cover more than a fraction of the brilliant men of Irish blood who led and bled in the long, hard, and strenuous struggle. The 69th New York Regiment was the mother of a dozen Irish regiments, including the Irish Brigade of Meagher and the Corcoran Legion. The 9th, 28th, and 29th regiments of Massachusetts were all Irish. A gallant Irishman, born at Fermoy, was Brigadier-General Thomas Smyth, who made a name and died in the battles around Richmond. There was not a regiment from the middle western and western States that did not hold its quota of Irishmen and sons of the

Irish. After the names of Porter and Farragut in the Navy stands next highest in honor that of Vice-Admiral Stephen C. Rowan, born in Dublin, of the famous family that produced Hamilton Rowan, one of the foremost of the United Irishmen. It was the son of the vice-admiral, a lieutenant in the army, who carried "the message to Garcia" from the United States War Department to the Cuban commander in the eastern jungle of Cuba, before the outbreak of the war with Spain, and did it so well and bravely through such difficulties and dangers that his name will stand for "the faithful messenger" forever.

As a consequence of their stand with the American people in the Civil War, the position of the whole mass of the Irish and Irish-American people was vastly uplifted in American eyes. The unlettered poverty of scores of thousands of Irish immigrants, who came in multitudes from 1846 on, had made an unfavorable and false impression; their red blood on the battle field washed it out.

On the southern side as well, Irish valor shone. While the great flood of the mid-century Irish immigration had spread itself mainly north, east, and west, the larger cities of the South also received a share. The slave system precluded the entry of free labor into the cotton, corn, lumber, and sugar lands of the South, but such cities as New Orleans, Mobile, Charleston, Savannah, Vicksburg, and Richmond gave varied employment to many of the Irish who made their homes in the Southland, and so they came to furnish thousands of recruits to the local Confederate levies. The "Louisiana Tigers", who fought so valiantly at Gettysburg on the Southern side, included many Irish. The Georgia brigade, that held the Confederate line atop of Marye's Heights at Fredericksburg, up which the Irish brigade so heroically charged, had whole companies of Irish. There were scores of Irish in many of the regiments that made Pickett's memorable charge at Gettysburg. All through the Confederate armies were valiant descendants of the earlier Irish immigration that settled the uplands of the Carolinas and Virginia and the blue grass region of Kentucky. Most famous, most glorious of these was "Stonewall" Jackson—Lieutenant-General Thomas Jonathan

Jackson—next to Robert E. Lee the greatest soldier on the southern side. No more splendid soldier-figure rises out of the contest. Educated at West Point, serving in Mexico, then a professor of philosophy—and artillery—next a volunteer with his State when Virginia took arms against the Union, his long and brilliant service included a large share in the victories at Bull Run, Gaines Mill, Malvern Hill, Cedar Mountain, Harper's Ferry, Antietam, Fredericksburg, and Chancellorsville, where he was accidentally wounded by his own men. He was once defeated by General Shields, as has been noted. The piety and purity of his life belie the supposed necessity for the coarser traits that are thought to go with the terrible trade. General Patrick R. Cleburne was born in 1828, near Cork, Ireland. He was in the English army three years, and, coming to the United States, became a lawyer at Helena, Ark. He enlisted in the Confederate army as a private, rose rapidly to the command of a brigade, and made a great name at Shiloh. As major-general he led divisions at Murfreesboro and Chickamauga, and was thanked by the Confederate Congress. He fell at the battle of Franklin—a soldier of commanding presence, skill, and daring, beloved by the whole Army of the West. The gallant colonel Thomas Claiborne was a striking cavalryman. It was Lieutenant Thomas A. Claiborne of the 1st South Carolina who, with Corporal B. Brannan, lashed the broken flagstaff on Fort Sumter in June, 1864, when, under a withering fire, the flag of the Confederacy had been shot away. The fighting of Major-General Gary of South Carolina around Richmond was desperate. He was the last to leave the city when it fell, as told by Captain Sullivan: "He galloped at night through the burning city, and at the bridge over the James cried out, 'We are the rear guard. It is all over; blow the bridge to h—l!' and went on into the night."

The story of the Civil War is a mine of honor to the Irish, and Irishmen should set it forth at length. Here it can be merely glanced at.

The war of 1898 with Spain—that great patriotic efflorescence—was brief in its campaigning. Immediately provoked by the blowing up of the U. S. S. *Maine* in Havana harbor on

February 15, war was declared on April 19. Admiral Dewey sank the Spanish fleet in Manila Harbor, May 1. The first troops landed on Cuban soil June 1. The first—and last—real land battle before Santiago occurred on July 1-2, with 13,500 troops on the American side against an available Spanish force somewhat less in number, but holding strongly fortified and entrenched positions around the town. The advance and charges uphill necessary to capture El Caney and the steep heights of San Juan called for desperate courage. It was there, however, and the Irish in the army exhibited dash and persistence, as duty demanded. In the second day's fighting the Spanish assaults on the American positions were repelled, and the land fighting was over. The Americans in the two days lost over 10 per cent killed and wounded. The destruction of Cervera's fleet on its attempt to escape from Santiago on July 3 ended the struggle. With the regiment of Rough Riders, under Theodore Roosevelt—who says he reckons "an O'Brien, a Redmond, and a man from Ulster" among his forbears—were many gallant Irishmen—Kellys, Murphys, Burkes, and Doyles, for instance. His favorite captain, "Bucky" O'Neill of Arizona, fell at the foot of San Juan. The white regiments of the regular army had their quota of Irish, as had most of the volunteers. The 9th Massachusetts was all Irish. The 69th New York, all Irish, never reached the front in the war, but shared the fate of the 150,000 troops cantoned through the Southern States, their only effective enemies being dysentery, typhoid, and malaria.

A little splash of Irish blood came with the Fenian dash into Canada on June 1, 1866. There had been active preparations for a real invasion by some 50,000 Irish-born or Irish-fathered soldiers who had served in the Civil War. The American government, using its army force, intervened to prevent the bellicose movement, not, however, before Colonel John O'Neill, who had served in the cavalry with Sherman on his march to the sea, with Captain Starr, one of Kilpatrick's cavalry, Captain O'Brien, and about 700 well-armed men, all Civil War veterans, had slipped across the Niagara River at Fort Erie. They made short work of all in sight, threw out a couple of hundred men who burned a bridge and tore up the railroad tracks.

Their scouts fired on a small British detachment, which ran. On the morning of June 2 news came of a larger Canadian force advancing, and O'Neill went out to meet them. Deploying his men in a field near the high road at a place called Ridgway, he sent his pickets forward. They found heavy ground in front and about three-quarters of a mile away some 1,400 men of the "Queen's Own" of Toronto and the Hamilton Volunteers advancing rapidly in line. O'Neill, after a few rounds, withdrew his pickets, and the Canadians, taking the movement for flight, came briskly on. As soon as they were clear of cover, O'Neill, firing a volley, gave orders for a charge. At it they went with a cheer, and the whole Canadian line gave way. They ran as fast as their legs could carry them, leaving some fifty killed and wounded. After chasing them for two miles, O'Neill halted his men and brought them back to Fort Erie, where they intrenched. The Canadians did not stop until they reached Colburne, eighteen miles away. The Fenian loss was twenty-five. In the night O'Neill learned that no help was coming from the United States' side, while news reached him that a force of 5,000 Canadian and British regulars was advancing on Fort Erie. Accordingly, at 2 a. m. on June 3, he surrendered to the United States forces with 400 of his men, who were detained for a few days on the U. S. S. *Michigan* and then let go. The balance of his force, about 250 men, escaped in groups across the river. There was another little victorious skirmish with the Canadians lower down under Captain Spear, who also slipped back over the border unpursued. What fighting took place was workmanlike and creditable.

There was a flicker of Irish fighting spirit in the Boer War. Many thousands, no doubt, were in the English army of 250,000 men brought against the 30,000 Boers, but there was a small "Irish Brigade" that fought on the Boer side, and was notably engaged at Spion Kop, where the English were driven so sweepingly from their position by desperate charges.

In the War of 1870, between France and Prussia, the good wishes of the Irish went with France, for the sake of the old friendship, largely helped, no doubt, by the fact that at the summit of army command was Marshal MacMahon, a descendant of a warrior of the old Irish Brigade. His service in Algiers; his skill and daring in the Crimean War before Sebastopol, where he led the division which stormed the Malakoff; his victories in the Italian War of 1859 against Austria, including the great battle of Magenta, all made him a striking, romantic figure. He failed in 1870 against the Prussians at Worth, and was made prisoner with his army at Sedan, but he suppressed the Commune after the war and was President of France from 1873 to 1879. The device by which 300 Irishmen took part on the French side in the war with Germany has a grim humor. They went as aides in an ambulance corps fitted out in Dublin by subscription, but, once on French soil, enlisted in the army. "Maybe we can kill as well as we can cure," said one of them. The *Compagnie irlandaise,* as it was called, did creditable work, and was in the last combat with the Prussians at Montbellard. Their captain, M. W. Kirwan, was offered a Cross of the Legion of Honor, but for some reason declined it. Dr. Constantine J. McGuire, who won the decoration for bravery before Paris during the siege of the Commune, did, however, accept it, receiving the cross from the hands of Marshal MacMahon, and, hale and hearty, wears the red ribbon on occasion in New York today.

Even as this chronicle of daring deeds and daring doers is being penned, in the ranks and as commanding officers on the side of the allies in the far-flung battle lines of the great European war, are men of Irish birth, and, let it not be forgotten, not a few of the opposing side are the descendants of the Irish military geniuses who, in days gone by, fought so gallantly across the continent "from Dunkirk to Belgrade". They are all, every man of them, bearing bravely, as of yore, their own part amid the dangers and chances of the fray.

If the inspiring story is of necessity here barely sketched in outline, it nevertheless clearly indicates that, as it has been for two thousand years of Irish history, so it will be to the end of the human chapter—the Irish race is the Fighting Race, and willing, even eager, to risk life itself for vital issues.

REFERENCES:

Keating's, MacGeoghegan's, Mitchel's Histories of Ireland; J. C. O'Callaghan: The Irish Brigades in the Service of France, The Green Book; Lossing: Field Book of the Revolution, Field Book of the War of 1812; Several Mexican War Histories; Battles and Leaders of the Civil War; The Irish at Home and Abroad (New York, 1856); Canon O'Hanlon: Irish-American History of the United States; O'Hart; Irish Pedigrees; Martin I. Griffin: Life of Commodore Barry; John D. Crimmins: Irish Miscellany; Joseph Denieffe: Fenian Recollections; Plowden: Historical Review of the State of Ireland (London, 1803); Hays: History of the Irish (1798) Rebellion; Macaulay: History of England; J. R. Young: Around the World with General Grant; several valuable articles and records of research by Michael J. O'Brien of New York.

THE SORROWS OF IRELAND

By John Jerome Rooney, A. M., LL.D.

"THE Sorrows of Ireland"! What a vision of woe the words conjure up. The late Goldwin Smith, himself an Englishman and a Unionist, in his *Irish History and the Irish Question,* finds that "of all histories, the history of Ireland is the saddest. For nearly seven centuries it was a course of strife between races, bloodshed, massacre, misgovernment, civil war, oppression, and misery."

The first of the great scourges of Erin was the coming of the Danes, the bloodthirsty and conquest-loving Vikings of the North, the worshipers of Thor and Odin, the gods of thunder and of strife. These warriors, in never-ending invasions, had for four hundred years overrun Britain and finally conquered the northern provinces of Gaul. Until the end of the eighth century Ireland had been free from the Scandinavian scourge. About this time the invaders made lodgments along the coasts, passed inward through the island, burned and looted religious houses and schools of learning, levied tribute upon the inhabitants, and at length established themselves firmly at Limerick, Waterford, Dublin, Wexford, and Carlingford. Fortified towns were built, trading communications with Britain and the continent were set up, and the Northman, though not in actual possession of the interior of the island, was apparently in substantial control of its destinies. Brian Borumha, or Boru, brother of the king of Munster, of the Dalcassian race of O'Brien, refused to submit, roused his brother, fought the Danes of Limerick at Sulchoid (A. D. 968), and captured Limerick. Brian later succeeded his brother, became sovereign of all Ireland (A. D. 1001), and, on Good Friday, A. D. 1014, joined battle with the Danes upon the famous field of Clontarf. Here the power of the Northmen was forever broken, Brian falling at the moment of victory, while in his tent, by the hand of a fugitive Dane.

With the death of Brian the united government dissolved. The provincial kings, or princes, resumed separate authority and a struggle arose among them, with varying success, for the national sovereignty. The central government never had been strong, as the nation was organized on a tribal or family basis. In this weakened condition Dermot MacMurrough, king of Leinster, abducted the wife of O'Rourke, prince of Breffni, while the latter was on a pilgrimage. MacMurrough was compelled to fly to England. He sought the protection of the Angevin English king, Henry Plantagenet. As a result of this appeal, a small expedition, headed by Strongbow (A. D. 1169), was sent to Ireland, and Waterford, Wexford, and Dublin were taken. Then came Henry himself, in 1171, with a fleet of 240 ships, 400 knights, and 4,000 men, landing at Waterford. This expedition was the beginning of the English attempted conquest of Ireland—a proceeding that, through all the ruin and bloodshed of 800 years, is not yet accomplished. Henry's first act was to introduce the feudal system into that southern half of the island which he controlled; he seized great tracts of land, which he in turn granted to his followers under feudal customs; he introduced the offices of the English feudal system and the English laws, and placed his followers in all the positions of power, holding their lands and authority under the feudal conditions of rendering him homage and military service.

This was the root of the alien "landlordism" and foreign political control of future times which became the chief curses of Ireland, the prolific source of innumerable woes. The succeeding years till the reign of Henry VIII. witnessed the extension, and at times the decline, of the Anglo-Norman rule. When Henry VII. became king of England the Anglo-Norman colony or "Pale" had shrunk to two counties and a half around Dublin, defended by a ditch. Many of the original Norman knights had become "more Irish than the Irish themselves." Such was the great family of the Geraldines or Fitzgerald—the most powerful, with the O'Neills of the North, in Ireland. A united attack at this time would most certainly have driven out the invader; for it must be remembered that Dublin, the "Pale"—"the Castle government" of later times— was the citadel of the English foreign power, and before a united nation would most certainly have succumbed.

When Henry VIII. ascended the throne of England, the policy of peace in Ireland was continued during the early portion of his reign. Then came Henry's break with the Pope over the royal divorce. The Irish beyond the Pale, and many within it, were loyal to the Church of their fathers, to the faith of Patrick, the faith of the Roman See. To Henry and his daughter Elizabeth, the daughter of Anne Boleyn, who displaced Henry's lawful wife, this was treason. Henceforth, to the bitterness of race hatred and the pride of the conqueror were to be added the blackest of religious feuds, the most cruel of religious persecutions in the history of the world. Again let Goldwin Smith, the English Unionist, describe the result: "Of all the wars waged by a civilized on a barbarous (sic) and despised race these wars waged by the English on the Irish seem to have been the most hideous. No quarter was given by the invader to man, woman, or child. The butchering of women and children is repeatedly and brutally avowed. Nothing can be more horrible than the cool satisfaction with which English commanders report their massacres." Famine was deliberately added to the other horrors. What was called law was more cruel than war: it was death without the opportunity for defense and with the hypocrisy of the forms of justice added.

Out of this situation came the infamous Penal Code, which, by the period of William the Third, about 1692, became a finished system. This is the "Irish Code" of which Lord Brougham said: "It was so ingeniously contrived that an Irish Catholic could not lift his hand without breaking it." And Edmund Burke said: "The wit of man never devised a machine to disgrace a realm or destroy a kingdom so perfect as this." Montesquieu, the great French jurist-philosopher, the author of the epoch-making *Spirit of the Laws,* commented: "It must have been contrived by devils; it ought to have been written in blood; and the only place to register it is in hell." Yet for two hundred years this code of death, national and individual, was the supreme law of Ireland.

Wendell Phillips, the great American orator, in his lecture on "Daniel O'Connell," summed up this Penal Code in words that will not soon be forgotten by the world. His reference to Mr. Froude is to James Anthony Froude, the English historian. He says:

"You know that, under it, an Irish Catholic could not sit in

(11)

the House of Commons; he could not hold any commission from the Crown, either civil or military; he could be a common soldier—nothing more. He could neither vote, nor sit on a jury, nor stand on a witness stand, nor bring a suit, nor be a doctor, nor be a lawyer, nor travel five miles from his own home without a permit from a justice of the peace. The nearest approach that ever was made to him was a South Carolina negro before the war. He had no rights that a Protestant needed to respect. If he was a land-holder, if all his children were Catholics, he was obliged to divide the land equally between them. This was the English plan for eliminating the Catholic tenure of the land and letting it slip out of their hands. Then, if any of the children, during their father's life, concluded to become Protestants, in such case they took the whole estate; or, indeed, they might compel the father to put his estate in trust for their benefit. So, if the Catholic wife would not go to an Episcopalian church once a month—which she deemed it a sin to do—she forfeited her dower. But if she went regularly, she could have all the estate. If a Catholic had a lease, and it rose one-quarter in value, any Protestant could take it from him by bringing that fact to the notice of a justice of the peace. Three justices of the peace might summon any Catholic before them, and oblige him to give up his faith, or quit the realm. Four justices could oblige him to abjure his faith or sell his estates. If a Protestant paid one dollar tax, the Catholic paid two. If a Protestant lost a ship, when at war with a' Catholic power—and at the time there was only *one* Protestant power in Europe, besides Great Britain; that was Holland: so that the chances were nine to one that, in case of war, Great Britain would be at war with a Catholic power—in such a case, if a Protestant lost a ship, he went home and assessed the value on his Catholic neighbors, and was reimbursed. So, of education. We fret a great deal on account of a class of Irishmen who come to our shores and are lacking in education, in culture, and refinement. But you must remember the bad laws, you must remember the malignant legislation, that sentenced them to a life of ignorance, and made education a felony in Catholic Ireland. If an Irishman sent his child to a Protestant schoolmaster, all right; but if the parent would not do so, and sent him to a Catholic school, the father was fined ten pounds a week; and the schoolmaster was fined five pounds a week; and for the third offense he was hung! But, if the father determined that his child should be educated, and sent him across the Channel to France, the boy forfeited his citizenship and became an alien; and, if discovered, the father was fined one hundred pounds; and anybody, except the father, who harbored him, forfeited all civil rights—that is, he could not sue in a court of law, nor could he vote. Indeed, a Catholic could not marry! If he married a Protestant, the marriage was void; the children were illegitimate. And, if one Catholic married another, it required the presence of a priest, and if a priest landed in Ireland for twenty minutes, it was death! To this ferocious 'Code', Sir Robert Peel, in our own day, added the climax, that no Catholic should quit his dwelling between the hours of sunset and sunrise, an exaggeration of the 'Curfew Law' of William the Conqueror. Now, you will hardly believe that this was enacted as a law. But Mr. Froude alludes to this code. Yes; he was very honest; he would paint England as black as she deserved. He said of Queen Elizabeth that she failed in her duty as a magistrate; she failed towards Ireland in her capability of being a great ruler. And then he proceeded, after passing sentence, to give us the history of her reign, and showed that, in very many cases, she could not have done any different. For instance—oh! it is the saddest, blackest, most horrible statement of all history; it makes you doubt the very possibility of human nature—when you read that Spenser, the poet, who had the most ardent, most perfect ideas in English poetry—Spenser sat at the council board that ordered the wholesale butchery of a Spanish regiment captured in Ireland, and, to execute the order, he chose Sir Walter Raleigh, the scholar, the gentleman, the poet, the author, and the most splendid Englishman of his age! And Norris, a captain under Sidney, in whose veins flowed the blood of Sir Philip, writing home to Elizabeth, begs and persuades her to believe in O'Neill's crimes, and asks for leave to send a hired man to poison him! And the Virgin Queen makes no objection! Mr. Froude quotes a letter from Captain Norris, in which he states that he found himself in an island where five hundred Irish

(all women and children; not a man among them) had taken
refuge from the war; and he deliberately butchered every
living soul! And Queen Elizabeth, in a letter still extant,
answers by saying: 'Tell my good servant that I will not
forget his good services.' He tells us that 'The English nobility and gentry would take a gun as unhesitatingly as a fowler,
and go out to shoot an Irishman as an Indian would a buf-
falo.' Then he tells us, with amazement, that you never could
make an Irishman respect an Englishman! He points to some
unhappy Kildare, the sole relic of a noble house, whose four
uncles were slaughtered in cold blood—that is the only word
for this kind of execution, *slaughtered*—and he, left alone, a
boy, grows up characterless and kills an archbishop. Every im-
petuous, impatient act is dragged before the prejudiced mind.
But when Mr. Froude is painting Sir Walter and Spenser,
blind no longer, he says: 'I regret—it is very sad to think—
that such things should ever have been!'"

Such was the cup from which Ireland drank even into the
days of men now living. Nor was this all. The rise of English manufactures brought a new chapter of woes to Ireland.
The Irish cattle trade had been killed by an Act of Charles II.
for the benefit of English farmers. The Irish then took up
the raising of wool and woolen manufactures. A flourishing
trade grew up. An English law destroyed it. In succession
the same greed killed the cotton, the glovemaking, the glass-
making, and the brewing trades. These were reserved for the
English maker and merchant. These crimes upon Irish industry surpassed a thousand-fold the later English attempts upon
the industries of the American colonies.

Under the Code, and through the extreme poverty produced thereby, substantially all the land of Ireland passed out
of the hands of the people. They became mere serfs upon the
soil. Their tribute was paid through a rapacious agent to a
foreign landlord. The improvement of the land by the labor
of the tenant brought increase of rent. There was no fixity
of tenure of the land. It was held at the will of the agent,
reflecting the rapacity of the non-resident landlord. Upon
these holdings the principal crop was the potato. A failure
of this crop was a failure to pay rent, eviction on the roadside,

and starvation. The results, after the enactment of the Penal Code, and during the greater part of the eighteenth century, are thus described by Goldwin Smith: "On such a scene of misery as the abodes of the Irish cotters the sun has rarely looked down. Their homes were the most miserable hovels, chimneyless, filthy. Of decent clothing they were destitute. Their food was the potato; sometimes they bled their cattle and mixed the blood with sorrel. The old and sick were everywhere dying by cold and hunger, and rotting amidst filth and vermin. When the potato failed, as it often did, came famine, with disease in its train. Want and misery were in every face, the roads were spread with dead and dying, there was sometimes none to bear the dead to the grave, and they were buried in the fields and ditches where they perished. Fluxes and malignant fevers followed, laying these villages waste. 'I have seen,' says a contemporaneous witness, 'the laborer endeavoring to work at his spade, but fainting for want of food and forced to quit it. I have seen the helpless orphan exposed on the dunghill, and none to take him in for fear of infection. And I have seen the hungry infant sucking at the breast of the already expired parent.' "

All these are not only the horrors of a hundred or two hundred years ago; they were repeated in ten thousand forms in the awful famine days of 1847. In 1841 the population of Ireland was 8,796,545 persons. In 1851, after four years of famine, the population was 6,551,970, leaving 2,244,575 persons to be accounted for, and taking no account of the natural increase of the population during the ten years. Not less than a million and a half of these died of starvation and the fevers brought on by famine. The remainder emigrated to foreign lands.

In this account of the Sorrows of Ireland nothing has been said of the vast emigrations, thousands upon thousands of persons in the seventeenth and eighteenth centuries leaving Ireland under forced deportations, in a practical selling into slavery. The sum total of this loss to Ireland cannot be less than 5,000,000 souls. The earlier deportations were carried out under the most atrocious circumstances. Families were broken up and scattered to distant and separate colonies, such as Barbados, the New England States, and later to the South Pacific.

This is but a glance at some of the wrongs to Ireland's religious, intellectual, and material welfare, wrongs that have plunged her into an age-long poverty. But one of the greatest of all her sorrows has been the denial of her national life, the attempt to strangle her rightful aspirations as a free people. Her autonomy was taken from her; her smallest legislative act was the act of a stranger; in fine, every mark of political slavery was put upon her. A foreign soldiery was, and still is, quartered upon her soil. The control of her revenues, of the system of taxation, was wrested from her. These became the function of a hateful resident oligarchy, alien in everything to the Irish people, and of the English parliament, to which she was not admitted until the days of Daniel O'Connell. And then she was admitted only through fear of revolution.

The dawn has come. The dark night is almost past; the heroic struggle of Ireland is about to close in triumph. Her loyalty to her ideals of freedom and religion is to meet its reward. The epitaph of Robert Emmet will soon be written, for at last Ireland is certain of "taking her place among the nations of the earth."

REFERENCES:

D'Alton: History of Ireland; J. P. Prendergast: Cromwellian Settlement; Barrington: Rise and Fall of the Irish Nation; McNevin: Confiscation of Ulster; R. R. Madden: History of the Penal Laws; Murphy: Cromwell in Ireland; T. A. Emmet: Ireland under English Rule, 2 vols.; Mrs. J. R. Green: Irish Nationality; Walpole: A Short History of the Kingdom of Ireland; A. M. Sullivan: Story of Ireland; Thomas Moore: History of Ireland; Edmund Spenser: View of the State of Ireland; C. Gavan Duffy: Four Years of Irish History, 1845-49; Isaac Butt: Land Tenure in Ireland; Justin McCarthy: History of our own Times; Johnston and Spencer: Ireland's Story; MacGeoghegan's History of Ireland and its continuation by John Mitchel; William Sampson: Memoirs of an Irish Exile, 1832; John Curry: A Historical and Critical Review of the Civil Wars in Ireland (1775); John Boyle: The Battlefields of Ireland (1879); Speeches of Edmund Burke, Daniel O'Connell, Henry Grattan; Wendell Phillips's Speech on Daniel O'Connell; Father Tom Burke: Lectures on Ireland.

Mitchel, as open advocate of physical force, became father to Fenianism. An honest conspirator and brilliant writer, he proved that the pen of journalism was sharper than the Irish pike. Carlyle described him as "a fine elastic-spirited young fellow, whom I grieved to see rushing on destruction palpable, by attack of windmills." Destruction came surely, but coupled with immortality. He was transported as a felon before the insurrection, while his writings sprang up in angry but unarmed men.

Mitchel and O'Connell both sought the liberation of Ireland, but their viewpoint differed. Mitchel thought only of Liberty; O'Connell not unnaturally considered the "Liberator." His refusal to allow a drop of blood to be shed caused Young Ireland to secede. Only when death removed his influence could the pent-up feelings of the country break out under Smith O'Brien. If Mitchel was an Irish Robespierre, O'Brien was their Lafayette. His advance from the level of dead aristocracy had been rapid. From defending Whigs in Parliament he passed to opposition and "contempt of the House." He resigned from the Bench from which O'Connell had been dismissed, became a Repealer, adding the words "no compromise," and finally gloried in his treason before the House. His next step brought a price upon his head.

Grave and frigid, but inwardly warmhearted and passionate, O'Brien had little aptitude for rebellion. But the death penalty (commuted to transportation) which he incurred went far to redeem his forlorn failure. Mitchel, who shared his Australian imprisonment, left a fine picture of "this noblest of Irishmen, thrust in among the off-scourings of England's gaols, with his home desolated and his hopes ruined, and defeated life falling into the sere and yellow leaf. A man, who cannot be crushed, or bowed, or broken; anchored immovably upon his own brave heart within; his clear eye and soul open as ever to all the melodies and splendors of heaven and earth, and calmly waiting for the angel, Death."

The Irish cause was not revived until the Fenian movement. Disgust with the politicians drove the noblest into their ranks. In Stephens they found an organizing chief, in Boyle

O'Reilly a poet, and in John O'Leary a political thinker, men who under other conditions had achieved mundane success. The Fenians were defended by Isaac Butt, a big-hearted, broad-minded lawyer, who afterwards organized a party to convince Englishmen that Repeal was innocuous, when called "Home Rule." The people stood his patient ways patiently, but when a more desperate leader arrived they transferred allegiance, and Butt died of a broken heart.

Parnell took his place and began to marshal the broken forces of Irish democracy against his own class. Butt had been a polite parliamentarian, reverencing the courtesy of debate and at heart loving the British Constitution. Parnell felt that his mission lay in breaking rather than interpreting the law. The well-bred House stared and protested when he defied their chosen six hundred. Parnell faced them with their own marble callousness. He outdid them in political cynicism and out-bowed them in frigid courtesy, while maintaining a policy before which tradition melted and a time-honored system collapsed. In one stormy decade he tore the cloak from the Mother of Parliaments, reducing her to a plain-speaking democratic machine. Through the breach he made, the English labor party has since entered.

He united priest and peasant, physical and moral force, under him. He could lay Ireland under storm or lull at his pleasure. His achievement equalled his self-confidence. He reversed the Irish land system and threw English politics out of gear. With the balance of power in his hand, he made Tory and Radical outbid each other for his support. He was no organizer or orator, but he fascinated able men to conduct his schemes, as Napoleon used his marshals. On a pregnant day he equaled the achievement of St. Paul and converted Gladstone, who had once been his gaoler. Gladstone became a Home Ruler, and henceforth English politics knew no peace.

Parnell stood for the fall and rise of many. Under his banner Irish peasants became human beings with human rights. He felled the feudal class in Ireland and undermined them in England. Incalculable forces were set to destroy him. A forged letter in the *Times* classed him with assassins, while an illegal Commission was sent to try his whole movement. It is history that his triumphant vindication was followed by a greater fall. The happiness of Ireland was sucked into the maelstrom of his ruin. He refused to retire from leadership at Gladstone's bidding, and Ireland staggered into civil war. The end is known—Parnell died as he had lived. Of his moral fault there is no palliation, but it may be said he held his country's honor dearer than his own, for he could not bear to see her win even independence by obeying the word of an Englishman.

REFERENCES:

Lecky: Leaders of Irish Opinion; Mitchel: Jail Journal; Duffy: Young Ireland; O'Brien: Life of Parnell; D'Alton: History of Ireland.

IRISH HEROINES

By Alice Milligan.

THE worth and glory of a nation may well be measured and adjudged by the typical character of its womanhood: not so much, I would say, by the eminence attained to by rarely gifted, exceptionally developed individuals, as by the prevalence of noble types at every period, and amongst all classes of the community, and by their recurrence from age to age under varying circumstances of national fortune.

Judged by such a standard, Ireland emerges triumphant and points to the roll of her chequered history, the story of her ancient race, with confidence and pride. Gaze into the farthest vistas of her legendary past, into the remotest eras of which tradition preserves a misty memory, and the figure of some fair, noble woman stands forth glimmering like a white statue against the gloom. At every period of stern endeavor, through all the generations of recorded time, the pages of our annals are inscribed with the names of mothers, sisters, wives, not unworthy to stand there beside those of the world-renowned heroes of the Gael.

In the ancient tales of Ireland we read of great female physicians and distinguished female lawyers and judges. There were *ban-file*, or women-poets, who, like the *file*, were at the same time soothsayers and poetesses, and there are other evidences of the high esteem in which women were held. There can be no doubt, to judge by the elaborate descriptions of garments in the saga-texts, that the women were very skilful in weaving and needlework. The Irish peasant girls of today inherit from them not a little of their gift for lacemaking and linen-embroidery. Ladies of the highest rank practiced needlework as an accomplishment and a recreation. Some of the scissors and shears they used have come to light in excavations.

In the stories of the loves of the ancient Irish, whether immortals or mortals, the woman's rôle is the more accentuated, while in Teutonic tradition man plays the chief part. Again, it has often been remarked that the feminine interest meekly disbanded, and the United Irishmen took their place. The brilliancy of Grattan's parliament never fulfilled national aspirations. Bristol was succeeded by another recruit from the aristocracy—Lord Edward Fitzgerald. With Wolfe Tone and Robert Emmet he has become legendary. All three attained popular canonization, for all three sealed their brief leadership with death.

Lord Edward was a dreamer, an Irish Bayard, too chivalrous to conspire successfully and too frankly courageous to match a government of guile. Tone was far more dangerous. He realized that foreign invasion was necessary to successful rebellion, and he allowed no scruple or obstacle in his path. He washed his hands of law and politics entirely. To divert Napoleon to Ireland was his object and the total separation of Ireland his ambition. The United Irishmen favored the invasion, which the Volunteers had been formed to repel. The feud between moral and physical force broke out. The failure of the sterner policy in 1798 did not daunt Emmet from his ill-starred attempt in 1803. He combined Lord Edward's chivalry with some abilities worthy of Tone, but he failed. The failure he redeemed by a swan-song from the dock and a demeanor on the scaffold which have become part of Irish tradition.

After the Union, Irish leaders sprang up in the English House, which Pitt had unwittingly made the cockpit of the racial struggle. Far from absorbing the Irish element, the Commons found themselves forced to resist, rally, and finally succumb.

The Irish House cannot be dismissed without mention of Curran. He was a brilliant enemy of corruption and servility. O'Connell said "there was never so honest an Irishman," which may account for his greater success as a lawyer than a politician. To be an Irish leader and a successful lawyer is given to no man. For the former the sacrifice of a great career is needed. This sacrifice Daniel O'Connell was prepared to make. His place in history will never be estimated, for few have been so loved or hated, or for stronger reasons. Never did a tribune rising to power lift his people to such sudden hope and success. Never did a champion leave his followers was fluent in epigram and most inspiring when condensed, and he had an immense moral advantage. The parliament which made him a grant was independent, but it was from one of subservience that Flood drew his salary. Henceforth Grattan was haunted by the jealous and discredited herald of himself. A great genius, Flood lacked the keen judgment and careless magnanimity without which leadership in Ireland brings misunderstanding and disaster. In the English House he achieved total failure. Grattan followed him after the Union, but retained the attention if not the power of Dublin days. Neither influenced English affairs, and their eloquence curiously was considered cold and sententious. Their rhapsody appeared artificial, and their exposition labored. The failure of these men was no stigma. What is called "Irish oratory" arose with the inclusion of the Celtic under strata in politics.

Burke's speeches were delivered to an empty house. Though he lived out of Ireland and never became an Irish leader in Ireland, Burke had an influence in England greater than that of any Irishman before or since. The beauty and diction of his speech fostered future parliamentary speaking. Macaulay, Gladstone, Peel, and Brougham were suckled on him. His farthest reaching achievement was his treatment of the French Revolution. His single voice rolled back that storm in Europe. But no words could retard revolution in Ireland herself. Venal government made the noblest conservative thinking seem treason to the highest interests of the country. The temporary success of Grattan's parliament had been largely won by the Volunteers. They had been drilled, ostensibly against foreign invasion, but virtually to secure reforms at home. Their power became one with which England had to reckon, and which she never forgave. Lord Charlemont, their president, was an estimable country gentleman, but not a national leader. A more dashing figure appeared in the singular Earl of Bristol. Though an Irish bishop and an English peer, he set himself in the front rank of the movement, assuming with general consent the demeanor and trappings of royalty. He would not have hesitated to plunge Ireland into war, had he obtained Charlemont's position. But it was not so fated.

After forcing parliamentary independence the Volunteers

is absent from the earlier heroic forms of some literatures. Not so, however, in the earliest saga-texts of the Irish. Many are the famous women to whom the old tales introduce us and who stand out and compel attention like the characters of the Greek drama. Everyone knows of the faithful Deirdre, the heroine of the touching story of the "Exile of the Sons of Usnech", and of her death; of the proud and selfish Medb, the ambitious queen of Connacht, the most warlike and most expert in the use of weapons of the women of the Gael—far superior in combat and counsel to her husband, Ailill; of Emer, the faithful wife of Cuchulainn; of Etain of the Horses (that was her name in Fairyland); and of many others too numerous to mention.

It is with the introduction of Christianity into Ireland that the Irish woman came into her rightful place, and attained the preponderating influence which she, ever since, has held among the Celtic people. In the period which followed the evangelization of the island many were the "women of worth" who upheld the honor and glory of "Inisfail the Fair", and women were neither the less numerous nor the less ardent who hung upon the lips of the Apostle of Ireland.

Amid the galaxy of the saints, how lustrous, how divinely fair, shines the star of Brigid, the shepherd maiden of Faughard, the disciple of Patrick the Apostle, the guardian of the holy light that burned beneath the oak-trees of Kildare! Over all Ireland and through the Hebridean Isles, she is renowned above any other. We think of her, moreover, not alone, but as the centre of a great company of cloistered maidens, the refuge and helper of the sinful and sorrowful, who found in the gospel that Patrick preached a message of consolation and deliverance. Let it be remembered that the shroud of Patrick is deemed to have been woven by Brigid's hand; that when she died, in 525, Columcille, the future apostle of Scotland, was a child of four. So she stands midmost of that trilogy of saints whose dust is said to rest in Down.

Who that hears of Columcille will forget how he won that name, "dove of the Church", because of his early piety, and that surely bespeaks a mother's guiding care. Ethne, mother of Columcille, remains a vague but picturesque figure, seen against the background of the rugged heath-clad hills of Tir-Conal by the bright blue waters of Gartan's triple lake. Her hearth-stone or couch is shown there to this day, where once in slumber, before the birth of her son, she saw in a glorious visionary dream a symbol of his future greatness. A vast veil woven of sunshine and flowers seemed to float down upon her from heaven: an exquisitely poetic thought, which gives us warrant to believe that Columcille's poetic skill was inherited from his mother.

Ronnat, the mother of his biographer, St. Adamnan, plays a more notable part in history, for, according to an ancient Gaelic text recently published, it was to her that the women of Ireland owed the royal decree which liberated them from military service. The story goes that once, as she walked beside the Boyne, after some sanguinary conflict, she came upon the bodies of two women who had fallen in battle. One grasped a reaping hook, the other a sword, and dreadful wounds disfigured them. Horrified at the sight, she brought strong pressure to bear upon her son, and his influence in the councils of the land availed to bring about the promulgation of the decree which freed women from war-service.

Our warrior kings had noble queens to rule their households, and of these none stands out so distinctly after long lapse of time as Gormlai, the daughter of Flann Siona, and wife of Nial Glondubh. Her story has in it that element of romance which touches the heart and wins the sympathy of all who hear it.

Her father was king of the Meathan branch of the Clan Nial, and *ard-ri* of Ireland for thirty-seven years. Nial Glondubh was king of Tir-Eoghain, and heir of Flann in the high kingship, for at that era it was the custom for the kings of Meath and of Tyrone to hold the supreme power alternately. In order to knit north and south, Flann betrothed his beautiful daughter to Cormac macCuillenan, king of Cashel, an ideal husband, one would have thought, for a poetess like Gormlai, for Cormac was the foremost scholar of the day; but his mind was so set on learning and religion that he took holy orders and became bishop-king of Cashel, repudiating his destined bride. Gormlai was then given as wife to Cearbhail, king of Leinster, and was was waged against Cormac who was killed in the battle of Ballymoon. Coming home wounded, Cearbhail lay on his couch, and while tended by Gormlai and her ladies told the story of the battle and boasted of having insulted the dead body of King Cormac. Gormlai reproached him for his ignoble conduct in such terms that his anger and jealousy flamed up, and striking her with his fist he hurled her to the ground.

Gormlai rose indignant and left his house forever, returning to the palace of King Flann, and on Cearbhail's death she at last found a true lover and worthy mate in Nial Glondubh, who brought her northward to rule over the famous palace of Aileach. In 916 Nial became high king, but the place of honor was also the place of danger, and soon he led the mustered hosts of the north against the pagan foreigners, who held Dublin and Fingal, and he fell in battle at Rathfarnham.

A poem, preserved for us ever since, tells us that Gormlai was present at his burial and chanted a funeral ode. Her long widowhood was a period of disconsolate mourning. At length it is said she had a dream or vision, in which King Nial appeared to her in such life-like shape that she spread her arms to embrace him, and thus wounded her breast against the carven head-post of her couch, and of that wound she died.

Many saintly, many noble, many hospitable and learned women lightened the darkness that fell over Ireland after the coming of the Normans.

I pass to the time when a sovereign lady filled the throne of England, "the spacious days of great Elizabeth," which were also the period of Ireland's greatest, sternest struggle against a policy of extermination towards her nobles and suppression of her ancient faith. Amid all the heroes and leaders of that wondrous age in Ireland, there appears, like a reincarnation of legendary Medb, a warlike queen in Connacht, Grace O'Malley, "Granuaile" of the ballads. Instead of a chariot, she mounts to the prow of a swift-sailing galley, and sweeps over the wild Atlantic billows, from isle to isle, from coast to coast, taking tribute (or is it plunder?) from the clans. First an O'Flaherty is her husband, then a Norman Burke. In Clare Island they show her castle tower, with a hole in the wall, through which they say she tied a cable from her ship, ready by day or night for a summons from her seamen. She voyaged as far as London town, and stood face to face with the ruffed and hooped Elizabeth, meeting her offer of an English title with the assertion that she was a princess in her own land.

The mother of Red Hugh O'Donnell, Ineen-dubh, though daughter of the Scottish Lord of the Isles, was none the less of the old Irish stock. Her character is finely sketched for us by the Franciscan chronicler who wrote the story of the captivity and mighty deeds of her son. When the clans of Tir-Conal assembled to elect the youthful chieftain, he writes: "It was an advantage that she came to the gathering, for she was the head of the advice and counsel of the Cinel-Conail, and, though she was slow and deliberate and much praised for her womanly qualities, she had the heart of a hero and the soul of a soldier." Her daughter, Nuala, is the "woman of the piercing wail" in Mangan's translation of the bard's lament for the death of the Ulster chieftains in Rome.

Modern critics like to interpret the "Dark Rosaleen" poem as an expression of Red Hugh's devotion to Ireland, but I think that Rose, O'Doherty's daughter, wife of the peerless Owen Roe, deserves recognition as she whose

"Holy delicate white hands should girdle him with steel."

The record has come down to us that she prompted and encouraged her husband to return from the low-countries and a position of dignity in a foreign court to command the war in Ireland, and in her first letter, ere she followed him over sea, she asked eagerly: "How stands Tir-Conal?" True daughter of Ulster was Owen's wife, so let us henceforth acknowledge her as the *Roisin* dubh, "dark Rosaleen", of the sublimest of all patriot songs.

In the Cromwellian and Williamite wars, we see the mournful mothers and daughters of the Gaeldom passing in sad procession to Connacht, or wailing on Shannon banks for the flight of the "Wild Geese." But what of Limerick wall, what of the valorous rush of the women of the beleaguered city to stem the inroads of the besiegers and rally the defenders

to the breach? The decree of St. Adamnan was quite forgotten then, and when manly courage for a moment was
daunted, woman's fortitude replaced and reinspired it.

And fortitude was sorely needed through the black years
that followed—the penal days, when Ireland, crushed in the
dust, bereft of arms, achieved a sublimer victory than did
even King Brian himself, champion of the Cross, against the
last muster of European heathendom.

Yes, her women have done their share in making Ireland
what she is, a heroic land, unconquered by long centuries of
wrath and wrong, a land that has not abandoned its Faith
through stress of direst persecution or bartered it for the lure
of worldly dominion; no—nor ever yielded to despair in face
of repeated national disaster.

It was this fidelity to principle on the part of the Irish
Catholic people which won for them the alliance of all that
were worthiest among the Protestants of north and south in
the days of the Volunteers and the United Irishmen. What
interesting and pathetic portraits of Irishwomen are added
to our roll at this period! None is more tenderly mournful
than that of Sarah Curran, the beloved of Robert Emmet.
The graceful prose of Washington Irving, the poignant verses
of Moore, have enshrined the memory of her, weeping for
him in the shadow of the scaffold, dying of heart-break at
last in a far-off land. No more need be said of her, for whom
the pity of the whole world has been awakened by song allied
to sweetest, saddest music. What of Anne Devlin, Emmet's
faithful servant, helping in his preparations for insurrection,
aiding his flight, shielding him in hiding, even when tortured,
scourged, half-hanged by a brutal soldiery, with stern-shut
lips refusing to utter a word to compromise her "Master
Robert"?

What of the sister of Henry Joy McCracken, Mary, the
friend and fellow-worker with the Belfast United Irishmen?
An independent, self-reliant business woman, she earned the
money which she gave so liberally in the good cause, or to
help the poor and distressed, through the whole period of a
long life. Some still living have seen Mary passing along the
streets of Belfast, an aged woman, clad in sombre gown, to

whom Catholic artisans raised their caps reverently, remembering how in '98 she had walked hand in hand with her brother to the steps of the scaffold, and how, in 1803, she had aided Thomas Russell in his escape from the north after Emmet's failure, had bribed his captors after arrest, provided for his defence, and preserved for futurity a record of his dying words. Madden's *History of the United Irishmen,* as far as it tells of the north, is mainly the record that she kept as a sacred trust in letters, papers, long-treasured memories of the men who fought and died to make Ireland a united nation.

And now a scene in America comes last to my mind. Wolfe Tone, a political fugitive who has served Ireland well and come through danger to safety, is busy laying the foundations of a happy and prosperous future, with a beloved wife and sister and young children to brighten his home. An estate near Princeton, New Jersey, has been all but bought, possibilities of a career in the new republic open before him, when a letter comes from Belfast, asking him to return to the post of danger, to undertake a mission to France for the sake of Ireland. Let his own pen describe what happened: "I handed the letter to my wife and sister and desired their opinion. . . . My wife especially, whose courage and whose zeal for my honor and interest were not in the least abated by all her past sufferings, supplicated me to let no consideration of her or our children stand for a moment in the way of my duty to our country, adding that she would answer for our family during my absence and that the same Providence which had so often, as it were, miraculously preserved us would not desert us now."

Inspired by the fortitude of this noble woman, Tone went forth on his perilous mission, and similarly the Young Ireland leaders, Mitchel and Smith O'Brien, were sustained by the courage of their nearest and dearest. "Eva," the poetess of the *Nation,* gave her troth-plight to one who had prison and exile to face ere he could claim her hand. Other names recur to me—"Speranza", with her lyric fire; Ellen O'Leary, fervent and still patient and wise; Fanny Parnell and her sister.

And what of the women of Ireland today? Shall they come short of the high ideal of the past, falter and fail, if devotion and sacrifice are required of them? Never: whilst they keep in memory and honor the illustrious ones of whom I have written. The name of Irishwoman today stands for steadfast virtue, for hospitality, for simple piety, for cheerful endurance, and in a changing world let us trust it is the will of God that in this there will be no change.

REFERENCES:

On Ethne, mother of St. Columcille: The Visions, Miracles, and Prophecies of St. Columba (Clarendon Press Series). On Ronnat: S. Mac an Bhaird, Life (in Irish) of Adamnan (Letterkenny); Reeves, St. Adamnan's Life of St. Columba; The Mother of St. Adamnan, an old Gaelic text, ed. by Kuno Meyer (Berlin). On Gormlai: Thomas Concannon, Gormfiath (in Irish; The Gaelic League, Dublin). On Granuaile: Elizabethan State Papers (Record Office Series); William O'Brien, A Queen of Men. On Ineen-Dubh: O'Clery's Life of Red Hugh (contemporary), ed. by Denis Murphy, S. J. (Dublin, 1894); Standish O'Grady, The Flight of the Eagle, or Red Hugh's Captivity. On Rose, wife of Owen Roe O'Neill, see references in Father Meehan's The Flight of the Earls, and in Sir John Gilbert's History of the Confederate War (Dublin, 1885). On the wife of Wolfe Tone, see Wolfe Tone's Autobiography, ed. by R. Barry O'Brien (London, 1894). The American edition has a fuller account of Tone's wife, her courage and devotion in educating her son, and her interviews with Napoleon, and life in America. The women of the United Irish period are fully dealt with in R. R. Madden's Lives and Times of the United Irishmen. On Mary Mc-Cracken, see Mrs. Milligan Fox, The Annals of the Irish Harpers. On the women of the Young Ireland period, see C. Gavan Duffy's Young Ireland (Dublin), and John O'Leary's Fenians and Fenianism. On the women of Limerick, see Rev. James Dowd, Limerick and its Sieges (Limerick, 1890). For the women under Cromwellian Plantation persecutions and the Penal Laws, see Prendergast's Cromwellian Settlement, Rev. Denis Murphy's Cromwell in Ireland, and R. R. Madden's History of the Penal Laws.

IRISH NATIONALITY

By Lord Ashbourne.

[NOTE.—This chapter was written by Lord Ashbourne in French, because he is so strong an Irishman that he objects to write in English. The translation has been made by the Editors.]

TO those of us who are interested in the future of our country there is at this very moment presented a really serious problem. The political struggle of the last century has been so intense that many of our people have come to have none but a political solution in view. For them the whole question is one of politics, and they will continue to believe that Ireland will have found salvation the moment we get Home Rule or something like it. Such an attitude seems natural enough when we remember what our people have suffered in the past. Nevertheless, on a little reflection, this error—for error it is, and an enormous one, too—will be quickly dissipated. In the first place, the political struggle of today is only the continuation of a conflict which has lasted seven hundred years, and in point of fact we have a right to be proud that after so many trials there still remains to us anything of our national inheritance. We find ourselves indeed on the battlefield somewhat seriously bruised, but we can console ourselves with the thought that our opponent is in equally doleful case, that he is beginning to suffer from a fatal weariness, and that he is anxious to make peace with us.

In order to place the present political situation in its true light and to take into account its comparatively limited importance, we must not lose sight of the fundamental fact that what Home Rule connotes is rather a tender of peace on the part of Ireland than a gift which England presents us of her own free will. In fact, our neighbor across the Channel has as much interest as ourselves, and perhaps even more, in bringing the struggle to an end. Through us, England has already lost much prestige, and that famous British Constitution, which in times past everyone admired while trying in vain to imitate it, has lost caste considerably. I am not now speaking of the danger which an Ireland discontented, and even hostile, and having nothing to lose, would constitute for England in case of war. It is especially from our neighbor's point of view that we can cry up Home Rule or any other solution that will bring peace. But let us leave to Great Britain the task of getting out of trouble as best she may. On our side, what shall we say of it?

In our conflict with the English we are not wearied; rather are we hardened for the fray. We have acquired the habit of fighting, and many of us can now scarcely regulate our conduct in a manner suitable to a state of peace with England. Nevertheless, as I have already said, we have not emerged unscathed from this war of the centuries. National sentiment remains with us, no doubt, and our traditions are not wholly lost, especially among the country people of the West. But our commerce is almost ruined and the national language is no longer spoken throughout the greater part of the country. It is true that a continuation of the hitherto existing state of war cannot do us much more harm; that for purposes of mere destruction all the advantages are on our side; and that on the other hand we can begin a reconstruction at home without waiting for a treaty of peace to be signed. But we have some things to do for which a home government would be useful to us, and further, in the absence of such a government, it would be difficult to imagine what means could be employed to turn the people away from their too exclusive absorption in Anglo-Irish politics.

It is, then, from a practical point of view that we wish for peace. But, we may lawfully ask, will not this peace bring with it a special danger, against which we ought to take precautions? As a matter of fact, there is such a danger, and it lies in the fact that the people have been to so great an extent obsessed by the political struggle that they run the risk, once their end is attained, of collapsing and of losing interest in the national question. Let us not forget that that question is to save our language and our civilization; without that, it is all over with our nationality. Let us endeavor to turn our parliament to account in order to work seriously on the reconstruction of our national life, and it is certain that Ireland will find therein her salvation.

We can, therefore, take advantage either of England's prolonged resistance or of peace. If England decides to continue the contest, she will suffer more from it than we. Her empire, her institutions, her safety, will be more and more impaired, while, as for us, there will result a strong growth in patriotism and in anti-British bitterness. What we have to do, right now, is to take our bearings in such a way that, no matter what happens to England, our own future shall be assured. We can do it if we wish it: the question is, shall we wish it?

Here it may be objected, *Cui bono?* The English language is quite enough for us. We have it now and we speak it, sometimes, even better than the English people themselves. We are proud of using the same language as Sheridan, Burke, and Grattan used. Such an opinion has its modicum of truth, though less now than a hundred years ago. Formerly there was in Ireland, and especially around Dublin, a little colony of Anglo-Irish. The members of this colony spoke a very pure and classic English, and this fact is largely responsible for the place which Ireland at one time held in English literature. But during the last century the remains of this colony have been swamped beneath a flood of half-Anglicized people, of Irishmen from the country districts, who were formerly excluded, and who brought with them such a mixture of expressions and of phonetic tendencies derived from the Gaelic that the language of Grattan, Sheridan, and Burke has well-nigh gone out of existence. The reason of this is that since the date of Catholic emancipation, most careers are open to everybody. The result has been that the newly enfranchised majority has ultimately absorbed the minority, and that the atmosphere of culture, of which we have just spoken, has disappeared. We thus reach an Ireland which, in a sense, has neither culture nor language, a country in which the Gaelic spoken by a people humiliated and deeply demoralized by an anti-Catholic legislation, which was both savage and degrading, tended to coalesce with an English already condemned to death. It is from the moment when the Catholics had finally triumphed over persecution that we must date the beginning of that political struggle with which we are familiar, a struggle which has resulted in absorbing all the energies of a great part of the population. That is why this tremendous problem presents itself to us, at the very time when we should be justified in feeling ourselves elated by triumph because of our victories in parliament. And let not England rejoice too much at our dilemma. If we are doomed to die, she will die with us, for before disappearing we shall prove to be a great destructive force, and out of the ruins of the British power we shall raise such a monument that future generations will know what it costs to murder a nation.

But, if possible, we must live and let live. The elements of reconstruction are always at hand. Anglo-Irish culture is indeed dead, but Gaelic culture is only seriously sick, and on that side there is always room for hope. Sooth to say, its sickness consists above all in the fact that the Irish language is no longer spoken in a great part of the country. But, on the other hand, where it is preserved, that same language is spoken in all its purity. By going there to find it all Ireland will gradually become Gaelic.

But, it will be objected, what a loss of time and energy! If it is a question of languages, why not learn one of the more useful ones? To this we may reply that, while English deforms the mouth and makes it incapable of pronouncing any language which is not spoken from the tip of the lips, Gaelic, on the contrary, so exercises the organs of speech that it renders easy the acquisition and the practice of most European idioms. Let us add, by way of example, that French, which is usually difficult for strangers, is much more within the compass of Irishmen who speak Irish, no less because of certain linguistic customs than from the original relationship between the two languages.

This remark brings us to another objection which is often lodged against our movement. It is urged that Ireland is already isolated enough, and that by making it a Gaelic-speaking nation, we shall make that state of affairs still worse. English, say the objectors, is spoken more or less everywhere, while Gaelic will never be able to claim the position of a quasi-universal language. To this line of reasoning it might be answered, for one thing, that no one can tell how far

Gaelic will go, in case our movement is a success, and that many a language formerly "universal" is today as dead as a door-nail. But we must look at the question from another point of view. John Bull's language is spread everywhere, while he himself retains the most exclusive insularity. He travels to every land and there finds his own language and his own customs. Now it goes without saying that from this very universalization his language is corrupted and becomes vulgarized. The idiom of Shakespeare and Milton gives place gradually to the idiom of the seaports. Furthermore, far from isolating us, Gaelic will tend to put us in touch with the civilization of the West. As a people Anglicised, and badly Anglicised at that, we share, and even exaggerate, the faults which I have just described. It is Anglo-Saxon speech which isolates us, and we wish on this ground to break with it and to hold out our hand to our brothers of the continent.

But, it may be said, what a pity to dig yet another abyss between Ireland and Great Britain, for it is with the latter that our geographical position will always link us for common defense. For, while it is true that history does not show us a single case of an empire which has not sooner or later fallen to pieces, nevertheless, whatever happens, the two islands will be necessarily forced to co-operate for the common good. Well, let us take it that things will so fall out, and let us suppose an Anglicised Ireland called upon to face such a situation. It would be a revolutionary Ireland, a restless Ireland, an Ireland seeking vaguely for revenge on someone, deprived of really national character, and, in a general way, suspecting England of responsibility for the disappearance from our country of everything that constitutes the idea of nationality. And let us remark that we are no longer living in those good old times when entire nations allowed themselves to be absorbed by their conquerors. The art of printing has changed all that. Today a "suppressed" nation is one that will sooner or later have its revenge. Thus let us suppose that we are destined to make political peace with England and to enter of our own accord into a Hiberno-Britannic confederation. From our point of view, what would be the result of that arrangement? The result would be strange. Here again, as in the case of Home

Rule, it is rather we who offer advantages to England than she who offers them to us. Only, in this latter case, the result depends on ourselves alone. If we die, it will be because we have wished it. Our language is not dead; on the contrary, although not widely spread, it is in itself much more alive than English, which as a literary language is in full decay. We may congratulate ourselves that our idiom is intact. Our civilization is old, but it has not yet lived its full life. If we wish, the future is ours. And let us truly believe that that is worth while, for the race which has produced epics like those of Ossian and all that magnificent literature which has been preserved for us through the ages, the race that gave to Europe that great impulse of missionary activity which is associated with the names of Columcille, Brendan, Columbanus, and Gall, not to mention men like the famous Scotus Erigena—that race is certainly called upon to play an important part in the modern world. But—let us repeat it—it must have the wish.

FAMOUS IRISH SOCIETIES

By JOHN O'DEA,

National Historian, A. O. H.

IN the social organization of no nation of antiquity were societies of greater influence than in pagan Ireland. During many centuries these societies, composed of the bards, ollamhs, brehons, druids, and knights, contended for precedence. In no country did the literary societies display greater vigor and exercise a more beneficent power than in pagan Ireland. Although the Hebrews and other Asiatic nations had societies organized from among the professions, yet in Ireland alone these societies seem to have been constructed with a patriotic purpose, and in Ireland alone they seem to have had ceremonies of initiation, with constitutions and laws. These societies existed from the earliest times until after the coming of St. Patrick. Traces of them are visible during all the centuries from the conversion of Ireland down to the Anglo-Norman epoch, and it is apparent that the clan system and the introduction of the feudal system by the English failed to eliminate completely their influence.

When the Irish emigration flowed towards the American colonies in the eighteenth century, the social instinct early found expression in societies. One of the earliest of these was founded in Boston, where, in 1737, twenty-six "gentlemen merchants and others, natives of Ireland or of Irish extraction", organized the Charitable Irish Society. In Pennsylvania, where the Irish emigration had been larger than in any other colony, the Hibernian Fire Company was organized in 1751. The Friendly Sons of St. Patrick was founded in Philadelphia in 1771, and about that time societies bearing this name were founded in Boston and New York, as convivial clubs welcoming Irish emigrants to their festive boards. These societies were formed upon the model of the Friendly Brothers of St. Patrick, which had existed in Dublin and other Irish cities a generation before, and was well and favorably known throughout Ireland.

The Society of the Friendly Sons of St. Patrick in Philadelphia contained some of the most prominent merchants and leading citizens of the city, and in 1780 they subscribed £103,000, or one-third of the sum collected, to supply the Continental army with food. Among its members were Commodore Barry, the Father of the American Navy; General Stephen Moylan; General Anthony Wayne; and the great merchants, Blair McClenachan, Thomas Fitzsimons, and Robert Morris. Washington, who was an honorary member, described it "as a society distinguished for the firm adherence of its members to the glorious cause in which we are embarked." Whether upon the field or upon the sea, in council or in the sacrifice of their wealth, their names are foremost in the crisis of the Revolution.

The Hibernian Society for the Relief of Emigrants from Ireland was founded in Philadelphia on March 3, 1790. Other Hibernian Societies, with the same title and organized for the same purpose, were founded in other cities along the Atlantic coast in the early years of the nineteenth century, but the Philadelphia Hibernian Society was, from the character of its members, the extent of its beneficence, and the length of its existence, the most famous. The emigrants from Ireland during the eighteenth century had pushed on to the frontier, or, in some instances, remained in the cities and engaged successfully in mercantile pursuits. The emigration which came after the Revolution was, however, in great part composed of families almost without means. Unable to subsist while clearing farms in the virgin forest, thousands were congested in the cities. The Hibernian Society extended a ready and strong hand to these helpless people, and not only aided the emigrants with gifts of money, but also secured for them employment, disseminated among them useful information, and provided them with medical attendance. While the Hibernian Society was regarded as the successor of the Friendly Sons of St. Patrick, yet the two societies, which contained largely a membership roll bearing the same names, flourished, in the work of patriotism, side by side. The first officers of the Hibernian Society for the Relief of Emigrants from Ireland were: President, Chief Justice Thomas McKean; Vice-President, General Walter Stewart; Secretary, Matthew Carey, the historian; Treasurer, John Taylor. It was said that no other society in America contained so many men distinguished in civil, military, and official life as the Hibernian Society. In almost every city where the Friendly Sons of St. Patrick and the Hibernian Society for the Relief of Emigrants were found, there was a close and intimate connection between them, which ultimately resulted in amalgamation.

The Ancient Order of Hibernians traces its origin to those orders which flourished in pagan Ireland, and which exercised so potent an influence upon the history of the Celtic race. The order of knighthood was the first of these orders to be founded. It existed from the earliest times, and is visible in the annals of the nation, until the Anglo-Normans invaded the land in the twelfth century. In pagan Ireland the knightly orders became provincial standing armies, and there are many glorious pages describing the feats of the Clanna Deagha of Munster, the Clanna Morna of Connacht, the Feni of Leinster, and the Knights of the Red Branch of Ulster. When the island was Christianized, these knightly orders were among the staunchest supporters of the missionary priests, and were consecrated to the service of the church in the sixth century, assuming the cross as their distinctive emblem, and becoming the defenders of religion.

Among the names which are upon the rolls of the ancient orders of knighthood are those of most of the kings, bards, saints, and statesmen, and in the long list there was no family of greater renown than that of Roderick the Great, to which belonged Conall Cearnach and Lugaidh, who, according to MacGeoghegan and others, were the direct ancestors of the O'Mores of Leix. In this family the ancient splendor of the knightly orders was a tradition which survived for centuries, and they were in almost continual rebellion against the English, from the siege of Dublin by Roderick O'Connor until the rebellion against Queen Elizabeth, led by Rory Oge O'More and his son Owen in the latter part of the sixteenth and the early seventeenth century. A nephew of Rory Oge, the sagacious and statesmanlike Rory O'More, revived the ancient orders in the Catholic Confederation of Kilkenny in 1642. A grandson of Rory O'More, Patrick Sarsfield, Earl of Lucan, was the most distinguished commander of Irish armies who opposed, in Ireland, the forces of William of Orange.

There is no stranger story in all history than the intimate connection of the O'More family with the annals of the Ancient Order of Hibernians. The lineage of this family furnishes the links connecting the ancient orders of pagan Ireland through the centuries with the Ancient Order in modern times. Under the names of Rapparees, Whiteboys, Defenders, Ribbonmen, etc., the Confederation of Kilkenny was carried on through the seventeenth and eighteenth centuries until the nineteenth. At various times the duties of these organizations were subject to local conditions. Thus the Defenders were occupied in protecting themselves and their priests against the hostility of the Penal Laws, engaging in armed conflict with the Orangemen in the north, while the Whiteboys were waging war against the atrocities of landlordism in the south. Between these two organizations there was a secret code, which operated until they were combined, under the name of Ribbonmen, in the early nineteenth century. The contentions of the Whiteboys regarding Irish landlordism have since been acknowledged to be just, and have been enacted into statutes. The Defenders joined with Wolfe Tone in the formation of the United Irishmen.

About 1825 the Ribbonmen changed their name to St. Patrick's Fraternal Society, and branches were established in England and Scotland under the name of the Hibernian Funeral Society. In 1836 a charter was received by members in New York City, and in Schuylkill County, Pennsylvania. The headquarters were for some years in Pennsylvania, but in 1851 a charter was granted to the New York Divisions under the name of "The Ancient Order of Hibernians." New York thus became the American headquarters. National conventions were held there until 1878, since which year they have been held in many other cities biennially. Many of the most distinguished leaders of the Irish race in America have been members of the Order, and from a humble beginning, with a few emigrants gathered together in a strange land, the membership has grown to nearly 200,000. General Thomas Francis Meagher, Colonel Michael Doheny, General Michael Corcoran, and Colonel John O'Mahony were among the members in the late '50's.

Among the organizations which have sprung from the ranks of the A. O. H. were the powerful Fenian Brotherhood, the Emmet Monument Association, and scores of smaller associations in all sections of the United States and Canada. During the Know Nothing riots, the Order furnished armed defenders for the Catholic churches in New York, Philadelphia, and Charleston, and it has ever been foremost in preserving its position as the hereditary defender of the faith. In 1894, the Ladies' Auxiliary was founded, and this body of women numbered in 1914 over 63,000, and had donated great sums to charity, education, and religion. The A. O. H. had, in 1914, assets of $2,230,000. It pays annually, for charity, sick and death benefits, and maintenance, over $1,000,000, and during its existence in America has donated nearly $20,000,000 to works of beneficence. One of the most celebrated of the gifts of the Order was the endowment of the Chair of Celtic in the Catholic University of America, and one of its greatest gifts to charity was its contribution of $40,000 to the sufferers from the San Francisco earthquake.

The Clan-na-Gael is a society organized to secure the independence of Ireland by armed revolution. Its organization is secret and it is the successor of the Irish Revolutionary Brotherhood, called in America the Fenian Brotherhood, which promoted many daring raids and risings in Ireland in 1867. The I. R. B. was perfected by James Stephens in Ireland, and by John O'Mahony in America, from 1857 to 1867. An invasion of Canada was made in great force under the general direction of Colonel William R. Roberts, president of the Fenian Brotherhood, but was unsuccessful owing to the attitude of the United States Government, which declared that the Fenians were violating the principles of neutrality. After the disorganization of the Fenian Brotherhood, the idea of revolution languished until revived by the founding of the Clan-na-Gael by Jerome J. Collins in 1869, and the membership during the twenty years from 1880 to 1900 included almost fifty thousand of the flower of the men of Irish blood in America. The principle of revolution was first given organized public expression in America through the formation in 1848 of the Irish Republican Union, which was succeeded by the Emmet Monument Association, these societies influencing the creation of the Sixty-Ninth and Seventy-Fifth Regiments of the New York State Militia, and the Ninth Massachusetts, which became so famous for valor during the Civil War. Although not putting forth all its strength, so as to allow full scope to the parliamentary efforts to ameliorate the state of the Irish people, the Clan-na-Gael is as vigorous a section as ever of the forces organized for the service of patriotism.

The Land League, founded in Ireland in 1879, was transplanted to America in 1880, when the first branch was established in New York City through the efforts of Patrick Ford, John Boyle O'Reilly, John Devoy, and others. Michael Davitt soon after came to America and travelled through the country founding branches of the League. In a few years the whole American continent was organized, and in this organization Michael Davitt declared that the members of the Ancient Order of Hibernians and the Clan-na-Gael were everywhere foremost. To the enormous sums collected by the League in this country, and to the magnificent labors of Parnell, Davitt, Redmond, Ferguson, Dillon, Kettle, Webb, and others in Ireland, is due in a large measure the present improved state of the people, resulting from the sacrifices made by those who supported this greatest of leagues devoted to the amelioration of unbearable economic conditions. A Ladies' Auxiliary to the Land League was established by the sisters of Parnell, and was for some years a brilliant vindication of the power and justice of feminine participation in public questions.

The Land League, the name of which was changed to the Irish National League in the early '80's, having prepared the path to eventual victory, declined in potency after the political movement was divided into Parnellites and Anti-Parnellites in 1890. The elements composing these rival parties were, through the initiative of William O'Brien, M. P., and in commemoration of the one hundredth anniversary of the United Irishmen of Wolfe Tone's day, joined in 1898 under the name of the United Irish League, John E. Redmond becoming the first president, and also the chairman of the Parliamentary Party which it had been instrumental in uniting. This organization is now a living, vital force in the affairs of Ireland on both sides of the Atlantic, Mr. Redmond being still its head, with Michael J. Ryan, of Philadelphia, as president of the American Branch.

The Knights of Columbus were organized in 1881 by Rev. Michael McGivney, in New Haven, Connecticut, and a charter was granted by the Connecticut Legislature on March 29, 1882. At first the activity of the organization was confined to Connecticut, but the time was ripe for its mission, and it soon spread rapidly throughout New England. In 1896 it began to attract the attention of Catholic young men in other parts of the nation, and during the next few years its appeal was made irresistibly in almost every State. It now exists in all the States of the Union, the Dominion of Canada, Nova Scotia, Newfoundland, Panama, Porto Rico, Mexico, Cuba, and the Philippine Islands, with a total membership of 328,000, of whom 108,000 are insurance members and 220,000 associate members. Its mortuary reserve fund is $4,500,000, being over $1,000,000 more than is required by law. It is one of the most successful fraternal societies ever organized, and the Irish-American Catholics have given to it the full strength of their enthusiasm and purpose.

The temperance movement among Catholics was, from the visit of Father Mathew in 1849, largely Irish. The societies first formed were united by no bond until 1871, when the Connecticut societies formed a State Union. Other States formed unions and a national convention in Baltimore in 1872 created a National Union. In 1878 there were 90,000 priests, laymen, women, and children in the Catholic Total Abstinence Benevolent Union. In 1883 the Union was introduced into Canada, and in 1895 there were 150,000 members on the American continent. From the C. T. A. B. U. were formed the Knights of Father Mathew, a total abstinence and semi-military body, first instituted in St. Louis in 1872.

The Catholic Knights of America, with a membership chiefly Irish-American, were organized in Memphis, Tennessee, in 1877, and the advantages offered for insurance soon attracted 20,000 members. The decade of the '70's was prolific of Irish

Catholic associations. The Catholic Benevolent Legion was founded in 1873, shortly followed by the Catholic Mutual Benevolent Association, the Catholic Order of Foresters (which started in Massachusetts and spread to other States), the Irish Catholic Benevolent Union, and the Society of the Holy Name, which latter, although tracing its origin to Lisbon in 1432, is yet dominantly Irish in America.

In the large industrial centres there are scores of Irish county and other societies composed of Irishmen and Irish-Americans, organized for the service of country and faith, beneficence and education, and all dedicated to the uplifting of humanity and to the progress of civilization. The ancient genius for organization has not been lost, the spirit of brotherhood pulsates strongly in the Irish heart, and through its powerful societies the race retains its place in the advance of mankind.

REFERENCES:

John M. Campbell: History of the Friendly Sons of St. Patrick and Hibernian Society; Maguire: The Irish in America; McGee: Irish Settlers in America; John O'Dea: History of the Ancient Order of Hibernians and Ladies' Auxiliary in America; Michael Davitt: The Fall of Feudalism in Ireland; Cashman: Life of Michael Davitt; T. P. O'Connor: The Parnell Movement; Joseph Denieffe; Recollections of the Irish Revolutionary Brotherhood; Articles in the Catholic Encyclopedia; Report of the Knights of Columbus, 1914; The Tidings, Los Angeles, 7th annual edition.

THE IRISH IN THE UNITED STATES

By Michael J. O'Brien,

Historiographer, American Irish Historical Society.

STUDENTS of early American history will find in the Colonial records abundant evidence to justify the statement of Ramsay, the historian of South Carolina, when he wrote in 1789, that:

"The Colonies which now form the United States may be considered as Europe transplanted. Ireland, England, Scotland, France, Germany, Holland, Switzerland, Sweden, Poland, and Italy furnished the original stock of the present population, and are generally supposed to have contributed to it in the order named. For the last seventy or eighty years, no nation has contributed so much to the population of America as Ireland."

It will be astonishing to one who looks into the question to find that, in face of all the evidence that abounds in American annals, showing that our people were here on this soil fighting the battles of the colonists, and in a later day of the infant Republic, thus proving our claim to the gratitude of this nation, America has produced men so ignoble and disingenuous as to say that the Irish who were here in Revolutionary days "were for the most part heartily loyal," that "the combatants were of the same race and blood", and that the great uprising became, in fact, "a contest between brothers"!

Although many writers have made inquiries into this subject, nearly all have confined themselves to the period of the Revolution. We are of "the fighting race", and in our enthusiasm for the fighting man the fact seems to have been overlooked that in other noble fields of endeavor, and in some respects infinitely more important, men of Irish blood have occupied prominent places in American history, for which they have received but scant recognition. The pioneers before whose hands the primeval forests fell prostrate; the builders, by whose magic touch have sprung into existence flourishing towns and cities, where once no sounds were heard save those of nature and her wildest offspring; the orators who roused the colonists into activity and showed them the way to achieve their independence; the schoolmasters who imparted to the American youth their first lessons in intellectuality and patriotism; all have their place in history, and of these we can claim that Ireland furnished her full quota to the American colonies.

It must now be accepted as an indisputable fact that a very large proportion of the earliest settlers in the American colonies were of Irish blood, for the Irish have been coming here since the beginning of the English colonization. It has been estimated by competent authorities that in the middle of the seventeenth century the English-speaking colonists numbered 50,000. Sir William Petty, the English statistician, tells us that during the decade from 1649 to 1659 the annual emigration from Ireland to the western continent was upwards of 6000, thus making, in that space of time, 60,000 souls, or about one-half of what the whole population must have been in 1659. And from 1659 to 1672 there emigrated from Ireland to America the yearly number of 3000 (Dobbs, on Irish Trade, Dublin, 1729). Prendergast, another noted authority, in the *Cromwellian Settlement of Ireland,* furnishes ample verification of this by the statistics which he quotes from the English records. Richard Hakluyt, the chronicler of the first Virginia expeditions, in his *Voyages, Navigations, Traffiques, and Discoveries of the English Nation* (London, 1600), shows that Irishmen came with Raleigh to Virginia in 1587 and, in fact, the ubiquitous Celts were with Sir John Hawkins in his voyage to the Gulf of Mexico twenty years earlier. The famous work of John Camden Hotten, entitled "The Original Lists of Persons of Quality, Emigrants, Religious Exiles, Political Rebels, Serving Men sold for a term of years," etc., who were brought to the Virginia plantations between 1600 and 1700, as well as his "List of the Livinge and the Dead in Virginia in 1623," contains numerous Celtic names, and further evidence of these continuous migrations of the Irish is contained in "A Booke of Entrie for Passengers passing beyond the Seas", in the year 1632. The Virginia records also show that as early as 1621 a colony of Irish people sailed from Cork in the *Flying Harte* under the patronage of Sir William Newce and located at what is now Newport News, and some few years later Daniel Gookin, a merchant of Cork, transported hither "great multitudes of people and cattle" from England and Ireland.

In the "William and Mary College Quarterly," in the transcripts of the original records published by the Virginia Historical Society, and in all County histories of Virginia, there are numerous references to the Irish "redemptioners" who were brought to that colony during the seventeenth century. But the redemptioners were not the only class who came, for the colonial records also contain many references to Irishmen of good birth and education who received grants of land in the colony and who, in turn, induced many of their countrymen to emigrate. Planters named McCarty, Lynch, O'Neill, Sullivan, Farrell, McDonnell, O'Brien, and others denoting an ancient Irish lineage appear frequently in the early records. Much that is romantic is found in the lives of these men and their descendants. Some of them served in the Council chamber and the field, their sons and daughters were educated to hold place, with elegance and dignity, with the foremost of the Cavaliers, and when in after years the great conflict with England began, Virginians of Irish blood were among the first and the most eager to answer the call. Those historians who claim that the South was exclusively an "Anglo-Saxon" heritage would be completely disillusioned were they to examine the lists of Colonial and Revolutionary troops of Celtic name who held the Indians and the British at bay, and who helped in those "troublous times" to lay the foundations of a great Republic.

There is no portion of the Atlantic seaboard that did not profit by the Irish immigrations of the seventeenth century. We learn from the "Irish State Papers" of the year 1595 that ships were regularly plying between Ireland and Newfoundland, and so important was the trade between Ireland and the far-distant fishing banks that "all English ships bound out always made provisions that the convoy out should remain 48 hours in Cork." In some of Lord Baltimore's accounts of his voyages to Newfoundland he refers to his having "sailed from Ireland" and to his "return to Ireland," and so it is highly probable that he settled Irishmen on his Avalon plantations.

After Baltimore's departure, Lord Falkland also sent out a number of Irish colonists, and "at a later date they were so largely reinforced by settlers from Ireland that the Celtic part of the population at this day is not far short of equality in numbers with the Saxon portion"—(Hatton and Harvey, *History of Newfoundland,* page 32). Pedley attributes the large proportion of Irishmen and the influence of the Catholics in Newfoundland to Lord Falkland's company, and Prowse, in his History (pp. 200-201), refers to "the large number of Irishmen" in that colony who fled from Waterford and Cork "during the troubled times" which preceded the Williamite war (1688). Many of these in after years are known to have settled in New England.

But it was to Maryland and Pennsylvania that the greatest flow of Irish immigration directed its course. In the celebrated "Account of the Voyage to Maryland," written in the year 1634 by Mutius Vitellestis, the general of the Jesuit Order, it is related that when the *Arke* and the *Dove* arrived in the West Indies in that year, they found "the island of Montserrat inhabited by a colony of Irishmen who had been banished from Virginia on account of their professing the Catholic faith." It is known also that there were many families in Ireland of substance and good social standing who, at their own expense, took venture in the enterprise of Lord Baltimore and afterwards in that of William Penn, and who applied for and received grants of land, which, as the deeds on record show, were afterwards divided into farms bought and settled by O'Briens, McCarthys, O'Connors, and many others of the ancient Gaelic race, the descendants of those heroic men whose passion for liberty, while causing their ruin, inspired and impelled their sons to follow westward "the star of empire."

After the first English colonies in Maryland were founded, we find in all the proclamations concerning these settlements by the proprietary government, that they were limited to "persons of British or Irish descent." The religious liberty established in Maryland was the magnet which attracted Irish Catholics to that Province, and so they came in large numbers in search of peace and comfort and freedom from the turmoil produced by religious animosities in their native land. The major part of this Irish immigration seems to have come in through the ports of Philadelphia and Charleston and a portion through Chesapeake Bay, whence they passed on to Pennsylvania and the southern colonies.

The "Certificates of Land Grants" in Maryland show that it was customary for those Irish colonists to name their lands after places in their native country, and I find that there is hardly a town or city in the old Gaelic strongholds in Ireland that is not represented in the nomenclature of the early Maryland grants. One entire section of the Province, named the "County of New Ireland" by proclamation of Lord Baltimore in the year 1684, was occupied wholly by Irish families. This section is now embraced in Cecil and Harford Counties. New Ireland County was divided into three parts, known as New Connaught, New Munster, and New Leinster. New Connaught was founded by George Talbot from Roscommon, who was surveyor-general of the Province; New Munster, by Edward O'Dwyer from Tipperary; and New Leinster, by Bryan O'Daly from Wicklow, all of whom were in Maryland prior to 1683. Among the prominent men in the Province may be mentioned Charles O'Carroll, who was secretary to the proprietor; John Hart from county Cavan, who was governor of Maryland from 1714 to 1720; Phillip Conner from Kerry, known in history as the "Last Commander of Old Kent"; Daniel Dulany of the O'Delaney family from Queen's County, one of the most famous lawyers in the American Colonies; Michael Tawney or Taney, ancestor of the celebrated judge, Roger Brooke Taney; the Courseys from Cork, one of the oldest families in the State; the Kings from Dublin; and many others.

The only place in the State bearing a genuine Irish name which has reached any prominence is Baltimore. Not alone has the "Monumental City" received its name from Ireland, but the tract of land on which the city is now situate was originally named (in 1695) "Ely O'Carroll," after the barony of that name in King's and Tipperary counties, the ancient home of the Clan O'Carroll. To subdivisions of the tract were given such names as Dublin, Waterford, Tralee, Raphoe,

Tramore, Mallow, Kinsale, Lurgan, Coleraine, Tipperary, Antrim, Belfast, Derry, Kildare, Enniskillen, Wexford, Letterkenny, Lifford, Birr, Galway, Limerick, and so on, all indicating the nationality of the patentees, as well as the places from which they came.

From such sources is the evidence available of the coming of the Irish to Maryland in large numbers, and so it is that we are not surprised to find on the rosters of the Maryland Revolutionary regiments 4633 distinctive Irish names, exclusive of the large numbers who joined the navy and the militia, as well as those who were held to guard the frontier from Indian raids, whose names are not on record. However, it is not possible now to determine the proportion of the Revolutionary soldiers who were of Irish birth or descent, for where the nationality is not stated in the rosters all non-Irish names must be left out of the reckoning. The first census of Maryland (1790), published by the United States Government, enumerates the names of all "Heads of Families" and the number of persons in each family. A count of the Irish names shows approximately 21,000 persons. This does not take into account the great number of people who could not be recorded under that head, as it is known there were many thousand Irish "redemptioners" in Maryland prior to the taking of the census, and while no precise data exist to indicate the number of Irish immigrants who settled in Maryland, I estimate that the number of people of Irish descent in the State in 1790 was not far short of 40,000.

The Land Records and Council Journals of Georgia of the last half of the seventeenth and the first half of the eighteenth century afford like testimony to the presence of the Irish, who crossed the sea and colonized the waste places of that wild territory, and whose descendants in after years contributed much of the strength of the patriot forces who confronted the armed cohorts of Carleton and Cornwallis. From the Colonial Records of Georgia, published under the auspices of the State Legislature, I have extracted a long list of people of Irish name and blood who received grants of land in that colony. They came with Oglethorpe as early as 1735 and continued to arrive for many years. It was an Irishman named Mitchell who laid out the site of Atlanta, the metropolis of the South; an O'Brien founded the city of Augusta; and a McCormick named the city of Dublin, Georgia.

From the records of the Carolinas we obtain similar data, many of an absorbingly interesting character, and the number of places in that section bearing names of a decidedly Celtic flavor is striking evidence of the presence of Irish people, the line of whose settlements across the whole State of North Carolina may be traced on the high roads leading from Pennsylvania and Virginia. Hawk, one of the historians of North Carolina, refers to the "Irish Romanists" who were resident in that Province as early as 1700, and Williamson says that "the most numerous settlers in the northwestern part of the Province during the first half of the eighteenth century were from Ireland." The manuscript records in the office of the Secretary of State refer to "a ship load of immigrants" who, in the year 1761, came to the Carolinas from Dublin. The names of the Irish pioneers in the Carolinas are found in every conceivable connection, in the parochial and court records, in the will books, in the minutes of the general Assembly, in the quaint old records of the Land and Registers' offices, in the patents granted by the colonial Government, and in sundry other official records. In public affairs they seem to have had the same adaptability for politics which, among other things, has in later days brought their countrymen into prominence. Florence O'Sullivan from Kerry was surveyor-general of South Carolina in 1671. James Moore, a native of Ireland and a descendant of the famous Irish chieftain, Rory O'More, was governor of South Carolina in 1700; Matthew Rowan from Carrickfergus was president of the North Carolina Council during the term of office of his townsman, Governor Arthur Dobbs (1754 to 1764); John Connor was attorney-general of the Province in 1730, and was succeeded in turn by David O'Sheall and Thomas McGuire. Cornelius Hartnett, Hugh Waddell, and Terence Sweeny, all Irishmen, were members of the Court, and among the members of the provincial assembly I find such names as Murphy, Leary, Kearney, McLewean, Dunn, Keenan,

McManus, Ryan, Bourke, Logan, and others showing an Irish origin. And, in this connection, we must not overlook Thomas Burke, a native of "the City of the Tribes", distinguished as lawyer, soldier, and statesman, who became governor of North Carolina in 1781, as did his cousin Aedanus Burke, also from Galway, who was judge of the Supreme Court of South Carolina in 1778. John Rutledge, son of Dr. John Rutledge from Ireland, was governor of South Carolina in 1776 and his brother Edward became governor of the State in 1788.

But there were Irishmen in the Carolinas long before the advent of these, and indeed Irish names are found occasionally as far back as the records of those colonies reach. They are scattered profusely through the will books and records of deeds as early as 1676 and down to the end of the century, and in a list of immigrants from Barbados in the year 1678, quoted by John Camden Hotten in the work already alluded to, we find about 120 persons of Irish name who settled in the Carolinas in that year. In 1719, 500 persons from Ireland transported themselves to Carolina to take the benefit of an Act passed by the Assembly by which the lands of the Yemmassee Indians were thrown open to settlers, and Ramsay (*History of South Carolina,* vol. I, page 20) says: "Of all countries none has furnished the Province with so many inhabitants as Ireland."

In the Pennsylvania records one is also struck with the very frequent mention of Irish names. William Penn had lived in Ireland for several years and was acquainted with the sturdy character of its people, and when he arrived on board *The Welcome* in 1682 he had with him a number of Irishmen, who are described as "people of property and people of consequence." In 1699 he brought over a brilliant young Irishman, James Logan from Lurgan, who for nearly half a century occupied a leading position in the Province and for some time was its governor. But the first Irish immigration to Pennsylvania of any numerical importance came in the year 1717. They settled in Lancaster County. "They and their descendants," says Rupp, an impartial historian, "have always been justly regarded as among the most intelligent people in the County and their progress will be found to be but little behind the boasted efforts of the Colony of Plymouth." In 1727, as the records show, 1155 Irish people arrived in Philadelphia and in 1728 the number reached the high total of 5600. "It looks as if Ireland is to send all her inhabitants hither," wrote Secretary Logan to the provincial proprietors in 1729, "for last week not less than six ships arrived. The common fear is that if they continue to come they will make themselves proprietors of the Province" (Rupp's *History of Dauphin County*).

The continuous stream of Irish immigration was viewed with so much alarm by the Legislature, that in 1728 a law was passed "against these crowds of Irish papists and convicts who are yearly powr'd upon us"—(the "convicts" being the political refugees who fled from the persecutions of the English Government!). But the operations of this statute were wholly nullified by the captains of the vessels landing their passengers at Newcastle, Del., and Burlington, N. J., and, as one instance of this, I find in the Philadelphia *American Weekly Mercury* of August 14, 1729, a statement to this effect: "It is reported from Newcastle that there arrived there this last week about 2000 Irish and an abundance more daily expected." This expectation was realized, for according to "An Account of Passengers and Servants landed in Philadelphia between December 25, 1728, and December 25, 1729", which I find in the *New England Weekly Journal* for March 30, 1730, the number of Irish who came in via the Delaware river in that year was 5655, while the total number of all other Europeans who arrived during the same period was only 553. Holmes, in his *Annals of America,* corroborates this. The Philadelphia newspapers down to the year 1741 also contained many similar references, indicating that the flood of Irish immigration was unceasing and that it was at all times in excess of that from other European countries. Later issues of the *Mercury* also published accounts of the number of ships from Ireland which arrived in the Delaware, and from these it appears that from 1735 to 1738 "66 vessels entered Philadelphia from Ireland and 50 cleared thereto." And in the *New York*

Gazette and Weekly Post-Boy of the years 1750 to 1752, I find under the caption, "Vessels Registered at the Philadelphia Custom House," a total of 183 ships destined from or to Ireland, or an average of five sailings per month between Irish ports and the port of Philadelphia alone. A careful search fails to disclose any record of the number of persons who came in these ships, but, from the fact that it is stated that all carried passengers as well as merchandise from Irish ports, we may safely assume that the "human freight" must have been very large.

Spencer, in his *History of the United States,* says: "In the years 1771 and 1772 the number of emigrants to America from Ireland was 17,350, almost all of whom emigrated at their own expense. A great majority of them consisted of persons employed in the linen manufacture or farmers possessed of some property, which they converted into money and brought with them. Within the first fortnight of August, 1773, there arrived at Philadelphia 3500 immigrants from Ireland. As most of the emigrants, particularly those from Ireland and Scotland, were personally discontent with their treatment in Europe, their accession to the colonial population, it might reasonably be supposed, had no tendency to diminish or counteract the hostile sentiments toward Britain which were daily gathering force in America." Marmion, in his *Ancient and Modern History of the Maritime Ports of Ireland,* verifies this. He says that the number of Irish who came during the years 1771, 1772, and 1773 was 25,000. The bulk of these came in by way of Philadelphia and settled in Pennsylvania and the Virginias.

The Irish were arriving in the Province in such great numbers during this period as to be the cause of considerable jealousy on the part of other settlers from continental Europe. They were a vigorous and aggressive element. Eager for that freedom which was denied them at home, large numbers of them went out on the frontier. While the war-whoop of the savage still echoed within the surrounding valleys and his council fires blazed upon the hills, those daring adventurers penetrated the hitherto pathless wilderness and passed through unexampled hardships with heroic endurance. They opened up the roads, bridged the streams, and cut down the forests, turning the wilderness into a place fit for man's abode. With their sturdy sons, they constituted the skirmish line of civilization, standing as a bulwark against Indian incursions into the more prosperous and populous settlements between them and the coast. From 1740 down to the period of the Revolution, hardly a year passed without a fresh infusion of Irish blood into the existing population, and, as an indication that they distributed themselves all over the Province, I find, in every Town and County history of Pennsylvania and in the land records of every section, Irish names in the greatest profusion. They settled in great numbers chiefly along the Susquehanna and its tributaries; they laid out many prosperous settlements in the wilderness of western Pennsylvania, and in these sections Irishmen are seen occupying some of the foremost and most coveted positions, and their sons in after years contributed much to the power and commercial greatness of the Commonwealth. They are mentioned prominently as manufacturers, merchants, and farmers, and in the professions they occupied a place second to none among the natives of the State. In several sections, they were numerous enough to establish their own independent settlements, to which they gave the names of their Irish home places, several of which are preserved to this day. It is not to be wondered at then that General Harry Lee named the Pennsylvania line of the Continental army, "the Line of Ireland"!

Ireland gave many eminent men to the Commonwealth, among whom may be mentioned: John Burns, its first governor after the adoption of the Constitution, who was born in Dublin; George Bryan, also a native of Dublin, who was its governor in 1788; James O'Hara, one of the founders of Pittsburgh; Thomas FitzSimmons, a native of Limerick, member of the first Congress under the Constitution which began the United States Government and father of the policy of protection to American industries; Matthew Carey from Dublin, the famous political economist; and many others who were prominent as nation-builders in the early days of the "Keystone State."

While the historians usually give all the credit to England and to Englishmen for the early colonization of New England, whose results have been attended with such important consequences to America and the civilized world, Ireland and her sons can also claim a large part in the development of this territory, as is evidenced by the town, land, church, and other colonial records, and the names of the pioneers, as well as the names given to several of the early settlements. That the Irish had been coming to New England almost from the beginning of the English colonization is indicated by an "Order" entered in the Massachusetts record under date of September 25, 1634, granting liberty to "the Scottishe and Irishe gentlemen who intend to come hither, to sitt down in any place upp Merimacke river." This, doubtless, referred to a Scotch and Irish company which, about that time, had announced its intention of founding a settlement on the Merrimac. It comprised in all 140 passengers, who embarked in the *Eagle Wing,* from Carrickfergus in September, 1636, bringing with them a considerable quantity of equipment and merchandise to meet the exigencies of their settlement in the new country. The vessel, however, never reached its destination and was obliged to return to Ireland on account of the Atlantic storms, and there is no record of a renewal of the attempt. In the Massachusetts records of the year 1640 (vol. I, p. 295) is another entry relating to "the persons come from Ireland," and in the Town Books of Boston may be seen references to Irishmen who were residents of the town in that year.

From local histories, which in many cases are but verbatim copies of the original entries in the Town Books, we get occasional glimpses of the Irish who were in the colony of Massachusetts Bay between this period and the end of the century. For example, between 1640 and 1660, such names as O'Neill, Sexton, Gibbons, Lynch, Keeney, Kelly, and Hogan appear on the Town records of Hartford, and one of the first schoolmasters who taught the children of the Puritans in New Haven was an Irishman named William Collins, who, in the year 1640, came there with a number of Irish refugees from Barbados Island. An Irishman named Joseph Collins with his wife and family came to Lynn, Mass., in 1635. Richard Duffy and

(14)

Matthias Curran were at Ipswich in 1633. John Kelly came to Newbury in 1635 with the first English settlers of the town. David O'Killia (or O'Kelly) was a resident of Old Yarmouth in 1657, and I find on various records of that section a great number of people named Kelley, who probably were descended from David O'Killia. Peter O'Kelly and his family are mentioned as of Dorchester in 1696. At Springfield in 1656 there were families named Riley and O'Dea; and Richard Burke, said to be of the Mayo family of that name, is mentioned prominently in Middlesex County as early as 1670. The first legal instrument of record in Hampden County was a deed of conveyance in the year 1683 to one Patrick Riley of lands in Chicopee. With a number of his countrymen, Riley located in this vicinity and gave the name of "Ireland Parish" to their settlement. John Molooney and Daniel MacGuinnes were at Woburn in 1676, and Michael Bacon, "an Irishman", of Woburn, fought in King Philip's war in 1675. John Joyce was at Lynn in 1637, and I find the names of Willyam Heally, William Reyle, William Barrett, and Roger Burke signed to a petition to the General Court of Massachusetts on August 17, 1664. Such names as Maccarty, Gleason, Coggan, Lawler, Kelly, Hurley, MackQuade, and McCleary also appear on the Cambridge Church records down to 1690. These are but desultory instances of the first comers among the Irish to Massachusetts, selected from a great mass of similar data.

In the early history of every town in Massachusetts, without exception, I find mention of Irish people, and while the majority came originally as "poor redemptioners", yet, in course of time and despite Puritanical prejudices, not a few of them rose to positions of worth and independence. Perhaps the most noted of these was Matthew Lyon of Vermont, known as "the Hampden of Congress," who, on his arrival in New York in 1765, was sold as a "redemptioner" to pay his passage-money. This distinguished American was a native of county Wicklow. Other notable examples of Irish redemptioners who attained eminence in America were George Taylor, a native of Dublin, one of Pennsylvania's signers of the Declaration of Independence; Charles Thompson, a native of county Tyrone, "the perennial Secretary of the Continental Congress", and

William Killen, who became chief justice and chancellor of Delaware. Some of the descendants of the Irish redemptioners in Massachusetts are found among the prominent New Englanders of the past hundred years. The Puritans of Massachusetts extended no welcoming hand to the Irish who had the temerity to come among them, yet, as an historical writer has truly said, "by one of those strange transformations which time occasionally works, it has come to pass that Massachusetts today contains more people of Irish blood in proportion to the total population than any other State in the Union."

So great and so continuous was Irish immigration to Massachusetts during the early part of the eighteenth century that on Saint Patrick's Day in the year 1737 a number of merchants, who described themselves as "of the Irish Nation residing in Boston," formed the Charitable Irish Society, an organization which exists even to the present day. It was provided that the officers should be "natives of Ireland or of Irish extraction," and they announced that the Society was organized "in an affectionate and Compassionate concern for their countrymen in these Parts who may be reduced by Sickness, Shipwrack, Old Age, and other Infirmities and unforeseen Accidents." I have copied from the Town Books, as reproduced by the City of Boston, 1600 Irish names of persons who were married or had declared their intentions of marriage in Boston between the years 1710 and 1790, exclusive of 956 other Irish names which appear on the minutes between 1720 and 1775.

In 1718, one of the largest single colonies of Irish arrived in Boston. It consisted of one hundred families, who settled at different places in Massachusetts. One contingent, headed by Edward Fitzgerald, located at Worcester and another at Palmer under the leadership of Robert Farrell, while a number went to the already established settlement at Londonderry, N. H. About the same time a colony of fishermen from the west coast of Ireland settled on the Cape Cod peninsula, and I find a number of them recorded on the marriage registers of the towns in this vicinity between 1719 and 1743. In 1720, a number of families from county Tyrone came to Shrewsbury, and eight years later another large contingent came to Leicester County from the same neighborhood, who gave the name of

Dublin to the section where they located. The annals of Leicester County are rich in Irish names. On the Town Books of various places in this vicinity and on the rosters of the troops enrolled for the Indian war, Irishmen are recorded, and we learn from the records that not a few of them were important and useful men, active in the development of the settlements, and often chosen as selectmen or representatives. On the minutes of the meetings of the selectmen of Pelham, Spencer, Sutton, Charlestown, Canton, Scituate, Stoughton, Salem, Amesbury, Stoneham, and other Massachusetts towns, Irish names are recorded many years before the Revolution. In local histories these people are usually called "Scotch-Irish," a racial misnomer that has been very much overworked by a certain class of historical writers who seem to be unable to understand that a non-Catholic native of Ireland can be an Irishman. In an exhaustive study of American history, I cannot find any other race where such a distinction is drawn as in the case of the non-Catholic, or so-called "Scotch," Irish. In many instances, this hybrid racial designation obviously springs from prejudice and a desire to withhold from Ireland any credit that may belong to her, although, in some cases, the writers are genuinely mistaken in their belief that the Scotch as a race are the antithesis of the Irish and that whatever commendable qualities the non-Catholic Irish are possessed of naturally spring from the Scotch.

The first recorded Irish settlement in Maine was made by families named Kelly and Haley from Galway, who located on the Isles of Shoals about the year 1653. In 1692, Roger Kelly was a representative from the Isles to the General Court of Massachusetts, and is described in local annals as "King of the Isles." The large number of islands, bays, and promontories on the Maine coast bearing distinctive Celtic names attests the presence and influence of Irish people in this section in colonial times. In 1720, Robert Temple from Cork brought to Maine five shiploads of people, mostly from the province of Munster. They landed at the junction of the Kennebec and Eastern rivers, where they established the town of Cork, which, however, after a precarious existence of only six years, was entirely destroyed by the Indians. For nearly a century the place was familiarly known to the residents of the locality as "Ireland." The records of York, Lincoln, and Cumberland counties contain references to large numbers of Irish people who settled in those localities during the early years of the eighteenth century. The Town Books of Georgetown, Kittery, and Kennebunkport, of the period 1740 to 1775, are especially rich in Irish names, and in the Saco Valley numerous settlements were made by Irish immigrants, not a few of whom are referred to by local historians as "men of wealth and social standing." In the marriage and other records of Limerick, Me., as published by the Maine Historical and Genealogical Recorder, in the marriage registers of the First Congregational Church of Scarborough, and in other similarly unquestionable records, I find a surprisingly large number of Irish names at various periods during the seventeenth and eighteenth centuries. In fact, there is not one town in the Province that did not have its quota of Irish people, who came either direct from Ireland or migrated from other sections of New England.

The records of New Hampshire and Rhode Island are also a fruitful source of information on this subject, and the Provincial papers indicate an almost unbroken tide of Irish immigration to this section, beginning as early as the year 1640. One of the most noted of Exeter's pioneer settlers was an Irishman named Darby Field, who came to that place in 1631 and who has been credited by Governor Winthrop as "the first European who witnessed the White Mountains." He is also recorded as "an Irish soldier for discovery," and I find his name in the annals of Exeter as one of the grantees of an Indian deed dated April 3, 1638, as well as several other Irish names down to the year 1664. In examining the town registers, gazeteers, and genealogies, as well as the local histories of New Hampshire, in which are embodied copies of the original entries made by the Town Clerks, I find numerous references to the Irish pioneers, and in many instances they are written down, among others, as "the first settlers." Some are mentioned as selectmen, town clerks, representatives, or colonial soldiers, and it is indeed remarkable that there is not one of these authorities that I have examined, out of more than two hundred, that does not contain Irish names. From these Irish pioneers sprang many men who attained prominence in New Hampshire, in the legislature, the professions, the military, the arts and crafts, and in all departments of civil life, down to the present time. In the marriage registers of Portsmouth, Boscawen, New Boston, Antrim, Londonderry, and other New Hampshire towns, are recorded, in some cases as early as 1716, names of Irish persons, with the places of their nativity, indicating that they came from all parts of Ireland. At Hampton, I find Humphrey Sullivan teaching school in 1714, while the name of John Sullivan from Limerick, schoolmaster at Dover and at Berwick, Me., for upwards of fifty years, is one of the most honored in early New Hampshire history.

This John Sullivan was surely one of the grandest characters in the Colony of Massachusetts Bay, and the record of his descendants serves as an all-sufficient reply to the anti-Irish prejudices of some American historians. He was the father of a governor of New Hampshire and of a governor of Massachusetts; of an attorney-general of New Hampshire and of an attorney-general of Massachusetts; of New Hampshire's only major-general in the Continental army; of the first judge appointed by Washington in New Hampshire; and of four sons who were officers in the Continental army. He was grandfather of an attorney-general of New Hampshire, of a governor of Maine, and of a United States Senator from New Hampshire. He was great-grandfather of an attorney-general of New Hampshire, and great-great-grandfather of an officer in the Thirteenth New Hampshire regiment in the Civil War.

In Rhode Island, Irish people are on record as far back as 1640, and for many years after that date they continued to come. Edward Larkin was an esteemed citizen of Newport in 1655. Charles McCarthy was one of the founders of the town of East Greenwich in 1677, while in this vicinity as early as 1680 are found such names as Casey, Higgins, Magennis, Kelley, Murphy, Reylie, Maloney, Healy, Delaney, Walsh, and others of Irish origin. On the rosters of the Colonial militia who fought in King Philip's war (1675) are found the names of 110 soldiers of Irish birth or descent, some of whom, for their services at the battle of Narragansett, received grants of land in New Hampshire and Massachusetts. The New England Historical and Genealogical Register for 1848 contains some remarkable testimony of the sympathy of the people of Ireland for the sufferers in this cruel war, and the "Irish Donation," sent out from Dublin in the year 1676, will always stand in history to Ireland's credit and as an instance of her intimate familiarity with American affairs, one hundred years prior to that Revolution which emancipated the people of this land from the same tyranny under which she herself has groaned. And yet, what a cruel travesty on history it reads like now, when we scan the official records of the New England colonies and find that the Irish were often called "convicts", and it was thought that measures should be taken to prevent their landing on the soil where they and their sons afterwards shed their blood in the cause of their fellow colonists! In the minutes of the provincial Assemblies and in the reports rendered to the General Court, as well as in other official documents of the period, are found expressions of the sentiment which prevailed against the natives of the "Island of Sorrows." Only twenty years before the outbreak of King Philip's war, the government of England was asked to provide a law "to prevent the importation of Irish Papists and convicts that are yearly pow'rd upon us and to make provision against the growth of this pernicious evil." And the colonial Courts themselves, on account of what they called "the cruel and malignant spirit that has from time to time been manifest in the Irish nation against the English nation," prohibited "the bringing over of any Irish men, women, or children into this jurisdiction on the penalty of fifty pounds sterling to each inhabitant who shall buy of any merchant, shipmaster, or other agent any such person or persons so transported by them." This order was promulgated by the General Court of Massachusetts in October, 1654, and is given in full in the American Historical Review for October, 1896.

With the "convicts" and the "redemptioners" came the Irish

schoolmaster, the man then most needed in America. And the fighting man, he too was to the fore, for when the colonies in after years called for volunteers to resist the tyranny of the British, the descendants of the Irish "convicts" were among the first and the most eager to answer the call.

Although it does not appear that Irish immigrants settled in the Province of New York in such large numbers as in other sections, yet, as far back as the third quarter of the seventeenth century, Irish names are found on the records of the Colony. O'Callaghan, the eminent archivist and historian, refers to "Dr. William Hayes, formerly of Barry's Court, Ireland," as one of New York's physicians in the year 1647, and from the same authority we learn that there were "settlers and Indian fighters in New Netherland" named Barrett, Fitzgerald, Dowdall, Collins, and Quinn in 1657. In records relating to the war with the Esopus Indians (1663), and in fact as early as 1658, frequent references are made to "Thomas the Irishman", whose name was Thomas Lewis, a refugee from Ireland to Holland after the Cromwellian war. Lewis is on record in 1683 as one of the wealthiest merchants of New York and a large owner of real estate in the present downtown portion of the city. Such names as Patrick Hayes, John Daly, John Quigly, and Dennis McKarty appear among its business men between 1666 and 1672, and in a "Census of the City of New York of the year 1703" we find people named Flynn, Walsh, Dooley, Gillen, Carroll, Kenne, Gurney, Hart, Mooney, Moran, Lynch, Kearney, and others, all "Freemen of the City of New York." In the "Poll List" of the city from 1741 to 1761, more than one hundred such names appear, while among the advertisers in the New York newspapers all through the eighteenth century I find a large number of characteristic Irish names.

One would scarcely expect to find an Irishman in the old Dutch settlement of Beverwyck as early as 1645. Yet such is the case, for "Jan Andriessen, de Iersman van Dublingh"—(John Anderson, the Irishman from Dublin)—is mentioned as the owner of considerable landed property in the neighborhood of Albany and Catskill, and in every mention of this ancient pioneer he is referred to as "the Irishman." At Albany, between 1666 and 1690, we find people named Connell, Daly, Larkin, Shaw, Hogan, and Finn, all Irishmen, and in Jonathan Pearson's "Genealogies of the First Settlers of the Ancient County of Albany" and·in his "Genealogies of the First Settlers of the Patent and City of Schenectady", I find 135 distinctive Irish names. These were mostly merchants, farmers, artisans, millers, and backwoodsmen, the pioneers, who, with their Dutch neighbors, blazed the trail of civilization through that section, rolled back the savage redman, and marked along the banks of the Hudson and Mohawk rivers the sites of future towns and cities. In the rate lists of Long Island between 1638 and 1675, I find Kelly, Dalton, Whelan, Condon, Barry, Powers, Quin, Kane, Sweeney, Murphy, Reilly, as well as Norman-Irish and Anglo-Irish names that are common to Irish nomenclature. Hugh O'Neale was a prominent resident of Newtown, L. I., in 1655. In a "Report to the Lord President," dated September 6, 1687, Governor Dongan recommended "that natives of Ireland be sent to colonize here where they may live and be very happy." Numbers of them evidently accepted the invitation, for many Irishmen are mentioned in the public documents of the Province during the succeeding twenty years.

That the Irish continued to settle in the Province all through the eighteenth century may be seen from the announcements in the New York newspapers of the time and other authentic records. The most important of these, in point of numbers and character of the immigrants, were those made in Orange County in 1729 under the leadership of James Clinton from Longford, and at Cherry Valley, in Otsego County, twelve years later. On the Orange County assessment and Revolutionary rolls, and down to the year 1800, there is a very large number of Irish names, and in some sections they constituted nearly the entire population. In the northwestern part of New York, Irishmen are also found about the time of the Franco-English war. They were not only among those settlers who followed the peaceful pursuits of tilling and building, but they were "the men behind the guns" who held the marauding Indians in check and repelled the advances of the French through that territory. In this war, Irish soldiers fought on both sides, and in the "Journals of the Marquis of Montcalm" may be seen references to the English garrison at Oswego, which, in August, 1756, surrendered to that same Irish Brigade by which they had been defeated eleven years before on the battlefield of Fontenoy. In the "Manuscripts of Sir William Johnson", are also found some interesting items indicating that Irishmen were active participants in the frontier fighting about that time, and in one report to him, dated May 28, 1756, from the commandant of an English regiment, reference is made to "the great numbers of Irish Papists among the Delaware and Susquehanna Indians who have done a world of prejudice to English interests."

The early records, with hardly an exception, contain Irish names, showing that the "Exiles from Erin" came to the Province of New York in considerable numbers during the eighteenth century. The baptismal and marriage records of the Dutch Reformed and Protestant churches of New York City; of the Dutch churches at Kingston, Albany, Schenectady, and other towns; the muster rolls of the troops enrolled for the French, Indian, and Revolutionary wars; the Land Grants and other provincial records at Albany; the newspapers; the Town, County, and family histories, and other early chronicles, supplemented by authoritative publications such as those of the New York Historical and Genealogical and Biographical Societies—these are the depositories of the evidence that thousands of Irish people settled in the Province of New York and constituted no inconsiderable proportion of the total population.

The majority of the Irish residents of New York whose marriages are recorded in the Dutch Reformed church were, doubtless, of the Catholic faith, but, as it was necessary to comply with the established law, and also so that their offspring might be legitimate, they could be bound in wedlock only by a recognized Minister of the Gospel. As there was no Catholic church in New York prior to 1786, the ceremony had to be performed in the Dutch Reformed or Protestant church. Many of these Catholics were refugees from Ireland on account of the religious persecutions. Like the people of Ireland in all ages, they were devoted to their religion, and while, no doubt, they eschewed for a while association with the established churches, yet, as time went on, they and their children were gradually drawn into religious intercourse with the other sects, until eventually they became regular communicants of those churches. The variations which from time to time were wrought in their names brought them further and further away from what they had been; in their new surroundings, both social and religious, they themselves changed, so that their children, who in many cases married into the neighboring Dutch and French families, became as wholly un-Irish in manner and sentiment as if they had sprung from an entirely different race. That fact, however, does not admit of their being now included in the category "Anglo-Saxon."

In a work entitled "Names of Persons for whom Marriage Licenses were issued by the Secretary of the Province of New York, previous to 1784," compiled by Gideon J. Tucker (when Secretary of State), and taken from the early records of the office of the Secretary of State at Albany, we find ample corroboration of the church records. Page after page of this book looks more like some record of the Province of Munster than of the Province of New York. It is a quarto volume printed in small type in double columns, and there are eleven pages wholly devoted to persons whose names commence with "Mac" and three to the "O's." Nearly every name common to Ireland is here represented.

New York, as a Province and as a State, is much indebted to Irish genius. Ireland gave the Province its most noted governor in the person of Thomas Dongan from Co. Kildare, and in later years Sir William Johnson from Co. Meath, governor of the Indians from New York to the Mississippi. It gave the State its first governor, George Clinton, son of an immigrant from Co. Longford, and to the city its first mayor after the Revolution, James Duane, son of Anthony Duane from Co. Galway. Fulton, an Irishman's son, gave America priority in the "conquest of the seas." Christopher Colles, a native of Cork, was the originator of the grand scheme which united the waters of the Atlantic and the Lakes—one of the greatest works of internal improvement ever effected in the United States—while the gigantic project was carried to a successful end through the influence and direction of Governor DeWitt Clinton, the grandson of an Irishman.

Many of the pioneer settlers of New Jersey were Irish. As early as 1683 "a colony from Tipperary in Ireland" located at Cohansey in Salem County, and in the same year a number of settlers, also described as "from Tipperary, Ireland," located in Monmouth County. In the County records of New Jersey, Irish names are met with frequently between the years 1676 and 1698. Several of the local historians testify to the presence and influence of Irishmen in the early days of the colony, and in the voluminous "New Jersey Archives" may be found references to the large numbers of Irish "redemptioners," some of whom, after their terms of service had expired, received grants of land and in time became prosperous farmers and merchants. Perhaps the most noted Irishman in New Jersey in colonial days was Michael Kearney, a native of Cork and ancestor of General Philip Kearney of Civil War fame, who was secretary and treasurer of the Province in 1723.

All through the west and southwest, Irishmen are found in the earliest days of authentic history. Along the Ohio, Kentucky, Wabash, and Tennessee rivers they were with the pioneers who first trod the wilderness of that vast territory. As early as 1690, an Irish trader named Doherty crossed the mountains into what is now Kentucky, and we are told by Filson, the noted French historian and explorer of Kentucky, that "the first white man who discovered this region" (1754) was one James McBride, who, in all probability, was an Irishman. The first white child born in Cincinnati was a son of an Irish settler named John Cummins; the first house built on its site was erected by Captain Hugh McGarry, while "the McGarrys, Dentons, and Hogans formed the first domestic circle in Kentucky." Prior to the Revolution, Indian traders from western Pennsylvania had penetrated into this region, and we learn from authentic sources that no small percentage of those itinerant merchants of the west were Irishmen. Among the leading and earliest colonists of the "Blue Grass State" who accompanied Daniel Boone, the ubiquitous Irish were represented by men bearing such names as Mooney, Mc-Manus, Sullivan, Drennon, Logan, Casey, Fitzpatrick, Dunlevy, Cassidy, Doran, Dougherty, Lynch, Ryan, McNeill, McGee, Reilly, Flinn, and the noted McAfee brothers, all natives of Ireland or sons of Irish immigrants.

Irishmen and their sons figured prominently in the field of early western politics. In the Kentucky legislature, I find such names as Connor, Cassidy, Cleary, Conway, Casey, Cavan, Dulin, Dougherty, Geohegan, Maher, Morrison, Moran, McMahon, McFall, McClanahan, O'Bannon, Powers, and a number of others evidently of Irish origin. On the bench we find O'Hara, Boyle, and Barry. Among the many distinguished men who reflecte d honor upon the west, Judge William T. Barry of Lexington ranks high for great ability and lofty virtues. Simon Kenton, famed in song and story, who "battled with the Indians in a hundred encounters and wrested Kentucky from the savage," was an Irishman's son, while among its famous Indian fighters were Colonels Andrew Hynes, William Casey, and John O'Bannon; Majors Bulger, McMullin, McGarry, McBride, Butler, and Cassidy; and Captains McMahon, Malarkie, Doyle, Phelon, and Brady. Allen, Butler, Campbell, Montgomery, and Rowan counties, Ky., are named after natives of Ireland, and Boyle, Breckinridge, Carroll, Casey, Daviess, Magoffin, Kenton, McCracken, Meade, Menifee, Clinton, and Fulton counties were named in honor of descendants of Irish settlers.

In the councils of the first territorial legislature of Missouri were Sullivan, Cassidy, Murphy, McDermid, McGrady, Flaugherty, McGuire, Dunn, and Hogan, and among the merchants, lawyers, and bankers in the pioneer days of St. Louis there were a number of Irishmen, the most noted of whom were Mullanphy, Gilhuly, O'Fallon, Connor, O'Hara, Dillon, Ranken, Magennis, and Walsh. In all early histories of Missouri towns and counties, Irish names are mentioned, and in many instances they are on record as "the first settlers."

And so it was all through the west. In Ohio, Indiana, Iowa, and Illinois, across the rolling prairies and the mountains, beyond the Mississippi and the Missouri, in the earliest days of colonization of that vast territory, we can follow the Irish "trek" in quest of new homes and fortunes. They were part of that irresistible human current that swept beyond the ranges of Colorado and Kansas and across the Sierra Nevada until it reached the Pacific, and in the forefront of those pathfinders and pioneers we find Martin Murphy, the first to open a wagon trail to California from the East. The names of Don Timoteo Murphy, of Jasper O'Farrell, of Dolans, Burkes, Breens, and Hallorins are linked with the annals of the coast while that territory was still under Spanish rule, and when Fremont crossed the plains and planted the "Bear flag" beyond the Sierras, we find Irishmen among his trusted lieutenants. An Irishman, Captain Patrick Connor, first penetrated the wilderness of Utah; a descendant of an Irishman, Hall J. Kelly, was the explorer of Oregon; Philip Nolan and Thomas O'Connor were foremost among those brave spirits "whose daring and persistency finally added the Lone Star State to the American Union"; and the famous Arctic explorer, scientist, and scholar, Dr. Elisha Kent Kane, was a descendant of John O'Kane who came from Ireland to the Province of New York in 1752.

To form any reliable estimate of the numerical strength of the Irish and their descendants in the United States would, I believe, be a hopeless task, and while several have attempted to do so, I am of the opinion that all such estimates should be discarded as mere conjecture. Indeed, there is no standard, or fixed rule or principle, by which a correct judgment of the racial composition of the early inhabitants of the United States can now be formed, and the available statistics on the subject are incomplete and confusing. The greatest obstacle in determining this question is found in the names of the immigrants themselves. With names such as Smith, Mason, Carpenter, and Taylor; White, Brown, Black, and Gray; Forrest, Wood, Mountain, and Vail, and other names that are similarly derived, the first thought is that they are of English origin. Yet we know that for centuries past such names have been numerous in Ireland, and there are many Irish

families so named who are of as pure Celtic blood as any
bearing the old Gaelic patronymics. By a law passed in the
second year of the reign of Edward IV., natives of Ireland
were forced to adopt English surnames. This Act was, substantially, as follows: "An Act that Irishmen dwelling in the
Counties of, etc. ....shall go appareled like Englishmen
and wear their beards in English manner, swear allegiance
and take English sirnames, which sirnames shall be of one
towne, as Sutton, Chester, Trim, Skryne, Cork, Kinsale; or
colours, as white, black, brown; or arts, or sciences, as smith
or carpenter; or office, as cook, butler, etc., and it is enacted
that he and his issue shall use his name under pain of for-
feyting of his goods yearly", etc.

This Act could be enforced only upon those Irish families
who dwelt within the reach of English law, and as emigrants
from those districts, deprived of their pure Celtic names, came
to America in an English guise and in English vessels, they
were officially recorded as "English." Moreover, numbers of
Irish frequently crossed the channel and began their voyage
from English ports, where they had to take on new names,
sometimes arbitrarily, and sometimes voluntarily for purposes
of concealment, either by transforming their original names
into English or adopting names similar to those above referred
to. These names were generally retained on this side of the
Atlantic so as not to arouse the prejudice of their English
neighbors. In complying with the statute above quoted, some
Irish families accepted the rather doubtful privilege of trans-
lating their names into their English equivalents. We have
examples of this in such names as Somers, anglicised from
McGauran (presumably derived from the Gaelic word signify-
ing "summer"); Smith from McGowan (meaning "the son of
the smith"); Jackson and Johnson, a literal translation from
MacShane (meaning "the son of John"); and Whitcomb from
Kiernan (meaning, literally, "a white comb").

In addition to this, in the case of some of those Irish immigrants whose family names were not changed in Ireland, their
descendants appear in a much disguised form in the colonial
records. Through the mistakes of clergymen, court clerks,
registrars, and others who had difficulty in pronouncing Gaelic

names, letters became inserted or dropped and the names were written down phonetically. In the mutations of time, even these names became still further changed, and we find that the descendants of the Irish themselves, after the lapse of a generation or two, deliberately changed their names, usually by suppressing the Milesian prefixes, "Mac" and "O". Thus we have the Laflin and Claflin families, who are descended from a McLaughlin, an Irish settler in Massachusetts in the seventeenth century; the Bryans from William O'Brian, a captain in Sarsfield's army, who, after the fall of Limerick in 1691, settled in Pasquetank County, N. C., and one of whose descendants is William Jennings Bryan, now Secretary of State; the Dunnels of Maine, from an O'Donnell who located in the Saco Valley; and at the Land Office at Annapolis I have found the descendants of Roger O'Dewe, who came to Maryland about 1665, recorded under the surnames of "Roger", "Dew", and "Dewey". I find Dennis O'Deeve or O'Deere written down on the Talbot County (Md.) records of the year 1667 with his name reversed, and today his descendants are known as "Dennis". Many such instances appear in the early records, and when we find a New England family rejoicing in the name of "Navillus" we know that the limit has been reached, and while we cannot admire the attempt to disguise an ancient and honorable name, we are amused at the obvious transposition of "Sullivan".

Thus we see, that, numerous though the old Irish names are on American records, they do not by any means indicate the extent of the Celtic element which established itself in the colonies, so that there is really no means of determining exactly what Ireland has contributed to the American Commonwealth. We only know that a steady stream of Irish immigrants has crossed the seas to the American continent, beginning with the middle of the seventeenth century, and that many of those "Exiles from Erin", or their sons, became prominent as leaders in every station in life in the new country.

Nor is the "First Census of the United States" any criterion in this regard, for the obvious reason that the enumerators made no returns of unmarried persons. This fact is important when we consider that the Irish exodus of the eighteenth century was largely comprised of the youth of the country. Although the First Census was made in 1790, the first regular record of immigration was not begun until thirty years later, and it is only from the records kept after that time that we can depend upon actual official figures. During the decade following 1820, Ireland contributed more than forty per cent. of the entire immigration to America from all European countries, and the Irish Emigration Statistics show that between 1830 and 1907 the number of people who left Ireland was 6,049,432, the majority of whom came to America.

The *Westminster Review* (vol. 133, p. 293), in an article on "The Irish-Americans", puts a series of questions as follows: "Is the American Republic in any way indebted to those Irish citizens? Have they with their large numbers, high social standing, great places of trust, contributed aught to her glory or added aught to her commercial greatness, refined her social taste or assisted in laying the foundations of the real happiness of her people, the real security of her laws, the influence of her civic virtues, which more than anything else give power and permanency to a naissant and mighty nation? The answer is unquestionably affirmative. We have only to look back on the past, and to scan the present state of American affairs, to feel certain of this." If it be further asked: "Does this statement stand the test of strict investigation?" the answer must also be in the affirmative, for in almost every line of progress the Irish in America have contributed their share of leaders and pioneers, thus proving that there are characteristics among even the poor Irish driven to emigration for an existence that are as capable of development as those possessed by any other race. When we scan the intellectual horizon, we see many men of great force of character: preachers and teachers; statesmen and scholars; philanthropists and founders of institutions; scientists and engineers; historians and journalists; artists and authors; lawyers and doctors, of Celtic race and blood, while, in the industrial field, as builders of steamships and railroads and promoters of public works, as merchants, manufacturers, and bankers, and in all other fields of endeavor, we find the

American Irish controlling factors in the upbuilding of the Republic.

Of the signers of the Declaration of Independence, Thornton, Taylor, and Smith were natives of Ireland; McKean, Read, and Rutledge were of Irish parentage; Lynch and Carroll were grandsons of Irishmen; Whipple and Hancock were of Irish descent on the maternal side; and O'Hart (*Irish Pedigrees*) declares that Robert Treat Paine was a great-grandson of Henry O'Neill, hereditary prince of Ulster, who "changed his name to that of one of his maternal ancestors so as to save his estates". It was an Irishman who first read the immortal Document to the public; an Irishman first printed it; and an Irishman published it for the first time with facsimiles of the signatures.

At least six American Presidents had more or less of the Celtic strain. President Jackson, whose parents came from Co. Down, more than once expressed his pride in his Irish ancestry. Arthur's parents were from Antrim, Buchanan's from Donegal, and McKinley's grandparents came from the same vicinity. Theodore Roosevelt boasts among his ancestors two direct lines from Ireland, and the first American ancestor of President Polk was a Pollock from Donegal. The present occupant of the White House, Woodrow Wilson, is also of Irish descent. Among the distinguished Vice-Presidents of the United States were George Clinton and John C. Calhoun, sons of immigrants from Longford and Donegal respectively, and Calhoun's successor as chairman of the committee on foreign relations was John Smilie, a native of Newtownards, Co. Down.

Among American governors since 1800, we find such names as Barry, Brady, Butler, Carroll, Clinton, Conway, Carney, Connolly, Curtin, Collins, Donaghey, Downey, Early, Fitzpatrick, Flannegan, Geary, Gorman, Hannegan, Kavanagh, Kearney, Logan, Lynch, Murphy, Moore, McKinley, McGill, Meagher, McGrath, Mahone, McCormick, O'Neal, O'Ferrall, Orr, Roane, Filey, Sullivan, Sharkey, Smith, Talbot, and Welsh, all of Irish descent. Today we have as governors of States, Glynn in New York, Dunne in Illinois, Walsh in Massachusetts, O'Neal in Alabama, Burke in North Carolina,

Carey in Wyoming, McGovern in Wisconsin, McCreary in Kentucky, and Tener in Pennsylvania, and not alone is the governor of the last-mentioned State a native of Ireland, but so also are its junior United States Senator, the secretary of the Commonwealth, and its adjutant-general.

In the political life of America, many of the sons of Ireland have risen to eminence, and in the legislative halls at the National Capital, the names of Kelly, Fitzpatrick, Broderick, Casserly, Farley, Logan, Harlan, Hannegan, Adair, Barry, Rowan, Gorman, Kennedy, Lyon, Fitzgerald, Fair, Sewall, Kernan, Butler, Moore, Regan, Mahone, Walsh, and Flannegan, are still spoken of with respect among the lawmakers of the nation. William Darrah Kelly served in Congress for fifty years, and it remained for James Shields to hold the unique distinction of representing three different States, at different times, in the Senate of the United States. Senator Shields was a native of Co. Tyrone.

In the judiciary have been many shining lights of Irish origin. The Chief Justice of the United States Supreme Court is Edward D. White, grandson of a '98 rebel, and one of his ablest associates is Joseph McKenna. No more erudite or profound lawyer than Charles O'Conor has adorned his profession and it can be said with truth that his career has remained unrivalled in American history. James T. Brady, Daniel Dougherty, Thomas Addis Emmet, and Charles O'Neill were among the most eminent lawyers America has known, while the names of Dennis O'Brien, Chief Justice of the New York Court of Appeals, John D. O'Neill, who occupied a like elevated place on the bench of South Carolina, John D. Phelan of the Alabama Supreme Court, Richard O'Gorman, Charles P. Daly, Hugh Rutledge, Morgan J. O'Brien, and others of like origin, are household words in the legal annals of America. There is no State in the Union where an Irish-American lawyer has not distinguished himself.

The history of medicine in the United States is adorned with the names of many physicians of Irish birth or blood. Several Irish surgeons rendered valuable services in the army of the Revolution, among whom are found Drs. McDonough, McHenry, McCloskey, McCalla, Burke, Irvine, and Williamson. Dr. John Cochran was appointed by Washington surgeon-general of the army. Dr. James Lynah of Charleston, a native of Ireland, became surgeon-general of South Carolina in recognition of his valuable services to the patriot army. Dr. John McKinley, a native of Ireland, who was a famous physician in his day, became the first governor of Delaware. Dr. Ephraim McDowell is known in the profession as the "Father of Ovariotomy", as is Dr. William J. McNevin the "Father of American Chemistry". Dr. John Byrne of New York had a world-wide fame, and his papers on gynecology have been pronounced by the medical press as "the best printed in any language". One of the most conspicuous figures in medicine in the United States was Dr. Jerome Cochran of Alabama. Drs. Junius F. Lynch of Florida; Charles McCreery of Kentucky; Hugh McGuire and Hunter McGuire of Virginia; Matthew C. McGannon of Tennessee; and James Lynch, Charles J. O'Hagan, and James McBride of South Carolina are mentioned prominently in the histories of their respective localities as the foremost medical men of their times, while in Wisconsin the pioneer physician was Dr. William H. Fox, and in Oregon, Dr. John McLoughlin. Among New York physicians who achieved high reputations in their profession were Drs. Thomas Addis Emmet, Frank A. McGuire, Daniel E. O'Neill, Charles McBurney, Isaac H. Reiley, Alfred L. Carroll, Howard A. Kelly, Joseph O'Dwyer, and James J. Walsh. These and many others of Irish descent have been honored by medical societies as leaders and specialists, while it can be said that no surgeon of the present day has achieved such a world-wide reputation as Dr. John B. Murphy of Chicago. Among experts in medico-legal science, the names of Drs. Benjamin W. McCreedy and William J. O'Sullivan of New York stand out prominently, and among the most noted contributors to medical journals in the United States, and recognized as men of great professional skill and authorities in their respective specialties, have been Drs. F. D. Mooney of St. Louis; Thomas Fitzgibbon of Milwaukee; John D. Hanrahan of Rutland; James McCann and James H. McClelland of Pittsburgh; John A. Murphy and John McCurdy of Cincinnati; John Keating of Philadelphia; John H. Murphy of St. Paul; John W. C.

O'Neal of Gettysburg; and Arthur O'Neill of Meadville, Pa. Indeed, it can be said that American medical science owes an incalculable debt to Irish genius.

Theodore Vail, the presiding genius of the greatest telephone system in the world, is Irish, and so is Carty, its chief engineer. Morse, the inventor of the telegraph, was the grandson of an Irishman; Henry O'Reilly built the first telegraph line in the United States; and John W. Mackey was the president of the Commercial Cable Company. John P. Holland, the inventor of the submarine torpedo boat, was a native of Co. Clare; and McCormick, the inventor of the reaping and mowing machine, was an Irishman's grandson.

Sons of Irishmen have stood in the front rank of American statesmen and diplomats who represented their country abroad. To mention but a few: Richard O'Brien, appointed by Jefferson American representative at Algiers; James Kavanagh, Minister to Portugal; and Louis McLane, Minister to England in 1829 and afterwards Secretary of State in 1832. In recent years, an O'Brien has represented American interests in Italy and Japan; a Kerens in Austria; an Egan in Chili and another of the same name in Denmark; an O'Shaughnessy in Mexico; a Sullivan in Santo Domingo; and an O'Rear in Bolivia.

Among historians were John Gilmary Shea, author of numerous historical works; Dr. Robert Walsh, a learned historian and journalist of the last century, whose literary labors were extensive; McMahon and McSherry, historians of Maryland; Burk, of Virginia; O'Callaghan, Hastings, and Murphy of New York; Ramsay of South Carolina; and Williamson of North Carolina, all native Irishmen or sons of Irish immigrants

In the field of American journalism have been many able and forcible writers of Irish birth or descent. Hugh Gaine, a Belfast man, founded the New York *Mercury* in 1775. John Dunlap founded the first daily paper in Philadelphia, John Daly Burk published the first daily paper in Boston, and William Duane edited the *Aurora* of Philadelphia in 1795. All these were born in Ireland. William Coleman, founder of the New York *Evening Post* in 1801, was the son of an Irish rebel of 1798; Thomas Fitzgerald founded the Philadelphia

Item; Thomas Gill, the New York *Evening Star*; Patrick Walsh, the Augusta *Chronicle;* Joseph Medill, the Chicago *Tribune*. Henry W. Grady edited the Atlanta *Constitution*; Michael Dee edited the Detroit *Evening News* for nearly fifty years; Richard Smith, the Cincinnati *Gazette;* Edward L. Godkin, the New York *Evening Post;* William Laffan, the New York *Sun;* and Horace Greeley, the New York *Tribune*. All of these were either natives of Ireland or sprung from immigrant Irishmen, as were Oliver of the Pittsburgh *Gazette,* O'Neill of the Pittsburgh *Despatch,* John Keating of Memphis, William D. O'Connor, and many other shining lights of American journalism during the last century. Fitz James O'Brien was "a bright, particular star" in the journalistic firmament; John MacGahan achieved fame as a war correspondent; Patrick Barry of Rochester, an extensive writer on horticultural and kindred subjects, was the recognized leader of his craft in the United States; and William Darby, son of Patrick and Mary Darby, and Michael Twomey were the ablest American geographers and writers on abstruse scientific subjects.

In the field of poetry, we have had Theodore O'Hara, the author of that immortal poem, "The Bivouac of the Dead"; John Boyle O'Reilly; Thomas Dunn English, author of "Ben Bolt"; Father Abram Ryan, "the poet priest of the South"; James Whitcomb Riley; Eleanor Donnelly; M. F. Egan; T. A. Daly; and Joseph I. C. Clarke, president of the American Irish Historical Society.

To recount the successful men of affairs of Irish origin it would be necessary to mention every branch of business and every profession. Recalling but a few, Daniel O'Day, Patrick Farrelly, John and William O'Brien, Alexander T. Stewart, John Castree, Joseph J. O'Donohue, William R. Grace, John McConville, Hugh O'Neill, Alexander E. Orr, William Constable, Daniel McCormick, and Dominick Lynch, all of New York, were dominant figures in the world of business. Thomas Mellon of Pittsburgh; John R. Walsh and the Cudahy brothers of Chicago; James Phelan, Peter Donahue, Joseph A. Donohoe, and John Sullivan of San Francisco; William A. Clark and Marcus Daly of Montaña; George Meade, the

Meases and the Nesbits, Thomas FitzSimmons and Thomas Dolan of Philadelphia; Columbus O'Donnell and Luke Tiernan of Baltimore, all these have been leading merchants in their day. Few American financiers occupy a more conspicuous place than Thomas F. Ryan, and no great industrial leader has reached the pinnacle of success upon which stands the commanding figure of James J. Hill, both sons of Irishmen. The names of Anthony N. Brady, Eugene Kelly, James S. Stranahan, and James A. Farrell, president of the United States Steel Corporation, are household words in business and financial circles.

John Keating, the first paper manufacturer in New York (1775); Thomas Faye, the first to manufacture wall-paper by machinery, who won for this distinction the first gold medal of the American Institute; John and Edward McLoughlin of New York, for many years the leading publishers of illustrated books; and John Banigan of Providence, one of the largest manufacturers of rubber goods in America, were natives of Ireland. John O'Fallon and Bryan Mullanphy of St. Louis, and John McDonough of Baltimore, who amassed great wealth as merchants, were large contributors to charitable and educational institutions; William W. Corcoran, whose name is enshrined in the famous Art Gallery at Washington, contributed during his lifetime over five million dollars to various philanthropic institutions; and one of the most noted philanthropists in American history, and the first woman in America to whom a public monument was erected, was an Irishwoman, Margaret Haughery of New Orleans.

Irishmen have shown a remarkable aptitude for the handling of large contracts, and in this field have been prominent John H. O'Rourke, James D. Leary, James Coleman, Oliver Byrne, and John D. Crimmins in New York; John B. McDonald, the builder of New York's subways; George Law, projector and promoter of public works, steamship and railroad builder; and John Roach, the famous ship-builder of Chester, Pa. John Sullivan, a noted American engineer one hundred years ago, completed the Middlesex Canal; and John McL. Murphy, whose ability as a constructing engineer was universally recognized, rendered valuable service to the United States during the Civil War. Among pioneer ship-builders in America are noted Patrick Tracy from Wexford and Simon Forrester from Cork, who were both at Salem, Mass., during the period of the Revolution and rendered most valuable service to the patriot cause; and the O'Briens, Kavanaghs, and Sewalls in Maine.

But it is not in the material things of life alone that the Irish have been in the van. Thousands of Americans have been charmed by the operas of Victor Herbert, a grandson of Samuel Lover, and with lovers of music the strains of Patrick Sarsfield Gilmore's band still linger as a pleasant memory. Edward A. MacDowell, America's most famous composer, was of Irish descent. The colossal statute of "America" on the dome of the National Capitol was executed by Thomas Crawford, who was born in New York of Irish parents in 1814; Henry Inman, one of the very best of portrait painters, was also born in New York of Irish parents; John Singleton Copley, the distinguished artist, came to Boston from Co. Clare in 1736; Thompson, the sculptor, was born in Queen's Co.; another noted sculptor was William D. O'Donovan of Virginia; and Augustus Saint Gaudens, one of the greatest sculptors of modern times, was born in Dublin. Other sculptors of Irish race have been elsewhere mentioned. Among America's most talented artists and portrait painters may be mentioned George P. Healy, William J. Hennessy, Thomas Moran, Henry Pelham, Henry Murray, John Neagle, and William Magrath, all of Irish birth or descent.

Ireland has given many eminent churchmen to the United States. The three American Cardinals, Gibbons, Farley, and O'Connell, stand out prominently, as do Archbishops Carroll, Hughes, McCloskey, Kenrick, Ryan, Ireland, Glennon, Corrigan, and Keane, all of whom have shed lustre on the Church. History has given to an Irishman, Francis Makemie of Donegal, the credit of founding Presbyterianism in America, while among noted Presbyterian divines of Irish birth were James Waddell, known as "the blind preacher of the wilderness," Thomas Smyth, John Hall, Francis Allison, William Tennant, and James McGrady, all men of great ability and influence in their day. Samuel Finley, President of Princeton College in

1761, was a native of Armagh, and John Blair Smith, famous as a preacher throughout the Shenandoah Valley and the first president of Union College (1795), was of Irish descent. Among the pioneer preachers of the western wilderness were McMahon, Dougherty, Quinn, Burke, O'Cool, Delaney, McGee, and many others of Irish origin.

Irishmen and their sons have founded American towns and cities, and the capital of the State of Colorado takes its name from General James Denver, son of Patrick Denver, an emigrant from county Down in the year 1795. Sixty-five places in the United States are named after people bearing the Irish prefix "O" and upwards of 1000 after the "Macs", and there are 253 counties of the United States and approximately 7000 places called by Irish family or place names. There are 24 Dublins, 21 Waterfords, 18 Belfasts, 16 Tyrones, 10 Limericks, 9 Antrims, 8 Sligos, 7 Derrys, 6 Corks, 5 Kildares, and so on.

Immigrant Irishmen have also been the founders of prominent American families. One of the most ancient of Irish patronymics, McCarthy, is found in the records of Virginia as early as 1635 and in Massachusetts in 1675, and all down through the successive generations descendants of this sept were among the leading families of the communities where they located. In Virginia, the McCormick, Meade, Lewis, Preston, and Lynch families; in the Carolinas, the Canteys, Nealls, Bryans, and Butlers; and in Maryland, the Carrolls and Dulanys are all descended from successful Irish colonizers.

Even from this very incomplete summary, we can see that Irish blood, brain, and brawn have been a valuable acquisition to the building of the fabric of American institutions, and that the sons of Ireland merit more prominent recognition than has been accorded them in the pages of American history. The pharisees of history may have withheld from Ireland the credit that is her due, but, thanks to the never-failing guidance of the records, we are able to show that at all times, whether they came as voluntary exiles or were driven from their homes by the persecutions of government, her sons have had an honorable part in every upward movement in American life. Testimony adduced from the sources from which this imperfect sketch is drawn cannot be called into question, and its perusal by those who so amusingly glorify the "Anglo-Saxon" as the founder of the American race and American institutions would have a chastening influence on their ignorance of early American history, and would reopen the long vista of the years, at the very beginning of which they would see Celt and Teuton, Saxon and Gaul, working side by side solidifying the fulcrum of the structure on which this great nation rests.

REFERENCES:

The archives, registers, records, reports, and other official documents mentioned in the text; the various Town, County, and State Histories; the collections and publications of the following societies: Massachusetts Historical Society, Genealogical Society of Pennsylvania, New York Historical Society (34 vols.), New York Genealogical and Biographical Society (44 vols.), Maine Historical Society, Rhode Island Historical Society, Connecticut Historical Society, South Carolina Historical Society, and American Historical Society; New England Historical and Genealogical Register (67 vols., Boston, 1847-1913); New England Historical and Biographical Record; Hakluyt: Voyages, Navigations, Traffiques, and Discoveries of the English Nation (London, 1607); Dobbs: The Trade and Improvement of Ireland (Dublin, 1729); Hutchinson: History of Massachusetts from the First Settlement in 1628 until 1750 (Salem, 1795); Proud: History of Pennsylvania, 1681-1770 (Philadelphia, 1797-1798); Savage: Genealogical Dictionary of the First Settlers of New England (Boston, 1860-1862); Morris (ed.): The Makers of New York (Philadelphia, 1895); Pope: The Pioneers of Massachusetts (Boston, 1900), The Pioneers of Maine and New Hampshire (Boston, 1908); Richardson: Side-lights on Maryland History (Baltimore, 1913); Spencer: History of the United States; Ramsay: History of the United States; Prendergast: Cromwellian Settlement of Ireland.

THE IRISH IN CANADA

By James J. Walsh, M.D., Ph.D., Litt.D., Sc.D.

WHEN Wolfe captured Quebec and Canada came under British rule, some of the best known of his officers and several of his men were Irish. After the Peace was signed many of them settled in Canada, not a few of them marrying French wives, and as a consequence there are numerous Irish, Scotch, and English names among the French speaking inhabitants of Lower Canada. Two of Wolfe's officers, Colonel Guy Carleton, born at Strabane in the county Tyrone, and General Richard Montgomery, born only seven miles away at Convoy, in the same county, were destined to play an important rôle in the future history of Canada. Montgomery was in command of the Revolutionary Army from the Colonies, when it attempted to take Quebec, and Carleton, who had been a trusted friend of General Wolfe, was in command of the Canadian forces. The two men were the lives of their respective commands, and with the death of Montgomery Carleton's victory was assured.

Carleton was made Governor-in-Chief of Canada, and during the trying years of the early British rule of New France and the American Revolution, his tact did more than anything else to save Canada for the British. Bibaud, the French historian, says, "the man to whom the administration of the government was entrusted had known how to make the Canadians love him, and this contributed not a little to retain at least within the bounds of neutrality those among them who might have been able, or who believed themselves able, to ameliorate their lot by making common cause with the insurgent colonies." Shortly after being made governor, Carleton went to England and secured the passage of the Quebec Act through the English parliament, which gave the Canadian French assurance that they were to be ruled without oppression by the British Government. Subsequently, in 1786, Carleton, as Lord Dorchester, became the first governor-general of Canada, being given jurisdiction over Nova Scotia and New Brunswick as well as Upper and Lower Canada, and to him more than to any other is due the early loyalty to the British crown in the Dominion.

After the army the next important source of Irish population in Canada were the loyalists who after the Revolution removed from the United States to the British Dominions in America. There were probably many thousands of them, more than enough to make up for the French who left Canada for France when the territory passed over to England. Among the Irish loyalists who went to Canada was the Rev. John Stuart, who had become very well known as a missionary in the Mohawk Valley before the Revolution, and who, though born a Presbyterian, was destined to win the title of the "Father of the Church of England in Upper Canada." When the first Canadian parliament met in December 1792, Edward O'Hara was returned for Gaspé, in Lower Canada, and D'Arcy McGee could boast that henceforward Lower Canada was never without an Irish representative in its legislative councils.

When the question of settling Upper Canada with British colonists came up, Colonel Talbot, a county Dublin man, was the most important factor. He obtained a large grant of land near what is now London and attracted settlers into what was at that time a wilderness. The tract settled under his superintendence now comprises twenty-nine townships in the most prosperous part of Canada.

The maritime Provinces had been under British rule before the fall of Quebec and contained a large element of Irish population. In Newfoundland in 1753 out of a total population of some thirteen thousand, Davin says that there were nearly five thousand Catholics, chiefly Irish. In 1784 a great new stimulus to Irish immigration to Newfoundland was given by Father O'Connell, who in 1796 was made Catholic bishop of the island. Newfoundland, for its verdure, the absence of reptiles, and its Irish inhabitants, was called at this time "Transatlantic Ireland", and Bonnycastle says that more than one half of the population was Irish.

In 1749 Governor Cornwallis brought some 4,000 disbanded soldiers to Nova Scotia and founded Halifax. Ten years later it was described as divided into Halifax proper, Irishtown or the southern, and Dutchtown or the northern, suburbs.

The inhabitants numbered 3,000, one-third of whom were Irish. They were among the most prominent men of the city and province. In the Privy Council for 1789 were Thomas Corcoran and Charles Morris. Morris was president of the Irish Society and Matthew Cahill the sheriff of Halifax in that year. A large number of Irish from the north of Ireland settled in Nova Scotia in 1763, calling their settlement Londonderry. They provided a fortunate refuge for the large numbers of Irish Presbyterians who were expelled from New England by the intolerant Puritans the following year. They also welcomed many loyalists who came from New York and the New England States after the acknowledgment of the independence of the American Colonies by Great Britain. Between the more eastern settlers around Halifax and those in the interior, the greater part of the population of Nova Scotia was probably Irish in origin.

It was in the Maritime Provinces that the first step in political emancipation for Catholics under British rule was made. In 1821 Lawrence Cavanaugh, a Roman Catholic, was returned to the Assembly of the Province for Cape Breton. He would not subscribe to the declaration on Transubstantiation in the oath of office tendered him, and as a consequence was refused admittance to the Assembly. But he was elected again and again, and six years afterwards Judge Haliburton, better known by his *nom de plume* of "Sam Slick", in an able speech, seconded the motion to dispense with the declaration, and Cavanaugh was permitted to take the oath without the declaration.

The War of 1812 brought over from Ireland a number of Irish soldiers serving in the British army, many of whom after the war settled down and became inhabitants of the country. They were allotted farm lands and added much to Canada's prosperity. A type of their descendants was Sir William Hingston, whose father was at this time a lieutenant adjutant in the Royal 100th Regiment, "the Dublins." Sir William's father died when his son was a mere boy, but the lad supported his mother, worked his way through the medical school, saved enough money to give himself two years in Europe, and became a great surgeon. He was elected three times mayor of Montreal, serving one term with great prestige under the most trying circumstances. He afterwards became a senator of the Dominion and was knighted by Queen Victoria.

Prince Edward Island was settled mainly by the Scotch and French, and yet many Irish names are to be found among its old families. It was ceded to Great Britain in 1763, and the first Governor appointed was Captain Walter Patterson, whose niece, Elizabeth Patterson, was married to Jerome Bonaparte in Baltimore in 1803. Captain Patterson was so ardent an Irishman that through his influence he had an act passed by the Assembly changing the name of the island to New Ireland, but the home Government refused to countenance the change. At this time the island was known as St. John's, and the name Prince Edward was given to it in honor of the Duke of Kent in 1789. One of the most popular governors of the island was Sir Dominick Daly, knighted while in office. He was a member of a well known Galway family, and first came to America as secretary to one of the governors. He afterwards became provincial secretary for Lower Canada.

Canada suffered from the aftermath of the revolutions which took place in Europe during the early part of the nineteenth century. The year 1837 saw two revolutions, one in Upper, the other in Lower, Canada, though neither of them amounted to more than a flash in the pan. As might be expected, there were not a few Irish among the disaffected spirits who fostered these revolutions. Their experience at home led them to know how little oppressed people were likely to obtain from the British Government except by a demonstration of force. There were serious abuses, especially "the Family Compact", the lack of anything approaching constitutional guarantees in government, and political disabilities on the score of religion. However, most of the Irish in Canada were ranged on the side of the government. Sir Richard Bonnycastle, writing in 1846, said "The Catholic Irish who have been long settled in the country are by no means the worst subjects in this transatlantic realm, as I can personally testify, having had the command of large bodies of them during the border troubles of 1837-8. They are all loyal and true." Above all Bonnycastle pledged himself for the loyalty of the Irish Catholic priesthood.

One of the Irishmen who came into prominence in the rebellions of 1837 was Edmund Bailey O'Callaghan, the editor of the *Vindicator,* the newspaper by means of which Papineau succeeded in arousing much feeling among the people of Lower Canada and fomented the Revolution. O'Callaghan escaped to the United States and settled at Albany, where he became the historian of New York State. To him, more than to any other, we owe the preservation of the historical materials out of which the early history of the State can be constructed. Rare volumes of the Jesuit Relations, to the value of which for historical purposes he had called special attention, were secured from his library for the Canadian library at Ottawa.

Towards the middle of the nineteenth century, when the population of Ireland reached its highest point of over 8,000,000, the pressure on the people caused them to emigrate in large numbers, and then the famine came to drive out great crowds of those who survived. In proportion to its population Canada received a great many more of these Irish emigrants than did the United States. Unfortunately the conditions on board the emigrant sailing vessels in those days cost many lives. They were often becalmed and took months to cross the ocean. My grandmother coming in the thirties was ninety-three days in crossing, landing at Quebec after seven weeks on half rations, part of the time living on nothing but oatmeal and water. Ship fever, the dreaded typhus, broke out on her vessel as on so many others, and more than half the passengers perished. Many, many thousands of the Irish emigrants thus died on ship-board or shortly after landing. In 1912, the Ancient Order of Hibernians erected near Quebec a monument to the victims. In spite of the untoward conditions, emigration continued unabated, and in 1875, in the population of Ontario, Quebec, New Brunswick, and Nova Scotia, it was calculated that the Irish numbered 846,414 as compared with 706,369 English and 549,946 Scotch (Hatton, quoted by Davin in *The Irishman in Canada*).

It had become clear that Canada would prosper more if united than in separate provinces jealous of each other. The first move in this direction came from the Maritime Provinces, where the Irish element was so much stronger than elsewhere, and when a conference of the leading statesmen of these

Provinces was appointed to be held at Charlottetown, P. E. I., September 1864, representatives of Upper and Lower Canada asked to be allowed to be present to bring forward a plan for a Federation of all the British Provinces in North America. The British North America Act was passed, and received the royal assent, the queen appointing July 1, 1867 as the formal beginning of the Dominion of Canada.

Among the men who were most prominent in bringing about federation and who came to be known as the Fathers of Confederation were several distinguished Irishmen. Thomas D'Arcy McGee was the best known and probably did more than any other Canadian to make the idea of confederation popular by his writings and speeches. He had come to Canada as a stranger, edited a newspaper in Montreal, and was elected to the Assembly after a brief residence, in spite of the opposition cries of "Irish adventurer" and "stranger from abroad," was subsequently elected four times by acclamation, and was Minister of Agriculture and Education and Canadian Commissioner to the Paris Exposition of 1867. His letters to the Earl of Mayo, pleading for the betterment of conditions in Ireland, were quoted by Gladstone during the Home Rule movement as "a prophetic voice from the dead coming from beyond the Atlantic."

Another of the Fathers of Confederation was the Honorable Edward Whalen, born in the county Mayo, who as a young man went to Prince Edward Island, where he gained great influence as a popular journalist. He was an orator as well as an editor, and came to have the confidence of the people of the island, and hence was able to do very much for federation. A third of the Fathers of Confederation from the Maritime Provinces was the Honorable, afterwards Sir, Edward Kenny, who, when the first Cabinet of the New Dominion was formed, was offered and accepted one of the portfolios in recognition of the influence which he had wielded for Canadian union.

At all times in the history of Canada the Catholic hierarchy has been looked up to as thoroughly conservative factors for the progress and development of the country. After the Irish immigration most of the higher ecclesiastics were Irish by birth or descent, and they all exerted a deep influence not only on their own people but on their city and province. One of the Fathers of Confederation was Archbishop Connolly, of Halifax, of whom the most distinguished Presbyterian clergyman of the Lower Provinces said the day after his death: "I feel that I have not only lost a friend, but as if Canada had lost a patriot; in all his big-hearted Irish fashion he was ever at heart, in mind, and deed, a true Canadian." Among his colleagues of the hierarchy were such men as his predecessor Archbishop Walsh, Archbishop Lynch, the first Metropolitan of Upper Canada when Toronto was erected into an archbishopric, Bishop Hogan of Kingston, Archbishop Hannan of Halifax, Archbishop Walsh of Toronto, and Archbishop O'Brien of Halifax, all of whom were esteemed as faithful Canadians working for the benefit of their own people more especially, but always with the larger view of good for the whole commonwealth of Canada.

The Irish continued to furnish great representative men to Canada. The first governor, Guy Carleton, was Irish, and his subsequent governor-generalship as Lord Dorchester did much to make Canada loyal to Great Britain. During the difficult times of the Civil War in the United States, Lord Monck, a Tipperary man, was the tactful governor-general, "like other Irish Governors singularly successful in winning golden opinions" (Davin). Probably the most popular and influential of Canada's governors-general was Lord Dufferin, another Irishman. Some of the most distinguished of Canadian jurists, editors, and politicians have been Irishmen, and Irishmen have been among her great merchants, contractors, and professional men. In our own time Sir William Hingston among the physicians, Sir Charles Fitzpatrick among the jurists, and Sir Thomas George Shaughnessy among the administrative financiers are fine types of Irish character.

REFERENCES:

Davin: The Irishman in Canada (Toronto, 1877); McGee: Works; Tracy: The Tercentenary History of Canada (New York, 1908); Walsh: Sir William Hingston, in the Amer. Catholic Quarterly (January, 1911), Edmund Bailey O'Callaghan, in the Records of the Amer. Catholic Historical Society (1907); McKenna: A Century of Catholicity in Canada, in the Catholic World, vol. 1, p. 229.

THE IRISH IN SOUTH AMERICA

By Marion Mulhall.

I.—From the Spanish Conquest to the War of Independence.

SOUTH AMERICA, although comparatively little known until recent times to the outside world, contains much to interest the missionary, the scientist, the historian, the traveler, and the financier. The twentieth century will probably see hundreds following in the footsteps of their predecessors. In the meantime, the brilliant achievements of numerous Irish men and women in that part of the world are falling into oblivion, and call for a friendly hand to collect the fragments of historical lore connected with their exploits.

This paper will cover three periods:—

(1). From the Spanish Conquest to the War of Independence: here the principal actors were maritime explorers, buccaneers, and mercantile adventurers;

(2). The War of Independence from 1810 to 1826: in this period Irishmen performed feats of valor worthy to rank with those in Greek or Roman history.

(3). Since the Independence; a period of commercial and industrial development, in which Irishmen have played a foremost part.

It has been said that George Barlow, the companion of Sebastian Cabot, was an Irishman. Cabot was the first Britisher to sail up the Rio de la Plata, and gave it its name just thirty-five years after the discovery of America. Barlow was in the service of the king of Spain, and in that country met Cabot, who had been appointed Pilot Major to his Majesty in the year 1518. In 1577 we read of the famous Admiral Drake's expedition to the River Plate, which he reached on April 14, 1578. Evidently it was a successful one in the opinion of Queen Elizabeth, for on Drake's return to Plymouth, September 26, 1580, she came aboard his ship and knighted him. There seem to have been three Irishmen on this expedition,

Fenton, Merrick, and Ward. Fenton, who was in command of two vessels, was attacked by a Spanish squadron between Brazil and the River Plate, and the battle continued by moonlight until one of the Spaniards was sunk. The Spanish historian adds that Fenton might have sunk another of the enemy's ships, but refrained because there were several women on board.

Lozana in his *History* mentions a revolution in Paraguay in 1555, which was headed by an Irishman named Nicholas Colman. This revolution was quickly suppressed by the Spanish viceroy, Yrala, but Colman led a second revolution in 1570, when Captain Rigueline was governor of Guayra. The mutineers named Colman for their chief, put their treasures into canoes, and floated down the Parana until their boats were capsized by some rapids, probably the falls of Apipe in Misiones. The viceroy, on hearing of the revolt, sent troops to bring back the fugitives, and the latter were treated with unusual clemency. Lozana describes Colman as a daring, turbulent buccaneer. For fifteen years he seems to have played an important part in Guayra; his subsequent fate is unknown.

In 1626 an expedition commanded by James Purcell, an Irishman, established itself on the island of Tocujos, in the mouth of the Amazon.

Captain Charles O'Hara was sent by Governor Arana from Montevideo in March, 1761, to destroy the old landmarks of Rio Negro and Ching between the dominions of Portugal and Spain. The officer next under him was Lieutenant Charles Murphy, afterwards governor of Paraguay. This expedition suffered great hardships.

Several of the expeditions of the privateers of the eighteenth century sailed from Ireland. Dampier, a skilful navigator, went on a cruise to intercept the Spanish galleons returning from the River Plate with booty supposed to be worth £600,000 sterling. He sailed from Kinsale in September, 1703, with two vessels, and no doubt amongst the crews were many Irishmen. It was on this expedition that Alexander Selkirk, a Scotch sailor, was put on shore at Juan Fernandez in 1704, where he remained until rescued by Captain Rogers, who commanded the *Duke*, a vessel of 320 tons, which sailed from

Cork on September 1, 1708, touched by chance at Juan Fernandez, and found the original of Defoe's remarkable story, *Robinson Crusoe,* who presented a wild appearance dressed in his goatskins.

In 1765 Captain Macnamara, with two vessels called the *Lord Clive* and the *Ambuscade,* mounting between them 104 guns, attempted to take Colonia, in front of Buenos Ayres, from the Spaniards. Having shelled the place for four hours, Macnamara expected every moment to see a white flag hoisted, when, by some mishap, the *Lord Clive* took fire, and 262 persons perished. The Spaniards fired upon the poor fellows in the water, only 78 escaping to land. Macnamara was seen to sink. His sword was found a few years ago by a Colonia fisherman, who presented it to the British consul at Montevideo. Most of the Irish names still extant in the Argentine provinces, such as Sarsfield, Carrol, and Butler, are probably derived from these captives. Among the descendants of the survivors of Macnamara's expedition may be mentioned the ablest lawyer ever known in Buenos Ayres and for many years Prime Minister, the late Dr. Velez Sarsfield, and also Governor O'Neill.

The year 1586 saw an expedition of a very different character, consisting of the first Jesuits sent to convert Paraguay, under the direction of Father Thomas Field, an Irishman, and son of a Limerick doctor. Their vessel fell into the hands of English privateers off the Brazilian coast, but the sea rovers respected their captives, and after sundry adventures the latter landed at Buenos Ayres, whence they proceeded over land to Cordoba. The year following they set out for Paraguay, where Father Field and his companions laid the foundation of the Jesuit commonwealth of Misiones, which had such wonderful development in the following two centuries as to cause Voltaire to admit that "the Jesuit establishment in Paraguay seems to be the triumph of humanity."

Another Irish Jesuit, Father Thaddeus Ennis, appears in authority in Misiones shortly before the downfall. In 1756, when Spain ceded San Miguel and other missions to Portugal, Father Ennis was entrusted with the removal lower down to

Parana of such tribes as refused to become Portuguese subjects.

Yet another Jesuit, Father Falkiner, son of an Irish Protestant doctor in Manchester, who had himself studied medicine, was one of the most successful travellers and missionaries of the 18th century. Among his friends in London was a ship-captain who traded from the coast of Guinea to Brazil, carrying slaves for the company recently established by Queen Anne's patent, and he it doubtless was who prevailed on the young physician to try a seafaring life. In one of his voyages as ship surgeon, from Guinea to Buenos Ayres, he fell ill at the latter port, and, there being no hotels, he had the good fortune to enjoy the hospitality of the Jesuit superior, Father Mahony, whose name proclaims his Irish nationality. Such was the impression made on Falkiner by the kindness of the Jesuits that he shortly afterwards was received into the Church and entered as a novice in the College of St. Ignatius at Buenos Ayres. He spent the first years of his missionary career in Misiones and Tucuman. Later on he was despatched by his superior to Patagonia, and his success there during 27 years was almost equal to what has already been mentioned of Father Field in Paraguay. He converted many tribes, and traversed nearly every part of Patagonia from Rio Negro to Magellan's Straits, and as far inland as the Andes. He knew most of the Indian tongues, and by his winning manners and knowledge of medicine gained a great influence over the savages. When he published his life and travels, such was the effect of his book upon the king of Spain that he at once ordered surveys and settlements to be made along the Patagonian coast, which Father Falkiner represented as exposed to seizure by the first adventurer who should land there. Father Falkiner's book has been translated into French, German, and Spanish. He returned to England and died at Spetchly, Worcestershire, near the end of the 18th century.

In 1774 the bishop of Ayachucho was Dr. James O'Phelan, who rebuilt the old Cathedral of Pasco. His father was an Irish officer in the Spanish army.

II.—THE WAR OF INDEPENDENCE.

Towards the close of the 18th century the Pitt administration lent a willing ear to a Venezuelan patriot, General Miranda, who proposed that Great Britain should aid South America to expel the Spanish rulers and set up a number of independent states. Spain being the ally of France and paying an annual subsidy to Napoleon, it became moreover the object of England to seize the treasure-ships periodically arriving from the River Plate.

Hostilities having broken out in Europe in 1803, an English squadron under an Irish commander, Captain Moore, captured in the following year some Spanish galleons laden with treasure at the mouth of the River Plate. In June, 1806, Major General William Carr Beresford with a British squadron cast anchor about twelve miles from Buenos Ayres, and with a force of only 1635 men took possession of that city of 60,000 inhabitants. The indignation which such a humiliation at first caused among the people was in large measure calmed by the manifesto which the conquering commander issued on the occasion. In the *Memoirs* of General Belgrano we read: "It grieved me to see my country subjugated in this manner, but I shall always admire the gallantry of the brave and honorable Beresford in so daring an enterprise." Beresford was, however, unable to hold his ground, for the Spaniards got together an army of 10,000 men, and re-took the city. Beresford was made prisoner, but after five months' detention he and his brother-officers, among whom was another Irishman, Major Fahy, managed to escape. Thus ended the expedition of this brave general, who nevertheless had covered himself and his little army with glory, for he held Buenos Ayres as a British colony for 45 days, and had he been properly supported from home the result would in all probability have been vastly different.

General Beresford was one of the most distinguished men of his time. He was the illegitimate son of the Marquis of Waterford, entered the army at 16, and served in every quarter of the globe. After his defeat at Buenos Ayres he captured Madeira, and was made governor of that island. In 1808 he successfully covered the retreat of Sir John Moore to Corunna, a difficult feat, for which he received a marshal's baton, and was made commander-in-chief in Portugal. In 1811 he defeated Marshal Soult at Albuera, and subsequently took part in the victories of Salamanca and Vittoria. For these services he was made Duke of Elvas, and the British government conferred on him in 1814 the title of Baron Beresford of Albuera and Dungannon. The same year he was sent as minister to Brazil, and on his return was created viscount. He married the widow of Thomas Hope the banker, and settled down on his estates in Kent, where he died in 1854.

The brilliancy of Beresford's achievement in capturing Buenos Ayres with a handful of men had dazzled the minds of English statesmen, who felt that 10,000 British troops were enough to subdue the whole of the vast continent of South America. In May, 1807, an expedition comprising several frigates and transports with 5,000 troops appeared off Montevideo from England. A month later Lieutenant-General Whitelock arrived with orders to assume the chief command, and among his officers were the gallant Irishmen, Major Vandeleur, who commanded a wing of the 88th Regiment, and Lieutenant-Colonel Nugent, of the 38th. Whitelock endeavored, but failed, to retake Buenos Ayres. During the siege a small detachment of Spanish troops under Colonel James Butler, after a terrific conflict, in which they sold their lives dearly, were all killed. Agreeably to Colonel Butler's request his remains were buried on the spot he had so valiantly defended, and his tombstone was visible there until 1818.

It is a remarkable fact that several of the South American countries, Mexico, Peru, and Chile, were governed by viceroys of Irish birth in the critical period preceding the Independence, although Spanish law forbade such office to any but Spaniards born. It was in recognition of gallant services in Spain, in combination with the Duke of Wellington, that General O'Donoghue was made viceroy of Mexico in 1821, but the elevation of the great viceroy of Peru, Ambrose O'Higgins, was due to the splendid talents of administration already displayed by him during twenty years of service in Chile. He was born at Summerhill, Co. Meath, about 1730. An uncle of his was one of the chaplains at the court of Madrid, and at his expense O'Higgins was educated at a college in Cadiz. He then entered the Spanish engineer corps, and in 1769 was given the command of the commission sent to Chile to strengthen the fortifications of Valdivia. He was made captain-general of Chile in 1788, was subsequently created marquis of Osorno, and in 1796 was nominated viceroy of Peru, a position which he held until his death in 1801.

The great viceroy left only one son, Bernard O'Higgins, who succeeded General Carreras in the supreme command of the patriot army against the Spaniards in 1813. In 1817 O'Higgins took a principal part in the victory of Chacabuco, and was almost immediately appointed supreme director of Chile, with dictatorial powers. During his administration, which lasted six years, he gave every proof of his fitness for the position. But, alas! it was the misfortune of South America to surpass the republics of antiquity in the ingratitude shown towards its greatest benefactors. It is then not surprising to find that the Father of his Country, as O'Higgins is affectionately styled, was deposed by a military revolution, and obliged to take refuge in Peru, from which country he never returned. General Miller and Lord Cochrane, in their *Memoirs,* give frequent testimony to the honesty and zeal of Bernard O'Higgins. He was always treated as an honored guest in Lima, in which city he died on October 24, 1842. He left a son, Demetrio O'Higgins, a wealthy land-owner, who contributed large sums for the patriot army against Spain.

Among other Irish commanders in Chile and Peru, who, during the War of Independence, fought their way to dignity and rank, was General MacKenna, the hero of Membrillar. He was born in 1771, at Clogher, Co. Tyrone; his mother belonged to the ancient Irish sept of O'Reilly, whose estates were confiscated after the fall of Limerick in 1691.

General Thomond O'Brien, who won his spurs at the battle of Chacabuco, seems to have been born in the south of Ireland about 1790. He joined the army of San Martin, and accompanied that general through the campaigns of Chile and Peru until the overthrow of the Spanish régime and the proclamation of San Martin as protector of Peru. On the day (July

28, 1821) when independence was declared at Lima, the protector took in his hand the standard of Pizarro and said,
"This is my portion of the trophies." Then, taking the state
canopy of Pizarro, a kind of umbrella always borne over the
viceroys in processions, he presented it to General O'Brien,
saying, "This is for the gallant comrade who fought so many
years by my side in the cause of South America." The inscription on the canopy, in O'Brien's hand, says that it was brought
to Peru on Pizarro's second journey from Spain. Little did
the viceroys think that its last owner would be an Irishman.

General O'Connor, one of the most distinguished soldiers of
the War of Independence, played an important part in the final
victory of Ayachucho. For his gallantry on that day he was
promoted to the rank of general by the commander-in-chief,
General Bolivar. After the War of Independence he became
Minister of War in Bolivia. General O'Connor went to South
America as an ensign in the Irish Legion under General
Devereux. He claimed direct descent from Roderic O'Conor,
last king of Ireland, 1186.

Captain Esmonde also fought in the War of Independence.
He was brother to the then baronet, Sir Thomas Esmonde,
of Co. Wexford. In later years Captain Esmonde was employed by the Peruvian government to report on some proposed canals at Tarapaca. The vessel in which he embarked
was never more heard of.

Colonel Charles Carroll had served in Spain, but joined the
Chilian army after independence was gained. He was one of
the most popular officers in the army, and met with a sad fate.
Being sent with too small a detachment against the savage
Indians, their commander, Benavides, cut his forces in pieces
and murdered all the officers in a most cruel manner. O'Carroll had his tongue cut out and was then butchered.

Lieutenant Colonel Moran, who commanded the Colombian
legion at the battle of Ayachucho, probably came out in the
legion of General Devereux.

Colonel (afterwards General) O'Leary was first aide-de-
camp to General Bolivar, the Liberator, and received his last
breath. He was nephew to the famous Father Arthur
O'Leary. Bolivar employed him on various missions of great

trust and says "he acquitted himself with great ability." After the war, General O'Leary was appointed British chargé d'affaires at Bogota, and died in Rome in 1868. General Arthur Sandes, a native of Dublin, was entrusted with an important garrison in Peru on the close of the War of Independence.

Admiral Brown, the distinguished commander and hero of the War of Independence, whose exploits may be ranked, like those of Nelson, "above all Greek, above all Roman fame," was born at Foxford, Co. Mayo, Ireland, on the 22nd of June, 1777. His father emigrated with his family to Pennsylvania. A ship captain who was about to sail from Philadelphia offered to take the intelligent Irish boy with him, and the offer was promptly accepted. During twenty years he seems to have voyaged to many countries; at one time we find him at Archangel. Brown had been in Buenos Ayres just two years when the patriot government offered him command of a squadron to commence hostilities against the Spanish navy, then mistress of all the coasts and waters of South America. On the memorable 8th of March, 1814, Brown sailed out of the port of Buenos Ayres with three ships to commence a campaign, which was destined to destroy the Spanish navy in this part of the waters of the New World. With him went his fellow-countrymen, Captains Seaver and Kearney. Brown's next exploits were against Spanish shipping in the Pacific, and his entirely successful campaign at sea against Brazil, in which he gained the mastery by his wonderful skill, courage, and perseverance, keeping at bay the great naval power of that country (which consisted at one time of fifty war vessels) with his few, small, ill-supplied, and ill-armed craft. After these great exploits Brown spent some months among the wild scenery of Mayo, so dear to him in boyhood, and, returning to Buenos Ayres, devoted himself to the quiet life of a country gentleman. He died surrounded by his family and friends on May 3, 1857, and the day of his funeral was one of national mourning. His widow erected a monument to his memory in the Recoleta cemetery, and in 1872 the municipality of Buenos Ayres granted a site for a public statue on the Paseo Julio, which so often rang with

the plaudits of the people as they welcomed this great Irishman returning from victory.

No brighter pages occur in the history of the New World
than those which commemorate the gallantry and self-devo-
tion of the Irish soldiers who aided South Americans to throw
off the yoke of Spain. In 1819 an Irish Legion of 1729 men
arrived under the command of General Devereux, a Wexford
landowner, called the Lafayette of South America, to fight in
the campaign of General Bolivar. Devereux was distinguished
for his great bravery. After the War of Independence he
returned to Europe, being commissioned to form a company
for mining operations in Colombia, which country had appointed him envoy extraordinary to various European courts.

Colonel Ferguson and Captain Talbot were both Irishmen
and among the last survivors of Devereux's Legion. It is
computed that one-third of the Irish who came out under
General Devereux died in hospital. It was this legion which
won the decisive battle of Carabobo, June 26, 1821, going into
action 1100 strong and leaving 600 on that hard-fought field.

Among the officers who composed Bolivar's Albion Rifles
we find the Irish names of Pigott, Tallon, Peacock, Phelan,
O'Connell, McNamara, Fetherstonhaugh, French, Reynolds,
Byrne, and Haig, and the medical officer was Dr. O'Reilly.
We find mention in General Millar's *Memoirs* of Dr. Moore,
an Irishman, who attended Bolivar in most of his campaigns
and was devotedly attached to the person of the Liberator.
Lieutenant-Colonel Hughes, Major Maurice Hogan, Lieuten-
ant William Keogh, Captain Laurence McGuire, Lieutenant-
Colonel S. Collins also served in the struggle for independence.

The period of independence found a small number of Irish
residents in Buenos Ayres, mostly patrician families, such as
Dillon, MacMurrough, Murphy, French, O'Gorman, Orr, Butler, O'Shee, who had been exiled or had fled from Ireland
and obtained the king of Spain's permission to settle in Spanish America. The descendants of these families are now so
intermarried in the country that they have mostly forgotten
the language and traditions of their ancestors; but they occupy
high positions in political, legal, and commercial circles.

III.—The Period After the Declaration of Independence.

A remarkable influx of settlers from Ireland occurred between 1825 and 1830, to work in the *saladeros,* or salt mines, of the Irish merchants, Brown, Dowdall, and Armstrong. Previous to this a few Irish mechanics and others had come from the United States. In 1813 Bernard Kiernan came from New Brunswick. He seems to have devoted himself to science, as the papers mention his discovery of a comet in the Magellan clouds on March 19, 1830. His son, James Kiernan, became editor of the government paper, *Gaceta Mercantil,* in 1823, and held this post for twenty years; his death occurred in 1857. There is reason to believe that the first Irishman who landed in Buenos Ayres in the 19th century, exclusive of Beresford's soldiers, was James Coyle, a native of Tyrone, who came in the *Agréable* in 1807, and died in 1876 at the age of 86.

In 1830 some survivors of an Irish colony of 300 persons in Brazil made their way to Buenos Ayres. They had come out from Europe in the barque *Reward* in 1829.

The banker, Thomas Armstrong, who arrived in Buenos Ayres in 1817, occupied the foremost place for half a century in the commerce of that city. He was of the ancient family of Armstrong in the King's county, one of whose members was General Sir John Armstrong, founder of Woolwich arsenal. Having married into the wealthy family of Villanueva he became intimately connected with all the leading enterprises of the day, such as railways, banks, loans, etc. He took no part in politics, but interested himself in charities of every kind.

In 1865 another Irishman, James P. Cahill, introduced into Peru from the United States the first complete machinery for sugar growing and refining.

Still another Irishman, Peter Sheridan, was one of the chief founders of the sheep farming industry in Argentina. His family claimed descent from the same stock in Co. Cavan as Richard Brinsley Sheridan, the great statesman and dramatist. Sheridan died at the age of 52, in 1844, and was succeeded in the *estancia* or sheep-farming business by his nephew,

James, whose brother Dr. Hugh Sheridan had served under Admiral Brown.

The number and wealth of the Irish *estancieros,* or sheep-farmers, in Argentina have never been exactly ascertained, but after the old Spanish families they are the most important. It would be impossible to give all the Irish names to be met with. Some of them own immense tracts of land. Men whose fathers arrived in Argentina without a shilling are to-day worth millions. Their *estancia* houses display all the comforts of an American or English home; their hospitality is proverbial; and most of them have built on their land fine schools and beautiful little chapels, in which the nearest Irish priest officiates.

Many of the *partidos* or districts of the various provinces of Argentina may be compared to Irish counties, the railway stations being called after the owners of the land on which they are situated. Among the earliest families settled in Argentina in the farming industries, we find Duggans, Torneys, Harringtons, O'Briens, Dowlings, Gaynors, Murphys, Moores, Dillons, O'Rorkes, Kennys, Raths, Caseys, Norrises, O'Farrells, Brownes, Hams, Duffys, Ballestys, Gahans, and Garaghans.

Dr. Santiago O'Farrell, son of one of the earliest Irish pioneers, holds a foremost position among the distinguished lawyers of the present day. An Irish engineer, Mr. John Coghlan, gave Buenos Ayres its first waterworks. The British hospital has at present for its leading surgeon a distinguished Irishman, Dr. Luke O'Connor. A son of Peter Sheridan, educated in England, has left the finest landscapes of South America by any artist born in America. He died at Buenos Ayres in his 27th year, 1861. Among the public men of Irish descent, fifty years ago, in Buenos Ayres, are to be mentioned the distinguished lawyer and politician, Dalmacio Velez Sarsfield, and John Dillon, commissioner of immigration. Dillon was the first to start a brewery in Buenos Ayres, for which purpose he brought out workmen and machinery from Europe. All of his sons occupied distinguished positions. Richard O'Shee, president of the Chamber of Commerce in Buenos Ayres, was born at Seville of an old Irish family banished by William III. Among the many valuable citizens of Buenos Ayres who perished during the cholera of 1868 was Dr. Leslie, a native of Cavan, whose benevolence to the poor was unceasing. Henry O'Gorman, for some years chief of police in Buenos Ayres and afterwards governor of the penitentiary, was descended from an Irish family which went to Buenos Ayres in the eighteenth century. His brother, Canon O'Gorman, was one of the dignitaries of the archdiocese, and director of the boys' reformatory. General Donovan, son of an Irish Dr. Donovan of Buenos Ayres, had command of one of the sections of the new Indian frontier.

The first Irish chaplain was Father Burke, a venerable friar mentioned by Mr. Love in 1820 as over 70 years of age and much esteemed. When Rivadavia suppressed the Orders in 1822, he allowed Father Burke to remain in the convent of Santo Domingo. After his death the Irish residents, in 1828, petitioned Archbishop Murray of Dublin for a chaplain. Accordingly the Rev. Patrick Moran was selected, and he arrived in Buenos Ayres in 1829. He died in the following year, and was succeeded by the Rev. Patrick O'Gorman from Dublin, who continued as chaplain during 16 years till his death in 1847.

The year 1843 is memorable for the arrival of Rev. Anthony Fahy, with whose name the advancement of the Irish in Argentina will be forever identified. This great patriarch was born at Loughrea, Co. Galway, in 1804, and made his ecclesiastical studies at St. Clement's convent of Irish Dominicans at Rome. Being sent to the western states of America, he passed ten years in Ohio and Kentucky, after which, on the invitation of the Irish community of Buenos Ayres and by permission of the superior of his Order, he came to the river Plate at a time when the prospects of the country and of the Irish residents were far from promising. The history of the Irish community since that time is in some measure a recital of the labors of Father Fahy. He it was who helped his countrymen to choose and buy their lands which now are of such enormous value. Their increasing numbers and prosperity in the camp districts obliged him to endow each of the provincial *partidos* was a resident chaplain. Most of these clergymen were educated in Dublin, and soon showed their zeal not merely in religious, but also in social spheres. Irish reading-rooms, libraries, and schools sprang up and laid the foundation for the refined Irish life of the present day in those districts. Among other services, Father Fahy founded the Irish convent, bringing out some Sisters of Mercy under Mrs. Mary Evangelist Fitzpatrick from Dublin, to whom he gave it in charge. Father Fahy died in harness in 1871 of yellow fever; he attended a poor Italian woman and on returning home was at once taken ill. He lasted only three days and expired peacefully, a martyr to his sacred calling. He died so poor that Mr. Armstrong had to discharge for him some small debts, and five others of his countrymen paid his funeral expenses. A fitting memorial of the deceased priest, the Fahy College for Irish orphan boys in Argentina, has been erected in Buenos Ayres, and a magnificent monument of Irish marble, carved in Ireland, also perpetuates his fame.

The priests, still living, who were co-workers with Father Fahy and appointed by him to various *partidos,* are Monsignor Samuel O'Reilly, deservedly beloved by his parishioners, and the Rev. Father Flannery, whose appointment to San Pedro brought a great influx of Irish farmers into that district. Among those who have gone to enjoy their eternal reward are the brothers, Rev. Michael and Rev. John Leahy, both of whom were indefatigable during the yellow fever in Buenos Ayres. Rev. Father Mulleady, Rev. Patrick Lynch, Rev. James Curran, and Monsignor Curley were also among the Irish priests of that time.

The Fahy College is entrusted to the care of the Marist Brothers, who are largely Irish. The community of Holy Cross of the Passionist Fathers, who have as provincial the distinguished North American scholar Father Fidelis Kent Stone, is almost entirely composed of Irish and Irish-Americans. They have several establishments in various provinces of Argentina. Irish priests are to be met with all over the country. In Patagonia and the Chaco we also find a number of Protestant missionaries sent out by the Irish branch of the South American Missionary Society.

Archdeacon Dillon succeeded Father Fahy as Irish chaplain in Buenos Ayres, and, although by birth and education an Irishman, he became one of the principal dignitaries of the archdiocese. He was for some time professor of theology in the ecclesiastical seminary of Buenos Ayres, and accompanied Archbishop Escalada as theologian to the Vatican Council in 1869. He was the founder of the *Southern Cross* in 1874, the Irish weekly paper which is now so ably edited by the gifted Irishman, Mr. Gerald Foley.

The first daily paper to appear in English in South America was the *Standard,* founded in 1861 by Michael G. Mulhall, the distinguished statistician, and it is still one of the leading papers in the country. In conducting it Michael G. Mulhall was joined by his brother, Edward T. Mulhall, in 1862, and for many years it was continuously under their care. The *Standard* still remains in the Mulhall family, and has for its editor a cousin of the former editor's, Mr. John Mulhall, who wisely directs its course. The *Argentina,* an important paper in Spanish, was founded a few years since by Edward T. Mulhall, Jr., a brilliant son of the late Edward Mulhall of the *Standard.* The *Hyberno-Argentine Review,* a new Irish weekly, is edited by another able Irishman, James B. Sheridan. In Rio Janeiro the *Anglo-Brazilian Times* was founded in 1864 by an Irishman, Mr. Scully, who also wrote an important book on Brazil.

Ireland had also its representatives in South American diplomacy and the making of treaties. As early as 1809 Colonel James Burke was sent by Lord Strangford, British minister at Rio, on a confidential mission to Buenos Ayres to negotiate the establishment of a separate kingdom on the river Plate, with the Princess Charlotte as queen. In 1867 Mr. Gould, an Irishman, British chargé d'affaires, endeavored to mediate between the allies, Brazil and Argentina, and President Lopez of Paraguay, but without success. Stephen H. Sullivan, British chargé d'affaires for Chile, signed the treaty of commerce and navigation between England and Chile on the 10th of May, 1852. He was afterwards appointed British minister at Lima, where he was murdered. The late Chilian ministers to Buenos Ayres and London, William Blest Gana and Albert Blest Gana, were the sons of an Irish

Doctor Blest from Sligo, who settled in Chile. In 1859 George Fagan signed a treaty with General Guido for compensation of losses to British subjects during the civil wars after the Independence.

The mining industry had among its pioneers brave sons of Erin. J. O. French went to Buenos Ayres in 1826, and after an arduous mountain journey arrived at the foot of the Cerro Morado, where he found auriferous ores. Chevalier Edmond Temple, an Irish gentleman who had served in Spain in a dragoon regiment, also landed in Buenos Ayres in 1826, and started across the Pampas, then almost uninhabited, until he came to the mountainous country where the Potosi mines were situated. In one of the defiles he lost his favorite horse, and in his book he bids a touching farewell to the friendly steed which had shared with him so many toils and dangers. Temple's successor in the Argentine mining provinces was Major Rickard Seaver, a member of an old Co. Dublin family.

Several books of travel in South America have been published by Irish writers during the last fifty years. MacCann's *Travels in the Argentine Provinces,* 1846-49, contains much that is valuable concerning the history and manners of the country. Major Rickard Seaver issued in 1863 an interesting narrative of his crossing the Andes. Consul Hutchinson, an Irishman, published in 1864 his book *Argentine Gleanings,* which was followed by another in 1869 called *South American Recollections.* Robert Crawford, an Irish engineer, led an expedition from Buenos Ayres in November, 1871, across the Indian Pampas and over the pass of the Planchon in the Andes, to survey an overland route to Chile, and subsequently published an interesting account of his journey. The first book printed and published in English, in South America, was the *Handbook of the River Plate,* written by Michael G. Mulhall and published by the *Standard,* in 1861. The same author also published the *Rural Code of Buenos Ayres* in 1867, and the *Handbook of Brazil* in 1877. In 1871 he published an account of his travels among the German colonies in Rio Grande do Sul. Twenty years ago the writer of this sketch published *Between the Amazon and the Andes* and the *Story of the Jesuit Missions of Paraguay.* These books derive special interest from the fact that she was the first foreign woman ever seen in Cuyaba, the capital of Matto Grosso, whither she accompanied her husband, 2500 miles from either the Atlantic or the Pacific seaboard. They arrived as far as the Diamantina Mountains, beyond Cuyaba, and saw the little rivers which form the sources of the mighty Amazon.

Casting a glance over South America, we see in every country and province evidences of Irish genius employed not only in fighting but in the development of natural resources. To quote Consul Cowper's report to the Foreign Office in London: "The progress of Buenos Ayres is mainly due to the industrious Irish sheep farmers." No other nationality contributed so largely to the export trade of the country. At one time it was shown by the tables of Mr. Duggan and other wool exporters that the quantity of this staple industry yearly sold by Irishmen in Buenos Ayres exceeded that sold by all other nationalities. In later years the Irish sheep farmers in the province of Buenos Ayres have turned their lands into wheat lands, and the great industries of the country, sheep and cattle, have been moved to the outside camps, especially to that wonderful grazing region in the Andine valleys recently visited by Col. Roosevelt and his party. It may be interesting to mention that at the first English races ever held in South America, on November 6, 1826, the principal event, in which ten horses ran, was easily won by an Irish horse with the appropriate name of "Shamrock."

REFERENCES:

Beaumont: Travels in Buenos Ayres (1828); Wilson: Travels in South America (1796); Pinkerton: Travels (1808); Captain Weddell: Cape Horn and South Atlantic Surveys; Major Gillespie: Buenos Ayres and Provinces; Mrs. Williams, on Humboldt's Travels (1826); Captain Master: At Home with the Patagonians (1891); Hadfield: Notes of Travel in Brazil and La plata (1863); Hinchcliff: South American Sketches (1862); Captain Burton: Highlands of Brazil; Ross Johnston: A Vacation in the Argentine Alps (1867); MacCann: Travels in the Argentine Provinces (1846-1849); Hutchinson: Argentine Gleanings and South American Recollections; Major Seaver: Crossing the Andes; Crawford: Across the Pampas; V. MacKenna: Life of O'Higgins; Life of Diego Rimagro; History of Santiago; History of Valparaiso; MacKenna: Archives of Spanish America, 50 vols.; Miller: Memoirs; Lives of Belgrano and San Martin; Mulhall: English in South America.

THE IRISH IN AUSTRALASIA

By Brother Leo, F.S.C., M.A.

SHOULD one be called upon to give in brief the history of the Irish in the land of the Southern Cross, he could do nothing more to the purpose than to relate the story of the "Holy House of Australia." The episode, indeed, is characteristic, not merely of the Irish in Australia, but of the Irish in every land and clime where they have striven and conquered.

On the fourteenth of November, 1817, there landed in Sydney an Irish Cistercian Father, Jeremiah F. Flynn. He had heard in Rome of the spiritual destitution of the Irish Catholics in Australia, and he secured the permission of his superiors to minister to the needs of his compatriots in the Antipodes. Shortly after his arrival he celebrated Mass in the house of an Irishman named William Davis, who had been transported for making pikes for the insurgents in the days of '98, and then, on the first opportunity that presented itself, he sought the authorization of the colonial governor to exercise the functions of his sacred ministry. Far from hospitable was the reception accorded him by Governor Macquarie. The priest was told, with the bluntness characteristic of British officialdom, that the presence of no "popish missionary" would be tolerated in the settlement, and that the profession of the Protestant form of belief was obligatory on every person in the penal colony.

With the example of the "priesthood hunted down like wolves" before him, Father Flynn saw but one consistent course to pursue. His fellow Catholics, his fellow Irishmen, were in sore need of his help; that help they must receive, even though the civil powers refused their sanction. So for several months he went about as secretly as he could, hearing confessions, offering the Holy Sacrifice, and breaking the bread of good counsel. During this trying period, Davis was his host and defender and friend. Eventually the presence of the priest was detected; he was arrested and promptly sent back to England. Before the ship sailed he tried repeatedly to return to the house of Davis where the Blessed Sacrament was preserved in a cedar clothes-press, but the surveillance of his captors was strict and unsleeping. So in the dwelling of the convict Irishman the Sacred Species remained. Before this unwonted repository Davis kept a light ever burning day and night; and day and night crept the loyal Irishmen of the settlement to kneel in prayer before the improvised shrine. The "Holy House of Australia", as the Davis dwelling came to be known, remained the only Catholic church in the colony until 1821, when two Irish priests, Father John Joseph Therry of Cork and Father Philip Connolly of Kildare, were permitted to attend to the spiritual needs of the Irish Catholics. Their coming marked the beginning of religious toleration in Australia and the termination of the sufferings and sacrifices of the Irish colonists, several of whom had had to pay dearly for their religious convictions. Davis himself had been twice flogged and once imprisoned for refusing to attend Protestant service.

Today, on the site of the "Holy House of Australia", stands the church of St. Patrick. Davis gave the land and the sum of one thousand pounds to the church, and his fellow exiles contributed according to their means. This episode in the history of the Irish in Australia pays a touchingly eloquent tribute to the spirit of loyalty to God and country which has characterized the sons and daughters of St. Patrick everywhere whither their feet have strayed. It is the spirit which has embodied itself in the imposing cathedral of St. Patrick in Melbourne and the splendidly equipped college of St. Patrick in Sydney. It is the spirit which has made the Irish play so conspicuous a rôle in the civic and commercial history of Australasia.

Originally known as New Holland, Australia became an English penal colony after the outbreak of the Revolutionary War in the United States of America. An Irish element came into the colony in the last decade of the eighteenth century when, during the Orange reign of terror, upwards of a thousand people from the west of Ireland were deported by the Ulster magistrates and by Lord Carhampton, the notorious "Satanides", who was charged with the pacification of Connacht. And during the first three decades of the nineteenth century the stream of Irish transportation flowed on. As a result of the Tithes agitation, the Charter and Reform movements, the Combination Laws and the Corn Laws, many more Irishmen were forced across the sea. It was not until 1868 that the convict system was permanently abolished.

It is difficult for us of a later day to realize the meaning of that word, transportation. Let us form some conception of what the Irish exiles suffered from the graphic picture painted in colors, somber but not untrue, by one who knew from first-hand experience the lot of the political prisoner. Writes Dr. Ullathorne in *The Horrors of Transportation:*

"Take any one of you, my dear readers; separate him from his wife, from his children, from all those whose conversation makes life dear to him; cast him on the ends of the earth; let him there fall amongst reprobates who are the last stain and disgrace of our common nature; give him those obscene-mouthed monsters for his constant companions and consolers; let the daily vision of their progress from infamy to infamy, until the demon that inspires them has exhausted invention and the powers of nature together, be his only example; house him, at night, in a bark hut on a mud floor, where he has less comfort than your cattle in their stalls; awake him from the troubled dreams of his wretched wife and outcast children, to feel how far he is from their help, and take him out at sunrise; work him under a burning sun, and a heartless overseer, and the threat of the lash until the night fall; give him not a penny's wages but sorrow; leave him no hope but the same dull, dreary round of endless drudgery for many years to come; let him see no opening by which to escape, but through a long, narrow prospect of police courts, of gaols, of triangles, of death cells, and of penal settlements; let him all the while be clothed in a dress of shame, that shows to every living soul his degradation; and if he dare to sell any part of that clothing, then flog him worse than any dog! And thus, whilst severed from all kindness and all love, whilst the stern harsh voice of his task-master is grating in incessant jars within his ear, take all rest out of his flesh, and plant the thorn; take all feeling out of his heart, and leave the withered core; take all peace out of his conscience, and leave the worm of remorse; and then let any one come and dare to tell me that the man is happy because he has bread and meat. Is it not here, if ever there was such a case, where the taste of bread is a taste of misery, and where to feed and prolong life is to feed and lengthen our sorrow? And in pondering these things, do not those strong words of Sacred Scripture bring down their load of truth in heavy trouble to our thoughts, that, 'Their bread is loathsome to their eye, and their meat unto their soul.'"

But the bright side of the story of the Irish in Australia and New Zealand unfolds in the subsequent years. The men who had been sent forth from Erin with the brand of the convict upon them became the founders of a new commonwealth. To them were joined the numerous voluntary settlers who, attracted by the natural resources of the island-continent and especially by the gold discoveries of the fifties, migrated to Queensland, Victoria, and New South Wales. When in 1858 William E. Gladstone sought to establish a new colony to be known as North Australia, he opened a fresh field for Irish initiative. As a result of his effort there stands today, on a terrace overlooking Port Curtis, the city of Gladstone, the terminal of the Australian railway system. It was here, according to Cardinal Moran, that in 1606, Mass was first celebrated in Australia, when the Spaniards sought shelter in the "Harbor of the Holy Cross." The first government resident at Gladstone was Sir Maurice Charles O'Connell, a relative of the great Liberator; he was four times acting-governor of Queensland.

The list of Irish pioneer settlers in Australasia is a lengthy one. The name of Thomas Poynton stands out prominently. He was a New Zealand pioneer who had married an Irish girl in Sydney. The devotion of Poynton and his wife to the faith of their fathers is evidenced by the fact that he several times made the long journey from his home to Sydney to interest the church authorities in the wants of the New Zealand Irish Catholics, and that she twice made the same arduous trip to have her children baptized. Thomas Mooney has the distinction of being the first Irish pioneer in Western Australia; and yet another Irishman, Cassidy by name, carried out a policy of benevolent assimilation by marrying the daughter of a Maori chief.

Among the pioneer ecclesiastics were Father William Kelly of Melbourne and Father John McEncroe, a native of Tipperary and a Maynooth man, who for thirty years and more was a prominent figure in the religious and civic life of New South Wales. Father John Brady, another pioneer priest, became Bishop of Perth. Irish names occupy a conspicuous and honored place in the roster of the Australian episcopate. Notable on the list are Bishop Francis Murphy of Adelaide, who was born in Co. Meath, and Archbishop Daniel Murphy of Sydney, a native of Cork, the man who delivered the eulogy on the occasion of Daniel O'Connell's funeral at Rome. But scant reference can here be made to the illustrious primate of Australia, Cardinal Moran, archbishop of Sydney from 1884 to 1911, who was such a potent force in the land of his adoption, and whose masterly *History of the Catholic Church in Australasia* puts him in the forefront of ecclesiastical historians. On his death he was succeeded in the see of Sydney by another Irishman, Archbishop Michael Kelly of Waterford. Archbishop O'Reily of Adelaide is a recognized authority on music, and has written several pamphlets on that subject. A Galway man, Dr. T. J. Carr, a great educator, is now (1914) archbishop of Melbourne, and a Clare man, Dr. J. P. Clune, holds sway in Perth.

Irishmen in Australia have figured largely in the iron and coal industries, in the irrigation projects, in the manufacturing activities, and in the working of the gold mines. But they have likewise distinguished themselves in other fields of endeavor. Prominent on the beadroll of Australian fame stand the names of Sir Charles Gavan Duffy (1816-1903), founder of the *Nation* newspaper in Dublin, member of the British house of commons, and afterwards premier of Victoria and speaker of the legislative assembly, and his sons, John Gavan Duffy and Frank Gavan Duffy, public-spirited citizens and authorities on legal matters. The Currans, father and son, active in the public life of Sydney, were afterwards members of the British parliament. Distinguished in the records of the Australian judiciary are Judges Quinlan, Casey, Brennan, and O'Dowd. The Rev. J. Milne Curran, F.G.S., is a geologist who has achieved more than local fame. Other Irishmen who have loomed large in Australasian affairs are Daniel Brophy, John Curnin, Augustus Leo Kenny, James Coghlan, Sir Patrick Buckley, Sir John O'Shannessy, and Nicholas Fitzgerald. Louis C. Brennan, C.B., who was born in Ireland in 1852, emigrated to Australia when a boy and while working in a civil engineer's office in Melbourne conceived the idea of the "Brennan Torpedo", which he afterwards perfected, and then in 1897 sold the invention to the British Admiralty for £110,000. Another Brennan, Frank by name, is president of the Knights of Our Lady of the Southern Cross and has been a labor member of the federal parliament since 1911; a third, Christopher John, is assistant lecturer in modern literature in the University of Sydney; and a fourth, James, of the diocese of Perth, was made a Knight of St. Silvester by Pius X. in 1912.

Young Australia and New Zealand may be as the world goes, but already both have much to their credit in the domains of music, art, and literature; and here, as usual, the Irish have been to the fore. In the writing of poetry, history, and fiction the Celtic element has been especially distinguished. Not to speak of the writers mentioned elsewhere in this sketch, scores of Irish men and women have been identified with the development of an Australian literature which, though delightfully redolent of the land whence it sprang, nevertheless possesses the universal note which makes it a truly human product. Many years ago one of the most gifted of Irish-Australian singers, "Eva" of the *Nation*, voiced a tentative plaint:

"O barren land! O blank, bright sky!
  Methinks it were a noble duty
To kindle in that vacant eye
  The light of spirit-beauty—
To fill with airy shapes divine
  Thy lonely plains and mountains,
The orange grove, the bower of vine,
  The silvery lakes and fountains;
To wake the voiceless, silent air
  To soft, melodious numbers;
To raise thy lifeless form so fair
  From those deep, spell-bound slumbers.
Oh, whose shall be the potent hand
  To give that touch informing,
And make thee rise, O Southern Land,
  To life and poesy warming?"

Mrs. O'Doherty herself, who long lived in that Queensland which she thus apostrophized, helped in no uncertain way to answer her own question. So did John Farrell, the author of the truly remarkable "Jubilee Ode" of 1897 and of a collection of poems which include the well known "How He Died." And so, long before, had the non-Catholic Irishman, Edward O'Shaughnessy, who went to Australia as a convict, but who laughed in lockstep and made music with his chains.

James Francis Hogan, author and journalist, was born in Tipperary in 1855 and shortly afterward was brought by his parents to Melbourne where he received his education. On his return to Ireland he was elected to represent his native county in parliament. He is an authority on Australian history and in his book on *The Gladstone Colony* has given us a fine specimen of modern historical method. With him must be mentioned Roderick Flanagan, whose *History of New South Wales* appeared in 1862.

Other Irish names distinguished in Australasian literature are those of the New Zealand poet, Thomas Bracken; Roderick Quinn; Desmond Byrne; J. B. O'Hara; the eccentric convict-writer, George "Barrington" Waldron; Victor J. Daley; Bernard O'Dowd; Edwin J. Brady; the Rev. J. J. Malone; and the Rev. W. Kelly.

Finally, the Irish in Australia have done more than their share in the work of education and social service. Under

Irish auspices several of the Catholic teaching congregations, including the Christian Brothers and the Presentation Nuns, were introduced, and their work has borne goodly fruit. A mighty power for good is the Hibernian Australasian Benefit Society. The organization, which was founded in 1871, has spread rapidly and has a large active membership.

Truly the land of the Southern Cross is not the dimmest jewel in the coronet of Ireland's glories.

References:

Hogan: The Irish in Australia (1888), The Gladstone Colony (1898); Mennell: Dictionary of Australian Biography (1892); Duffy: Life in Two Hemispheres (1903); Kenny: The Catholic Church in Australia to the Year 1840; Moran: History of the Catholic Church in Australasia (1898); Davitt: Life and Progress in Australasia (1898); Bonwick: The First Twenty Years of Australia (1883); Flanagan: History of New South Wales (1862); Byrne: Australian Writers (1896); Wilson: The Church in New Zealand (1910); Hocken: A Bibliography of the Literature Relating to New Zealand (1909).

THE IRISH IN SOUTH AFRICA

By A. HILLIARD ATTERIDGE.

THE tide of emigration from Ireland has set chiefly towards America and Australia. In South Africa, therefore, the Irish element among the colonists has never been a large one. But, despite its comparatively small numbers, it has been an important factor in the life of South Africa. Here, as in so many other countries, it has been the glory of the sons of Erin to be a missionary people. To their coming is due the very existence of the Catholic Church in these southern lands.

When Dr. Ullathorne touched at the Cape on his way to Australia in 1832, he found at Cape Town "a single priest for the whole of South Africa," an English Benedictine, who soon afterwards returned to Europe in broken health. Few Irish immigrants had by that time found their way to the Cape. They began to arrive in numbers only after the famine year.

The founder of the Catholic hierarchy in South Africa was the Irish Dominican, Patrick R. Griffith, who, in 1837, was sent to Cape Town by Gregory XVI. as the first Vicar Apostolic of Cape Colony. His successors at the Cape, Bishops Grimley, Leonard, and Rooney, have all been Irishmen, and nine in every ten of their flock have from the first been Irish by birth or descent. In the earlier years of Bishop Griffith's episcopate there was a large garrison in South Africa on account of the Kaffir wars. Many of these soldiers were Irishmen. At Grahamstown in 1844 the soldiers of an Irish regiment stationed there did most of the work of building St. Patrick's Church, one of the oldest Catholic churches in South Africa. They worked without wages or reward of any kind, purely out of their devotion to their Faith, giving up most of their leisure to this voluntary labor.

Ten years after Bishop Griffith's appointment, Pius IX. separated Natal and the eastern districts of Cape Colony from Cape Town, and erected the Eastern Vicariate Apostolic. Once more an Irish prelate was the first Bishop—Aidan Devereux, who was consecrated by Bishop Griffith at Cape Town in the

Christmas week of 1847. The great emigration from Ireland had now begun, and a stream of immigrants was arriving at the Cape. Bishop Devereux fixed his residence at Port Elizabeth, and of his four successors up to the present day three have been Irish. Bishop Moran, who went out to Port Elizabeth in 1854, was consecrated at Carlow in Ireland by Archbishop (afterwards Cardinal) Cullen. The third Vicar Apostolic was Bishop Ricards, and the present bishop is another Irishman, Dr. Hugh McSherry, who received his consecration from the hands of Cardinal Logue in St. Patrick's Cathedral at Armagh.

Until the discovery of the diamond deposits in what is now the Kimberley district, some forty years ago, the Irish immigrants had chiefly settled in the ports and along the coast. But among the crowds who went to seek their fortunes at the diamond fields were large numbers of adventurous Irishmen. The mission church established at Kimberley became the centre of a new bishopric in 1886, when the Vicariate of Kimberley, which for some time included the Orange Free State, was established, and an Irish Oblate, Father Anthony Gaughran, was appointed its first bishop. He was succeeded in 1901 by his namesake and fellow countryman, the present Bishop Matthew Gaughran.

The gold discoveries on the Witwatersrand about Johannesburg produced another rush into the interior in the days after the first Transvaal war. A great city of foreign immigrants— the "Uitlanders"—grew up rapidly on the upland, where a few months before there had been only a few scattered Boer farms. Irishmen from Cape Colony and Natal, from Ireland itself, and from the United States formed a large element in the local mining and trading community. They were mostly workers. Few of them found their way into the controlling financier class, which was largely Jewish. The Irish were better out of this circle of international gamblers, whose intrigues finally produced the terrible two years' bloodshed of the great South African war. Many engineers of the mines were Irish-Americans. Huge consignments of mining machinery arrived from the United States, and many of the engineers who came to fit it up remained in the employ of the mining companies. Until after the war, the Transvaal and Johannesburg had depended ecclesiastically on the Vicar Apostolic of Natal, but in 1904 a Transvaal Vicariate was erected, and once more the first bishop was an Irishman, Dr. William Miller, O. M. I.

We have seen how Irish the South African episcopate has been from the very outset. Most of the clergy belong to the same missionary race, as also do the nuns of the various convents, and the Christian Brothers, who are in charge of many of the schools. Of the white Catholic population of the various states of the South African Union, the greater part are Irish. There are about 25,000 Irish in Cape Colony in a total population of over two millions. There are some 7,000 in Natal, 1,500 in Kimberley, and about 2,000 in the Orange River Colony. In the Transvaal, chiefly in and about Johannesburg, there are some 12,000 Irish. A few thousand more are to be found scattered in Griqualand and Rhodesia.

As has been already said, the total numbers are not large in proportion to that of the population generally, and they belong chiefly to the industrial and trading classes. The most notable names among them are those of prelates, priests, and missionaries, who have founded and built up the organization of the Catholic Church in South Africa. But there are some names of note also in civil life. Sir Michael Gallwey was for many years Chief Justice of Natal; the Hon. A. Wilmot, who has not only held high official posts, but has also done much to clear up the early history of South Africa, is Irish on the mother's side; Mr. Justice Shiel is a judge of the Cape Courts; Eyre and Woodbyrne are Irish names among the makers of Rhodesia; and amongst those who have done remarkable work in official life may also be named Sir Geoffrey Lagden, Sir William St. John Carr, and the Hon. John Daverin. Lagden was for many years British Resident in Basutoland, the Switzerland of South Africa, where the native tribes are practically independent under a British protectorate. Griffith, the paramount chief of the Basuto nation, has been a Catholic since 1911. Sir Geoffrey's tactful policy and wise counsels did much to promote the prosperity of this native state, and during the trying days of the South African War, he was able to secure the neutrality of the tribesmen.

In the Boer wars, Irishmen fought with distinction on both sides. General Colley, who fell at Majuba in the first Boer War, was a distinguished Irish soldier. Another great Irishman, General Sir William Butler, has written the story of Colley's life. Butler himself was in command of the troops at the Cape before the great war. If his wise counsels had been followed by the Government, the war would undoubtedly have been avoided. He refused to have any part in the war-provoking policy of Rhodes and Chamberlain, and warned the Home Government that an attack on the Dutch republics would be a serious and perilous enterprise. When the war came, England owed much to the enduring valor of Irish soldiers and to the leadership of Irish generals. One need only name General Hart, of the Irish Brigade; General French, who relieved Kimberley, and who is now (1914) Field-Marshal and Commander-in-Chief of the British army in France; General Mahon, who raised the siege of Mafeking; Colonel Moore, of the famous Connaught Rangers, now (1914) commandant and chief military organizer of the Irish National Volunteers; and, finally, Lord Roberts, who took over the chief command and saved the situation after the early disasters. Lord Kitchener, who acted as Roberts's chief-of-staff, succeeded him in the command, and brought the war to an end by an honorable treaty with the Boer leaders, is a native of Ireland, but of English descent, and he passed most of his boyhood in Ireland, in Co. Kerry, where his father had bought a small property. I used to know an Irish Franciscan lay brother who told me he had taught the future soldier "many games" when he was quite a little fellow.

Of the regiments which took part in the war none won a higher fame than the Munster and the Dublin Fusiliers and the Connaught Rangers. It was in recognition of their splendid valor that the new regiment of Irish Guards was added to the British Army.

But the majority of Irishmen sympathized with the Boer republics, and many of them fought under the Boer flag. Some of these were legally British subjects, but many were naturalized burghers of the Transvaal, and many more were United States citizens, Irish-Americans from the Rand gold mines. There were two small Irish brigades under the Boer flag, those of McBride and Lynch (the latter now a member of the British House of Commons), and an engineer corps commanded by Colonel Blake, an American. At the first battle before Ladysmith it was one of the Irish brigades that kept the Boer guns in action, bringing up ammunition under a rain of shellfire. During the Boer retreat and Roberts's advance on Pretoria, Blake's engineers were always with the Boer rearguard and successfully destroyed every mile of the railway as they went back. Blake had served in the United States cavalry, had learned mining while on duty in Nevada, and had then gone to seek his fortune at Johannesburg. The great leader of the Boer armies, now the Prime Minister of the new South Africa which has happily arisen out of the storm of war, has Irish connections. Louis Botha lived before the war in the southeast Transvaal, not far from Laings Nek, and near neighbors of his were a family of Irish settlers bearing the honored name of Emmet. The Emmets and the Bothas were united by ties of friendship and intermarriage, and one of the Emmets served with Louis Botha during the war.

The Irish colonists of South Africa keep their love for faith and fatherland, but, as in the United States, they have thoroughly and loyally thrown in their lot with the new country of which they have become citizens. Few in number though they are, they are an important factor in the new Dominion, for their national tradition inspires them with civic patriotism, and their religion gives them a high standard of conduct and puts before them, as guides in the work of life and the solution of the problems of the day, the Christian principles of justice and charity.

REFERENCES:

Government Census Returns, South Africa; Catholic Directory for British South Africa (Cape Town, since 1904); The Catholic Magazine, Cape Town; Wilmot and Chase: History of Cape Colony (London, 1896); Theal: History of South Africa (5 vols., London, 1888-1893); for the war period, the *Times* History of the South African War, and the British Official History.

IRISH LANGUAGE AND LETTERS

By Douglas Hyde, LL.D., M. R. I. A.

THE Celtic languages consist of two divisions, (a) the Gaelic or Irish division, and (b) the Kymric or Welsh division. Between them they comprise (a) Irish, Scotch-Gaelic, and Manx, and (b) Welsh, Armorican, and Cornish. All these languages are still alive except Cornish, which died out about a hundred years ago.

Of all these languages Irish is the best preserved, and it is possible to follow its written literature back into the past for some thirteen hundred years; while much of the most interesting matter has come down to us from pagan times. It has left behind it the longest, the most luminous, and the most consecutive literary track of any of the vernacular languages of Europe, except Greek alone.

For centuries the Irish and their language were regarded by the English as something strange and foreign to Europe. It was not recognized that they had any relationship with the Greeks or Romans, the French, the Germans, or the English. The once well-known statesman, Lord Lyndhurst, in the British parliament denounced the Irish as aliens in religion, in blood, and in language. Bopp, in his great Comparative Grammar, refused them recognition as Indo-Europeans, and Pott in 1856 also denied their European connection. It was left for the great Bavarian scholar, John Caspar Zeuss, to prove to the world in his epoch-making "Grammatica Celtica" (published in Latin in 1853) that the Celts were really Indo-Europeans, and that their language was of the highest possible value and interest. From that day to the present it is safe to say that the value set upon the Irish language and literature has been steadily growing amongst the scholars of the world, and that in the domain of philology Old Irish now ranks close to Sanscrit for its truly marvellous and complicated scheme of word-forms and inflections, and its whole verbal system.

The exact place which the Celtic languages (of which Irish is philologically far the most important) hold in the Indo-European group has often been discussed. It is now generally agreed upon that, although both the Celtic and Teutonic languages may claim a certain kinship with each other as being both of them Indo-European, still the Celtic is much more nearly related to the Greek and the Latin groups, especially to the Latin.

All the Indo-European languages are more or less related to one another. We Irish must acknowledge a relationship, or rather a very distant connecting tie, with English. But, to trace this home, Irish must be followed back to the very oldest form of its words, and English must be followed back to Anglo-Saxon and when possible to Gothic. The hard mutes (p, t, c) of Celtic (and, for that matter, of Sanscrit, Zend, Greek, Latin, Slavonic, and Lithuanian) will be represented in Gothic by the corresponding soft mutes (b, d, g), and the soft mutes in Celtic by the corresponding hard mutes in Gothic. Thus we find the Irish *dia* (god) in the Anglo-Saxon *tiw*, the god of war, whose name is perpetuated for all time in Tiwes-däg, now "Tuesday", and we find the Irish *déad* in the Anglo-Saxon "toth", now "tooth", and so on. But of all the Indo-European languages Old Irish possesses by far the nearest affinity to Latin, and this is shown in a great many ways, not in the vocabulary merely, but in the grammar, which for philologists is of far more importance,—as, for example, the *b*-future, the passive in-*r*, the genitive singular and nominative plural of "o stems", etc. Thus the Old Irish for "man", nom. *fer*, gen. *fir*, dat. *fiur*, acc. *fer n*—, plur. nom. *fir*, gen. *fer n*—, is derived from the older forms *viros*, *viri*, *viro*, *viron*, nom. plur. *viri*, gen. plur. *viron*, which everyone who knows Latin can see at a glance correspond very closely to the Latin inflections, *vir*, *viri*, *viro*, *virum*, nom. plur. *viri*, etc.

So much for the language. When did this language begin to be used in literature? This question depends upon another— When did the Irish begin to have a knowledge of letters; when did they begin to commit their literature to writing; and whence did they borrow their knowledge of this art?

The oldest alphabet used in Ireland of which remains exist appears to have been the Ogam, which is found in numbers of stone inscriptions dating from about the third century of our era on. About 300 such inscriptions have already been found, most of them in the southwest of Ireland, but some also in Scotland and Wales, and even in Devon and Cornwall. Wherever the Irish Gael planted a colony, he seems to have brought his Ogam writing with him.

The Irishman who first invented the Ogam character was probably a pagan who obtained a knowledge of Roman letters. He brought back to Ireland his invention, or, as is most likely, invented it on Irish soil. Indeed, the fact that no certain trace of Ogam writing has been found upon the European continent indicates that the alphabet was invented in Ireland itself. An inscription at Killeen Cormac, Co. Kildare, survives which seems to show that the Roman alphabet was known in Ireland in pagan times. Ogam is an alphabet suitable enough for chiselling upon stones, but too cumbrous for the purposes of literature. For this the Roman alphabet must have been used. The Ogam script consists of a number of short lines straight or slanting, and drawn either below, above, or through one long stem-line. This stem-line is generally the sharp angle between two faces or sides of a long upright rectangular stone. Thus four cuts to the right of the long line stand for S; to the left of it they mean C; passing through it, half on one side and half on the other, they mean Z. The device was rude, but it was applied with considerable skill, and it was undoubtedly framed with much ingenuity. The vowels occurring most often are also the easiest to cut, being scarcely more than notches on the edge of the stone. The inscription generally contains the name of the dead warrior over whom the memorial was raised; it usually begins on the left corner of the stone facing the reader and is to be read upwards, and it is often continued down on the right hand angular line as well.

The language of the Ogam inscriptions is very ancient and nearly the same forms occur as in what we know of Old Gaulish. The language, in fact, seems to have been an antique survival even when it was first engraved, in the third or fourth century. The word-forms are probably far older than those used in the spoken language of the time. This is a very important conclusion, and it must have a far-reaching bearing upon the history of the earliest epic literature. Because if forms of language much more ancient than any that were then current were employed on pillar-stones in the third or fourth century, it follows that this obsolescent language must have survived either in a written or a regularly recited form. This immediately raises the probability that the substance of Irish epic literature (which was written down on parchment in the sixth or seventh century) really dates from a period much more remote, and that all that is purely pagan in it was preserved for us in the same antique language as the Ogam inscriptions before it was translated into what we now call "Old Irish."

The following is the Ogam alphabet as preserved on some 300 ancient pillars and stones, in the probably ninth-century treatise in the Book of Ballymote, and elsewhere:

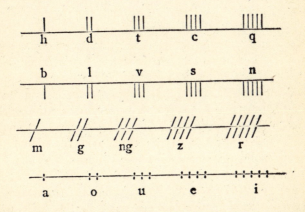

There are a great many allusions to this Ogam writing in the ancient epics, especially in those that are purely pagan in form and conception, and there can be no doubt that the knowledge of letters must have reached Ireland before the island became Christianized. With the introduction of Christianity and of Roman letters, the old Ogam inscriptions, which were no doubt looked upon as flavoring of paganism, quickly fell into disuse and disappeared, but some inscriptions at least are as late as the year 600 or even 800. In the thoroughly pagan poem, *The Voyage of Bran,* which such authorities as Zimmer and Kuno Meyer both consider to have been committed to parchment in the seventh century, we find it stated that Bran wrote the fifty or sixty quatrains of the poem in Ogam. Cuchulainn constantly used Ogam writing, which he cut upon wands and trees and standing stones for Queen Medb's army to read, and these were always brought to his friend Fergus to decipher. Cormac, king of Cashel, in his glossary tells us that the pagan Irish used to inscribe the wand they kept for measuring corpses and graves with Ogam characters, and that it was a source of horror to anyone even to take it in his hand. St. Patrick in his Confession, the authenticity of which no one doubts, describes how he dreamt that a man from Ireland came to him with innumerable letters.

In Irish legend Ogma, one of the Tuatha De Danann who was skilled in dialects and poetry, seems to be credited with the invention of the Ogam alphabet, and he probably was the equivalent of the Gaulish god Ogmios, the god of eloquence, so interestingly described by Lucian.

We may take it then that the Irish pagans knew sufficient letters to hand down to Irish Christians the substance of their pagan epics, sagas, and poems. We may take it for granted also that the greater Irish epics (purely pagan in character, utterly untouched in substance by that Christianity which so early conquered the country) really represent the thoughts, manners, feelings, and customs of pagan Ireland.

The effect of this conclusion must be startling indeed to those who know the ancient world only through the medium of Greek and Roman literature. To the Greek and to his admiring master, the Roman, all outside races were simply barbarians, at once despised, misinterpreted, and misunderstood. We have no possible means of reconstructing the ancient world as it was lived in by the ancestors of some of the leading races in Europe, the Gauls, Spaniards, Britons, and the people of all those countries which trace themselves back to a Celtic ancestry, because these races have left no literature or records behind them, and the Greeks and Romans, who tell us about them, saw everything through the false medium of their own prejudices. But now since the discovery and publication of the Irish sagas and epics, the descendants of these great races no longer find it necessary to view their own past through the colored and distorting glasses of the Greek or the Roman, since there has now opened for them, where they least expected to find it, a window through which they can look steadily at the life of their race, or of one of its leading offshoots, in one of its strongholds, and reconstruct for themselves with tolerable accuracy the life of their own ancestors. It is impossible to overrate the importance of this for the history of Europe, because neither Teutons nor Slavs have preserved pictures of their own heroic past, dating from pagan times. It is only the Celts, and of these the Irish, who have handed down such pictures drawn with all the fond intimacy of romance, and descriptions which exhibit the life of western Europeans at an even earlier culture-stage in the evolution of humanity than do the poems of Homer.

This conclusion, to which a study of the literature invites us, falls in exactly with that arrived at from purely archaeological sources. Professor Ridgeway of Cambridge University, working on archaeological lines, expresses himself as follows: "From this survey of the material remains of the *la Tène* period found actually in Ireland, and from the striking correspondence between this culture and that depicted in the *Táin Bó Cúalnge,* and from the circumstance that the race who are represented in the epic as possessing this form of culture resemble in their physique the tall, fair-haired, grey-eyed Celts of Britain and the continent, we are justified in inferring (1) that there was an invasion (or invasions) of such peoples from Gaul in the centuries immediately before Christ, as is ascribed by the Irish traditions, and (2) that the poems themselves originally took shape when the *la Tène* culture was still flourishing in Ireland. But as this could hardly have continued much later than A. D. 100, we may place the first shaping of the poems not much later than that date and possibly a century earlier."

This conclusion would make the earliest putting together of the Irish epics almost contemporaneous with Augustus Cæsar.

So much for the history and growth of Irish letters.

REFERENCES:

Brash: Ogam inscribed Monuments of the Gaedhil (1879); Mac-Alister: Studies in Irish Epigraphy, vol. 1 (1897), vol. 2 (1902), vol. 3 (1907); Rhys: in Proceedings of the Scottish Society of Antiquaries (Edinburgh, 1892); Ridgeway: Date of the First Shaping of the Cuchulain Saga (1905), in Proceedings of the British Academy, vol. II; Joyce: Social History of Ancient Ireland, vol. I, Chap. 2; Preface to fac-simile edition of the Book of Ballymote.

NATIVE IRISH POETRY

By Professor Georges Dottin.

[Note.—This chapter was written in French by M. Dottin, who is a distinguished professor and dean at the University of Rennes, France. The translation into English has been made by the Editors.]

BY the year 1200 of the Christian era, a time at which the other national literatures of Europe were scarcely beginning to develop, Ireland possessed, and had possessed for several centuries, a Gaelic poetry, which was either the creation of the soul of the people or else was the work of the courtly bards. This poetry was at first expressed in rhythmical verses, each containing a fixed number of accented syllables and hemistichs separated by a pause:

Crist lim,	Crist reum,	Crist in degaid
Crist indium	Crist issum	Crist úasum
	Crist dessum	Crist úasum

This versification, one of the elements of which was the repetition of words or sounds at regular intervals, was transformed about the eighth century into a more learned system. Thenceforward alliteration, assonance, rhyme, and a fixed number of syllables constituted the characteristics of Irish verse:

> Mésse ocus Pángur bán
> cechtar náthar fria sáindAN
> bith a *ménma* sam fri seilGG
> mu *ménma* céin im sáinchEIRDD.

As we see, the consonants in the rhyme-words were merely related: *l, r, n, ng, m, dh, gh, bh, mh, ch, th, f* could rime together just as could *gg, dd, bb.* Soon the poets did not limit themselves to end-rhymes, which ran the risk of becoming monotonous, but introduced also internal rhyme, which set up what we may call a continuous chain of melody:

> is aire caraim DOIRE
> ar a reidhe ar a ghloINE
> 's ar iomad a aingel fIND
> ó 'n cIND go soich arOILE.

This harmonious versification was replaced in the seventeenth century by a system in which account was no longer taken of consonantal rhyme or of the number of syllables.

The rules of Irish verse have nothing in common with classical Latin metres, which were based on the combination of short and long syllables. In Low-Latin, indeed, we find occasionally alliteration, rhyme, and a fixed number of syllables, but these novelties are obviously of foreign origin, and date from the time when the Romans borrowed them from the nations which they called barbarous. We cannot prove beyond yea or nay that they are of Celtic origin, but it is extremely probable that they are, for it is among the Celts both of Ireland and of Wales that the harmonizing of vowels and of consonants has been carried to the highest degree of perfection.

This learned art was not acquired without long study. The training of a poet (*filé*) lasted twelve years, or more. The poets had a regular hierarchy. The highest in rank, the *ollamh,* knew 350 kinds of verse and could recite 250 principal and 100 secondary stories. The *ollamhs* lived at the court of the kings and the nobles, who granted them freehold lands; their persons and their property were sacred; and they had established in Ireland schools in which the people might learn history, poetry, and law. The bards formed a numerous class, of a rank inferior to the *filé;* they did not enjoy the same honors and privileges; some of them even were slaves; according to their standing, different kinds of verse were assigned to them as a monopoly.

The Danish invasions in the ninth century set back for some time the development of Irish poetry, but, when the Irish had driven the fierce and aggressive sea-rovers from their country, there was a literary renascence. This was in turn checked by the Anglo-Norman invasion in the twelfth century, and thereafter the art of versification was no longer so refined as it had formerly been. Nevertheless, the bardic schools still existed in the seventeenth century, more than four hundred years after the landing of Strongbow, and, in them, students followed the lectures of the *ollamhs* for six months each year, or until the coming of spring, exercising both their talents for composition and their memory.

A catalogue of Irish poets, which has recently been made out, shows that there were more than a thousand of them. We have lost many of the oldest poems, but the Irish scribes often modernized the texts which they were copying. Hence the language is not always a sufficient indication of date, and it is possible that, under a comparatively modern form, some very ancient pieces may have been preserved. Even if the poems attributed to Amergin do not go back to the tenth century B. C., as has been claimed for them, they are in any case old enough to be archaic, and certain poems of the mythological cycle are undoubtedly anterior to the Christian era.

We have reason to believe that there have been preserved some genuine poems of Finn macCumaill (third century), a hymn by St. Patrick (d. 461), some greatly altered verses of St. Columcille (d. 597), and certain hymns written by saints who lived from the seventh to the ninth century. The main object of the most celebrated of the ancient poets up to the end of the twelfth century was to render history, genealogy, toponomy, and lives of saints readier of access and easier to retain by putting them into verse-form; and it is the names of those scholars that have been rescued from oblivion, while lyric poetry, having as its basis nothing more than sentiment, has remained for the most part anonymous. After the Anglo-Norman invasion, the best poet seems to have been Donnchadh Mór O'Daly (d. 1244). Of later date were Teig MacDaire (1570-1652), Teig Dall O'Higinn (d. 1615), and Eochaidh O'Hussey, who belonged to the seventeenth and eighteenth centuries. The new school, which abandoned the old rules and whose inspiration is now personal, now patriotic, is represented by *caoine* (keens or laments), *abran* (hymns), or *aislingi* (visions), composed, among others, by Geoffrey Keating (d. c. 1650), David O'Bruadair (c. 1625-1698), Egan O'Rahilly (c. 1670-c. 1734), John MacDonnell (1691-1754), William O'Heffernan (fl. 1750), John O'Tuomy (1706-1775), and Andrew MacGrath (d. c. 1790). The greatest of the eighteenth century Irish poets was Owen Roe O'Sullivan (c. 1748-1784), whose songs were sung everywhere, and who, in the opinion of his editor, Father Dinneen, is the literary glory of his country and deserves to be ranked among the few supreme lyric poets of all time.

If, in order to study the subjects treated by the poets, we lay aside didactic poetry and confine ourselves to the ancient poems from the seventh to the eleventh century, we shall find in the latter a singular variety. They were at first dialogues or monologues, now found incorporated with the sagas, of which they may have formed the original nucleus. Thus, in the *Voyage of Bran,* we have the account of the Isles of the Blessed and the discourse of the King of the Sea; in the *Expedition of Loégaire MacCrimthainn,* the brilliant description of the fairy hosts; in *The Death of the Sons of Usnech,* the touching farewell of Deirdre to the land of Scotland and her lamentation over the dead bodies of the three warriors; and in the *Lay of Fothard Canann,* the strange and thrilling speech of the dead lover, returning after the battle to the tryst appointed by his sweetheart. Other poems seem never to have figured in a saga, like the Song of Crede, daughter of Guaire, in which she extols the memory of her friend Dinertach, and the affecting love-scenes between Liadin and Curithir; or like the bardic songs designed to distribute praise or blame: the funeral panegyric on King Niall, in alternate verses, the song of the sword of Carroll, and the satire of MacConglinne against the monks of Cork.

Religious poetry comprised lyric fragments, which were introduced into the lives of the saints and there formed a kind of Christian saga, or else were based on Holy Writ, like the *Lamentation of Eve;* hymns in honor of the saints, like *The Hymn to St. Michael,* by Mael Isu; pieces such as the famous Hymn of St. Patrick; and philosophic poems like that keen analysis of the flight of thought which dates from the tenth century.

At a time when the poets of other lands seem wholly engrossed in the recital of the deeds of men, one of the great and constant distinguishing marks of poetry in Ireland, whether we have to do with a short note set down by a scribe on the margin of a manuscript or with a religious or profane poem, is a deep, personal, and intimate love of nature expressed not by detailed description, but more often by a single picturesque and telling epithet. Thus we have the hermit who prays God to give him a hut in a lonely place beside a clear spring in the wood, with a little lark to sing overhead; or we have Marban, who, rich in nuts, crab-apples, sloes, water-cress, and honey, refuses to go back to the court to which the king, his brother, presses him to return. Now, we have the description of the summer scene, in which the blackbird sings and the sun smiles; now, the song of the sea and of the wind, which blows tempestuously from the four quarters of the sky; again, the winter song, when the snow covers the hills, when every furrow is a streamlet and the wolves range restlessly abroad, while the birds, numbed to the heart, are silent; or yet again the recluse in his cell, humorously comparing his quest of ideas to the pursuit of the mice by his pet cat. This deep love of inanimate and animate things becomes individual-ized in those poems in which every tree, every spring, every bird is described with its own special features.

If we remember that these original poems, which, before the twelfth century, expressed thoughts that were scarcely known to the literature of Europe before the eighteenth, are, besides, clothed in the rich garb of a subtle harmony, what admiration, what respect, and what love ought we not to show to that ancient Ireland which, in the darkest ages of western civilization, not only became the depositary of Latin knowl-edge and spread it over the continent, but also had been able to create for herself new artistic and poetic forms!

REFERENCES:

Hyde: Love Songs of Connacht (Dublin, 1893), Irish Poetry, an Essay in Irish with Translation in English and a Vocabulary (Dub-lin, 1902), The Religious Songs of Connacht (London, 1906); Meyer: Ancient Gaelic Poetry (Glasgow, 1906), a Primer of Irish Metrics with a Glossary and an Appendix containing an Alphabetical List of the Poets of Ireland (Dublin, 1909); Dottin-Dunn: The Gaelic Literature of Ireland (Washington, 1906); Meyer: Selections from Ancient Irish Poetry (2d edition, London, 1913); Best: Bibliography of Irish Philology and of Printed Irish Literature (Dublin, 1913); Loth: La métrique galloise (Paris, 1902); Thurneysen: Mittelirische Verslehren, Irische Texte III.; Buile Suibhne (Dublin, 1910).

IRISH HEROIC SAGAS

By Eleanor Hull.

IRELAND has the unique distinction of having preserved for mankind a full and vivid literary record of a period otherwise, so far as native memorials are concerned, clouded in obscurity. A few fragmentary suggestions, derived from ancient stone monuments or from diggings in tumuli and graves, are all that Gaul or Britain have to contribute to a knowledge of that important period just before and just after the beginning of our era, when the armies of Rome were over-running western Europe and were brought, for the first time, into direct contact with the Celtic peoples of the West. Almost all that we know of the early inhabitants of these countries comes to us from the pens of Roman writers and soldiers—Poseidonius, Cæsar, Diodorus, Tacitus. We may give these observers credit for a desire to be fair to peoples they some-times admired and often dreaded, but conquerors are not always the best judges of the races they are engaged in sub-duing, especially when they are ignorant of their language, unversed in their lore and customs, and unused to their ways. Valuable as are the reports of Roman authorities, we feel at every point the need of checking them by native records; but the native records of Gaul, and in large part also those of Britain and Wales, have been swept away. Cæsar is probably right in saying that the Druids, who were the learned men of their race and day, committed nothing to writing; if they did, whatever they wrote has been irrecoverably lost.

But Ireland was exempt from the sweeping changes brought about through long periods of Roman and Saxon occupation; no great upheaval from without disturbed the native political and social conditions up to the coming of the Norse and Danes about the beginning of the ninth century. Agricola, standing on the western coast of Britain, looked across the dividing channel, and reflected upon "the beneficial connection that the conquest of Ireland would have formed between the most powerful parts of the Roman Empire," but, fortunately for the literature of Ireland, if not for her history, he never came. The early incursions of the Scotti or Irish were east-ward into England, Wales, and Gaul, and there seem to have been few return movements towards the west. Ireland pur-sued her path of native development undisturbed. It is to this circumstance that she owes the preservation of so much of her native literature, a great body of material, historical, religious, poetic, romantic, showing marks of having originated at a very early time, and of great variety and interest.

At what period this literature first began to be written down we do not know. Orosius tells us that a traveler named Aethicus spent a considerable time in Ireland early in the fifth century "examining their volumes", which tends to prove that there was writing in Ireland before St. Patrick. But the native bard must have made writing superfluous. The man who could, at a moment's notice, recite any one out of the 350 stories which might be called for, besides poetry, genealogies, and tribal records, was worth many books. Only a few were expert enough to read his writings, but all could enjoy his tales.

The earliest written records that we have now existing date from the seventh or eighth century; but undoubtedly there is preserved for us, in these materials, a picture of social con-ditions going back to the very beginning of our era, and coeval with the stage of civilization known in archaeology as *La Tène* or "Late Celtic".

To help his memory the early "shanachie" or story-teller grouped his romantic story-store under different heads, such as "Táins" or Cattle-spoils, Feasts, Elopements, Sieges, Bat-tles, Destructions, Tragical Deaths; but it is easier for us now to group them in another way, and to class together the series of tales referring to the Tuatha De Danann or ancient deities, those belonging to the Red Branch cycle of King Conchobar and Cuchulainn, those relating to Finn, and the Legends of the Kings. The hundred or more tales belonging to the second group are especially valuable for social history on account of the detailed descriptions they give of customs, dress, weapons, habits of life, and ethical ideas. To the historian, folklorist, and student of primitive civilizations they are documents of the highest importance.

It seems likely that the Red Branch cycle of tales, including the epic tale of the Táin or Cattle-spoil of Cualnge, which has gathered round itself a number of minor tales, had some basis of historical fact, and arose in the period of Ulster's predominance to celebrate the deeds of a band of warlike champions who flourished in the north about the beginning of the Christian era. No one who has visited the raths of Emain Macha, near Armagh, where stood the traditional site of the ancient capital of Ulster, or has followed the well-defined and massive outworks of Rath Celtchair and the forts of the other heroes whose deeds the tales embody, could doubt that they had their origin in great events that once happened there. The topography of the tales is absolutely correct. Or again, when we cross over into Connacht, the remains at Rath Croghan, near the ancient palace of the Amazonian queen, Medb, testify to similar events. She it was who in her "Pillow Talk" with her husband Ailill declared that she had married him only because in him did she find the "strange bride-gift" which her imperious nature demanded, "a man without stinginess, without jealousy, without fear." It was in her desire to surpass her husband in wealth that she sent the combined armies of the south and west into Ulster to carry off a famous bull, the Brown Bull of Cooley, the only match in Ireland for one possessed by her spouse. This raid forms the central subject of the *Táin Bó Cúalnge*. The motif of the tale and the kind of life described in it alike show the primitive conditions out of which it had its rise. It belongs to a time when land was plenty for the scattered inhabitants to dwell upon, but stock to place upon it was scarce. The possession of herds was necessary, not only for food and the provisioning of troops, but as a standard of wealth, a proof of position, and a means of exchange. Everything was estimated, before the use of money, by its value in kine or herds. When Medb and Ailill compare their possessions, to find out which of them is better than the other, their herds of cattle, swine, and horses are driven in, their ornaments and jewels, their garments and vats and household appliances are displayed. The pursuit of the cattle of neighboring tribes was the prime cause of the innumerable raids which made every man's life one of perpetual war-

fare, much more so than the acquisition of land or the aveng-
ing of wrongs. Hence a motif that may seem to us insufficient
and remote as the subject of a great epic arose out of the
necessities of actual life. Cattle-driving is the oldest of all
occupations in Ireland.

The conditions we find described in these tales show us an
open country, generally unenclosed by hedges or walls. The
chariots can drive straight across the province. There are no
towns, and the stopping places are the large farmers' dwell-
ings, open inns known as "houses of hospitality", fortified by
surrounding raths or earthen walls, the only private property
in land, in a time when the tribe-land was common, that we
hear of at this period. Within these borders lay the pleasure
grounds and gardens and the cattle-sheds for the herds, which
the great landowner or chief loaned out to the smaller men
in return for services rendered. Here were trained in arts of
industry and fine needlework the daughters of the chief men of
the tribe and their foster-sisters, drawn from the humbler
families around them. The rivers as a rule formed the boundaries of the provinces, and the fords were constantly guarded by
champions who challenged every wayfarer to single combat,
if he could not show sufficient reason for crossing the border-
land. These combats were fought actually in the ford itself,
and all wars began in a long series of single hand-to-hand combats between equal champions before the armies as a whole
engaged each other.

To fight was every man's prime duty, and the man who had
slain the largest number of his fellows was acclaimed as the
greatest hero. It was the proud boast of Conall Cernach, "the
Victorious", that seldom had a day passed in which he had
not challenged a Connachtman, and few nights in which a Connachtman's head had not formed his pillow. It shows the
primitive savagery of the period that skulls of enemies were
worn dangling from the belt, and were stored up in one of
the palaces of Emain Macha as trophies of valor. So warlike were the heroes that even during friendly feasts their
weapons had to be hung up in a separate house, lest they
should spring to arms in rivalry with their own fellows.

Yet in spite of this rude barbarism of outward life, the warriors had formed for themselves a high and exacting code of honor, which may be regarded as the first steps toward what in later times and other countries became known as "chivalry"; save that there is in the acts of the Irish heroes a simplicity and sincerity which puts them on a higher level than the obligatory courtesies of more artificial ages. Generosity between enemies was carried to an extraordinary pitch. Twice over in fights with different foes, Conall Cernach binds his right hand to his side in order that his enemy, who had lost one hand, may fight on equal terms with him. The two severest combats sustained by Cuchulainn, the youthful Ulster champion, in the long war of the Táin are those with Loch the Great and Ferdiad, both first-rate warriors, who had been forced by the wiles of Medb into unwilling conflict against their young antagonist. In their youth they had been fellow-pupils in the school of the Amazon Scathach, who had taught them both alike the arts of war. When Loch the Great, as a dying request, prays Cuchulainn to permit him to rise, "so that he may fall on his face and not backwards towards the men of Erin," lest hereafter it should be said that he fell in flight, Cuchulainn replies: "That will I surely, for it is a warrior's boon thou cravest," and he steps back to allow the wounded man to reverse his position in the ford. The tale of Cuchulainn's combat with Ferdiad has become classic; nothing more pathetic or more full of the true spirit of chivalry is to be found in any literature. Each warrior estimates nobly the prowess of the other, each sorrowfully recalls the memory of old friendships and expeditions made together. When Ferdiad falls, his ancient comrade pours out over him a passionate lament. Each night, when the day's combat is over, they throw their arms round each other's neck and embrace. Their horses are put up in the same paddock and their charioteers sleep beside the same fire; each night Cuchulainn sends to his wounded friend a share of the herbs that are applied to his own wounds, while to Cuchulainn Ferdiad sends a fair half of the pleasant delicate food supplied to him by the men of Erin. We may recall, too, Cuchulainn's act of compassion towards Queen Medb near the close of the Táin. Her army is flying in rout homeward across the Shannon, closely pursued by Cuchulainn. As he approaches the ford he finds Queen Medb lying prostrate on the bank, unable any longer to guard the retreat of her army. She appeals to her enemy to aid her; and Cuchulainn, with that lovable boyish delight in acts of supreme generosity which is always ascribed to him, undertakes to shield the retreat of the disordered host from his own troops and to see them safely across the river, while Medb reposes peacefully in a field hard by. The spirit which actuates the heroes is well expressed by Cuchulainn when his friends would restrain him from going forth to his last fight, knowing that in that battle he must fall: "I had rather than the whole world's gold and than the earth's riches that death had ere now befallen me, so would not this shame and testimony of reproach now stand recorded against me; for in every tongue this noble old saying is remembered, 'Fame outlives life.'"

The Irish tales surpass those of the Arthurian cycle in simplicity, in humor, and in human interest; the characters are not mere types of fixed virtues and vices, they have each a strongly marked individuality, consistently adhered to through the multitude of different stories in which they play a part. This is especially the case with regard to the female characters. Emer, Deirdre, Etain, Grainne may be said to have introduced into European literature new types of womanhood, quite unlike, in their sprightliness and humor, their passionate affection and heroic qualities, to anything found elsewhere. Stories about women play a large part in ancient Irish literature; their elopements, their marriages, their griefs and tragedies, form the subject of a large number of tales. Among the list of tales that any bard might be called upon to recite, the "Courtships" or "Wooings" probably formed a favorite group; they are of great variety and beauty. The Irish, indeed, may be called the inventors of the love-tale for modern Europe.

The gravest defect of this literature (a defect which is common to all early literature before coming under the chastening hand of the master) is undoubtedly its tendency to extravagance; though much depended upon the individual writer, some being stylists and some not, all were prone to frequent

(19)

and grotesque exaggerations. The lack of restraint and self-criticism is everywhere apparent; the old Irish writer seems incapable of judging how to shape his material with a view to presenting it in its best form. Thus, we have the feeling, even with regard to the *Táin Bó Cúalnge,* that what has come down to us is rather the rough-shaped material of an epic than a completed design. The single stories and the groups of stories have been handled and rehandled at different times, but only occasionally, as in the Story of Deirdre (the "Sorrowful Tale of the Sons of Usnech"), or in the later versions of the "Wooing of Emer", or the Book of Leinster version of the "Wooing of Ferb", do we feel that a competent artist has so formed his story that the best possible value has been extracted from it. Yet, in spite of their defects, the old heroic sagas of Ireland have in them a stimulating force and energy, and an element of fine and healthy optimism, which is strangely at variance with the popular conception of the melancholy of Irish literature, and which, wherever they are known, make them the fountain-head of a fresh creative inspiration. This stimulating of the imagination is perhaps the best gift that a revived interest in the old native romance of Ireland has to bestow.

REFERENCES:

The originals of many of the Tales of the Cuchulainn cycle of romances will be found, usually accompanied by English or German translations, in the volumes of *Irische Texte; Revue Celtique; Zeitschrift für Celt. Phil.; Eriu;* Irish Texts Society, vol. II; *Atlantis;* Proceed. of the R. Irish Academy (Irish MSS. Series and Todd Lecture Series). English translations: of the Táin Bó Cúalnge (LU. and Y.B.L. versions), by Miss Winifred Faraday (1904); (LL. version with conflate readings), by Joseph Dunn (1914); of various stories: E. Hull, The Cuchulain Saga in Irish Literature (1898); A. H. Leahy, Heroic Romances of Ireland (1905-6), the Courtship of Ferb (1902). French translations in Arbois de Jubainville's *Epopée celtique en Irlande;* German translations in Thurneysen's *Sagen aus dem alten Irland* (1901); free rendering by S. O'Grady in The Coming of Cuchullain (1904), and in his History of Ireland, the Heroic Period (1878). For full bibliography, see R. I. Best's Bibliography of Irish Philology and Printed Literature (1913), and Joseph Dunn's *Táin Bó Cúalnge,* pp. xxxii-xxxvi (1914).

IRISH PRECURSORS OF DANTE

By Sidney Gunn, M. A.

O NE of the supreme creations of the human mind is the *Divine Comedy* of Dante, and undoubtedly one of its chief sources is the literature of ancient Ireland. Dante himself was a native of Florence, Italy, and lived from 1265 to 1321. Like many great men, he incurred the hatred of his countrymen, and he spent, as a result, the last twenty years of his life in exile with a price on his head. He had been falsely accused of theft and treachery, and his indignation at the wrong thus done him and at the evil conduct of his contemporaries led him to write his poem, in which he visits Hell, Purgatory, and Paradise, and learns how God punishes bad actions, and how He rewards those who do His will.

To the writing of his poem Dante brought all the learning of his time, all its science, and an art that has never been surpassed, perhaps never equalled. Of course, he did not know any Irish, but he knew Italian and the then universal tongue of the learned—Latin, in both of which were tales of visits to the other world; and the greater part of these tales, as well as those most resembling Dante's work in form and spirit, were Irish in origin.

All peoples have traditions of persons visiting the realms of the dead. Homer tells of Odysseus going there; Virgil does the same of Aeneas; and the Oriental peoples, as well as the Germanic races, have similar tales; but no people have so many or such finished accounts of this sort as the ancient Irish. In pagan times in Ireland one of the commonest adventures attributed to a hero was a visit to "tír na m-beó," the land of the living, or to "tír na n-óg," the land of the young; and this supernatural world was reached in some cases by entering a fairy mound and going beneath the ground to it, and in others by sailing over the ocean.

Of the literature of pagan Ireland, though much has come down to us, we have only a very small fraction of what once existed, and what we have has been transmitted and modified by persons of later times and different culture, who, both consciously and unconsciously, have changed it, so that it is very different from what it was in its original form; but the subject and the main outlines still remain, and we have many accounts of both voyages and underground journeys to the other world.

The oldest voyage is, perhaps, that of Maelduin, which Tennyson has transmuted into English under the title *The Voyage of Maeldune*. This is a voyage undertaken for revenge; but vengeance, as Sir Walter Scott has pointed out in his preface to *The Two Drovers,* springs in a barbarous society from a passion for justice; and it is this instinct for justice that inspires the Irish hero to endure and to achieve what he does. Christianity has preserved this legend and added to it its own peculiar quality of mercy; and this illustrates one of the characteristics of Ireland's pagan literature— it is imperfectly Christian and can readily be made to express the Christian point of view.

Another voyage of pagan Irish literature is the *Voyage of Bran.* In this tale idealism is the inspiration that leads the hero into the unknown world. A woman appears who is invisible to all but Bran, and whose song of the beauteous supernatural land beyond the wave is heard by none but him; so that, after refusing to go with her the first time she appears, at length he steps into her boat of glass and sails away to view the wonders and taste the joys of the other world.

In these tales we have two main elements, one real and one ideal. The real element is the fact that the ancient Irish unquestionably made voyages and visited lands which the fervid Celtic imagination and the lapse of time transformed into the wonderful regions of the legends. The stories are thus early geographies, and they show unmistakably a knowledge of western Europe and of the Canary Islands or some other tropical regions; perhaps also, some have gone so far as to claim, they are reminiscent of voyages to America.

The ideal element is no less important as indicating achievement, for it shows that the Irish poets of pagan times had not only realized, but had succeeded in making their national traditions embody, the fact that love of justice and aspiration for knowledge are the foundations of all enduring human achievement and all perfect human joy. Christianity there-

fore found moral and spiritual ideas of a highly developed
order in pagan Ireland, and it did not hesitate to adopt whatever in the literature of the country illustrated its own teachings, and not only were these stories of visits to the other
world full of suggestions as to ways of enforcing Christian
doctrine, but the Irish church and men of Irish birth were the
most active in spreading the faith in the early centuries of its
conquest of western Europe.

For these reasons it is not strange that all the earliest Christian visions of the spirit-world were of Irish origin. We find
the earliest in the *Ecclesiastical History* of the "Venerable
Bede," who died in 735. It is the story of how an Irishman
of great sanctity, Furseus by name, was taken in spirit by
three angels to a place from which he looked down and saw
the four fires that are to consume the world: those of false-
hood, avarice, discord, fraud and impiety. In this there is
the germ of some very fundamental things in Dante's poem,
and we know that Dante knew Bede and had probably read
his history, for he places him in Paradise and mentions him
elsewhere in his works.

In Bede's work there is also another vision, and though in
this second case the man who visits the spirit-world is not an
Irishman, but a Saxon named Drithelm, yet the story came to
Bede through an Irish monk named Haemgils; so it, too, is
connected with Ireland, and it also contains much that is
developed further in the *Divine Comedy.*

One of the most celebrated of the works belonging to this
class of so-called "visionary" writings is the *Fis* or "Vision"
which goes under the name of the famous Irish saint, Adamnan, who was poetically entitled the "High Scholar of the
Western World." This particular vision, the *Fis Adamnáin,* is
remarkable among other things for its literary quality, which is
far superior to anything of the time, and for the fact that it represents "the highest level of the school to which it belonged,"
and that it is "the most important contribution made to the
growth of the legend within the Christian Church prior to the
advent of Dante."

Another Irish vision of great popularity all over Europe in
the Middle Ages is the *Voyage of Saint Brendan.* This is

known as the Irish Odyssey, and it is similar to the pagan tales of Maelduin and Bran, except that instead of its hero being a dauntless warrior seeking vengeance or a noble youth seeking happiness, he is a Christian saint in quest of peace; and instead of the perils of the way being overcome by physical force or the favor of some capricious pagan deity, they are averted by the power of faith and virtue.

The *Voyage of Saint Brendan,* like its pagan predecessors, has a real and an ideal basis; and in both respects it shows an advancement over its prototypes. It contains some very poetic touches, and is credited with being the source of some of the most effective features of Dante's poem. Its great popularity is shown by the fact that Caxton, the first English printer, published a translation of it in 1483; so that it was among the first books printed in English, and for that reason must have been one of the best-known works of the time. Dante undoubtedly knew it, for he was a great scholar in the learning of his day, and especially in ecclesiastical history and the biography of saints.

Another vision of Irish origin that Dante and other writers have borrowed from is that of an Irish soldier named Tundale. He is said to have been a very wicked and proud man, who refused to a friend who owed him for three horses an extension of time in which to pay for them. For this he was struck down by an invisible hand so that he remained apparently dead from Wednesday till Saturday, when he revived and told a story of a visit to the world of the dead that has many features later embodied in the *Divine Comedy.* Tundale's vision is said to have taken place in 1149; Dante probably wrote his poem between 1314 and 1321.

The Irish also produced another legend of this sort that was enormously and universally popular, and became the chief authority on the nature of heaven and hell, in the story of *Saint Patrick's Purgatory.* Saint Patrick was said to have been granted a view of heaven and hell, and a certain island in Lough Derg in Donegal was reputed to be the spot in which he had begun his journey; and there, it was said, those who desired to purge themselves of their sins could enter as he had entered and come back to the world again, provided their faith was strong enough.

This legend was probably known in Ireland from a very early time, but it had spread over all western Europe by the twelfth century. Henry of Saltrey, a Benedictine monk of the Abbey of that name in England, wrote an account in Latin of the descent of an Irish soldier named Owen into Saint Patrick's Purgatory in 1153; and this story soon became the subject of poetic treatment all over Europe. We have several French versions, one by the celebrated French poetess Marie de France, who lived about 1200; and there are others in all the languages of Europe, besides evidence of its wide circulation in the original Latin. Its importance is shown by the fact that it is mentioned by Matthew Paris, the chief English historian of the thirteenth century, and also by Froissart, the well-known French annalist of the fourteenth; while Calderon, the great Spanish dramatist, has written a play based on the legend. Dante undoubtedly knew of Marie de France's version as well as the original of Henry of Saltrey and probably others besides.

From what has been said it will be seen that Dante's masterpiece is largely based on literature of Irish origin; but there are other superlative exhibitions of human genius of which the same is true. One of these is the story of Tristan and Isolde. Tristan is the paragon of all knightly accomplishments, the most versatile figure in the entire literature of chivalry; while Isolde is an Irish princess. By a trick of fate these two drink a love potion inadvertently and become irresistibly enamored of each other, although Isolde is betrothed to King Mark of Cornwall, and Tristan is his nephew and ambassador. The story that follows is infinitely varied, intensely dramatic, delicately beautiful, and tenderly pathetic. It has been treated by several poets of great genius, among them Gottfried of Strassburg, the greatest German poet of his time, and Richard Wagner; but all the beauty and power in the works of these men existed in the original Celtic form of the tale, and the later writers have only discovered it and brought it to light.

The same thing is true of the Arthurian Legend and the story of the Holy Grail. Dante knew of King Arthur's fame, and mentions him in the *Inferno*. To Dante he was a Christian hero, and the historical Arthur may have been a Christian; but much in the story goes back to the pagan Celtic religion. We can find in Irish literature many references that indicate a belief in a self-sustaining, miraculous object similar to the Holy Grail, and the fact that this object was developed into a symbol of some of the deepest and most beautiful Christian truths shows the high character of the civilization and literature of ancient Ireland.

REFERENCES:

Wright: St. Patrick's Purgatory (London, 1844); Krapp: The Legend of St. Patrick's Purgatory (Baltimore, 1900); Becker: Mediaeval Visions of Heaven and Hell (Baltimore, 1899); Shackford: Legends and Satires (Boston, 1913); Meyer and Nutt: The Voyage of Bran, edited and translated by K. Meyer, with an Essay on the Irish Version of the Happy Other World and the Celtic Doctrine of Rebirth, by A. Nutt, 2 vols. (London, 1895); Boswell: An Irish Precursor of Dante (London, 1908).

IRISH INFLUENCE ON ENGLISH LITERATURE

By E. C. Quiggin, M.A.

AMONG the literary peoples of the west of Europe, the Irish, in late medieval and early modern times, were singularly little affected by the frequent innovations in taste and theme which influenced Romance and Teutonic nations alike. To such an extent is this true, that one is often inclined to think that far-off Iceland was to a greater degree in the general European current than the much more accessible Erin. During the age of chivalry, conditions in Ireland were not calculated to promote the growth of epic and lyric poetry after the continental manner. Some considerable time elapsed before the Norman barons became fully Hibernicised, previous to which their interest may be assumed to have turned to the compositions of the trouvères. In the early Norman period, the poets of Ireland might well have begun to imitate Romance models. But, strange to say, they did not, and, for this, various reasons might be assigned. The flowing verses of the Anglo-Norman were impossible for men who delighted in the trammels of the native prosody; and in the heyday of French influence, the patrons of letters in Ireland probably insisted on hearing the foreign compositions in their original dress, as these nobles were doubtless sufficiently versed in Norman-French to be able to appreciate them. But a still more potent factor was the conservatism of the hereditary Irish poet families. A close corporation, they appear to have resented every innovation, and were content to continue the tradition of their ancestors. The direct consequence of this tenacious clinging to the fashions of by-gone days rendered it impossible, nay almost inconceivable, that the literary men of Ireland should have exerted any profound or immediate influence upon England or western Europe. Yet, nowadays, few serious scholars will be prepared to deny that the island contributed in considerable measure to the common literary stock of the Middle Ages.

We might expect to find that direct influence, as a general rule, can be most easily traced in the case of religious themes. Here, in the literature of vision, so popular in Ireland, a chord was struck which continued to vibrate powerfully until the time of the Reformation. In this branch the riotous fancy of the Celtic monk caught the medieval imagination from an early period. Bede has preserved for us the story of Fursey, an Irish hermit who died in France, A. D. 650. The greatest Irish composition of this class with which we are acquainted, the *Vision of Adamnan,* does not appear to have been known outside the island, but a later work of a similar nature met with striking success. This was the *Vision of Tundale* (Tnudgal), written in Latin by an Irishman named Marcus at Regensburg, about the middle of the twelfth century. It seems probable that this work was known to Dante, and, in addition to the numerous continental versions, there is a rendering of the story into Middle English verse.

Closely allied to the Visions are the *Imrama* or "voyages" (Lat. *navigationes*). The earliest romances of this class are secular, *e. g., Imram Maelduin,* which provided Tennyson with the frame-work of his well-known poem. However, the notorious love of adventure on the part of the Irish monks inevitably led to the composition of religious romances of a similar kind. The most famous story of this description, the *Voyage of St. Brendan,* found its way into every Christian country in Europe, and consequently figures in the South English Legendary, a collection of versified lives of saints made in the neighborhood of Gloucester towards the end of the thirteenth century. The episode of St. Brendan and the whale, moreover, was probably the ultimate source of one of Milton's best known similes in his description of Satan. Equally popular was the visit of Sir Owayn to the Purgatory of St. Patrick, which is also included in the same Middle English Legendary. Ireland further contributed in some measure to the common stock of medieval stories which were used as illustrations by the preachers and in works of an edifying character.

When we turn to purely secular themes, we find ourselves on much less certain ground. Though the discussion as to the origins of the "romance of Uther's son", Arthur, continues with

unabated vigor, many scholars have come to think that the
Celtic background of these stories contains much that is derived from Hibernian sources. Some writers in the past have
argued in favor of an independent survival of common Celtic
features in Wales and Ireland, but now the tendency is to
regard all such coincidences as borrowings on the part of
Cymric craftsmen. At the beginning of the twelfth century a
new impulse seems to have been imparted to native minstrelsy
in Wales under the patronage of Gruffydd ap Cynan, a prince
of Gwynedd, who had spent many years in exile at the court of
Dublin. Some of the Welsh rhapsodists apparently served a
kind of apprenticeship with their Irish brethren, and many
things Irish were assimilated at this time which, through this
channel, were shortly to find their way into Anglo-French.
Thus it may now be regarded as certain that the name of the
"fair sword" Excalibur, by Geoffrey called Caliburnus (Welsh
caletfwlch), is taken from Caladbolg, the far-famed broad-
sword of Fergus macRoig. It does not appear that the whole
framework of the Irish sagas was taken over, but, as Windisch
points out, episodes were borrowed as well as tricks of imagery.
So, to mention but one, the central incident of *Syr Gawayn and
the Grene Knyght* is doubtless taken from the similar adventure of Cuchulainn in *Bricriu's Feast*. The share assigned to
Irish influence in the *matière de Bretagne* is likely to grow
considerably with the progress of research.

The fairy lore of Great Britain undoubtedly owes much to
Celtic phantasy. Of this Chaucer, at any rate, had little doubt,
as he writes:

> In th' olde dayes of the King Arthour,
> Of which that Britons speken greet honour,
> Al was this land fulfild of fayerye;
> The elf-queen, with hir joly companye,
> Daunced ful ofte in many a grene med.

And here again there is a reasonable probability that certain
features were borrowed from the wealth of story current in
the neighboring isle. Otherwise it is difficult to understand
why the queen of fayerye should bear an Irish name (Mab,
from Irish Medb), and curiously enough the form of the name
rather suggests that it was borrowed through a written medium

and not by oral tradition. On the other hand it is incorrect
to derive Puck from Irish *puca,* as the latter is undoubtedly
borrowed from some form of Teutonic speech.

So all embracing a mind as that of the greatest English
dramatist could not fail to be interested in the gossip that must
have been current in London at the time of the wars in Ulster.
References to kerns and gallowglasses are fairly frequent. He
had evidently heard of the marvellous powers with which the
Irish bards were credited, for, in *As You Like It,* Rosalind
exclaims:

"I was never so be-rhymed since Pythagoras' time, that I
was an Irish rat, which I can hardly remember."

Similarly, in *King Richard III,* mention is made of the pro-
phetic utterance of an Irish bard, a trait which does not appear
in the poet's source. Any statements as to Irish influence in
Shakespeare that go beyond this belong to the realm of con-
jecture. Professor Kittredge has attempted to show that in Syr
Orfeo, upon which the poet drew for portions of the plot of
A Midsummer Night's Dream, the Irish story of Etain and
Mider was fused with the medieval form of the classical tale of
Orpheus and Eurydice. Direct influence is entirely wanting,
and it is difficult to see how it could have been otherwise.

Even in the case of the Elizabethan poet who spent many
years in the south of Ireland, there is no trace of Hibernian
lore or legend. Spenser, indeed, tells us himself that he had
caused some of the native poetry to be translated to him, and
had found that it "savoured of sweet wit and good invention."
But Ireland plays an infinitesimal part in the *Faerie Queene.*
The scenery round Kilcolman Castle forms the background of
much of the incident in Book V. "Marble far from Ireland
brought" is mentioned in a simile in the second Book, where
we also read:

> As when a swarme of gnats at eventide
> Out of the fennes of Allan do arise.

But Ireland supplied no further inspiration.

The various plantations of the seventeenth century produced an Anglo-Irish stock which soon asserted itself in literature. As a typical example, we may take the author of *The*

Vicar of Wakefield. At his first school at Lissoy, Oliver Goldsmith came under Thomas Byrne, a regular shanachie, possessed of all the traditional lore, with a remarkable gift for
versifying. It was under this man that the boy made his first
attempts at verse, and his memory is celebrated in *The Deserted
Village*:

> There, in his noisy mansion, skilled to rule,
> The village master taught his little school.
> A man severe he was, and stern to view.

Unfortunately Goldsmith was removed to Elphin at the age of
nine, and although he retained an affection for Irish music all
his life, his intimate connection with Irish Ireland apparently
ceased at this point. "Sweet Auburn! loveliest village of the
plain" is doubtless full of reminiscences of the poet's early
years in Westmeath, but the sentiments, the rhythm, and the
language are entirely cast in an English mould. We may
mention, in passing, that it has been suggested that Swift derived the idea of the kingdom of Lilliput from the Irish story
of the Adventures of Fergus macLeide amongst the lepre-
chauns. All that can be said is that this derivation is not impossible, though the fact that the tale is preserved only in a
single manuscript rather points to the conclusion that the story
did not enjoy great popularity in the seventeenth and eighteenth
centuries.

We have seen that Goldsmith was removed from an Irish
atmosphere at a tender age, and this is not the only instance of
the frowning of fortune upon the native literature. When the
fame of the ancient bards of the Gael was noised from end to
end of Europe, it was through the medium of Macpherson's
forgeries. *Fingal* caught the fleeting fancy of the moment in
a manner never achieved by the true Ossianic lays of Ireland.
The *Reliques of Irish Poetry*, published by Miss Brooke by
subscription in Dublin in 1789 to vindicate the antiquity of the
literature of Erin, never went into a second edition. And
although some of the pieces contained in that volume have
been reprinted in such undertakings of a learned character as
the volumes of the Dublin Ossianic Society, J. F. Campbell's
Leabhar na Feinne, and Cameron's *Reliquiae Celticae,* they

have aroused little interest amongst those ignorant of the Irish
tongue.

During the nineteenth century, the number of poets who
drew upon Ireland's past for their themes increased considerably. The most popular of all is unquestionably the author
of the *Irish Melodies*. But, here again, the poet owes little
or nothing to vernacular poetry, the mould is English, the
sentiments are those of the poet's age. Moore's acquaintance
with the native language can have been but of the slightest, and
in the case of Mangan we are told that he had to rely upon
literal versions of Irish pieces furnished him by O'Donovan
or O'Curry. Of the numerous attempts to reproduce the over-
elaboration of rhyme to which Irish verse has ever been prone,
Father Prout's *Bells of Shandon* is perhaps the only one that
is at all widely known. When the legendary lore of Ireland
became accessible to men of letters, owing to the labors of
O'Curry, O'Donovan, and Hennessy, and the publication of
various ancient texts by the Irish Archæological Society, it
was to be expected that an attempt would be made by some
poet of Erin to do for his native land what the Wizard of the
North had accomplished for Scotland. The task was undertaken by Sir Samuel Ferguson, who met with conspicuous success. His most ambitious effort, *Congal,* deals in epic fashion
with the story of the battle of Moyra. Others in similar strain
treat the story of Conaire Mór and Deirdre, whilst others
such as the *Tain-Quest* are more in the nature of ballads.
Ferguson did more to introduce the English reading public to Irish story than would have been accomplished by
any number of bald translations. His diction is little affected
by the originals, and he sometimes treats his materials with
great freedom, but his achievement was a notable one, and he
has not infrequently been acclaimed as the national poet.

Is it perhaps invidious to single out any living author for
special mention, but this brief survey cannot close without
noticing the dramatic poems of W. B. Yeats, the latest poet
who attempts to present the old stories in an English dress.
His plays *On Baile's Strand, Deirdre,* and others, have become
familiar to English audiences through the excellent acting of
the members of the Abbey Theatre Company. The original

texts are now much better known than they were in Ferguson's day, and Mr. Yeats consequently cannot permit himself the same liberties. Similarly, it is only during the last twenty-five years that the language of Irish poetry has been carefully studied, and Mr. Yeats has this advantage over his predecessors that on occasion, *e. g.,* in certain passages in *The King's Threshold,* he is able to introduce with great effect reminiscences of the characteristic epithets and imagery which formed so large a part of the stock-in-trade of the medieval bard.

REFERENCES:

Friedel and Meyer: La Vision de Tondale (Paris, 1907); Boswell: An Irish Precursor of Dante (London, 1908); Cambridge History of English Literature, vol. I, chaps. xii and xvi; Windisch: *Das Keltische Brittannien* (Leipzig, 1912), more especially chap. xxxvii; Dictionary of National Biography; Gwynn: Thos. Moore ("English Men of Letters" Series, London, 1905).

IRISH FOLKLORE

By Alfred Perceval Graves.

A MONG savage peoples there is at first no distinction of a definite kind between good and bad spirits, and when a distinction has been reached, a great advance in a spiritual direction has been made. For the key to the religion of savages is fear, and until such terror has been counteracted by belief in beneficent powers, civilization will not follow. But the elimination of the fear of the unseen is a slow process: indeed, it will exist side by side with the belief in Christianity itself, after a modification through various stages of better pagan belief.

Ireland still presents, in its more out-of-the-way districts, evidence of that strong persistence in the belief in maleficent or malicious influences of the pre-Christian powers of the air, which it seems difficult to eradicate from the Celtic imagination. In the celebrated poem entitled *The Breastplate of St. Patrick,* there is much the same attitude on the part of Patrick towards the Druids and their powers of concealing and changing, of paralyzing and cursing, as was shown by Moses towards the magicians of Egypt. Indeed, in Patrick's time a belief in a world of fairies existed even in the king's household, for "when the two daughters of King Leary of Ireland, Ethnea the fair and Fedelma the ruddy, came early one morning to the well of Clebach to wash, they found there a synod of holy bishops with Patrick. And they knew not whence they came, or in what form, or from what people, or from what country; but they supposed them to be *Duine Sidh,* or gods of the earth, or a phantasm."

Colgan explains the term *Duine Sidh* thus: "Fantastical spirits," he writes, "are by the Irish called men of the *Sidh,* because they are seen, as it were, to come out of the beautiful hills to infest men, and hence the vulgar belief that they reside in certain subterranean habitations: and sometimes the hills themselves are called, by the Irish, *Sidhe* or *Siodha.*"

No doubt, when the princesses spoke of the gods of the earth, reference was made to such pagan deities as Beal;

Dagda the great or the good god; Aine, the Moon, goddess of the water and of wisdom; Manannan macLir, the Irish Neptune; Crom, the Irish Ceres; and Iphinn, the benevolent, whose relations to the Irish Oirfidh resembled those of Apollo towards Orpheus; and to the allegiance they owed to the Elements, the Wind, and the Stars. But besides these pagan divinities and powers, and quite apart from them, the early Irish believed in two classes of fairies: in the first place, a hierarchy of fairy beings, well and ill disposed, not differing in appearance, to any great degree at any rate, from human beings—good spirits and demons, rarely visible during the daytime; and, in the second place, there was the magic race of the De Danann, who, after conquest by the Milesians, transformed themselves into fairies, and in that guise continued to inhabit the underworld of the Irish hills, and to issue thence in support of Irish heroes, or to give their aid against other fairy adversaries.

There is another theory to account for the fairy race. It is that they are angels who revolted with Satan and were excluded from heaven for their unworthiness, but were not found evil enough for hell, and therefore were allowed to occupy that intermediate space which has been called "the Other World." It is still a moot point with the Irish peasantry, as it was with the Irish saints of old, whether, after being compelled to dwell without death among rocks and hills, lakes and seas, bushes and forest, till the day of judgment, the fairies then have the chance of salvation. Indeed, the fairies are themselves believed to have great doubts of a future existence, though, like many men, entertaining undefined hopes of happiness; and hence the enmity which some of them have for mankind, who, they acknowledge, will live eternally. Thus their actions are balanced between generosity and vindictiveness towards the human race.

Mr. W. Y. Evans Wentz, A. M., of Leland Stanford University, California, and Jesus College, Oxford, has received an honorary degree from the latter university for his thesis, "The Fairy Faith in Celtic Countries: Its Psychical Origin and Nature", a most laborious as well as ingenious work, whose object is to prove "that the origin of the fairy faith is psychical, and that fairyland, being thought of as an invisible world within which the visible world is immersed as an island in an unexplored ocean, actually exists, and that it is peopled by more species of living beings than this world, because incomparably more vast and varied in its possibilities." This may be added as a fourth theory to account for the existence of fairies, and it may be further stated here that the Irish popular belief in ghosts attributes to some of their departed spirits much of the same violence and malice with which fairies are credited. Mr. Jeremiah Curtin gives striking instances of this kind in his book, the *Folk Lore of West Kerry*.

It became necessary, therefore, for the Gaels who believed in the preternatural powers of the fairies for good and ill to propitiate them as far as possible. On May eve, accordingly, cattle were driven into raths and bled there, some of the blood being tasted, the rest poured out in sacrifice. Men and women were also bled on these occasions. The seekers for buried treasure, over which fairies were supposed to have influence, immolated a black cock or a black cat to propitiate them. Again, a cow, suffering from sickness believed to be due to fairy malice, was bled and then devoted to St. Martin. If it recovered, it was never sold or killed. The first new milk of a cow was poured out on the ground to propitiate the fairies, and especially on the ground within a fairy rath. The first drop of any drink is also thrown out by old Irish people. If a child spills milk, the mother says, "that's for the fairies, leave it to them and welcome." Slops should never be thrown out of doors without the warning, "Take care of water!" lest fairies should be passing invisibly and get soiled by the discharge. Eddies of dust upon the road are supposed to be caused by the fairies, and tufts of grass, sticks, and pebbles are thrown into the centre of the eddy to propitiate the unseen beings. Some fairies of life size, who live within the green hills or under the raths, are supposed to carry off healthy babes to be made fairy children, their abstractors leaving weak changelings in their place. Similarly, nursing mothers are sometimes supposed to be carried off to give the breast to fairy babes, and handsome young men are spirited away to become bridegrooms to fairy brides. Again, folk suffering

from falling sickness are supposed to be in that condition
owing to the fatigue caused by nocturnal rides through the air
with the fairies, whose steeds are bewitched rushes, blades of
grass, straws, fern roots, and cabbage stalks. The latter, to be
serviceable for the purpose, should be cut into the rude shapes
of horses before the metamorphosis can take place.

Iron of every kind keeps away malignant fairies: thus, a
horseshoe nailed to the bottom of the churn prevents butter
from being bewitched. Here is a form of charm against the
fairies who have bewitched the butter: "Every window should
be barred, a great turf fire should be lit upon which nine irons
should be placed, the bystanders chanting twice over in Irish,
'Come, butter, come; Peter stands at the gate waiting for a
buttered cake.' As the irons become heated the witch will
try to break in, asking the people to take the irons, which are
burning her, off the fire. On their refusing, she will go and
bring back the butter to the churn. The irons may then be
removed from the fire and all will go well."

If a neighbor or stranger should enter a cottage during the
churning, he should put his hand to the dash, or the butter
will not come. A small piece of iron should be sewed into an
infant's clothes and kept there until the child is baptized, and
salt should be sprinkled over his cradle to preserve the babe
from abduction. The fairies are supposed to have been conquered by an iron-weaponed race, and hence their dread of
the metal.

To recover a spell-bound friend, stand on All Hallows' eve
at cross roads or at a spot pointed out by a wise woman or
fairy doctor. When you have rubbed fairy ointment on your
eyelids, the fairies will become visible as the host sweeps by
with its captive, whom the gazer will then be able to recognize. A sudden gust announces their approach. Stooping
down, you will then throw dust or milk at the procession,
whose members are then obliged to surrender your spell-
bound friend. If a man leaves home after his wife's confine-
ment, some of his clothes should be spread over the mother
and infant, or the fairies may carry them off. It is good for a
woman, but bad for a man, to dream of fairies. It betokens

marriage for a girl, misfortune for a man, who should not undertake serious business for some time after such dreaming.

Fairy changelings may be recognized by tricky habits, constant crying, and other unusual characteristics. It was customary to recover the true child in the following way: The changeling was placed upon an iron shovel over the fire, when it would go shrieking up the chimney, and the *bona fide* human child would be restored. It was believed that fairy changelings often produced a set of small bagpipes from under the clothes and played dance music upon them, till the inmates of the cottage dropped with exhaustion from the effects of the step dancing they were compelled to engage in.

On Samain eve, the night before the first of November, or, as it is now called, All Hallows' night or Hallowe'en, all the fairy hills or *shees* are thrown wide open and the fairy host issues forth, as mortals who are bold enough to venture near may see. Naturally therefore people keep indoors so as not to encounter the spectral host. The superstition that the fairies are abroad on Samain night still exists in Ireland and Scotland, and there is a further belief, no doubt derived from it, that the graves are open on that night and that the spirits of the dead are abroad.

Salt, as already suggested, is regarded to be so lucky that if a child falls, it should always be given three pinches of salt, and if a neighbor calls to borrow salt, it should not be refused, even though it be the last grain in the house.

An infant born with teeth should have them drawn by the nearest smith, and the first teeth when shed should be thrown into the fire, lest the fairies should get hold of what had been part of you.

Those who hear fairy music are supposed to be haunted by the melody, and many are believed to go mad or commit suicide in consequence.

The fairies are thought to engage in warfare with one another, and in the year 1800 a specially sanguinary battle was believed to have been fought between two clans of the fairies in county Kilkenny. In the morning the hawthorns along the fences were found crushed to pieces and drenched with blood.

In popular belief fairies often go hunting, and faint sounds of fairy horns, the baying of fairy hounds, and the cracking of fairy whips are supposed to be heard on these occasions, while the flight of the hunters is said to resemble in sound the humming of bees.

Besides the life-sized fairies who are reputed to have these direct dealings with human beings, there are diminutive preternatural beings who are also supposed to come into close touch with men. Among these is the Luchryman (*Leithphrogan*), or brogue maker, otherwise known as Leprechaun. He is always found mending or making a shoe, and, if grasped firmly and kept constantly in view, will disclose hidden treasure to you, or render up his *sparan na sgillinge,* or purse of the (inexhaustible) shilling. He can only be bound by a plough chain or woolen thread. He is the symbol of industry which, if steadily faced, leads to fortune, but, if lost sight of, is followed by its forfeiture.

Love in idleness is personified by another pigmy, the *Geancanach* (love-talker). He does not appear, like the Leprechaun, with a purse in one of his pockets, but with his hands in both of them, and a *dudeen* (short pipe) in his mouth, as he lazily strolls through lonely valleys making love to the foolish country lasses and "gostering" with the idle "boys." To meet him meant bad luck, and whoever was ruined by ill-judged love was said to have been with the *Geancanach*.

Another evil sprite was the *Clobher-ceann,* "a jolly, red-faced, drunken little fellow," always "found astride of a wine-butt" singing and drinking from a full tankard in a hard drinker's cellar, and bound by his appearance to bring its owner to speedy ruin.

Then there were the *Leannan-sighes,* or native Muses, to be found in every place of note to inspire the local bard, and the *Beansighes* (Banshees, fairy women) attached to each of the old Irish families and giving warning of the death of one of its members with piteous lamentations.

Black Joanna of the Boyne (*Siubhan Dubh na Boinne*) appeared on Hallowe'en in the shape of a great black fowl, bringing luck to the home whose *Banithee* (woman of the house) kept the dwelling constantly clean and neat.

The Pooka, who appeared in the shape of a horse, and whom Shakespeare is by many believed to have adapted as "Puck," was a goblin who combined "horse-play" with viciousness, but also at times helped with the housework.

The *Dullaghan* was a churchyard demon whose head was of a movable kind. Dr. Joyce writes: "You generally meet him with his head in his pocket, under his arm, or absent altogether; or if you have the fortune to light upon a number of *Dullaghans*, you may see them amusing themselves by flinging their heads at one another or kicking them for footballs."

An even more terrible churchyard demon is the fascinating phantom that waylays the widower at his wife's very tomb, and poisons him by her kiss when he has yielded to her blandishments.

Of monsters the Irish had, and still believe in, the *Piast* (Latin *bestia*), a huge dragon or serpent confined to lakes by St. Patrick till the day of judgment, but still occasionally seen in their waters. In old Fenian times, namely, the days of Finn and his companion knights, the *Piasts*, however, roamed the country, devouring men and women and cattle in large numbers, and some of the early heroes are recorded to have been swallowed alive by them and then to have hewed their way out of their entrails.

Merrows, or Mermaids, are also still believed in, and many folk tales exist describing their intermarriage with mortals.

According to Nicholas O'Kearney, "It is the general opinion of many old persons versed in native traditional lore, that, before the introduction of Christianity, all animals possessed the faculties of human reason and speech; and old story-tellers will gravely inform you that every beast could speak before the arrival of St. Patrick, but that the saint having expelled the demons from the land by the sound of his bell, all the animals that, before that time, had possessed the power of foretelling future events, such as the Black Steed of *Binn-each-labhra,* the Royal Cat of *Cloughmagh-righ-cat* (Clough), and others, became mute, and many of them fled to Egypt and other foreign countries."

Cats are said to have been appointed to guard hidden treasures; and there are few who have not heard old Irish people

tell about strange meetings of cats and violent battles fought
by them in the neighborhood. "It was believed," adds O'Kearney, "that an evil spirit in the shape of a cat assumed command over these animals in various districts, and that when
those wicked beings pleased they could compel all the cats belonging to their division to attack those of some other district.
The same was said of rats; and rat-expellers, when commanding a colony of those troublesome and destructive animals to
emigrate to some other place, used to address their 'billet' to
the infernal rat supposed to hold command over the rest. In a
curious pamphlet on the power of bardic compositions to charm
and expel rats, lately published, Mr. Eugene O'Curry states
that a degraded priest, who was descended from an ancient
family of hereditary bards, was enabled to expel a colony of
rats by the force of satire!"

Hence, of course, Shakespeare's reference to rhyming Irish
rats to death.

It will thus be seen that Irish Fairy Lore well deserves to
have been called by Mr. Alfred Nutt, one of the leading
authorities on the subject, "as fair and bounteous a harvest of
myth and romance as ever flourished among any race."

REFERENCES:

Alex. Carmichael: Carmina Gadelica; David Comyn: The Boyish
Exploits of Finn; the Periodical, "Folklore"; Lady Gregory: Cuchu-
lain of Muirthemne, Gods and Fighting Men; Miss Eleanor Hull: The
Cuchulain Saga in Irish Literature; Douglas Hyde: Beside the Fire,
(a collection of Irish Gaelic Folk Stories), *Leabhar Sgeulaicheachta*,
(Folk Stories in Irish); "Irish Penny Journal"; Patrick Kennedy:
The Fireside Stories of Ireland, Legendary Fictions of the Irish Celt;
Standish Hayes O'Grady: Silva Gadelica; Wood-Martin: Traces of
the Elder Faiths in Ireland, Pagan Ireland; W. Y. Wentz: The
Fairy Faith in Celtic Countries; Lady Wilde: Charms, Incantations,
etc.; Celtic articles in Hastings' Dictionary of Religion and Ethics.

IRISH WIT AND HUMOR

By Charles L. Graves.

NO record of the glories of Ireland would be complete without an effort, however inadequate, to analyze and illustrate her wit and humor. Often misunderstood, misrepresented, and misinterpreted, they are nevertheless universally admitted to be racial traits, and for an excellent reason. Other nations exhibit these qualities in their literature, and Ireland herself is rich in writers who have furnished food for mirth. But her special pre-eminence resides in the possession of what, to adapt a famous phrase, may be called an *anima naturaliter jocosa*. Irish wit and Irish humor are a national inheritance. They are inherent in the race as a whole, independent of education or culture or comfort. The best Irish sayings are the sayings of the people; the greatest Irish humorists are the nameless multitude who have never written books or found a place in national dictionaries of biography. None but an Irishman could have coined that supreme expression of contempt: "I wouldn't be seen dead with him at a pig-fair," or rebuked a young barrister because he did not "squandher his carcass" (*i. e.*, gesticulate) enough. But we cannot trace the paternity of these sayings any more than we can that of the lightning retort of the man to whom one of the "quality" had given a glass of whisky. "That's made another man of you, Patsy," remarked the donor. "'Deed an' it has, sor," Patsy flashed back, "an' that other man would be glad of another glass." It is enough for our purpose to note that such sayings are typically Irish and that their peculiar felicity consists in their combining both wit and humor.

To what element in the Irish nature are we to attribute this joyous and illuminating gift? No one who is not a Gaelic scholar can venture to dogmatize on this thorny subject. But, setting philology and politics aside, it is hard to avoid the conclusion that Ireland has gained rather than lost in this respect by the clash of races and languages. Gaiety, we are told, is not the predominating characteristic of the Celtic temperament, nor is it reflected in the prose and verse of the "old ancient days" that have come down to us. Glamour and magic and passion abound in the lays and legends of the ancient Gael, but there is more melancholy than mirth in these tales of long ago. Indeed, it is interesting to note in connection with this subject that the younger school of Irish writers associated with what is called the Celtic Renascence have, with very few exceptions, sedulously eschewed anything approaching to jocosity, preferring the paths of crepuscular mysticism or sombre realism, and openly avowing their distaste for what they consider to be the denationalized sentiment of Moore, Lever, and Lover. To say this is not to disparage the genius of Yeats and Synge; it is merely a statement of fact and an illustration of the eternal dualism of the Irish temperament, which Moore himself realized when he wrote of "Erin, the tear and the smile in thine eye."

A reaction against the Donnybrook tradition was inevitable and to a great extent wholesome, since the stage Irishman of the transpontine drama or the music-halls was for the most part a gross and unlovely caricature, but, like all reactions, it has tended to obscure the real merits and services of those who showed the other side of the medal. Lever did not exaggerate more than Dickens, and his portraits of Galway foxhunters and duellists, of soldiers of fortune, and of Dublin undergraduates were largely based on fact. At his best he was a most exhilarating companion, and his pictures of Irish life, if partial, were not misleading. He held no brief for the landlords, and in his later novels showed a keen sense of their shortcomings. The plain fact is that, in considering the literary glories of Ireland, we cannot possibly overlook the work of those Irishmen who were affected by English influences or wrote for an English audience.

Anglo-Irish humorous literature was a comparatively late product, but its efflorescence was rapid and triumphant. The first great name is that of Goldsmith, and, though deeply influenced in technique and choice of subjects by his association with English men of letters and by his residence in England, in spirit he remained Irish to the end—generous, impulsive, and improvident in his life; genial, gay, and tenderhearted in his works. The Vicar of Wakefield was Dr.

Primrose, but he might just as well have been called Dr. Shamrock. No surer proof of the pre-eminence of Irish wit and humor can be found than in the fact that, Shakespeare alone excepted, no writers of comedy have held the boards longer or more triumphantly than Goldsmith and his brother Irishman, Sheridan. *She Stoops to Conquer, The Rivals, The School for Scandal,* and *The Critic* represent the sunny side of the Irish genius to perfection. They illustrate, in the most convincing way possible, how the debt of the world to Ireland has been increased by the fate which ordained that her choicest spirits should express themselves in a language of wider appeal than the ancient speech of Erin.

On the other hand, English literature and the English tongue have gained greatly from the influence exerted by writers familiar from their childhood with turns of speech and modes of expression which, even when they are not translations from the Gaelic, are characteristic of the Hibernian temper. The late Dr. P. W. Joyce, in his admirable treatise on English as spoken in Ireland, has illustrated not only the essentially bilingual character of the Anglo-Irish dialect, but the modes of thought which it enshrines. There is no better known form of Irish humor than that commonly called the "Irish bull," which is too often set down to lax thinking and faulty logic. But it is the rarest thing to encounter a genuine Irish "bull" which is not picturesque and at the same time highly suggestive. Take, for example, the saying of an old Kerry doctor who, when conversing with a friend on the high rate of mortality, observed, "Bedad, there's people dyin' who never died before." Here a truly illuminating result was attained by the simple device of using the indicative for the conditional mood—as in Juvenal's famous comment on Cicero's second Philippic: *Antoni gladios potuit contemnere si sic omnia dixisset.* The Irish "bull" is a heroic and sometimes successful attempt to sit upon two stools at once, or, as an Irishman put it, "Englishmen often make 'bulls,' but the Irish 'bull' is always pregnant."

Though no names of such outstanding distinction as those of Goldsmith and Sheridan occur in the early decades of the nineteenth century, the spirit of Irish comedy was kept vigorously alive by Maria Edgeworth, William Maginn, Francis

Mahony (Father Prout), and William Carleton. Sir Walter Scott's splendid tribute to the genius of Maria Edgeworth is regarded by some critics as extravagant, but it is largely confirmed in a most unexpected quarter. Turgenief, the great Russian novelist, proclaimed himself her disciple, and has left it on record that but for her example he might never have attempted to give literary form to his impressions of the classes in Russia corresponding to the poor Irish and the squireens and the squires of county Longford. Maginn and Mahony were both scholars—the latter happily called himself "an Irish potato seasoned with Attic salt"—wrote largely for English periodicals, and spent most of their lives out of Ireland. In the writings of all three an element of the grotesque is observable, tempered, however, in the case of Mahony, with a vein of tender pathos which emerges in his delightful "Bells of Shandon." Maginn was a wit, Mahony was the hedge-school-master *in excelsis,* and Carleton was the first realist in Irish peasant fiction. But all alike drew their best inspiration from essentially Irish themes. The pendulum has swung back slowly but steadily since the days when Irish men of letters found it necessary to accommodate their genius to purely English literary standards. Even Lever, though he wrote for the English public, wrote mainly about Ireland. So, too, with his contemporary Le Fanu, whose reputation rests on a double basis. He made some wonderful excursions into the realm of the bizarre, the uncanny, and the gruesome. But in the collection known as *The Purcell Papers* will be found three short stories which for exuberant drollery and "diversion" have never been excelled. That the same man could have written *Uncle Silas* and *The Quare Gander* is yet another proof of the strange dualism of the Irish character.

The record of the last fifty years shows an uninterrupted progress in the invasion of English *belles lettres* by Irish writers. Outside literature, perhaps the most famous sayer of good things of our times was a simple Irish parish priest, the late Father Healy. Of his humorous sayings the number is legion; his wit may be illustrated by a less familiar example—his comment on a very tall young lady named Lynch: "Nature gave her an inch and she took an ell." In the House of Commons today there is no greater master of irony and sardonic humor than his namesake, Mr. Tim Healy. On one occasion he remarked that Lord Rosebery was not a man to go tiger-shooting with—except at the Zoo. On another, being anxious to bring an indictment against the "Castle" *régime* in Dublin and finding the way blocked by a debate on Uganda, he successfully accomplished his purpose by a judicious geographical transference of names, and convulsed the House by a speech in which the nomenclature of Central Africa was applied to the government of Ireland.

But wit and humor are the monopoly of no class or calling in Ireland. They flourish alike among car-drivers and K. C.'s, publicans and policemen, priests and parsons, beggars and peers. It is a commonplace of criticism to deny these qualities in their highest form to women. But this is emphatically untrue of Ireland, and was never more conclusively disproved than by the recent literary achievements of her daughters. The partnership of two Irish ladies, Miss Edith Somerville and Miss Violet Martin, has given us, in *Some Experiences of an Irish R. M.* (*i. e.*, Resident Magistrate), the most delicious comedy, and in *The Real Charlotte* the finest tragi-comedy, that have come out of Great Britain in the last thirty years. The *R. M.*, as it is familiarly called, is already a classic, but the Irish *comédie humaine*—to use the phrase in the sense of Balzac—is even more vividly portrayed in the pages of *The Real Charlotte.* Humor, genuine though intermittent, irradiates the autumnal talent of Miss Jane Barlow, and the long roll of gifted Irishwomen who have contributed to the gaiety of nations may be closed with the names of Miss Hunt, author of *Folk Tales of Breffny;* of Miss Purdon and Miss Winifred Letts, who in prose and verse, respectively, have moved us to tears and laughter by their studies of Leinster peasant life; and of "Moira O'Neill" (Mrs. Skrine), the incomparable singer of the Glens of Antrim. To give a full list of the living Irish writers, male and female, who are engaged in the benevolent work of driving dull care away would be impossible within the space at our command. But we cannot end without recognition of the exhilarating extravaganzas of

"George A. Birmingham" (Canon Hannay), the freakish and elfin muse of James Stephens, and the coruscating wit of F. P. Dunne, the famous Irish-American humorist, whose "Mr. Dooley" is a household word on both sides of the Atlantic.

REFERENCES:

Goldsmith: Vicar of Wakefield, She Stoops to Conquer; Sheridan: The Rivals, The School for Scandal, The Critic; R. Edgeworth: Essay on Irish Bulls; M. Edgeworth: Castle Rackrent, The Absentee; Maginn: Miscellanies in Prose and Verse; Carleton: Traits and Stories of the Irish Peasantry; Mahony (Father Prout): Reliques of Father Prout; John and Michael Banim: Tales of the O'Hara Family; Lover: Legends and Stories of Ireland, Handy Andy; Lever: Harry Lorrequer, Charles O'Malley, Lord Kilgobbin; Le Fanu: The Purcell Papers; Barlow: Bogland Studies, Irish Idylls, Irish Neighbours; Birmingham: The Seething Pot, Spanish Gold, The Major's Niece, The Red Hand of Ulster, General John Regan; Stephens: The Crock of Gold, Here are Ladies; Hunt: The Folk Tales of Breffny; Purdon: The Folk of Furry Farm; Somerville and Ross: The Real Charlotte, Some Experiences of an Irish R. M., All on the Irish Shore, Dan Russel the Fox.

THE IRISH THEATRE

By Joseph Holloway.

THE Irish theatre and secular drama may be said to begin with the production of James Shirley's historical play, *St. Patrick for Ireland,* in Werburgh Street Theatre, about 1636-7; and though Dublin was a great school for acting, and supplied many of the best players to the English stage, such as Quin, Macklin, Peg Woffington, Miss O'Neill, and hosts of others, it never really possessed a creative theatre (save at the Capel Street Theatre for a few years during the Grattan Parliament) until the modern movement in Ireland came into being and the Abbey Theatre became its headquarters.

Of course, innumerable plays by Irish writers were written, but most of them were not distinctively Irish in character; and the names of Goldsmith, Sheridan, O'Keeffe, Farquhar, Sheridan Knowles, Oscar Wilde, and dozens of others will always be remembered as great Irish writers for the stage. And when fine impersonators of Irish character like Tyrone Power, John Drew, or Barney Williams arrived, there were always to be found several clever writers to fit them with parts, the demand always creating the supply.

Even before Dion Boucicault took to writing Irish dramas of a more palatable and less "stage-Irish" character than those of his immediate predecessors, some excellent plays, Irish in character and tone, had from time to time found their way to the stage. However, Boucicault sweetened our stage by the production of *The Colleen Bawn, Arrah-na-Pogue,* and *The Shaughraun,* and showed by his rollicking impersonations of Myles, Shan, and Conn, how good-humored, hearty, and self-sacrificing Irish boys in humble life can be. He had great technical knowledge of stagecraft, and that has helped to make his Irish plays live in the popular goodwill right up to today.

A revolt against Boucicault's Irish boys, all fun and frolic, and charming colleens, who could do no wrong, has made our modern playwrights go to the other extreme; so that now we find our stage peopled with peasants, cruel, hard, and forbidding for the most part, and with colleens who are the reverse of lovable in thought or act. Neither picture is quite true of our people. What is really wanted is the happy medium, which few, if any, of our new playwrights have yet given us.

If our great popular Irish drama has yet to come, I think the Fays have made it possible to say that a distinct and really fine dramatic school has arisen in Ireland, evolved out of their wonderful skill in teaching, producing, and acting; and if we are not always really delighted with what our playwrights give us, the almost perfect way in which the plays are served up by the actors invariably wholly satisfies. It is the actors who have made the Abbey Theatre famous, and not the plays. Such acting as theirs cast a spell over all who see them. What pleasing memories do the names of W. G. Fay, Frank J. Fay, Dudley Digges, Sara Allgood, Arthur Sinclair, Maire O'Neill, Maire ni Shuiblaigh, J. M. Kerrigan, Fred O'Donovan, Eileen O'Doherty, Una O'Connor, Eithne Magee, Nora Desmond, and John Connolly recall!

With the production of W. B. Yeats's poetic one-act play, *The Land of Heart's Desire,* at the Avenue Theatre, London, on March 29, 1894, began the modern Irish dramatic movement. When the poet had tasted the joys of the footlights, he longed to see an Irish Literary Theatre realized in Ireland. Five years later, in the Antient Concert Rooms, Dublin, on May 9, 1899, his play, *The Countess Cathleen,* was produced, and his desire gratified. The experiment was tried for three years and then dropped; plays by Yeats, Edward Martyn, George Moore, and Alice Milligan were staged with English-trained actors in the casts; and a Gaelic play—the first ever presented in a theatre in Ireland—was also given during the third season. It was *The Twisting of the Rope,* by Dr. Douglas Hyde, and was played at the Gaiety Theatre, Dublin, on October 21, 1901, by a Gaelic Amateur Dramatic Society coached by W. G. Fay. The author filled the principal part with distinction.

It was while rehearsing this play that the thought came to Fay: "Why not have my little company of Irish-born actors— the Ormond Dramatic Society—appear in plays by Irish writers instead of in the ones they have been giving for years?" And the thought soon ripened into realization. His brother, Frank, had dreamed of such a company since he read of the small beginnings out of which the Norwegian Theatre had grown; and just then, seeing some of "Æ's" (George Russell's) play, *Deirdre,* in the *All Ireland Review,* he asked the author if he would allow them to produce it, and, consent being given, the company put it into rehearsal at once. "Æ" got for them from Yeats *Kathleen-Ni-Houlihan,* to make up the programme. Thus it was that this company of amateurs and poets, now known as the Abbey Players, came into existence, and at St. Teresa's Hall, Clarendon Street, Dublin, gave their first performance on April 2, 1902.

Shortly afterwards they took a hall at the back of a shop in Camden Street, where they rehearsed and gave a few public performances. On "Æ" declining to be their president, Frank Fay suggested the name of W. B. Yeats, and he was elected, and in that way came again into the movement in which he has figured so largely ever since.

The company played occasionally in the Molesworth Hall, and produced there, among other pieces, Synge's *In the Shadow of the Glen* (October 8, 1903) and *Riders to the Sea* (February 25, 1904); Yeats's *The Hour Glass* (March 14, 1903) and *The King's Threshold* (October 8, 1903); Lady Gregory's *Twenty-five* (March 14, 1903); and Padraic Colum's *Broken Soil* (December 3, 1903).

On March 26, 1904, the company paid a flying one-day visit to the Royalty, London, and Miss A. E. F. Horniman, who had given Shaw, Yeats, and Dr. John Todhunter their first real start as playwrights at the Avenue, London, in March-April, 1894 (Shaw had had his first play, *Widowers' Houses,* played by the Independent Theatre in 1892), saw the performance, and was so impressed that she thought she would like to find a suitable home for such talent in Dublin, and fixed upon the old Mechanics' Institute and its surrounding buildings, and there the Abbey Theatre soon afterwards—on December 27, 1904—came into existence.

In writing of this Irish dramatic movement, one must always bear in mind that it was Yeats who first conceived the idea of such a movement; the Fays who founded the school of Irish acting; and Miss Horniman who, like a fairy god-mother, waved the wand, and gave it a habitation and a name—the Abbey Theatre—and endowed it for six years.

Play followed play with great rapidity, and dramatic socie-ties sprang up all over the country, playing home-made pro-ductions in Gaelic and English. All Ireland seemed to be play-acting and play-writing; so much so that Frank Fay was heard to say that "he thought everyone had a play in his pocket, and that anyone in the street could be picked up and shaped into an actor or actress with a little training, Ireland was so teeming with talent!"

Dramatic Ireland had slumbered for a long while, and awoke with tremendous vigor for work. New dramatists sprang up in all parts of Ireland; The Ulster Literary Theatre started in Belfast; The Cork Dramatic Society, in Cork; The Theatre of Ireland, in Dublin; and others in Galway and Waterford soon followed. In Dublin at present more than half a dozen dramatic societies are continually producing new plays and discovering new acting talent. There are also two Gaelic dramatic societies. And nearly every town in Ireland now has its own dramatic class and its own dramatists. All this activity has come about within the last ten or twelve years, where, before, in many places, drama and acting were almost unknown.

Many Gaelic societies throughout the country put on Gaelic plays by Dr. Douglas Hyde, Pierce Beasley, Thomas Haynes, Canon Peter O'Leary, and others; and the *Oireachtas* (the Gaelic musical and literary festival) held each year in Dublin usually presents several Irish plays and offers prizes for new ones at each festival.

Of all the Irish playwrights who have arisen in recent years, Lady Gregory has produced most and W. B. Yeats is the most poetic. He is more a lyric poet than a dramatist, and is never satisfied with his work for the stage, but keeps eternally chop-ping and changing it. His *Kathleen-Ni-Houlihan*, though a dream-play, always appeals to an audience of Irish people. Perhaps his one-act *Deirdre* is the nearest approach to real drama he has done. Some of Lady Gregory's earlier one-act farces, such as *The Workhouse-Ward,* are very amusing; *The Rising of the Moon* is a little dramatic gem, and *The Gaol Gate* is touched with genuine tragedy. Synge wrote only one play— *Riders to the Sea*—that acts well. The others are admired by critics for the strangeness of their diction and the beauty of the nature-pictures scattered through them. His much-discussed *Playboy of the Western World* has become famous for the rows it has created at home and abroad from its very first production on January 26, 1907. William Boyle, who gets to the heart of those he writes about, has produced the most popular play of the movement in *The Eloquent Dempsey,* and a perfectly constructed one in *The Building Fund.* W. F. Casey's two plays—*The Man Who Missed the Tide* and *The Suburban Groove*—are both popular and actable. Padraic Colum's plays—*The Land* and *Broken Soil* (the latter rewritten and renamed *The Fiddler's House*)—are almost idyllic scenes of country life. Lennox Robinson's plays are harsh in tone, but dramatically effective, and T. C. Murray's *Birthright* and *Maurice Harte* are fine dramas, well constructed and full of true knowledge of the people he writes about. Seumas O'Kelly has written two strong dramas in *The Shuiler's Child* and *The Bribe,* and Seumas O'Brien one of the funniest Irish farces ever staged in *Duty.* R. J. Ray's play, *The Casting Out of Martin Whelan,* is the best this dramatist has as yet given us, and George Fitzmaurice's *The Country Dressmaker* has the elements of good drama in it. St. John G. Ervine has written a very human drama in *Mixed Marriage.* He hails from the north of Ireland; but Rutherford Mayne is the best of the Northern playwrights, and his plays, *The Drone* and *The Turn of the Road,* are splendid homely county Down comedies.

Bernard Shaw's *John Bull's Other Island,* as Irish plays go, is a fine specimen; Canon Hannay has written two successful comedies, *Eleanor's Enterprise* and *General John Regan*—the latter not wholly to the taste of the people of the west. James Stephens and Jane Barlow have also tried their hands at playwriting, with but moderate success. Perhaps the modern drama that made the most impression when first played was *The Heather Field,* by Edward Martyn. It gripped and remains a lasting memory with all who saw it in 1899. But I think I have written enough to show that the Irish Theatre of today is in a very alive condition, and that if the great National Dramatist has not yet arrived, he is sure to emerge. When that time comes, the actors are here ready to interpret such work to perfection.

An article, however brief, on the Irish Theatre, would be incomplete without mention of the world-famous tragedians, John Edward MacCullough, Lawrence Patrick Barrett, and Barry Sullivan; of genial comedians like Charles Sullivan and Hubert O'Grady; of sterling actors like Shiel Barry, John Brougham, Leonard Boyne, J. D. Beveridge, and Thomas Nerney; or of operatic artists like Denis O'Sullivan and Joseph O'Mara—many of whom have passed away, but some, fortunately, are with us still.

References:

John Genest: Some Account of the English Stage from the Restoration to 1830 (1832; vol. 10 is devoted to the Irish Stage); Chetwood: General History of the Stage, more particularly of the Irish Theatre (Dublin, 1749); Molloy: Romance of the Irish Stage; Baker: Biographia Dramatica (Dublin, 1782); Hitchcock: An Historical View of the Irish Stage from its Earliest Period down to the Season of 1788; Doran: Their Majesties' Servants, or Annals of the English Stage (London, 1865); Hughes: The Pre-Victorian Drama in Dublin; The History of the Theatre Royal, Dublin (Dublin, 1870); Levey and O'Rourke: Annals of the Theatre Royal (Dublin, 1880); O'Neill: Irish Theatrical History (Dublin, 1910); Brown: A Guide to Books on Ireland (Dublin, 1912); Lawrence: The Abbey Theatre (in the Weekly Freeman, Dublin, Dec., 1912), Origin of the Abbey Theatre (in Sinn Fein, Dublin, Feb. 14, 1914); Weygandt: Irish Plays and Playwrights (London, 1913); Lady Gregory: Our Irish Theatre (London, 1914); Bourgeois: John M. Synge and the Irish Theatre (London, 1913); Moore: Hail and Farewell, 3 vols. (London, 1911-1914); Esmore: The Ulster Literary Theatre (in the Lady of the House, Dublin, Nov. 15, 1913); the Reviews, Beltaine (1899-1900) and Samhain (1901-1903).

IRISH JOURNALISTS

By Michael MacDonagh.

THE most splendid testimony to the Irish genius in journalism is afforded by the London press of the opening decades of the twentieth century. One of the greatest newspaper organizers of modern times is Lord Northcliffe. As the principal proprietor and guiding mind of both the *Times* and the *Daily Mail,* he directly influences public opinion, from the steps of the Throne and the door of the Cabinet, to the errand boy and the servant maid. T. P. O'Connor, M. P., is the most popular writer on current social and political topics, and so amazing is his versatility that every subject he touches is illumined by those fine qualities, vision and sincerity. The most renowned of political writers is J. L. Garvin of the *Pall Mall Gazette* and the *Observer.* By his leading articles he has done as much as the late Joseph Chamberlain by his speeches to democratize and humanize the old Tory party of England. The authoritative special correspondent, studying at first hand all the problems which divide the nations of Europe, and knowing personally most of its rulers and statesmen, is E. J. Dillon of the *Daily Telegraph.* And when the quarrels of nations are transferred from the chancelleries to the stricken field there is no one among the war correspondents more enterprising and intrepid in his methods, or more picturesque and vivid with his pen, than M. H. Donohoe of the *Daily Chronicle.* All these men are Irish. Could there be more striking proof of the natural bent and aptitude of the Irish mind for journalism?

Dean Swift was the mightiest journalist that ever stirred the sluggish soul of humanity. Were he alive today and had he at his command the enormous circulation of a great daily newspaper, he would keep millions in a perpetual mental ferment, such was the ferocious indignation into which he was aroused by wrong and injustice and his gift of savage ironical expression. Swift, as a young student in Trinity College, Dublin, saw the birth of the first offspring of the Irish mind in journalism. The *Dublin News Letter* made its appearance in June, 1685, and was published every three or four days for the circulation of news and advertisements. Only one copy of the first issue of this, the earliest of Irish newspapers, is extant. It is included in the Thorpe collection of tracts in the Royal Dublin Society. Dated August 26, 1685, it consists of a single leaf of paper printed on both sides, and contains just one item of news, a letter brought by the English packet from London, and two local advertisements. As I reverently handled it, I was thrilled by the thought that from this insignificant little seed sprang the great national organ, the *Freeman's Journal;* the *Press* of the United Irishmen; the *Nation* of the Young Irelanders; the *United Ireland* of the Land League; the *Irish World* and the *Boston Pilot* of the American Irish; and the *Irish Independent,* the first half-penny Dublin morning paper, and the most widely circulated of Irish journals. If Swift did not write for the *Dublin News Letter,* he certainly wrote for the *Examiner,* a weekly miscellany published in the Irish capital from 1710 to 1713, and the first journal that endeavored to create public opinion in Ireland. It was at Swift's instigation that this paper was started, and he was doubtless encouraged to suggest it by the success that attended his articles in the contemporary London publication of the same name, the Tory *Examiner,* in which his journalistic genius was fully revealed. As it has been expressively put, he wrote his friends, Harley and St. John, into a firm grip of power, and thus, as in other ways, contributed his share to the inauguration and maintenance of that policy which in the last four years of Queen Anne so materially recast the whole European situation. About the same time there appeared in London the earliest forms of the periodical essay in the *Tatler* and the *Spectator,* which exhibit the comprehensiveness of the Irish temperament in writing by affording a contrast between the Irish force and vehemence of Swift and the Irish play of kindly wit and tender pathos in the deft and dainty periods of Richard Steele.

Dr. Charles Lucas was, even more than Swift perhaps, the precursor of that type of Irish publicist and journalist, of which there have been many splendid examples since then in Ireland, England, and America. Lucas first started the *Censor,* a weekly journal, in 1748. Within two years his paper was suppressed for exciting discontent with the government, and to avoid a prosecution he fled to England. In 1763 the *Freeman's Journal* was established by three Dublin merchants. Lucas, who had returned from a long exile and was a member of the Irish parliament, contributed to it, sometimes anonymously but generally over the signature of "A Citizen" or "Civis." The editor was Henry Brooks, novelist, poet, and playwright. His novel, *The Fool of Quality,* is still read. His tragedy, *The Earl of Essex,* was, wrongly, supposed to contain a precept, "Who rules o'er freemen should himself be free," which led to the more famous parody of Dr. Samuel Johnson, "Who drives fat oxen should himself be fat." The object of Lucas and Brooke, as journalists, was to awaken national sentiment, by teaching that Ireland had an individuality of her own independently of England. But they were more concerned with the assertion of the constitutional rights of the parliament of the Protestant colony as against the domination of England. Therefore, the first organ of Irish Nationality, representative of all creeds and classes, was the *Press,* the newspaper of the United Irishmen, which was started in Dublin in 1797, by Arthur O'Connor, the son of a rich merchant who had made his money in London. Its editor was Peter Finnerty, born of humble parentage at Loughrea, afterwards a famous parliamentary reporter for the London *Morning Chronicle,* and its most famous contributor was Dr. William Drennan, the poet, who first called Ireland "the Emerald Isle."

Irishmen did not become prominently associated with American journalism until after the Famine and the collapse of the Young Ireland movement in 1848. The journalist whom I regard as having exercised the most fateful influence on the destinies of Ireland was Charles Gavan Duffy, the founder and first editor of the *Nation,* a newspaper of which it was truly and finely said that it brought a new soul into Erin. Among its contributors, who afterwards added lustre to the journalism of the United States, was John Mitchel. In the *Southern Citizen* and the *Richmond Enquirer* he supported the South against the North in the Civil War. The Rev. Abram Joseph Ryan, who was associated with journalism in New Orleans, not only acted as a Catholic chaplain with the Confederate army, but sang of its hopes and aspirations in tuneful verse. Serving in the army of the North was Charles G. Halpine, whose songs signed "Private Miles O'Reilly" were very popular in those days of national convulsion in the United States. Halpine's father had edited the Tory newspaper, the Dublin *Evening Mail;* and Halpine himself, after the war, edited the *Citizen* of New York, famous for its advocacy of reforms in civic administration. Perhaps the two most renowned men in Irish-American journalism were John Boyle O'Reilly of the *Boston Pilot* and Patrick Ford of the *Irish World.* O'Reilly was a troop-sergeant in the 10th Hussars (Prince of Wales's Own), and during the Fenian troubles of 1866 had eighty of his men ready armed and mounted to take out of Island Bridge Barracks, Dublin, at a given signal, to aid the projected insurrection. Detected, he was brought to trial, summarily convicted, and sentenced to be shot. This sentence was commuted to twenty-five years' penal servitude; but O'Reilly survived it all to become a brilliant man of letters and make the *Boston Pilot* one of the most influential Irish and Catholic newspapers in the United States. Ford, who had served his apprenticeship as a compositor in the office of William Lloyd Garrison at Boston, founded the *Irish World* in 1870. This newspaper gave powerful aid to the Land League. A special issue of 1,650,000 copies of the *Irish World* was printed on January 11, 1879, for circulation in Ireland; and money to the amount of $600,000 altogether was sent by Ford to the headquarters of the agitation in Dublin. A journalist of a totally different kind was Edwin Lawrence Godkin. Born in County Wicklow, the son of a Presbyterian clergyman, Godkin in 1865 established the *Nation* in New York as an organ of independent thought; and for thirty-five years he filled a unique position, standing aside from all parties, sects, and bodies, and yet permeating them all with his sane and restraining philosophy.

In Canada, Thomas D'Arcy Magee won fame as a journalist on the *New Era* before he became even more distinguished as a parliamentarian. When the history of Australian journalism is written it will contain two outstanding Irish names: Daniel Henry Deniehy, who died in 1865, was called by Bulwer Lytton "the Australian Macaulay" on account of his brilliant writings as critic and reviewer in the press of Victoria. Gerald Henry Supple, another Dublin man, is also remembered for his contributions to the *Age* and the *Argus* of Melbourne. In India one of the first—if not the first—English newspapers was founded by a Limerick man, named Charles Johnstone, who had previously attained fame as the author of *Chrysal, or the Adventures of a Guinea,* and who died at Calcutta about 1800.

Stirring memories of battle and adventure leap to the mind at the names of those renowned war correspondents, William Howard Russell, Edmond O'Donovan, and James J. O'Kelly. Russell, a Dublin man, was the first newspaper representative to accompany an army into the field. He saw all the mighty engagements of the Crimea—Alma, Balaclava, Inkerman, Sebastopol—not from a distance of 60 or 80 miles, which is the nearest that correspondents are now allowed to approach the front, but at the closest quarters, riding through the lines on his mule, and seeing the engagements vividly, so that he was able to describe them in moving detail for readers of the *Times*. O'Donovan—son of Dr. John O'Donovan, the distinguished Irish scholar and archaeologist—was in the service of the London *Daily News*. That dashing campaigner—as his famous book, *The Merv Oasis,* shows him to have been—perished with Hicks Pasha's Army in the Sudan in November, 1883. At the same time James O'Kelly, also of the *Daily News,* was lost in the desert, trying to join the forces of the victorious Sudanese under the Madhi. Ten years before that he had accomplished, for the New York *Herald,* the equally daring and hazardous feat of joining the Cuban rebels in revolt against Spain. He escaped the perils of the Mambi Land and the Sudan, and survived to serve Ireland for many years as a Nationalist member in the British parliament. John Augustus O'Shea, better known, perhaps, as "The Irish Bohemian", also deserves remembrance for his quarter of a century's work as special correspondent in Europe—including Paris during the siege—for the London *Standard*.

Indeed, no matter to what side of journalism we turn, we find Irishmen filling the foremost and the highest places. John Thaddeus Delane, under whose editorship the *Times* became for a time the most influential newspaper in the world, was of Irish parentage. The first editor of the *Illustrated London News* (1842)—one of the pioneers in the elucidation of news by means of pictures—was an Irishman, Frederick Bayley. Among the projectors of *Punch,* and one of its earliest contributors, was a King's county man, Joseph Sterling Coyne. The founder of the *Liverpool Daily Post* (1855), the first penny daily paper in Great Britain, was Michael Joseph Whitty, a Wexford man. His son, Edward M. Whitty, was the originator of that interesting feature of English and Irish journalism, the sketch of personalities and proceedings in parliament. Of the editors of the *Athenaeum*—for many years the leading English organ of literary criticism—one of the most famous was Dr. John Doran, who was of Irish parentage. "Dod" is a familiar household word in the British Parliament. It is the name of the recognized guide to the careers and political opinions of Lords and Commons. Its founder was an Irishman, Charles Roger Dod, who for twenty-three years was a parliamentary reporter for the *Times*. And what name sheds a brighter light on the annals of British journalism for intellectual and imaginative force than that of Justin MacCarthy, novelist and historian, as well as newspaper writer?

At home in Ireland the name of Gray is inseparably associated with the *Freeman's Journal*. Under the direction of Dr. John Gray this newspaper became in the sixties and seventies the most powerful organ of public opinion in Ireland; and in the eighties it was raised still higher in ability and influence by his son and successor, Edmund Dwyer Gray. In the south of Ireland the most influential daily newspaper is the *Cork Examiner,* which was founded in 1841 by John Francis Maguire, who wrote in 1868 *The Irish in America*. It is doubtful whether any country ever produced a more militant and able political journal than was *United Ireland* in the stormy years during which it was edited by William O'Brien as the organ of the Land League.

The Irish mood is gregarious, expansive, glowing, and eager to keep in intimate touch with the movements and affairs of humanity. That, I think, is the secret of its success in journalism.

REFERENCES :

Madden: Irish Periodical Literature (1867) ; Andrews: English Journalism (1855) ; North: Newspaper and Periodical Press of the United States (1884) ; MacDonagh: The Reporter's Gallery (1913).

THE IRISH LITERARY REVIVAL

By Horatio S. Krans, Ph.D.

IN the closing decade of the nineteenth century and in the opening years of the twentieth, no literary movement has awakened a livelier interest than the Irish Literary Revival, a movement which, by its singleness and solidarity of purpose, stood alone in a time of confused literary aims and tendencies. Movements, like individuals, have their ancestry, and that of the Irish Literary Revival is easily traced. It descends from Callanan and Walsh, and from the writers of '48. It is to this descent that the lines in William Butler Yeats's "To Ireland in Coming Times" allude:

> Know that I would accounted be
> True brother of that company,
> Who sang to sweeten Ireland's wrong,
> Ballad and story, rann and song.

With the passing of the mid-nineteenth-century writers, the old movement waned, and in the field of Irish letters there was, in the phrase of a famous bull, nothing stirring but stagnation. A witty critic of the period, commenting upon this unhappy state of affairs, declared that, though the love of learning in Ireland might still be, as the saying went, indestructible, it was certainly imperceptible. But after the fall of Parnell a new spirit was stirring. Politics no longer absorbed the whole energy of the nation. Groups of men inspired with a love of the arts sprang up here and there. In 1890 Yeats proved himself a real prophet when he wrote: "A true literary consciousness—national to the centre—seems gradually to be forming out of all this disguising and prettifying, this penumbra of half-culture. We are preparing likely enough for a new Irish literary movement—like that of '48—that will show itself in the first lull in politics."

Responsive to the need of the young writers associated with Yeats, the National Literary Society was founded in Dublin in 1892, and a year later London Irishmen, among them men already distinguished in letters, founded in the English metropolis the Irish Literary Society. From the presses in Dublin, in London, and in New York as well, books began to appear in rapid succession—slender volumes of verse, novels, short stories, essays, plays, translations, and remakings of Irish myths and legends, all inspired by, and closely related to, the past or the present of Ireland, voicing an essentially national spirit and presenting the noblest traits of Irish life and character.

Not content with the organization of the two literary societies, Yeats, with courage and relentless tenacity, cast about to realize his long-cherished dream of a theatre that should embody the ideals of the Revival. In Lady Gregory, and in Edward Martyn, an Irishman of large means, who with both pen and purse lent a willing hand, he found two ardent laborers for his vineyard. George Moore, who in the event proved a fish out of water in Ireland, Yeats and Martyn contrived to lure from his London lodgings and his cosmopolitan ways, and to enlist in the theatrical enterprise. The practical knowledge of the stage which this gifted *enfant terrible* of literature contributed was doubtless of great value in the early days of the dramatic adventure, though Moore's free thoughts, frank speech, and mordant irony brought an element of discord into Dublin literary circles, which may well have left Yeats and his associates with a feeling that they had paid too dear for a piper to whose tunes they refused to dance. Be that as it may, in 1899 Yeats's dream was measurably realized, and the Irish Literary Theatre established, to be succeeded a little later by the Irish National Theatre Society. Enough, however, of the dramatic aspect of the Revival, which receives separate treatment elsewhere in these pages, as does also the dramatic work of certain of the authors considered here.

From what has already been said, it should be plain that in the last decade of the last century the ranks of the Irish Literary Revivalists filled rapidly, and that the movement was really under way. The renascent spirit took various forms. To one group of poets the humor, pathos, and tragedy of peasant life deeply appealed, and found expression in a poetry distinctively and unmistakably national, from which a kind of pleasure could be drawn unlike anything else in other litera-

tures. In this group Alfred Perceval Graves and Moira
O'Neill cannot pass unmentioned. Who would ask anything
racier in its kind than the former's "Father O'Flynn"?

> Of priests we can offer a charmin' variety,
> Far renowned for larnin' and piety,
> Still I'd advance you without impropriety,
> Father O'Flynn as the flower of them all.
>   Here's a health to you, Father O'Flynn,
>   Slainte,* and slainte, and slainte agin.
>   Powerfullest preacher,
>   And tinderest teacher,
> And kindliest creature in Old Donegal.

Or was the homing instinct, the homesick longing for the
old sod, ever more truly rendered than in Moira O'Neill's
song of the Irish laborer in England?

> Over here in England I'm helpin' wi' the hay,
> An' I wish I was in Ireland the livelong day;
> Weary on the English, an' sorra take the wheat!
> Och! Corrymeela an' the blue sky over it.

> D'ye mind me now, the song at night is mortial hard to raise,
> The girls are heavy-goin' here, the boys are ill to plase;
> When ones't I'm out this workin' hive, 'tis I'll be back again—
> Aye, Corrymeela in the same soft rain.

Here, too, should be named Jane Barlow, whose poems and
stories are faithful imaginative transcripts of the face of
nature and the hearts of men as she knew them in Connemara.
Finally there is William Butler Yeats, who, on the whole,
is the representative man of the Revival. Except in the translator's sphere, his writings have given him a place in almost
all the activities of this movement. As a lyric poet, he has
expressed the moods of peasant and patriot, of mystic, sym-
bolist, and quietist, and it is safe to say that in lyric poetry
no one of his generation writing in English is his superior.
We cannot resist the pleasure of quoting here from his "Innis-
free", which won the praise of Robert Louis Stevenson, and

---

*"Your health."

which, if not the high mark of Yeats's achievement, is still a flawless thing in its way:

> I will arise and go now, and go to Innisfree,
>   And a small cabin build there, of clay and wattles made;
> Nine bean rows will I have there, a hive for the honey bee,
>   And live alone in the bee-loud glade.

> And I shall have some peace there, for peace comes dropping slow,
>   Dropping from the veils of the morning to where the cricket sings;
> There midnight's all a glimmer, and noon a purple glow,
>   And evening full of the linnets' wings.

In this place, and for convenience sake, it may be permitted to speak of aspects of Yeats's work other than that by virtue of which he is to be classed with the group we have just considered. In his narrative poem, "The Wanderings of Usheen", as well as in his plays and lyrics, he is of the best of those—among them we may mention by the way Dr. John Todhunter, Nora Hopper (Mrs. W. H. Chesson), and William Larminie—who have revealed to our day the strange beauty of the ancient creations of the Gaelic imagination. In prose he has written short stories, a novelette, *John Sherman and Dhoya,* and essays that reveal a subtle critical insight, and a style of beautiful finish and grace, suggestive of the style of Shelley's *Defence of Poetry.* Yeats's plays constitute a considerable and an important part of his work, but these must be reserved for treatment elsewhere in this book. In prefaces to anthologies of prose and verse of his editing, in the pages of reviews, and elsewhere, he appears as the chief apologist of the aims of the Literary Revival, and in particular of the methods of the dramatists of the Revival. Whatever he has touched he has lifted into the realm of poetry, and this is in large measure true of his prose, which proceeds from the poet's point of view and breathes the poetic spirit. A man of rare versatility, a finished artist with a scrupulous artistic conscience, he has done work of high and sustained quality, and is certain to exert a good and lasting influence upon the literature of his country.

In a literary movement in the "Isle of Saints", we look naturally for religious poetry, and we do not look in vain.

This poetry, chiefly Catholic, has a quality of its own as distinctive as that of the writers of the group we have just left. Now it voices a naïve, devoted simplicity of Christian faith; now it attains to a high and keen spirituality; now it is mystic and pagan. Among the religious poets, Lionel Johnson easily stands first—perhaps the Irish poet of firmest fibre and most resonant voice of his generation. A note of high courage and of spiritual triumph rings through his verse, even from the shadow of the wings of the dark angel that gives a title to one of the saddest of his poems. Often he strikes a note of genuine religious ecstasy and exaltation rarely heard in English, as in "Te Martyrum Candidatus":

Ah, see the fair chivalry come, the companions of Christ!
  White Horsemen, who ride on white horses, the Knights of God!
They, for their Lord and their Lover who sacrificed
  All, save the pleasure of treading where He first trod.

These through the darkness of death, the dominion of night,
  Swept, and they woke in white places at morning tide:
They saw with their eyes, and sang for joy of the sight,
  They saw with their eyes the Eyes of the Crucified.

Among the men of the Revival, no personality is stronger or more attractive than that of G. W. Russell—"Æ", as he is always called—who may be regarded as the hero of George Moore's *Hail and Farewell,* and who alone in that gallery of wonderful pen-portraits looks forth with complete amiability. He is a pantheist, a mystic, and a visionary, with what would seem a literal and living faith in many gods, though strongly prepossessed in favor of the ancient divinities of the Gael, now long since in exile. Impressive and striking by a certain spiritual integrity, so to say, "Æ" unites gifts and faculties seldom combined. He is a poet of rare subtlety, a painter in whose genius so good a judge as George Moore believed, and a most practical man of affairs, who, as assistant to Sir Horace Plunkett, held up the latter's hands in his labors on behalf of co-operative dairies and the like. His poems have their roots in a pantheism which half reveals the secrets of an indwelling spirit, speaking alike "from the dumb brown lips of earth" and from the passions of the heart of man.

Of novelists, both men and women, the Irish Revival can, in the words of "Father O'Flynn", offer a charming variety, and among their novels and short stories are some books of high quality and not a few in a high degree interesting and entertaining. To Standish O'Grady we turn for tales, with a kind of bardic afflatus about them, of the hero age of legendary Ireland—tales which drew attention to the romantic Celtic past of myth and saga, and must have been an inspiration to more than one writer of the younger generation. In contrast to the broad epic sweep and remote romantic backgrounds of O'Grady, are the stories of Jane Barlow, whose *genre* pictures of peasant life in the west of Ireland, like her poems mentioned above, show how sympathetically she understands the ways of thinking, feeling, and acting of her humble compatriots. A like minute and faithful knowledge is evident in the work of two story-tellers of the north, Seumas MacManus and Shan Bullock. The former's outlook is humorous and pathetic. He tells fairy and folk tales well, and is a past master of the dialect and idiom that combine to give his old-wives' yarns an honest smack of the soil. Let him who doubts it read *Through the Turf Smoke* or *Donegal Fairy Stories*. If Shan Bullock walks the same fields as Seumas MacManus, he does so with a different air and with a more definite purpose. Sometimes he turns to the squireens, small farmers, or small country gentry, and lays bare the hardness and narrowness that are a part of their life. Or, again, in pictures whose sadness and gloom are lightened, to be sure, with humor or warmed with love, he studies the necessitous life of the poor. *The Squireen, The Barrys,* and *Irish Pastorals* are some of his representative books.

In the novel as in poetry the ladies have worked side by side with their literary brethren. Miss Hermione Templeton, in her *Darby O'Gill,* and elsewhere, has written pleasantly and gracefully of the fairies. In a very different vein are the novels of the collaborators, Miss Somerville and "Martin Ross" (Miss Violet Martin), over which English and American readers have laughed as heartily as their own fellow countrymen. *The Experiences of an Irish R. M.* remains, perhaps, their best book. The work of these ladies, be it said by the way, is in the line of descent from that group of older Irish novelists who wrote in the spirit of the devil-may-care gentry, the novelists from Maxwell to Lover and Lever, who were ever questing "divilment and divarshion," and who in their moods of boisterous fun forgot the real Irishman, and presented in his place a caricature—him of the Celtic screech and the exhilarating whack of the shillelagh, the famous stage Irishman who has made occasional appearances in English literature from the time of Shakespeare's *Henry V.*, on through the works of Fielding and the plays of Sheridan, to the present moment of writing.

Of a very different stripe from the work of the collaborating ladies just mentioned are the novels of the recently deceased Canon Sheehan—notable among them *Luke Delmege* and *My New Curate*—rambling, diffuse, and a trifle provincial from the artistic standpoint, but interesting as studies of manners, and for the pictures they afford of the priesthood of modern Ireland in the pleasantest light. If the stories of Miss Somerville and "Martin Ross" are related to the comic stories of the old novelists of the gentry, those of Canon Sheehan must be associated with the work of the older novelists who wrote more or less in the spirit of the peasantry, that is, with Gerald Griffin, the Banim brothers, and William Carleton, less famous than he deserves to be by his *Traits and Stories* and a long line of novels and tales.

No survey of Irish novelists, however brief, can afford to forget the Rev. James Owen Hannay ("George A. Birmingham"), canon of St. Patrick's Cathedral, Dublin, whose work is as distinctively Protestant in its point of view as Father Sheehan's is Catholic. His more substantial novels are a careful transcript of the actualities of Irish life today, and in them one meets, incognito but easily recognizable, many Irishmen now prominent in literature or politics in Ireland. Of his numerous books may be mentioned *The Seething Pot, Hyacinth,* and *Northern Iron.*

Finally there is George Moore, whose enlistment in the Revival was responsible for the novel *The Lake* and the short stories of *The Untilled Field,* and for a largely autobiographic and entirely indiscreet trilogy entitled *Hail and Farewell,* the separate volumes appearing as *Ave, Salve, Vale,* and the last of them as late as 1914. George Moore's anti-Catholic bias is strong, but his is the pen of an accomplished artist. He has the story-teller's beguiling gift, and he bristles with ideas which his books cleverly embody and to which the dramatic moments of his novels give point and relief.

Not the least important work of the Irish Literary Revival has been done by translators, who have put into English the old Gaelic romances and the folklore still current among the little remnant of Irish-speaking country folk. Dr. Douglas Hyde is in the forefront of this group. He it was who organized the Gaelic League, a band of enthusiasts zealous for the revival of the Irish language both as a spoken tongue and as the medium for a national literature, and eager, also, to breed up a race of Celtic scholars. The lyrics in his *Love Songs of Connacht* are full of grace, tenderness, and fire, and indicate the kind of gems which he and his fellow laborers have added to the treasury of poetry in English. But it is Lady Gregory, especially in her *Cuchulain of Muirthemne* and *Gods and Fighting Men,* who more than any other has found a way to stir the blood of readers of to-day by the romantic hero tales of Ireland. From the racy idiom of the dwellers on or about her own estate in Galway, she happily framed a style that gave her narratives freshness, novelty, and a flavor of the soil. Upon the work of scholars she drew heavily in making her own renderings, but she has justified all borrowings by breathing into her books the breath and the warmth of life, and her adaptation to epic purposes of the dialect of those who still retain the expiring habit of thinking in Gaelic was a real literary achievement. She has, indeed, in sins of commission and of omission, taken liberties with the old legends, but this may render them not less, and perhaps more, delightful to the general reader, however just complaints may be from the standpoint of the scholar.

Even so brief a sketch as this may suffice to bring home to those not already aware of it a realization of the delights to be drawn from the creations of a living literary movement, which is perhaps the most notable of its generation, and which has gathered together a remarkable group of poets, novelists, and dramatists, who, as men and women, are a most interesting company—a fact to which even George Moore's *Hail and Farewell,* with its quick eye for defects and foibles and its ironic wit, bears abundant testimony.

REFERENCES:

Brooke and Rolleston: Treasury of Irish Poetry (New York and London, 1900) ; Krans: William Butler Yeats and the Irish Literary Revival (New York and London, 1904) ; Yeats: Ideas of Good and Evil (London, 1903) ; Moore: Hail and Farewell, 3 vols. (London and New York, 1912-1914) ; Lady Gregory: Our Irish Theatre (New York and London, 1913) ; Weygandt: Irish Plays and Playwrights (New York, 1913) ; Yeats: Introduction to Fairy and Folk Tales of the Irish Peasantry (London, 1889), Representative Irish Tales (London, 1890), Book of Irish Verse (London, 1895). There is much of interest, though chiefly as regards the drama, in the reviews, Beltaine (London and Dublin, 1899-1900) and Samhain (London and Dublin, 1901-1903).

IRISH WRITERS OF ENGLISH

By P. J. LENNOX, B.A., Litt.D.

THE Gaelic literature of Ireland is not only of wonderful volume and priceless worth, but is also of great antiquity, whereas the English literature of Ireland, while also of considerable extent and high value, is of comparatively modern origin. The explanation of this fact is that for more than six centuries after the Anglo-Norman invasion of 1169 the Irish language continued to be both the spoken and, with Latin, the written organ of the great mass of the Irish people, and that for nearly the whole of that period those English settlers who did not become, as the well-known phrase has it, more Irish than the Irish themselves by adopting the native language, customs, and sentiments, were kept too busy in holding, defending, and extending their territory to devote themselves to literary pursuits. Hence we need not wonder if, leaving out of account merely technical works like Lionel Power's treatise on music, written in 1395, we find that the English literature of Ireland takes its comparatively humble origin late in the sixteenth century. For more than two centuries thereafter, owing to the fact that the native Irish, because they were Catholics, were debarred by law from an education, the writing of English remained almost exclusively in the hands of members or descendants of the Anglo-Irish colony, who, with scarcely an exception, were Protestants and had as their principal Irish seat of learning the then essentially Protestant institution, Trinity College, Dublin. Alien in race and creed though these writers mainly were, they have nevertheless spread a halo of glory around their adopted country, and have won the admiration, and often the affection, of Irishmen of every shade of religious and political belief. For example, there is no Irishman who is not proud of Molyneux and Swift, of Goldsmith and Burke, of Grattan and Sheridan. From the nineteenth century onward Irish Catholics have taken their full share in the production of English literature. Here, however, it will be necessary to consider the writers of none but the sixteenth, seventeenth, and eighteenth centuries, as in other pages of this volume considerable attention has been given to those of later date.

I. Sixteenth Century.

Richard Stanyhurst (1547-1618), born in Dublin but educated at Oxford, is the first representative of the sixteenth century with whom we are called upon to deal. He belonged to a family long settled in or near Dublin and of some note in municipal annals. Under the direction of the Jesuit martyr, Edmund Campion, Stanyhurst wrote a *Description*, as well as a portion of the *History*, of Ireland for Holinshed's *Chronicles*, published in 1577. He also translated (1582) the first four books of *Virgil his Aeneis* into quantitative hexameters, on the unsound pedantic principles which Gabriel Harvey was at that time trying so hard to establish in English prosody; but the experiment, which turned out so badly in the master's hands, fared even worse in those of the disciple, and Stanyhurst's lines will always stand as a noted specimen of inept translation and ridiculous versification. Equally inartistic was his version of some of the Psalms in the same metre. In Latin he wrote a profound commentary on Porphyry, the Neo-Platonic mystic. Stanyhurst, who was uncle to James Ussher, the celebrated Protestant archbishop of Armagh, was himself a convert to Catholicity, and on the death of his second wife became a priest and wrote in Latin some edifying books of devotion. Two of his sons joined the Jesuit order. He died at Brussels in 1618. Stanyhurst viewed Ireland entirely from the English standpoint, and in his *Description* and *History* is, consciously or unconsciously, greatly biased against the native race.

If we may take it as certain that modern investigation is correct in asserting that Thomas Campion was a native of Dublin, a notable addition will have been made to the ranks of Irish-born writers of English at this period. Thomas Campion (1567-1620), wherever born, spent most of his life in London. He was a versatile genius, for, after studying law, he took up medicine, and, although practising as a physician, he yet found time to write four masques and many lyrics and to compose a goodly quantity of music. Some of his songs appeared as early as 1591. Among his works is a treatise entitled *Observations in the Art of English Poesie* (1602), in which, strange to say, he, a born lyrist, advocated unrhymed verse and quantitative measures, but fortunately his practice did not usually square with his theory. His masques were written for occasions, such as the marriage of Lord Hayes (1607), the nuptials of the Princess Elizabeth and the Elector Palatine (1613), and the ill-starred wedding of Somerset and the quondam Countess of Essex in the same year. In these masques are embedded some of his best songs; others of his lyrics appeared in several *Bookes of Ayres* between 1601 and 1617. Many of them were written to music, sometimes music of his composing. Such dainty things as "Now hath Flora robb'd her bowers" and "Harke, all you ladies that do sleep" possess the charms of freshness and spontaneity, and his devotional poetry, especially "Awake, awake, thou heavy Spright" and "Never weather-beaten Saile more willing bent to shore", makes almost as wide an appeal.

II. SEVENTEETH CENTURY.

Passing by with regret the illustrious seventeenth century names of Philip O'Sullivan Beare, Sir James Ware, Luke Wadding, Hugh Ward, John Colgan, and John Lynch, because their bearers wrote in Latin, and those of "The Four Masters" and Geoffrey Keating, because they wrote in Irish, we are first brought to a pause in the seventeenth century by the imposing figure of him, whom, in a later day, Johnson justly called the "great luminary of the Irish [Protestant] church", none other than the archbishop of Armagh and primate of Ireland, James Ussher himself. James Ussher (1581-1656), born in Dublin and among the earliest students of the newly-founded Trinity College, was in intellect and scholarship one of the greatest men that Ireland has ever produced. Selden describes him as "learned to a miracle" (*ad miraculum doctus*), and Canon D'Alton in his *History of Ireland* says of him that "he was not unworthy to rank even with Duns Scotus, and when he died he left in his own Church neither an equal nor a second." Declining the high office of provost of Trinity, Ussher was made bishop of Meath and was afterwards promoted to the primatial see. His fine intellect was unfortunately marred by narrow religious views, and in many ways he displayed his animus against those of his countrymen who did not see eye to eye with him in matters of faith and doctrine. For example, it was he who in 1626 drew up the Irish Protestant bishops' protest against toleration for Catholics, therein showing a bigotry which consorted badly with his reputation as a scholar. On account of his well-known attitude towards Catholicism, he was naturally unpopular with those who professed the ancient creed, and hence, when the rebellion of 1641 broke out, much of his property was destroyed by the enraged insurgents. His person escaped violence, for he happened to be in England at the time engaged in the vain task of trying to effect an accommodation between Charles I. and the English parliament. He never returned to his see and died in London.

Ussher's collected works fill seventeen stately volumes. His *magnum opus* is undoubtedly the *Annales Veteris et Novi Testamenti*. It is written in Latin, and is a chronological compendium of the history of the world from the Creation to the dispersion of the Jews under Vespasian. Published at Leyden, London, Paris, and Oxford, it gained for its author a European fame. His books written in English deal mostly with theological or controversial subjects, and while they display wide reading, great acumen, and keen powers of argumentation, they yet do not do full justice to his genius. Those which he published in Dublin are *A Discourse of the Religion anciently professed by the Irish and British* (1622), in which he tried to show that the ritual and discipline of the Church as originally established in the British Isles were in agreement with the Church of England and opposed to the Catholic Church on the matters in dispute between them; *An Answer to a Challenge made by a Jesuite in Ireland* (1624), in which his aim was to disprove the contention set forth earlier in the same year by a Jesuit that uniformity of doctrine had always been maintained by the Catholic Church; and *Immanuel, or the Mysterie of the Incarnation*. He published in England *The Originall of Bishops*, *A Body of Divinitie*, *The Principles of*

Christian Religion, and other works. So great was Ussher's reputation that when he died Cromwell relaxed in his favor one of the strictest laws of the Puritans and allowed him to be buried with the full service of the Church of England, and with great pomp, in Westminster Abbey.

Among Ussher's other claims to distinction, it should be noted that it was he who in 1621 discovered the celebrated Book of Kells, which had long been lost. This marvel of the illuminator's art passed with the remainder of his collection of books and manuscripts to Trinity College, Dublin, in 1661, and to this day it remains one of the most treasured possessions of the noble library of that institution.

Sir John Denham (1615-1669), a Dublin man by birth, took an active part on the side of Charles I. against the parliament during the Civil War, and subsequently was conspicuous in the intrigues that led to the restoration of Charles II. In his own day he had a great reputation as a poet. His tragedy, *The Sophy,* and his translation of the Psalms are now forgotten, but he is still remembered for one piece, *Cooper's Hill,* in which occur the well-known lines addressed to the River Thames:

> O could I flow like thee, and make thy stream
> My great example, as it is my theme!
> Though deep, yet clear; though gentle, yet not dull;
> Strong, without rage; without o'erflowing, full.

Another Dublin-born man was Wentworth Dillon, Earl of Roscommon (1633-1684). He had the good fortune to win encomiums both from Dryden and from Pope. One of his merits, as pointed out by the latter, is that

> In all Charles's days
> Roscommon only boasts unspotted bays.

He translated from Virgil, Lucan, Horace, and Guarini; wrote prologues, epilogues, and other occasional verses; but is now principally remembered for his poetical *Essay on Translated Verse* (1681), in which he develops principles previously laid down by Cowley and Denham. To his credit be it said, he condemns indecency, both as want of sense and bad taste. He was honored with a funeral in Westminster Abbey. Johnson records that, at the moment of his death, Roscommon uttered with great energy and devotion the following two lines from his own translation of the *Dies Irae*:

My God, my Father, and my Friend,
Do not forsake me in my end!

Robert Boyle (1627-1691), one of the founders of the Royal Society (1662), was son of the "great" Earl of Cork and was born at Lismore, Co. Waterford. He takes rank among the principal experimental philosophers of his age, and he certainly rendered valuable services to the advancement of science. Most of his writings, which are very voluminous, are naturally of a technical character and therefore do not properly belong to literature; but his *Occasional Reflections on Several Subjects* (1665), a strange mixture of triviality and seriousness, was germinal in this sense that it led to two celebrated *jeux d'esprit*, namely, Butler's *Occasional Reflection on Dr. Charlton's feeling a Dog's Pulse at Gresham College* and Swift's *Pious Meditation upon a Broomstick, in the Style of the Honourable Mr. Boyle*. Indeed, one of Boyle's *Reflections*, that "Upon the Eating of Oysters", is reputed to have rendered a still more signal service to literature, for in its two concluding paragraphs is contained the idea which, under the transforming hand of the master satirist, eventually took the world by storm when it appeared, fully developed, as *Gulliver's Travels*.

His brother, Roger Boyle (1621-1679), who figures largely as a soldier and a statesman in Irish and English history under his title of Lord Broghill, was an alumnus of Trinity College, Dublin. During the Civil War he was a royalist until the death of Charles I., when he changed sides and aided Cromwell materially in his Irish campaign. When the Lord Protector died, Broghill made another right-about-face, and crossing to his native country worked so energetically and successfully that he made Ireland solid for the restoration of Charles II. For this service he was rewarded by being created Earl of Orrery. He was the author of six tragedies and two comedies, some of which when produced proved gratifyingly popular. He is noted for having been the first to write tragedy in rhyme, thereby setting an example that was followed with avidity for a time by Dryden and others. He also wrote poems, a romance called *Parthenissa* (1654), and a *Treatise on the Art of War* (1677). From whatever point of view considered, Lord Orrery was a remarkable member of a remarkable family. His son, John Boyle, Earl of Cork and Orrery (1707-1762), in virtue of his translation of Pliny's *Letters,* his *Remarks on the Life and Writings of Swift,* and his *Letters from Italy,* has some claims to recognition in the field of literature.

Charles Leslie (1650-1722), a Dubliner by birth, was son of that John Leslie, bishop of Raphoe and Clogher, who lived through a whole century, from 1571 to 1671, and who was 79 years of age when Charles, his sixth son, was born. Educated first at Enniskillen and afterwards at Trinity College, Dublin, Charles Leslie studied law in London, but eventually abandoned that profession and entered the ministry. He was of a disputatious character and in particular went to great lengths in opposing the pro-Catholic activities of James II. Nevertheless, when the Revolution of 1688 came, he took the side of the deposed monarch, and loyally adhered to his Jacobite principles for the remainder of his life. He even joined the Old Pretender on the continent, and endeavored to convert him to Protestantism, but, failing therein, he returned to Ireland, where he died at Glasslough in county Monaghan. Many years of Leslie's life were devoted to disputes with Catholics, Quakers, Socinians, and Deists, and the seven volumes which his writings fill prove that he was an extremely able controversialist. His best known work is the famous treatise, *A Short and Easy Method with the Deists,* published in 1698.

The Irish note, tone, or temper is not conspicuous in any of the writings so far named unless when it is conspicuous by its absence; but it appears plainly, for the first time, in Molyneux's *Case of Ireland being bound by Laws [made] in England Stated* (1698). William Molyneux (1656-1698) has always ranked as an Irish patriot. His was one of the spirits invoked by Grattan in his great speech (1782) on the occasion on which he carried his celebrated Declaration of Independence in the Irish parliament. When the English Act of

1698, which was meant to destroy, and did destroy, the Irish woolen industry, came before the Irish house of commons for ratification, Molyneux's was the only voice raised against its adoption. His protest was followed by the publication of his *Case Stated,* which is a classic on the general relations between Ireland and England, and contained arguments so irrefutable that it drove the English parliament to fury and was by that body ordered to be burned by the common hangman. It is a remarkable coincidence that Molyneux opens his argument by laying down in almost identical words the principles which stand at the beginning of the American Declaration of Independence.

John Toland (1669-1722) was born near Redcastle, in Co. Derry, and was at first a Catholic but subsequently became a free-thinker. His *Christianity not Mysterious* (1696) marks an epoch in religious disputes, for it started the deistical controversy which was so distinctive a feature of the first half of the eighteenth century. It shared a similar fate to that of the *Case Stated,* though on very different grounds, and was ordered by the Irish parliament to be burned by the hangman. Toland wrote many other books, among which are *Amyntor* (1699); *Nazarenus* (1702); *Pantheisticon; History of the Druids;* and *Hypatia.* All his books show versatility and wide reading and are characterized by a pointed, vigorous, and aggressive style.

George Farquhar (1678-1707), a Derry man, and Thomas Southerne (1660-1746), born near Dublin, were distinguished playwrights, who began their respective careers in the seventeenth century. Farquhar left Trinity College, Dublin, as an undergraduate and became an actor, but owing to his accidental killing of another player he left the stage and secured a commission in the army. He soon turned his attention to the writing of plays, and was responsible in all for eight comedies. He has left us some characters that are very humorous and at the same time true to life, such as Scrub the servant in *The Beaux' Stratagem* and Sergeant Kite in *The Recruiting Officer.* His Boniface, the landlord in the former of these two plays, has become the type, as well as the ordinary quasi-facetious nickname, of an innkeeper. He was advancing in his art, for his last comedy, *The Beaux' Stratagem* (1707), is undoubtedly his best, and had he lived longer—he died before he was thirty—he might have bequeathed to posterity something even more noteworthy. As Leigh Hunt says of him: "He was becoming gayer and gayer, when death, in the shape of a sore anxiety, called him away as if from a pleasant party, and left the house ringing with his jest."

Southerne was also a student of Trinity College, Dublin. At the age of eighteen, however, he left his *alma mater,* and went to London to study law. This profession he in turn abandoned for the drama. His first play, *The Persian Prince, or the Loyal Brother,* had remarkable success when performed, and secured him an ensign's commission in the army (1685). Here promotion came to him rapidly and by 1688 he had risen to captain's rank. The Revolution of that year, however, cut off all further hope of advancement, and he once more turned his attention to the writing of plays. His productions number ten. His tragedies *Isabella, or the Fatal Marriage* (1694) and *Oroonoko* (1696), both founded on tales by Mrs. Aphra Behn, are powerful presentations of human suffering. His comedies are amusing, but gross. Southerne had business ability enough to make play-writing pay, and the amounts he received for his productions fairly staggered his friend Dryden. It is to this faculty that Pope alludes when he says that Southerne was one whom

> heaven sent down to raise
> The price of prologues and of plays.

He was apparently of amiable and estimable character, for he secured and retained the friendship not only of Dryden—a comparatively easy matter—but also that of Pope, a much more difficult task. Known as "the poets' Nestor", Southerne spent his declining years in peaceful retirement and in the enjoyment of the fortune which he had amassed by his pen.

Nahum Tate (1652-1715), a Dubliner by birth, and Nicholas Brady (1659-1726), a Bandon man, have secured a certain sort of twin immortality by their authorized metrical version of the Psalms (1696), which gradually took the place of the older rendering by Sternhold and Hopkins. Tate became poet-laureate in 1690 in succession to Shadwell and was appointed historiographer-royal in 1702. He wrote the bulk of the second part of *Absalom and Achitophel* with a wonderfully close imitation of Dryden's manner, besides several dramatic pieces and poems. Between Tate, Shadwell, Eusden, and Pye lies the unenviable distinction of being the worst of the laureates of England. Brady was a clergyman who, after the pleasant fashion of that day, was a pluralist on a small scale, for he had the living of Richmond for thirty years from 1696, and while holding that held also in succession the livings of Stratford-on-Avon and Clapham. He added further to his income, and doubtless to his anxieties, by keeping a school at Richmond. He wrote a tragedy entitled *The Rape,* a *History of the Goths and Vandals,* a translation of the *Aeneid* into blank verse, and an *Ode for St. Cecilia's Day;* but, unless for his share in the version of the Psalms, his literary reputation is well nigh as dead as the dodo.

Ireland somewhat doubtfully claims to have given birth to Mrs. Susannah Centlivre (c. 1667-1723), who, after a rather wild youth, settled down to literary pursuits and domestic contentment when, in 1706, she married Queen Anne's head-cook, Joseph Centlivre, with whom she lived happily ever after. Her first play, *The Provoked Husband,* a tragedy, was produced in 1700, and then she went on the stage as an actress. She wrote in all nineteen dramatic pieces, some of which had the honor of being translated into French and German. Her most original play was *A Bold Stroke for a Wife* (1717).

III. EIGHTEENTH CENTURY.

We have now fairly crossed the border of the eighteenth century, and, as we met Ussher early in the seventeenth, so we are here confronted with the colossal intellect and impressive personality of Swift, one of the greatest, most peculiar, and most original geniuses to be found in the whole domain of English literature. Jonathan Swift (1667-1745), born in Dublin, was educated at Trinity College, where he succeeded in graduating only by special favor. After some years spent in the household of Sir William Temple in England, he entered the ministry of the Irish Church. During the early years of the century he spent much time in London, and took an active part in bringing about that political revolution which seated the Tories firmly in power during the last four years of the reign of Queen Anne. His services in that connection on the *Examiner* newspaper were so great that it would be difficult to dispute the assertion, which has been made, that he was one of the mightiest journalists that ever wielded a pen. He also stood loyally by his party in his great pamphlets, *The Conduct of the Allies* (1711), *The Barrier Treaty* (1712), and *The Public Spirit of the Whigs* (1714). When the time came for his reward, he received not, as he had hoped, an English bishopric, but the deanery of St. Patrick's in Dublin. On resuming his residence in Ireland he was at first very unpopular, but his patriotic spirit as shown in the *Drapier Letters* (1723-1724), written in connection with a coinage scheme known as "Wood's halfpence", not only caused the withdrawal of the obnoxious project but also made Swift the idol of all classes of his countrymen. In many others of his writings he showed that pro-Irish leaning which caused Grattan to invoke his spirit along with that of Molyneux on the occasion already referred to. Nothing more mordant than the irony contained in his *Modest Proposal* has ever been penned. In his plea for native manufactures he struck a keynote that has vibrated down the ages when he advised Irishmen to burn everything English except coal!

Swift's greater works are *The Battle of the Books,* his contribution to the controversy concerning the relative merits of the ancients and the moderns; the *Tale of a Tub,* in which he attacked the three leading forms of Christianity; and, above all, *Gulliver's Travels.* In this last work he let loose the full flood of his merciless satire and lashed the folly and vices of mankind in the most unsparing way. He also wrote verses which are highly characteristic and some of them not without considerable merit. His life was unhappy and for the last five years of it he was to all intents and purposes insane. His relations with Stella (Hester Johnson) and Vanessa (Esther Vanhomrigh) have never been quite satisfactorily explained. The weight of evidence would seem to show that he was secretly married to Stella, but that they never lived together as husband and wife.

Many novels and plays have been written round those entanglements. He lies buried in his own cathedral, St. Patrick's, Dublin, and beside him lies Stella. Over his tomb there is an epitaph in Latin, written by himself, in which, after speaking of the *saeva indignatio* which tore his heart, he bids the wayfarer go and imitate, if he can, the energetic defender of his native land.

Contemporary with the Dean there was another Anglo-Irishman, who fills a large space in the history of English literature, and of whom his countrymen are justly proud. Sir Richard Steele (1672-1729), who was born in Dublin and educated at the Charterhouse in London and afterwards at Oxford, started the *Tatler* in 1709, and thereby popularized, though he did not exactly originate, the periodical essay. Aided by his friend, Addison, he carried the work to perfection in the *Spectator* (1711-1712) and the *Guardian* (1713). Since then these essays have enlightened and amused each succeeding generation. Of the two, Addison's is the greater name, but Steele was the more innovating spirit, for it is to him, and not to Addison, that the conception and initiation of the plan of the celebrated papers is due. Steele had had a predecessor in Defoe, whose *Review* had been in existence since 1704, but the more airy graces which characterized the *Tatler* and the *Spectator* gave the "lucubrations" of "Isaac Bickerstaffe" and of "Mr. Spectator" a greater hold on the public than Defoe's paper was ever able to establish. Steele was responsible for many more periodicals, such as the *Englishman,* the *Lover,* the *Reader, Town Talk,* the *Tea-Table, Chit-Chat,* the *Plebeian,* and the *Theatre,* most of which had a rather ephemeral existence. Among his other services to literature he helped to purify the stage of some of its grossness, and he became the founder of that sentimental comedy which in the days of the early Georges took the place of the immoral comedy of the Restoration period, when, in Johnson's famous phrase,

> Intrigue was plot, obscenity was wit.

Steele's four comedies are *The Funeral; or Grief à la mode* (1701); *The Lying Lover* (1703); *The Tender Husband* (1705); and *The Conscious Lovers* (1722). Although he held various lucrative offices, Steele was never really prosperous and was frequently in debt; like most of the contemporary Englishmen with whom his lot was thrown, he was rather addicted to the bottle; but, on the whole, it may fairly be advanced that unnecessary stress has been laid on these aspects of his life by Macaulay, Thackeray, and others. After a chequered career, he died near Carmarthen, in Wales, on September 1, 1729.

Member of a family and bearer of a name destined to secure immense fame in later Irish history, Thomas Parnell (1679-1718) was born in Dublin and educated at Trinity College. Entering the ministry in 1700, he was rapidly promoted to be archdeacon of Clogher and some years later was made rector of Finglas. An accomplished scholar and a delightful companion, he was one of the original members of the famous Scriblerus Club and wrote or helped to write several of its papers, he contributed to the *Spectator* and the *Guardian,* and he rendered sterling assistance to Pope in the translation of Homer. As will be inferred, he spent much of his time in England, and on one of his journeys to Ireland he died in his thirty-ninth year at Chester, where he was buried. He wrote a great deal of verse—songs, hymns, epistles, eclogues, translations, tales, and occasional trifles; but three poems, *A Hymn to Contentment,* which is fanciful and melodious, *A Night-piece on Death,* in which inquisitorial research seems to have found the first faint dawn of Romanticism, and *The Hermit,* which has been not inaptly styled "the apex and *chef d'œuvre* of Augustan poetry in England", constitute his chief claim to present remembrance.

Francis Hutcheson (1694-1746), the son of a Presbyterian minister, was born at Armagh, and studied at Glasgow University. He opened in Dublin a private academy, which succeeded beyond expectation. The publication of his *Inquiry into the Original of our Ideas of Beauty and Virtue* (1720) and his *Essay on the Nature and Conduct of the Passions* (1728) brought him great fame, and in 1729 he was elected to the professorship of moral philosophy in the University of Glasgow. Others of his works are a treatise on *Logic* and *A System of Moral Philosophy,* the latter not published till 1755, nine

years after his death. Hutcheson fills a large space in the
history of philosophy, both as a metaphysician and as a moral-
ist. He is in some respects a pioneer of the "Scotch school"
and of "common sense" philosophy. He greatly developed the
doctrine of "moral sense", a term first used by the third Earl
of Shaftesbury; indeed, much of his whole moral system may
be traced to Shaftesbury. Hutcheson's influence was widely
felt: it is plainly perceptible in Hume, Adam Smith, and
Reid. He was greater as a speaker even than as a writer, and
his lectures evoked much enthusiasm.

George Berkeley (1685-1753), bishop of Cloyne, was born
at Dysert Castle, near Thomastown, Co. Kilkenny, and was
educated first at Kilkenny school and afterwards at Trinity
College, Dublin. Having taken Anglican orders, he visited
London, where he wrote nine papers for the *Guardian* and was
admitted to the companionship and friendship of the leading
literary men of the age—Swift, Pope, Addison, Steele,
and Arbuthnot. This connection proved of great assistance to
him, for Pope not only celebrated him as possessing "every
virtue under heaven", but also recommended him to the Duke
of Grafton, Lord-Lieutenant of Ireland, who appointed him
his chaplain and subsequently obtained for him the deanery of
Derry. In furtherance of a great scheme for "converting the
savage Americans to Christianity", Berkeley and some friends,
armed with a royal charter, came to this country, landing at
Newport in Rhode Island in January, 1729. All went well for
a while: Berkeley bought a farm and built a house; but when
the hard-hearted prime minister refused to forward the £20,000
which had been promised, the project came to an end,
and Berkeley returned to London in February, 1732. In 1734
he was appointed bishop of Cloyne, and later refused the see
of Clogher, though its income was fully double that of his
own diocese. In 1752 he resigned his bishopric and settled
at Oxford, where he died in 1753.

Berkeley's works are very numerous. His *Essay towards a
New Theory of Vision* (1709), which was long regarded in
the light of a philosophical romance, in reality contains speculations which have been incorporated in modern scientific
optics. In his *Three Dialogues between Hylas and Philonous*
(23)

(1713) he sets forth his famous demonstration of the immateriality of the external world, of the spiritual nature of the soul, and of the all-ruling and direct providence of God. His tenets on immateriality have always been rejected by "common-sense" philosophers; but it should be remembered that the whole work was written at a time when the English-speaking world was disturbed by the theories of sceptics and deists, whose doctrines the pious divine sought as best he could to confute. In 1732 appeared his *Alciphron, or the Minute Philosopher,* in which, dialogue-wise, he presents nature from a religious point of view and in particular gives many pleasing pictures of American scenery and life. These dialogues have frequently been compared to the dialogues of Plato. To Berkeley's credit be it said that while he ruled in Cloyne he devoted much thought to the amelioration of conditions in his native land. Many acute suggestions in that direction are found in the *Querist* (1735-1737). By some extraordinary ratiocinative process he convinced himself that tar-water was a panacea for human ills, and in 1744 he set forth his views on that subject in the tract called *Siris,* and returned to the charge in 1752 in his *Further Thoughts on Tar-Water.* Whatever may be thought of the value of Berkeley's philosophical or practical speculations, there is only one opinion of his style. It is distinguished by lucidity, ease, and charm; it has the saving grace of humor; and it is shot through with imagination. Taken all in all, this eighteenth century bishop is a notable figure in literary annals.

Charles Macklin (c. 1697-1797), whose real name was MacLaughlin, was a Westmeath man, who took to the stage in early life and remained on the boards with considerable and undiminished reputation for some seventy years, not retiring until 1789 when he was at least 92 years old. To him we are indebted for what is now the accepted presentation of the character of Shylock in *The Merchant of Venice.* He wrote a tragedy and many comedies and farces: those by which he is now best remembered are the farce, *Love-à-la-Mode* (1760), and his masterpiece, the farcical comedy, *The Man of the World* (1764). In Sir Pertinax MacSycophant, Macklin has given us one of the traditional burlesque characters of the English stage.

Thomas Amory (1691?—1788), if not born in Ireland, was at least of Irish descent and was educated in Dublin. He is known in literature for two books. The first, with the very mixed title of *Memoirs containing the Lives of several Ladies of Great Britain; A History of Antiquities; Observations on the Christian Religion,* was published in 1755, and the second, *The Life of John Buncle, Esq.,* came out in two volumes in 1756-1766. It appears to have been the author's aim in both works to give us a hotch-potch in which he discourses *de omnibus rebus et quibusdam aliis.* We have dissertations on the cause of earthquakes and of muscular motion, on the Athanasian Creed, on fluxions, on phlogiston, on the physical cause of the Deluge, on Irish literature, on the origin of language, on the evidences for Christianity, and on all other sorts of unrelated topics. Hazlitt thought that the soul of Rabelais had passed into Amory, while a more recent critic can see in his long-winded discussions naught but the "light-headed ramblings of delirium." If we try to read *John Buncle* consecutively, the result is boredom; but if we open the book at random, we are pretty sure to be interested and even sometimes agreeably entertained.

The bizarre figure of Laurence Sterne (1713-1768) next claims our attention. The son of a captain in the British army, he was born at Clonmel, Co. Tipperary. Of him almost more than of any of the writers so far dealt with, it may be said that he was Irish only by the accident of birth. His parents were English on both sides, and practically the whole life of their son was spent out of Ireland. He was sent to school at Halifax, in Yorkshire, and thence went to Cambridge University, where he graduated in due season. Taking Anglican orders in 1738, he was immediately appointed to the benefice of Sutton-in-the-Forest, near York, and on his marriage in 1741 with Elizabeth Lumley he received the additional living of Stillington. He was also given sundry prebendal and other appointments in connection with the chapter of the archdiocese of York. He spent nearly twenty years in the discharge of his not very onerous duties and in reading,

painting, shooting, and fiddling, without showing the least sign
of any literary leanings. Then suddenly, in 1760, he took the
world by storm with the first two volumes of *Tristram Shandy*.
He at once became the lion of the hour, was fêted and dined to
his heart's content, and had his nostrils tickled with the daily
incense of praise from his numerous worshippers. He repeated the experiment with equal success the following year
with two more volumes of *Tristram,* and so at intervals until
1767, when he published the ninth and last volume of this most
peculiar story. In 1768 he brought out *A Sentimental Journey,*
and within three weeks he died in his lodgings in London. His
other publications include *Sermons* and *Letters. Tristram
Shandy* is unique in English literature—it stands *sui generis*
for all time. There is scarcely any consecutive narrative, and
what there is is used merely as a peg on which to hang endless
digressions. But while there are many faults of taste and
morals, there are also genuine humor and pathos, and without
Walter Shandy, Dr. Slop, the Widow Wadman, Yorick, Uncle
Toby, and Corporal Trim, English literature would certainly
be very much the poorer.

Hugh Kelly (1739-1777), born in Dublin, was the son of a
publican and himself became a staymaker, a trade from which
he developed through the successive stages of attorney's clerk,
newspaper-writer, theatrical critic, and essayist, into a novelist
and playwright. His novel, *Memoirs of a Magdalen* (1767),
was translated into French. His first comedy, a sentimental
one entitled *False Delicacy* (1768), achieved a remarkable
success on the stage and was even a greater success in book
form, 10,000 copies being sold in a year, so that its author
was raised from poverty to comparative affluence. In addition,
it gave him a European reputation, for it was translated into
German, French, and Portuguese. Strange to say, his later
comedies, *A Word to the Wise, A School for Wives,* and *The
Man of Reason,* were practically failures, and the same is
true of his tragedy, *Clementina.* Kelly ultimately withdrew
from stage work, and for the last three years of his life practised as a barrister without, however, achieving much distinction in his new profession.

Charles Coffey (d. 1745), an Irishman, was the author of several farces, operas, ballad operas, ballad farces, and farcical operas, the best known of which was *The Devil to Pay, or the Wives Metamorphosed* (1731).

Henry Brooke (1703?—1783), a county Cavan man and the son of a clergyman, was educated at Trinity College, Dublin, and afterwards studied law in London. Becoming guardian to his cousin, a girl of twelve, he put her to school for two years and then secretly married her. Of his large family of twenty-two children, three of whom were born before their mother was eighteen years old, but one survived him. Appointed by Lord Chesterfield barrack-master at Mullingar, Brooke afterwards settled in Co. Kildare. It was there that he wrote his celebrated work, *The Fool of Quality, or the History of the Earl of Moreland* (5 vols., 1766-1770), which won the commendations of men so widely different as John Wesley and Charles Kingsley. It is, indeed, a remarkable book, combining, as it does, many of the characteristics of Sterne, Mackenzie, Borrow, and George Meredith. It is not very well known nowadays, but it will always bear, and will well repay, perusal. Brooke also wrote a poem on *Universal Beauty* (1735) and the tragedies *Gustavus Vasa* (1739), the production of which was forbidden in London but which was afterwards staged in Dublin as *The Patriot,* and *The Earl of Essex* (1749), which was played both in London and in Dublin, and has been made famous by the parody of one line in it by Samuel Johnson. Another novel, *Juliet Grenville, or the History of the Human Heart,* published in 1774, was not nearly up to the standard of *The Fool of Quality.* Brooke was a busy literary man. He made a translation of part of Tasso, drafted plans for a History of Ireland, projected a series of old Irish tales, wrote one fragment in a style very like that subsequently adopted by Macpherson in his *Ossian,* and for a while was editor of the *Freeman's Journal.* In the beginning, Brooke was violently anti-Catholic; but, as time progressed, he became more liberal-minded, and advocated the relaxation of the penal laws and a more humane treatment of his Catholic fellow-countrymen. Like Swift and Steele, he fell into a state of mental debility for some years before his death. His daughter,

Charlotte Brooke (1740-1793), deserves mention as a pioneer of the Irish literary revival, for she devoted herself to the saving of the stores of Irish literature which in her time were rapidly disappearing. One of the fruits of her labors was *The Reliques of Irish Poetry,* published in 1789. She also wrote *Emma, or the Foundling of the Wood,* a novel, and *Belisarius,* a tragedy.

Charles Johnstone (c. 1719-1800), a Co. Limerick man, was educated in Dublin and called to the English bar, but owing to deafness was more successful as a chamber counsel than as a pleader. Emigrating to India in 1782, he became joint proprietor of a newspaper in Calcutta, and there he died. He wrote several satirical romances, such as *Chrysal, or the Adventures of a Guinea; The Reverie, or a Flight to the Paradise of Fools;* and *The History of Arsaces, Prince of Betlis.* Of these the first was the best. Samuel Johnson, who read it in manuscript, advised its publication, and his opinion was vindicated, for it proved a huge success. Sir Walter Scott afterwards said that the author of *Chrysal* deserved to rank as a prose Juvenal. Johnstone also wrote *The Pilgrim, or a Picture of Life* and a picaresque novel, *The History of John Juniper, Esquire, alias Juniper Jack.*

Arthur Murphy (1727-1805), born at Cloonquin, Co. Roscommon, was educated at St. Omer. At first an actor, he afterwards studied law and was called to the English bar in 1762. He made a translation of Tacitus, and wrote several farces and comedies, among which may be mentioned *The Apprentice; The Spouter; The Upholsterer; The Way to Keep Him;* and *All in the Wrong.* He also wrote three tragedies, namely, *The Orphan of China; The Grecian Daughter;* and *Arminius.* For the last-named, which was produced in 1798, and which had a strongly political cast, he received a pension of £200 a year. His plays long held the stage.

Oliver Goldsmith (1728-1774), essayist, poet, novelist, playwright, historian, biographer, and editor, was a many-sided genius, who, as Johnson said in his epitaph, left scarcely any kind of writing untouched, and touched none that he did not adorn. Born, probably, in Co. Longford, the son of a poor clergyman, he was educated at various country schools until, in 1744, he secured a sizarship in Trinity College, Dublin. There he had a somewhat stormy career, but eventually took his degree in 1749. He then lounged at home for a while in his widowed mother's cottage at Ballymahon, until he was persuaded to take orders, but spoiled his already sufficiently poor chances of ordination by appearing before the bishop of Elphin in scarlet breeches. After other adventures in search of a profession, he went to Edinburgh in 1752 to study medicine, and two years later transferred himself to Leyden for the same purpose. It was from Leyden that, with one guinea in his pocket, one shirt on his person, and a flute in his hand, he started on his celebrated walking tour of Europe, during which he gained those impressions which he was afterwards to embody in some of his greater works. In 1756 he arrived in England, where for three years he had very varied experiences —as a strolling player, an apothecary's journeyman, a practising physician, a reader for the press, an usher in an academy, and a hack-writer. In 1759 he published anonymously his *Enquiry into the Present State of Polite Learning in Europe,* which was well received and helped him to other literary work. *The Bee,* a volume of essays and verses, appeared in the same year. He was made editor of the *Lady's Magazine;* he published *Memoirs of Voltaire* (1761), a *History of Mecklenburgh* (1762), and a *Life of Richard Nash* (1762). In 1762 also he brought out his *Citizen of the World,* a collection of essays, which takes an extremely high rank. In 1764 his poem, *The Traveller, or a Prospect of Society,* made its appearance; and in 1766 he gave to the world his famous novel, *The Vicar of Wakefield.* His reputation as a writer was now established; he was received into Johnson's circle and was a member of the Literary Club; Reynolds and Burke were proud to call him friend. In 1768 he had his comedy, *The Good Natured Man,* produced at Covent Garden Theatre, where it achieved a fair measure of success and brought him in £400. In 1770 he repeated his triumph as a poet with *The Deserted Village.* He wrote a *History of Animated Nature,* a *History of England,* and a *History of Rome,* all compilations couched in that easy style of which he was master. He also wrote a *Life of Parnell* and a *Life of Bolingbroke.* Finally, in 1773, his great comedy, *She Stoops to Conquer,* was staged at Covent Garden, and met with wonderful success. A little more than a year later Goldsmith died of a nervous fever, the result of overwork and anxiety, and was buried in the burial ground of the Temple Church. His unfinished poem, *Retaliation,* a series of epigrams in epitaph form on some of his distinguished literary and artistic friends, was issued a few days after his death, and added greatly to his reputation as a wit and humorist, a reputation which was still further enhanced when, in 1776, *The Haunch of Venison* made its appearance. In the latter year a monument, with a medallion and Johnson's celebrated Latin epitaph attached, was erected to his memory in Westminster Abbey.

Goldsmith's renown, great in his own day, has never since diminished. His essays, his novel, and his poems are still read with avidity and pleasure; his comedy is still acted. It is his statue that stands along with Burke's at the entrance gate to Trinity College, Dublin, the *alma mater* seeking to commemorate in a striking manner two of her most distinguished sons by placing their effigies thus in the forefront of her possessions and in full view of all the world. Personally, Goldsmith was a very amiable and good-hearted man, dear to his own circle and dear to that "Mr. Posterity" to whom he once addressed a humorous dedication. He had his faults, it is true, but they are hidden amid his many perfections. Everyone will be disposed to agree with what Johnson wrote of him: "Let not his frailties be remembered; he was a very great man."

Edmund Burke (1729-1797), born in Dublin, the son of a Protestant father and a Catholic mother whose name was Nagle, was educated first at a Quaker school in Ballitore, Co. Kildare, and afterwards at Trinity College, Dublin. He became a law student in London, but he did not eventually adopt the law as a profession. He brought out in 1756 a *Vindication of Natural Society,* in which he so skilfully imitated the style and the paradoxical reasoning of Bolingbroke that many were deceived into the belief that the *Vindication* was a posthumously published production of the viscount's pen. In the following year Burke published in his own name *A*

Philosophical Inquiry into the Origin of our Ideas of the Sublime and Beautiful, which attracted widespread attention, was translated into German and French, and brought its author into touch with all the leading literary men of London. He was instrumental with Dodsley the publisher in starting the *Annual Register* in 1759, and for close on thirty years he continued to supply it with the "Survey of Events." He entered public life in 1760 by accompanying "Single-Speech" Hamilton to Dublin when the latter was appointed Chief Secretary for Ireland. In 1765 he was made private secretary to the prime minister, the Marquis of Rockingham, and, as member for Wendover, entered parliament, where he speedily made a name for himself. During Lord North's long tenure of office (1770-1782) Burke was one of the minority and opposed the splendid force of his genius to the corruption, extravagance, and mal-administration of the government. To this period belong, in addition to lesser works, his great speeches *On American Taxation* (1774) and *On Conciliation with America* (1775), as well as his spirited *Letter to the Sheriffs of Bristol* (1777). He had been elected member of parliament for Bristol in 1774, but he lost his seat in 1780 because he had advocated the relaxation of the restrictions on the trade of Ireland with Great Britain and of the penal laws against Catholics. In the second administration of Rockingham (1782) and in that of Portland (1783) he was paymaster of the forces, a position which he lost on the downfall of the Whigs in the latter year, and he never again held public office. His speech on the impeachment of Warren Hastings in 1788 is universally and justly ranked as a masterpiece of eloquence. When the French Revolution broke out, he opposed it with might and main. His *Reflections on the French Revolution* (1790) had an enormous circulation, reached an eleventh edition inside of a year, was read all over the continent as well as in the British Isles, and helped materially not only to keep England steady in the crisis, but also to incite the other powers to continue their resistance to French aggression. He continued his campaign in *Thoughts on French Affairs* and *Letters on a Regicide Peace.* He was given two pensions in 1794, and would have been raised to the peerage as Lord Beaconsfield, had not the succession to the title been cut off by the premature death of his only son. He himself died in 1797 and was buried at Beaconsfield, where, as far back as 1768, he had purchased a small estate.

As an orator and a deep political thinker, Burke holds a foremost place among those of all time who distinguished themselves in the British parliament. His keen intellect, his powerful imagination, his sympathy with the fallen, the down-trodden, and the oppressed, and his matchless power of utterance of the thoughts that were in him have made an impression that can never be effaced. His wise and statesman-like views on questions affecting the colonies ought to endear him to all Americans, although, if his counsels had been hearkened to, it is probable that the separation from the mother country would not have occurred as soon as it did. For his native land he used his best endeavors when and how he could, and although, as her defender, he was faced by obloquy as well as by the loss of that parliamentary position which was as dear to him as the breath of his nostrils, he did not flinch or shrink from supporting her material and spiritual interests in his own generous, manly, whole-hearted way. Trinity College, Dublin, has done well in placing his statue at her outer gates as representing the greatest Irishman of his generation.

A political associate of Burke's for many years was Richard Brinsley Sheridan (1751-1816). Of Co. Cavan descent, Sheridan was born in Dublin, and was educated partly in his native city and partly at Harrow, and the remainder of his life was spent in England. He was distinguished first as a playwright and afterwards as a parliamentary orator. In 1775 his comedy, *The Rivals*, was produced at Covent Garden Theatre; his farce, *St. Patrick's Day, or the Scheming Lieutenant,* and his comic opera, *The Duenna,* were staged in the same year. His greatest comedy, *The School for Scandal,* was acted at Drury Lane Theatre in 1777, and it was followed in 1779 by *The Critic.* His last dramatic composition was the tragedy, *Pizarro,* produced in 1799. Elected to parliament in 1780, Sheridan was made under-secretary for foreign affairs in the Rockingham administration of 1782, and in 1783 he was secretary to the treasury in the Coalition Ministry. He sprang into repute as a brilliant orator during the impeachment of Warren Hastings, 1787-1794. His speech on the Begums of Oude was one of the greatest ever delivered within the walls of the British parliament. In 1806, on the return of the Whigs to power, he was appointed treasurer in the navy. In 1812 his long parliamentary career came to a close when he was defeated for the borough of Westminster. He died in 1816, and was honored with a magnificent funeral in Westminster Abbey.

To give an idea as to how Sheridan's oratorical powers impressed his contemporaries, it is perhaps enough to repeat what Burke said of his second speech against Warren Hastings, namely, that it was "the most astonishing effort of eloquence, argument, and wit united of which there is any record or tradition", and to add that when, after three hours of impassioned pleading, he brought his first speech against Hastings to an end, the effect produced was so great that it was agreed to adjourn the house immediately and defer the final decision until the members should be in a less excited mood. As a dramatist Sheridan is second in popularity to Shakespeare alone. *The School for Scandal* and *The Rivals* are as fresh and as eagerly welcomed today as they were a hundred and forty years ago. Like Burke, he was true to the land of his birth and his oppressed Catholic fellow-countrymen. Almost his last words in the house of commons were these: "Be just to Ireland. I will never give my vote to any administration that opposes the question of Catholic emancipation."

Sheridan belonged to a family that was exceptionally distinguished in English literature. Among those who preceded him as litterateurs were his grandfather, the Rev. Thomas Sheridan, D.D.; his father, Thomas Sheridan; and his mother, Frances Sheridan. Rev. Dr. Sheridan (1684-1738), the friend and confidant of Dean Swift, kept a fashionable school in Dublin, edited the *Satires* of Persius in 1728, wrote a treatise on *The Art of Punning,* and figures largely in Swift's correspondence. Thomas Sheridan (1721-1788) was at first an actor of considerable reputation, both in Dublin and in London; was next a teacher of elocution; and finally came forward with an improved system of education, in which oratory was to have a conspicuous part. In this connection he published an elaborate *Plan of Education* in 1769, but his ideas, some of which are in accord with modern practice, were not taken up. He also compiled a pronouncing *Dictionary of the English Language,* with a prosodic grammar, and in 1784 published an entertaining *Life of Swift.* Frances Sheridan (1724-1766), wife of Thomas and mother of Richard Brinsley, who as Frances Chamberlaine had been known as a poetess, wrote after her marriage two plays, *The Discovery* and *The Dupe,* and two novels, *The Memoirs of Miss Sidney Biddulph,* which was a great success and was translated by the Abbé Prévost into French, and *The History of Nourjahad,* an Oriental tale. In 1775 the singular spectacle was presented of the son's play running at Covent Garden while the mother's was being acted at Drury Lane.

Among Sheridan's descendants who earned a niche in the temple of literary fame were his grand-daughters, the Countess of Dufferin (1807-1867) and the Hon. Mrs. Norton, afterwards Lady Stirling Maxwell (1808-1877), and his great-grandson, the first Marquis of Dufferin and Ava (1826-1902). Lady Dufferin's *Lament of the Irish Emigrant* ("I'm sittin' on the style, Mary") has moved the hearts and brought tears to the eyes of countless thousands since it was published more than fifty years ago.

Sir Philip Francis (1740-1818), born in Dublin, was the son of a clergyman of like name who attained some literary eminence as the translator of Horace and as a political writer. After filling various important government positions, Philip Francis, the son, was in 1773 made a member of the Council of Bengal, where his relations with the governor-general, Warren Hastings, were of an extremely strained character, amounting at times almost to a public scandal. He returned to England in 1781, entered parliament, made a name as a speaker, took part in the impeachment of Hastings, and composed numerous political pamphlets. He is generally supposed to have been the writer of the celebrated *Letters of Junius,* which appeared at intervals in the *Public Advertiser* between January 21, 1769, and January 21, 1772. These letters are distinguished for their polished style, their power of invective, their galling sarcasm, their knowledge of state secrets, and their unparalleled boldness. Every prominent man connected with the government was attacked: even the king himself was not spared. As revised by their pseudonymous writer in a reprint made in 1772, they number 70; a later edition, in 1812, contained 113 more. Their authorship has been the subject of much controversy, nor is the question yet finally settled. In his *Essay on Warren Hastings,* written in 1841, Macaulay went to considerable trouble to prove, by the cumulative method, that Francis was the writer, and since then that opinion has been generally, but not universally, maintained.

Isaac Bickerstaffe (c. 1735—c. 1812) was an Irishman, whose name, strange to say, had no connection with the *nom de guerre* of the same style under which Swift had masqueraded in his outrageously satirical attacks on Partridge the almanac maker, or with the more celebrated imaginary Isaac Bickerstaffe under cover of whose personality Steele conducted the *Tatler.* The real Bickerstaffe was a prolific playwright. His best known pieces are *The Sultan, The Maid of the Mill, Lionel and Clarissa,* and *Love in a Village.* In the last-mentioned occurs the famous song, beginning "We all love a pretty girl—under the rose."

William Drennan (1754-1820), who has been called the Tyrtaeus of the United Irishmen, was the son of a Presbyterian clergyman, was born in Belfast, and was educated at Glasgow and Edinburgh universities, taking a medical degree from the latter. He practised his profession in the north of Ireland. When the Irish Volunteers were established, Drennan entered heart and soul into the movement. Removing to Dublin in 1789, he associated with Tone and other revolutionary spirits, and became one of the founders of the Society of United Irishmen, the first statement of whose objects was the product of his pen. His *Letters of Orellana* helped materially to enlist the men of Ulster in the ranks of the Society. He also wrote a series of stirring lyrics which, voicing as they did the general sentiment in Ireland at the time, became extremely popular and had a widespread effect. These were afterwards (1815) collected under the title of *Fugitive Pieces.* All his political hopes being blasted with the failure of the rebellion of 1798 and of Emmet's insurrection in 1803, Drennan returned in 1807 to Belfast and there founded the *Belfast Magazine*. "The Wake of William Orr", a series of noble and affecting stanzas commemorating the judicial murder of a young Presbyterian Irish patriot in 1798, is one of his best known pieces. He also celebrated the ill-fated brothers Sheares. His song "Erin" was considered by Moore to be one of the most perfect of modern songs. It was in this piece that he fixed upon Ireland the title of the Emerald Isle:

> When Erin first rose from the dark swelling flood,
> God bless'd the green island, and saw it was good;
> The em'rald of Europe, it sparkled and shone—
> In the ring of the world the most precious stone.

Mary Tighe (1772-1810), whose maiden name was Blachford, was born, the daughter of a clergyman, in Co. Wicklow. She contracted an unhappy marriage with her cousin who represented Kilkenny in the Irish house of commons. By all accounts she was of great beauty and numerous accomplishments. She wrote many poems: her best, and best known, is *Psyche, or the Legend of Love,* an adaptation of the story of Cupid and Psyche from the *Golden Ass* of Apuleius. The metre she employed in this piece was the Spenserian stanza, which she handled with great power, freedom, and melody. *Psyche,* which first appeared in 1795, had a wonderful vogue, running rapidly through edition after edition. Among others to whom it appealed and who were influenced by it was Keats. Mrs. Tighe's talent drew from Moore a delicate compliment in "Tell me the witching tale again"; and in "The Grave of a Poetess" and "I stood where the life of song lay low", Mrs. Hemans bewailed her untimely death.

Edmund Malone (1741-1812), the son of an Irish judge, was born in Dublin and studied at Trinity College. He was called to the Irish bar in 1767, but coming into a fortune, he abandoned his profession and gave himself over to literary work. In 1790 he brought out an edition of Shakespeare which was deservedly praised for its learning and research. His critical acumen led him to doubt the genuineness of Chatterton's *Rowley Poems,* and he was one of the first to expose Ireland's Shakespearean forgeries in 1796. Among other services to literature he wrote a *Life of Sir Joshua Reynolds* and edited Dryden. He also left a quantity of materials afterwards utilized for the "Variorum Shakespeare" by James Boswell the younger in 1821.

John O'Keeffe (1747-1833), a Dublin man, was at first an art student, but soon became an actor, and then developed into a playwright. His pen was most prolific; he published a collection of over fifty pieces in 1798. His plays are mostly comic operas or farces, and some of them had great success. Lingo, the schoolmaster in *The Agreeable Surprise,* is a very amusing character. *The Positive Man, The Son-in-Law, Wild Oats, Love in a Camp,* and *The Poor Soldier* are among his compositions. His songs are well known, such as "I am a friar of orders grey", and there are few schoolboys who have not sooner or later made the acquaintance of his "Amo, amas, I loved a lass". For the last fifty-two years of his life O'Keeffe was blind, an affliction which he bore with unfailing cheerfulness. In 1826 he was given a pension of one hundred guineas a year from the king's privy purse.

George Canning (1770-1827), prime minister of England, properly belongs here, for, although born in London, he was a member of an Irish family long settled at Garvagh in Co. Derry. Entering parliament on the side of Pitt in 1796, he was made secretary of the navy in 1804 and in 1812 secretary of State for foreign affairs. He became prime minister in 1827, but died within six months, leaving a record for scarcely surpassed eloquence. In addition to his speeches, he is known in literature for his contributions to the *Anti-Jacobin, or Weekly Examiner,* which ran its satirical and energetic career for eight months (November, 1797—July, 1798.) Some of the best things that appeared in this ultra-conservative organ were from Canning's pen. Few there are who have not laughed at his *Loves of the Triangles,* in which he caricatured Erasmus Darwin's *Loves of the Plants;* at *The Needy Knife-Grinder;* or at the song of Rogero in *The Rovers,* with its comic refrain of the

U-
niversity of Gottingen.

Like most of the great Anglo-Irishmen of his time, Canning favored Catholic emancipation. It is interesting to note that it was a letter of Canning's that led to the formulation of the Monroe Doctrine.

Henry Grattan (1746-1820), the hero of Grattan's parliament, was born in Dublin and studied at Trinity College. His history belongs to that of his country. Suffice it here to say that not only did he by great eloquence and real statesmanship secure a free parliament for Ireland in 1782, but also that he fought energetically, if unavailingly, against the abolition of that parliament in 1800, and that thenceforward he devoted his abilities to promoting the cause of Catholic emancipation. Dying in London, he was honored by being buried in Westminster Abbey. In an age of great orators he stands out among the very foremost. His speeches have become classics, and are constantly quoted.

Another brilliant Irish orator, as well as an eminent wit, of this period, was John Philpot Curran (1750-1817), who, born at Newmarket, Co. Cork, and educated at Trinity College, Dublin, achieved a wonderful success at the Irish bar. He defended with rare insight, eloquence, and patriotism those who were accused of complicity in the rebellion of 1798. As a member of Grattan's parliament, he voiced the most liberal principles, and, though a Protestant himself, he worked hard in the Catholic cause. He held the great office of Master of the Rolls in Ireland from 1806 to 1814. The memory of few Irish orators, wits, or patriots is greener today than that of Curran. His daughter Sarah, whose fate is so inextricably blended with that of the ill-starred Robert Emmet, has been rendered immortal by Moore in his beautiful song, "She is far from the land where her young hero sleeps".

Mary Wollstonecraft Godwin (1759-1797), the first advocate of the rights of women, though born in London, was of Irish extraction. Into the details of her extraordinary and chequered career it is not possible, or necessary, here to enter. Her published works include *Thoughts on the Education of Daughters* (1787); *Answer to Burke's Reflections on the French Revolution* (1791); *Vindication of the Rights of Women* (1792); and an unfinished *Historical and Moral View of the French Revolution* (Vol. I., 1794). Having in August, 1797, borne to her husband, William Godwin, a daughter who afterwards became Shelley's second wife, Mary Godwin died in the following month. Whatever her faults—and they were perhaps not greater than her misfortunes—she had something of the divine touch of genius, and, in a different environment, might easily have left some great literary memento which the world would not willingly let die.

Maria Edgeworth (1767-1849), though born at Blackbourton in England, belonged to a family which had been settled in different parts of Ireland and finally at Edgeworthstown, Co. Longford, for nearly two hundred years. She was the daughter of Richard Lovell Edgeworth (1744-1817), who was distinguished for his inventions, for his eccentricity, and for his varied matrimonial experiences, and who himself figures in literature as the author of *Memoirs,* posthumously published in 1820, and as the partner with his daughter in *Practical Education* (1798) and in an *Essay on Irish Bulls* (1802). Maria had a busy literary career and was before the public for fifty-two years from 1795 to 1847. She wrote *Moral Tales; Popular Tales; Tales from Fashionable Life;* and *Harrington;* but she is now best remembered for her three masterpieces dealing with Irish life and conditions, namely, *Castle Rackrent* (1800); *The Absentee* (1812); and *Ormond* (1817). By these works she inspired Scott, as he himself tells us, to attempt for his own country something "of the same kind with that which she had so fortunately achieved for Ireland", and in a later day she inspired Turgenief to do similarly for Russia. She excels in wit and pathos and gives a true and vivid presentation of the times and conditions as she viewed them.

Andrew Cherry (1762-1821), born in Limerick, became an actor, a theatrical manager, and a playwright. He wrote nine or ten plays, several of which were moderately successful. The one that is now remembered is *The Soldier's Daughter*. Some of his songs, such as "The Bay of Biscay", "Tom Moody, the Whipper-in", and, especially, "The Green Little Shamrock of Ireland", bid fair to be immortal.

Other Irish song-writers were Thomas Duffet (fl. 1676), author of "Come all you pale lovers"; Arthur Dawson (1700?-

1775), author of "Bumpers, Squire Jones"; George Ogle (1742-1814), author of "Molly Asthore"; Richard Alfred Millikin (1767-1815), author of the grotesque "Groves of Blarney"; Edward Lysaght (1763-1811), author of "Our Ireland", "The Gallant Man who led the van Of the Irish Volunteers", and "Kate of Garnavilla"; George Nugent Reynolds (1770?-1802), author of "Kathleen O'More"; Thomas Dermody (1775-1802), author of the collection of poems and songs known as *The Harp of Erin;* James Orr (1770-1816), author of "The Irishman"; Henry Brereton Code (d. 1830), author of "The Sprig of Shillelah"; Charles Wolfe (1791-1823), author of "If I had thought thou couldst have died", and of "The Burial of Sir John Moore"; and Charles Dawson Shanly (1811-1875), author of "Kitty of Coleraine".

Theobald Wolfe Tone (1763-1798), born in Dublin, educated at Trinity College, and called to the Irish bar in 1789, fills a large space in the history of his country from 1790 to his death in 1798. Intrepid, daring, and resourceful, he was one of the most dangerous of the enemies to English domination in Ireland that arose at any time during the troubled relations between the two countries. Taken prisoner on board a French ship of the line bound for Ireland on a mission of freedom, he committed suicide in prison rather than submit to the ignominy of being hanged to which he had been condemned. He sleeps his last sleep in Bodenstown churchyard, in that county of Kildare to which he was connected by many ties. His grave is still the Mecca of many a pilgrimage, and the corner-stone of a statue to his memory has been laid for some years on a commanding site in the city of his birth. He is known in literature for his *Journals* and his *Autobiography,* both containing sad, but inspiring, reading for the Irishman of today.

. . .

Here this rapid survey of Irish writers of English must close. To tell in any sort of appropriate detail the story of the English literature of Ireland in the nineteenth and twentieth centuries would require a separate volume—a volume which is now under way and will, it is hoped, be speedily forthcoming. There is all the less need to attempt the agreeable task here, because in other portions of this book much more than passing reference is made to the chief Irish authors who, in the last hundred and fifteen years, have distinguished themselves and shed lustre on their country. During that period Irish poets, playwrights, novelists, essayists, historians, biographers, humorists, critics, and scholars have fully held their own both in the quantity and the quality of the work produced, and have left an impression of power and personality, of graceful style and vivifying imagination, that in itself constitutes, and must for ever constitute, one of the distinctive Glories of Ireland.

REFERENCES :

Irish Literature (10 vols., New York, 1904) ; Chambers's Cyclopaedia of English Literature (3 vols., Philadelphia and London, 1902-1904) ; Dictionary of National Biography ; Encyclopaedia Britannica ; Cambridge History of English Literature ; D'Alton: History of Ireland (London, 1910) ; Lennox: Early Printing in Ireland (Washington, 1909), Addison and the Modern Essay (Washington, 1912), Lessons in English Literature (21st edition, Baltimore, 1913) ; Macaulay: Essays, History of England ; Brown: A Reader's Guide to Irish Fiction (London, 1910), A Guide to Books on Ireland (Dublin, 1912).